Diction in Context

SINGING IN ENGLISH, ITALIAN, GERMAN, AND FRENCH

Diction in Context

SINGING IN ENGLISH, ITALIAN, GERMAN, AND FRENCH

Brenda Smith, DMA

PLURAL
PUBLISHING
INC.

PLURAL PUBLISHING
INC.

5521 Ruffin Road
San Diego, CA 92123

Email: information@pluralpublishing.com
Website: https://www.pluralpublishing.com

Typeset in 11/14 Stone Informal by Flanagan's Publishing Services, Inc.
Printed in the United States of America by Integrated Books International

For permission to use material from this text, contact us by
Telephone: (866) 758-7251
Fax: (888) 758-7255
Email: permissions@pluralpublishing.com

Every attempt has been made to contact the copyright holders for material originally printed in another source. If any have been inadvertently overlooked, the publishers will gladly make the necessary arrangements at the first opportunity.

Library of Congress Cataloging-in-Publication Data:

Names: Smith, Brenda (Brenda Jo) author.
Title: Diction in context : singing in English, Italian, German, and French
  / Brenda Smith.
Description: San Diego : Plural Publishing, Inc., 2019. | Includes
  bibliographical references and index.
Identifiers: LCCN 2019029717 | ISBN 9781635501209 (paperback) | ISBN
  9781635501247 (ebook)
Subjects: LCSH: Singing--Diction. | English language--Pronunciation. |
  French language--Pronunciation. | German language--Pronunciation. |
  Italian language--Pronunciation.
Classification: LCC MT883 .S66 2019 | DDC 783/.043--dc23
LC record available at https://lccn.loc.gov/2019029717

Contents

4 GERMAN

159

Introduction

In the preface to his book, *Rumi: The Book of Love: Poems of Ecstasy and Longing*, Coleman Banks states that "Poetry and music are two great mysteries of human consciousness" (Banks, 2003). A composer unites poetry with music for a singer to perform. In composing vocal works of any kind, a composer approaches an existing artwork—a poem—and infuses it with expanded artistic possibilities. Whether folk song, art song, oratorio, or opera aria, every work composed for singing is the result of the composer's encounter with words. You, the singer, interpret the text and music. To do so, you must discern the intention of the composer's interpretation. The goals of this book are to provide you with the tools needed to delve deeply into the poetry and music you sing, to pronounce text accurately, and to feel confident in expressing it.

Every poetic text offers myriad avenues that lead to meaning. With each new song, you embark on a personal journey to answer questions that will inform your performance. You may wonder what caused the composer to be drawn to this poem or poet. Were there events in the life of the composer that made a text particularly attractive? What was it about the text that inspired the composer to make a musical adaptation? Does the title of the song give clues to the composer's interpretation? Might there be specific repetitions of text that reveal what most fascinated the composer? Does the text contain literary symbols that are reflected in the musical setting? Are there aspects of the culture or current events that may have influenced the composer's musical language? Whether you are a student, a teacher of singing, or a vocal coach, *Diction in Context* should serve you as a source for answers to such questions.

Effective, expressive diction for singing requires more than just a mastery of pronunciation rules. What a word means in the context of a phrase determines much about how it is to be spoken, pronounced, and sung. Diction and interpretation are intimate, reciprocal partners, both utterly essential to a meaningful performance. For each style period and every culture, the events of the heart are expressed in unique ways. In these pages, you will find pertinent biographical, historical, and literary sources along with diction rules and textual examples of English, Italian, German, and French song. For each language, there is a section on sentence structure and syntax intended to assist you with poetic analysis and word-by-word translations. Representative song texts are provided for the purpose of comparative listening and phonetic transcription. Comparative listening reveals subtle differences in expression and diction. The texts are presented in a workbook format, allowing space for IPA dictation practice. You can verify the accuracy of your IPA transcriptions through online and published sources that are readily available.[1] Resources

---

[1]www.ipasource.com and *Exploring Arts Song Lyrics: Translation and Pronunciation of Italian, German, & French Repertoire,* by Jonathan Retzlaff with IPA transcription by Cheri Montgomery, are available through most academic libraries at no cost.

for further reading and study are given at the conclusion of the book. As you supplement the usual didactic material with contextual knowledge, you can build a firm foundation and deepen your mastery of vocal repertoire. It is hoped that *Diction in Context* will be a lively and inspiring companion on your journey as a student, teacher, and performer.

A Message to Students

Dear Students of Singer's Diction,

After studying singing and teaching others for more than three decades, I have come to believe that the key to satisfying performance is a thorough understanding of the texts. The meaning of the text informs everything about the singing. There is a famous saying from the early Bel Canto masters: "To breathe is to sing." In your singing life, you will hear many interpretations of the phrase. For me, it means that the nature of a singer's inhalation determines much about the success a singer will have in the presentation of a phrase. There is a deep connection between meaning and delivery in spoken language. If it is your task to bring exciting, joyful news to a peer, you will instinctively inhale swiftly and speak the words vigorously. In sharing thoughts that are less favorable, it is likely you take time to breathe so that you can deliver the words carefully, with attention to timing and tone. In other words, you begin on the "inside" of the text to bring its meaning to the "outside" world. Expressive singing generates from the same thought process. To communicate the thoughts of poets and librettists in any language, singers use a variety of tools to discern the meaning buried beneath the surface of the text. This book is intended to help you understand what the texts mean and how they should sound, so that you can breathe and sing them intuitively and beautifully.

As a beginning student of singing, you must learn to sing poetic texts in the four basic languages: English, Italian, German, and French. There are many excellent resources in the form of pronouncing dictionaries, diction handbooks, and websites that you can access to determine the proper pronunciation of each word that has been set to music. You will study vocal technique to establish a healthy approach to the basics of singing: relaxation, posture, breathing, and resonance. These two elements, pronunciation and singing skill, form the foundation for vocal performance. The missing element is the meaning of the words within the poetic context. Though the subjects of poetry are universal, the specific use of words is exquisite to the poet and the culture. The more confident you can be about the intended meaning of a poetic idea, the more successful you will be in expressing it in performance. As you study the artistic, literary, and philosophical ideas contained in the poetry set by composers of various times and nationalities, you will begin to grow as a citizen of the world. With this understanding, your performances will gain depth and artistry. You will become a powerfully poetic singer.

Within these pages, you will find what I have shared with first-year students for many years. In my courses, weekly class periods contain the study of diction anatomy and mechanics, exercises in the imitation of sounds and poetic analysis, and lessons in cultural history and comparative listening. The repertoire represents what is considered age and size appropriate for beginning students at the collegiate level. This introductory course should ground you in the skills you need to explore all repertoire as you advance to upper-level study. The songs and arias discussed here are mere examples of the many musical masterpieces that await further exploration. Please consider this book an invitation to a life of discovery.

The book concludes with resource material for further study and a glossary of terms. May these pages inspire and equip you for a lifetime of singing in English, Italian, German, and French!

A Message to Teachers

Dear Teachers of Singer's Diction,

This book is a collection of the materials I have gathered over three decades of teaching. I use these materials to invite first-year students into the world of art song and early opera. Singer's diction is much more than accurate pronunciation of words. To sing any language meaningfully, a performer must comprehend which words carry the poetic essence and what components of vowel color and consonant articulation deliver it. The main goal for each student of singer's diction should be to read a poetic text with the inflection suggested by the musical setting. Such a reading could be called a "lyric" one, one that promises the expressive qualities to be heard in performance. The format of the course I teach is that of a so-called "flipped classroom," where students will participate with the teacher in comparative listening, IPA dictation practice, and class discussion.

Voice teachers and singers are fortunate to have excellent resources for determining the proper sounds and articulation for words in English, Italian, German, and French. At the conclusion of this book, you will find an extensive list of online and printed resources. The publisher has designed a website through which you can access PowerPoints and additional teaching materials to supplement the contents of this book.

The implementation of these resources is only the first step toward mastery of texts set to music. Students must investigate the culture depicted in poetry and music to build a deeper layer of understanding. The study of representative poets and composers and their styles gives students further assurance. A thorough inquiry into poetic form and symbolism helps determine which words are significant and worthy of expression. (Please be aware that all word-by-word translations and poetic equivalents contained in this book are my work.) The internet allows everyone the opportunity to listen and compare the musical interpretations of reliable singers, both historical and contemporary. Along with this body of knowledge, students must gather the phonetic and grammatical tools to speak and sing texts confidently. In studying the publications, websites and demonstrations, I find that many resources are based upon the phonetic spellings for spoken language. As singers and singing teachers, we adjust the pronunciation of the spoken text to the melodic contours of the musical setting. We consider vocal technical issues such as phrase shape, tuning and tessitura. To create a well-sung phrase, a singer may need to modify the vowel, delay the consonant, or make myriad other adjustments. This text hopes to honor the artistic freedom of the singing teacher and vocal coach, while suggesting basic practical solutions for the achievement of impeccable singer's diction in English, Italian, German, and French.

Many first-year students have little experience with English grammar, sentence structure, and syntax or with poetry and textual interpretation. The exercise of comparative listening, class discussion, and peer review opens the door to creative thinking and critical analysis. By listening to representative performances and discussing the poetic symbols, idioms, and practices of each time period and nationality, students develop a framework for interpreting assigned vocal repertoire. The lively circumstance of listening, discussing, transcribing, and performing makes clear that the interpretation of text and music is never static. The daily classroom experience becomes an exploration of spontaneous thought and feeling based on good aural models and confirmed in writing through a solid acquaintance with the International Phonetic Alphabet (IPA).

The textbook is intended to serve a yearlong sequence of four segments (English and Italian in fall semester, and German and French in spring term). At the university where I teach, each segment consists of 8 weeks of classes with three meetings weekly. I divide the 8 weeks into two larger historical units, representing repertoire composed before and after 1800, respectively. Within each unit, the first 3 weeks are spent introducing the target language, its music and cultural history, and vocal literature. During the 4th and 7th week of the English, Italian, and German diction courses, students perform representative repertoire as assigned. Because of the nature of the French language and the complexity of its musical settings, students research and prepare only one *mélodie* to be presented in the 7th week of the term. (Sample repertoire lists for student presentations are included in each chapter.)

Prior to each presentation, students prepare a phonetic transcription in IPA that identifies the proper pronunciation of each word as it would be spoken. Students should be encouraged to use printed and/or online resources to prepare the transcriptions and to cite the sources properly. Students are asked to note any vowel modifications suggested by their studio teacher. Any modification should be included in the IPA transcription as variants intended for the singing of the text. For all texts in foreign languages, students are required to create a word-by-word as well as poetic translation. The texts, transcriptions, and translations are submitted in advance to be corrected and duplicated for class use. An able pianist rehearses the repertoire with each student prior to the presentation and performs with the student in class.

Because the poetry and music for the first segment of each language is generally unfamiliar to students, I present orally the program notes for each selection during the first presentation in English, Italian, and German. The first presentation in English, Italian, and German is graded pass/fail and serves as a "dress rehearsal" for the second, graded one. For the French presentation, each student receives private diction coaching and is guided to the pertinent resources for the investigation of the musical style and composer's/poet's lives. Because there is only one presentation in the French segment of the course, the private coaching session mentioned above serves the same purpose as the pass/fail first presentations in the other languages.

The second presentation in each language is a graded event. Students prepare their assigned text as described above and formulate a brief introduction to the musical style period, the lives of the composer and poet to be given orally as program notes. After the presentation, the introductions are collected, edited, and distributed electronically to the class for future use. (Sample presentation assessment sheets are included at the appendix of this book.)

For all presentations, the student performer explains briefly what the text means and what words or musical phrases are particularly expressive. Before the student performer sings, the entire class reads aloud the text from the corrected IPA transcription that has been distributed. This allows every class member to engage with the poem and to practice its sounds and symbols. The student performer follows with a "solo" reading of the text. Each student singer is encouraged to read the target text with the inflection intended for the sung performance. Finally, the student sings the assigned work accompanied by the collaborative pianist. After each performance, class members comment on the diction challenges that were successfully met.

With each language, the students participate in a cultural celebration of the target language. In English, this might be an afternoon tea with a poetry reading and musicale. It could be the viewing of a film that contains a performance of an early English song. At the conclusion of the Italian segment of the course, the students gather for an Italian dinner. This event coincides with the holiday season. Between the main course and dessert, the class carols in the neighborhood before returning for panettone and warm cider. At the midpoint of the German diction course, the students enjoy a "Kaffeetrinken" that includes cake and coffee along with the singing of a part song, solo performances of Lieder, and the reading aloud of a German fairytale. It has become a tradition to conclude by singing Schubert's "An die Musik" together. The academic year ends with a four-course luncheon of French food. After the meal, we discuss how our course material will be used in future years of study.

Perfect diction is grounded in the careful imitation of exquisite models. In this textbook, you will find representative poems in each language with suggestions for comparative listening with a rubric for listening and transcribing. The foreign language texts are presented in a format conducive to dictation practice along with a word-by-word translation. A poetic equivalent appears at the end of each dictation practice page. The strategies described should help each student "divide and conquer" the texts. The strategies include the identification of parts of speech, familiar words, rhyme scheme, word repetition, and expressive elements. In this format, students encounter poems first as texts and second as musical settings. Through comparative listening, students apply pronunciation rules and IPA symbols to confirm what they have heard sung by qualified performers. (As noted above, the accuracy of phonetic transcriptions can easily be verified by online or published resources.) Discussion often arises between classmates about what vowel sound a performer has sung. Because singing is not an exact science, the class eventually arrives at a consensus that defines the "range of normal." The effort made to arrive at a workable solution for problematic words or phrases involves engagement by every member of the class.

It has been my experience that the final presentations in each language demonstrate the positive results of this active, attentive learning. Students recognize the choices to be made in pronunciation and interpretation. Having gathered the tools for good decision making regarding musical and literary style as well as diction, students present their assigned repertoire with understanding, artistry, and confidence.

I strive to select repertoire that is age and size appropriate for the average first-year student in a collegiate setting. Each selection is approved in advance by the studio teacher. In this book as in my course, it is not possible to study every worthy poem set to music in any language or time period. I have sought to include representative works by standard composers in each language. The works I have chosen, with few exceptions, can be sung by most voice types. The majority of study repertoire is accessible for performance with piano. Vocal works that demand an orchestral accompaniment are included for historical purposes; they are given less space than those works appropriate for study at the beginning of a collegiate career. I hope you will find here a basic structure that can be adapted to suit the songs and arias that are of special interest to you.

Acknowledgments

I wish to express my sincerest gratitude to Nicole Hodges, Valerie Johns, and Elaine Murphy for their encouragement and help in the creation of this textbook. I appreciate the expert advice I have received from Dr. Robert T. Sataloff, MD, DMA, not only on this publication but on numerous other projects. I am very grateful to Janna Bruene and Lurray Myers, two collaborative pianists with whom I have had the privilege of making meaningful music. I value our friendship and cherish our endless interchange of ideas about text and music in rehearsal and performance. I am especially indebted to Sabrina Baêta for her tireless assistance with the mechanics of this manuscript. As always, I thank Ronald Burrichter, my husband and best singing friend, who contributes his knowledge and insights to my work. My warmest thanks to a lifelong singer and wordsmith Dr. R. Allen Shoaf for the poem "Music's Mirror Calls."

Music's Mirror Calls

ὅτι/ὀργῆς νοσούσης εἰσὶν ἰατροὶ λόγοι;
[Don't you know] words are healers of the nausea of pride?
Aeschylus *Prometheus Bound 379**

We evolved with melodies, they with us,
Since we must cooperate in nature
To compose our special opera together—
Melody fuses us, we work in unison.

But when melody couples with language
Inw<u>o</u>rdness unfolds to ins<u>o</u>nuate
Particy<u>ou</u>larity, individy<u>ou</u>al
<u>ME</u>anings, d<u>I</u>v<u>I</u>ded—but *tutti* by partis<u>o</u>n.

As music's mirror calls, sound echoes words,
Mixing colors audible and visible,
And in this sea of sound, from life evolving,
Love articulates its lyrical chants.

R. Allen Shoaf

*Literally, "that of the disease of swelling are healers words?"

Reviewers

Thomas Bandy, MM, DMA
Associate Professor of Collaborative
  Piano
Oberlin Conservatory of Music
Oberlin, Ohio

Byron Johnson, MM, DMA
Associate Professor of Music, Vocal Area
  Head
Alcorn State University
Lorman, Mississippi

Kathleen M. Maurer, BM, MM, DMA
Associate Professor of Voice
Ball State University School of Music
Muncie, Indiana

Brady R. McElligott, BM, MM
Associate Professor of Music in Opera
  and Voice
The University of Tulsa
Tulsa, Oklahoma

Helen Dewey Reikofski, DMA
English Diction for Singers
College of Music
University of North Texas
Denton, Texas

Daniel Shirley, BM, MM, DM
Assistant Professor of Vocal Studies
East Carolina University School of Music
Greenville, North Carolina

Valerie Trollinger, BME, MM, DME
Professor of Music
Kutztown University of Pennsylvania
Professor (Adjunct) of Otolaryngology-
  Head and Neck Surgery
Drexel University College of Medicine
Philadelphia, Pennsylvania

Melanie Williams, MM, DMA
University of Montevallo
Montevallo, Arizona

Dedicated to Dr. Joseph Ross Flummerfelt
(1937–2019)
Emeritus Professor of Conducting and Conductor Laureate
Westminster Choir College

"Song, as you teach us, is not a grasping,
Not a seeking for some final consummation.
To sing is to be."

Rainer Maria Rilke, *Sonnets to Orpheus* I, 3

Gathering the Tools

Introduction

As a student of singing, you will confront a world of unfamiliar poetry and music in at least three languages besides your native English. From the outset, you will be hearing and learning vocal repertoire in Italian, German, and French. The first English works you study might be Shakespeare texts with archaic words, the meaning of which you may not comprehend. There are several tools you will need. The tools are: meaning, pronunciation, articulation, enunciation, punctuation, and cultural context.

Meaning

Since vocal repertoire, unlike other musical forms, is based on the text, its rhythm and meaning, the first tool you require is a means of grasping the meaning of the poem. In many ways, this is the most important tool. As you immerse yourself in each language and its poetry, you analyze, maybe even learn to savor, every vowel and consonant. You will notice how its subtle, hidden meaning awakens your heart. When you speak aloud or sing the poem, its message is translated instinctively into shades of vocal color.

To understand what the poem means, you will need to study its form as well as its content. Within the form, you will notice certain combinations of vowels and consonants that require special care. The rhyme scheme, the rhythmic patterns, and the use of alliteration often drive poetic phrases to points of tension or climax. This poetic momentum demands the perfect pronunciation of each word.

Pronunciation

The International Phonetic Alphabet (IPA) is the tool that will assist you in pronouncing each word with confidence. Every student of IPA learns the symbols by associating them with sounds found in words from the native language. The words associated with each IPA symbol become "points of departure" for documenting the sounds of words in foreign languages. Think of the IPA symbols as a code that will help you "decode" unfamiliar words. If you select your associative words with care and memorize them with diligence, you will equip yourself for an exciting journey of discovery in the world of singer's diction.

Articulation

To pronounce well, you must learn the physical aspects of each vowel and consonant. Articulation in diction refers to the "anatomy" and "mechanics" of creating sounds. Vowels and consonants occur through movements of the tongue and lips along with the vocal tract. If these movements are intentional and efficient, you will be able to sing well and be understood clearly. Vowels are created through neurological signals you send when you imagine or "audiate" the sound. Consonants are formed by adjustments you make. For example, "d," "l," "n," and "t" occur when the tip of your tongue interacts with the alveolar ridge behind your teeth. The back of your tongue forms the consonants "g" and "k." You control the speed and character of these interactions. Effective articulation requires a thorough understanding of the physical movements that cause each vowel and consonant in every language. The study of articulatory anatomy and mechanics helps you "divide and conquer" the pronunciation of words. We speak of persons as "articulate" when they use language well. An articulate singer sings text with clarity and crispness. Such a singer sings the right vowels and consonants in a clearly audible, vocally efficient manner. Your voice teacher or vocal coach will be the extra "eyes and ears" that help you fine tune your skills.

Enunciation

Enunciation and articulation are related terms that are frequently used interchangeably. To enunciate a word, you must articulate it clearly. When a speaker or singer "enunciates" a word, the listener hears specific elements of a word presented with special care. The enunciated word receives an emphasis that causes the word to rise above other words in a spoken or sung phrase. To enunciate a word dramatically, a speaker or singer may delay the delivery of a syllable, a vowel, or a consonant. In summary, enunciation is an intentional, emphatic form of articulation.

Punctuation

Punctuation marks are valuable tools for determining how you gather meaning from a text. Punctuation marks such as commas and semicolons delineate phrases, while periods confirm complete thoughts. Certain kinds of punctuation marks indicate how a phrase should be performed. For example, parentheses, exclamation marks, and question marks signify the need to adjust one's tone of voice. Dashes or colons imply time spent before the next phrase begins. Punctuation can determine the nature of a breath or pace the drive toward a climatic word. Punctuation marks act as guideposts that help a reader follow an author or poet's path. When setting a text to music, vocal composers recognize punctuation marks as messages sent by the poet to the poem's interpreters. Adherence to punctuation often unravels mysteries hidden within a text.

Cultural Context

Singing any text set to music requires an understanding of the literary and musical style period in which the work was conceived. When you seek to determine the tempo, pacing, or inflection of a spoken or sung text, the style of the period will provide you with valuable clues. In reading a text aloud or silently, you often encounter unfamiliar words or idioms. The use of language is indicative of the poet's time, place, and mannerisms. In creating a musical setting, a composer may choose to represent the elements of the poem's original style or to demonstrate the timeless value of the text's message by designing a new, modern context for it. The more you know about the original circumstances of a poem or its musical setting, the more confident you will be in your interpretation.

The Anatomy of Diction

Most books about vocal technique or singer's diction begin with an explanation of the anatomical parts involved in singing and speech. Correct posture is foundational to good singing and speaking practice. Learning to sing well involves the memorization of physical sensations; therefore, it makes sense to position your body in the same way for practice and performance. Careful repetition develops skill mastery and confidence. A solid vocal technique promises stability in your stance, flexibility in your breath, consistency in your resonance, and precision in your articulations. The physiology of the voice is complex, involving the interaction of brain centers that coordinate the larynx or "voice box," chest and abdominal muscles, and the vocal tract articulators (Smith & Sataloff, 2013). The vocal tract is the resonating system that includes the larynx, the pharynx, and the oral cavity. (See the Glossary for definitions of these terms.) An alert, focused mind governs every step of speaking and singing. At every point in the process of vocal production, efficiency is the goal.

The Mechanics of Diction

The mechanics of diction are difficult to describe in words. The singing voice is the only musical instrument that cannot be seen or touched. The actions of the voice are the results of signals from the brain. Phonation or "sound making" involves the interaction of breath energy with the vocal folds and the resonators. The complex, intricate movements of the tongue, lips, jaw, and palate cause the utterance of vowels and consonants.

Through computer imaging and MRI technology, it is possible to see the shape of the vocal tract during the phonation of individual vowels and consonants. Many excellent online and published resources contain explanations, charts or drawings to demonstrate the movements of the tongue, lips, jaw, and palate. A variety of terms have been applied to the positions of vowels along the vocal tract. Vowels have been described as "front," "central," and "back"; "fronting" and "backing"; or "bright" and "dark." Vowels are sometimes called "lip" versus "tongue" vowels, referring to the location of the sensations in the mouth. These are not conflicting terms, but they can be very confusing. The words are intended to convey the situation within the mouth when a vowel is spoken or sung. The charts, drawings, and images remind you of what your body did.

We learn our languages by imitating the sounds made by others. As described above, the vocal tract responds to signals and replicates the sound the respondent has heard. Your body knows what to do to create each sound. As singers, we do not learn to "make" vowels and consonants. We learn to understand the natural production of vowels and consonants and to facilitate its efficiency.

Singing any vowel or consonant is somewhat different than speaking it. In singing, you strive for a relaxed jaw, while in speaking, a relaxed jaw, though desirable, is not essential to the task. You sing higher and lower pitches than you speak. Because the vocal tract arranges itself differently for each note we sing, the position and stability of the vocal tract during singing are major vocal technical considerations. When you sing, dynamic, instantaneous changes occur that involve mental agility, breath pressure, and physical responses. Each adjustment will have an impact on the shape of your vocal tract. Your teacher will help you develop the strategies required to cope with these subtle changes. Because of the adjustments necessary for each sound you make, there is no single way to create any vowel or consonant. Once you are aware of what the body does to produce a vowel or consonant sound, you will aim for efficiency and avoid any intrusion on the natural process.

Vowels and consonants have been "classified" to compare the means by which they are produced. Vowels may be classified as "closed" or "open." A "closed" vowel is one that is created by a rounding or tightening of the lips. The sound of the letter "a" in the word *chaos* is such a vowel and has the IPA symbol of [e]. The "open" version of the same sound is found in the word *bed* and is identified with the IPA symbol [ɛ]. The "open" sound does not require the rounding or tightening of the lips. Some vowels are classified as "pure." A pure vowel occurs without any conscious effort of the tongue, lips, jaw or palate. The pure vowels are the basic sounds of [a] as in *father*, [ɛ] as in *bed*, [i] as in *me*, [ɔ] as in *awe*, and [u] as in *shoe*. Because the formation of "pure" vowels is uncomplicated, pure vowels are easy to sustain in singing.

Consonants are classified by points of origin and contact and by voice use. By understanding how each consonant is formed, you can plan the efficient use of each one in combination with vowels that precede or follow. A full description of consonants and consonant clusters is found below.

Classifications of Vowels

The basic vowel sounds that are unique to the English language are: [æ] as in *cat*, [ɜ] as in *learn* and any of its "r" related shapes such as [ɚ] and [ɝ], the vowel [ʌ] as in *up*, the adjusted version of [I] written as [ɪ] or [ɨ] and associated with unaccented "-ly" or "-y" endings, the voiceless or voiced "-th" [θ] as in *breath*, [ð] as in *breathe*, and the vowel sound spelled in English "w" [w] as in *weep, wonder,* or *wandering*. The spelling "wh" [ʍ] or [hw] also appears only in the English language.

Italian has fewer vowel sounds than English. In German, vowels used in English but not in Italian such as [I] and [ʊ] and [ə] appear along with mixed vowels called "umlauts" and consonant sounds known as the "ich-laut" [ç] and the "ach-laut" [x]. The French language contains mixed vowels that are very similar to the German ones plus four additional nasal vowel sounds [ã], [ɛ̃], [õ], and [œ̃].

Classifications of Consonants

Consonants are classified based upon how they are produced. Consonants that require the voice are called "voiced" consonants. Those that do not require the voice are called "unvoiced" or "voiceless" consonants. In English, the voiced single consonants are: b [b], d [d], g [g], l [l], m [m], n [n], v [v], and z [z], and the unvoiced or voiceless single consonants are: f [f], k [k], p [p], s [s], and t [t]. When voiced as in the English word *breathe*, "th" is indicated by the symbol [ð]. When unvoiced as in *breath*, the "th" is indicated by the IPA symbol [θ]. Note that the unvoiced symbol is the same as the Greek letter for "theta," a word that is pronounced with an unvoiced "th." The consonant "w" is voiced in the word *wonder* and unvoiced in the word *why*. The voiced "w" is identified by the IPA symbol [w] and the unvoiced one as [ʍ] or [hw]. The letter "h" [h] is also an unvoiced or voiceless consonant. The letter "y" in certain words such as *yes* functions as a consonant that is indicated by the symbol [j] in the IPA. The letter "r" enjoys a wide range of expressive possibilities. The extent to which the sound of "r" is to be heard determines the kind of symbol you will use. In general, an "r" is flipped or tapped between vowel sounds. This kind of "r" is indicated by the symbol [ɾ]. When the language or the circumstance requires a rolled or trilled "r," the symbol [r] is used. You will discover language and situation specific uses of the letter "r" indicated by one of the following symbols: [ʁ], [ɹ], [ɚ], or [ɝ].

There are consonant clusters that are expressed clearly through the symbols chosen to designate them. For example, there are nasal sounds that create "ng" [ŋ] as in *sing* or [ɲ] as in *Tanya*. Compare the sound [ʃ] heard in the word *sugar* with [tʃ] in the word *char*. Note the differences in voicing between the consonant [ʒ] representing the sound in *pleasure* and the cluster [dʒ] as in *jam*. There are also consonants that appear in foreign languages but not in English, such as the [ç] or "ich-laut" in German found in the word *ich* and the [x] or "ach-laut" found in *ach*. The letter "z" in German is pronounced as a consonant cluster with the symbol [ts] as heard in the term name of the insect, the "tse-tse" fly, in English. In Italian, the letter "z" is pronounced in certain words as [ts] in some words and as [dz] in others.

Classifications of Consonant Articulations

Each consonant is created or "articulated" by moving the tongue, the palate or the lips or some combination of these elements. Consonants are classified or "grouped together" by the method of their articulation. In principle, a consonant is formed when an articulator (e.g., tongue, lip, teeth, palate, etc.) interrupts the flow of air as it moves through the vocal tract. The "point of articulation" refers to where the interruption takes place. It might be at the level of the lip or "labial" and is called a "bilabial" consonant. If the interruption takes place at the level of the teeth, it is called a "dental" consonant. "Labiodental" refers to a sound made by combining the lips and teeth. The "alveolar ridge," the ridge between your teeth and your hard palate, is another location where consonants interrupt the flow of air. There are consonants that are formed along the hard palate and called "palate" or "palatal" consonants. Some occur in front of the hard palate and have the name "prepalate" or "prepalatal." "Velar" and "uvular" consonants are those formed by adjustments to the soft palate.

Points of Articulation

Here are the points of articulation and examples of their IPA spelling and use:

Alveolar ridge	[l]	lo!
Bilabial	[b]	bee
Dental	[θ]	thin
Labiodental	[f]	fee
Nasal	[m], [n]	mine
Palate	[j]	yes
Prepalate	[ʒ]	measure
Uvular	[ŋ]	sing
Velar	[k]	could

Manners of Articulation

How the formation of a consonant interrupts the flow of air is referred as the "manner" of articulation. The terms used to describe them are:

♦ *Fricative* refers to consonants that require some "friction" between the air and the point of articulation. In English, the fricatives are [f], [v], [θ], [h], [ʃ], and [ʒ].

♦ *Glide* refers to consonants created by the movement of articulators from one place to another. In English, there are three glides. They are [j], [ɹ], and [w].

♦ *Lateral* is the term used to describe the tip of the tongue when it is lifted to contact the teeth and alveolar ridge. In English, the consonant [l] is only one "lateral" consonant.

♦ *Nasal* consonants are those created when the lowered velum allows the flow of air to move to the nasal passages. In English, this occurs to form [m], [n], and [ŋ].

♦ *Plosive or Stop-Plosive* describes a manner of articulation in which the flow of air is stopped and then released as in [b,] [p], [d], [t], [g], and [k].

♦ *Affricative* is a term related to "fricative." Such a consonant cluster requires a stoppage of the flow of air before producing a fricative. There are two affricative consonant clusters in English. They are [ʤ] and [ʧ].

For more detailed information on terms, see the specific reference materials for each target language at the end of this book.

Diction and Vocal Health

"To sing is to breathe" is a wise saying that comes to us from 17th-century singing masters. Healthy singing involves careful use of our voices as singers and speakers. The act of singing begins with an aural image in your brain. The syllable you hear belongs to a word that is a part of a larger phrase. The more familiar you are with the sounds of each language you sing, the more facile you will become at recreating the sound with your voice. Singer's diction is an important element in your singing life.

As a student of singing, you engage very intentionally in your vocal exercises and repertoire study. Not every singer considers speaking voice activities with the same attention to function and ease. Should your speaking habits be less than optimal, they may inhibit your growth as a singer. As you practice the pronunciation of English, Italian, German, and French vowels, notice the "onset" or the instant of phonation. Was the onset balanced and easy? Was there any undue pressure or discomfort? We singers are taught to time the onset of sound perfectly the movement of air with the beginning of the musical phrase. In speech, we rarely "practice" the delivery of our thoughts before we utter them. The resulting negative behavior is called a "glottal stop" or "hard glottal attack."

The "glottis" is the space between the vocal folds that occurs during respiration. Singing training teaches us to close the glottis in tandem with the flow of air in the act of phonation. If the glottis is forced to close through undue pressure, the vocal folds are squeezed together harshly (Stemple, Glaze, & Klaben, 2010). This behavior can put your vocal instrument at risk of injury.

Below is an example of a text designed to identify the frequency with which a speaker produces a glottal stop or attack. As you read the passage aloud, you will notice phrases containing words that begin with open vowels, such as "in the air" or "and its ends apparently." Be careful to coordinate your thoughts with your breath and voice as you approach these phrases. If you find it difficult to read the phrases with a gentle onset of sound, speak to your voice teacher about seeking help. Remember that we are born with an innate ability to breathe healthfully and to produce appropriately normal speech (Sataloff, 2005). The coordination of your breath for phonation is a skill you will master with the aid of your teacher.

The Rainbow Passage

> When the sunlight strikes raindrops *in the air*, they act *like a prism* and *form a rainbow*. The rainbow *is a* division of white *light into* many beautiful colors. These take the shape of *a* long round arch, *with its* path *high above*, *and its ends apparently* beyond the horizon. *There is, according* to legend, *a* boiling pot *of* gold *at one end*. People look, but *no one ever* finds *it*. When *a* man looks for something beyond his reach his friends say *he is* looking for the pot *of* gold *at the end of* the rainbow.

Interpretation: Where to Begin

What Do Singers Sing About?

Have you ever thought about what singers sing about? Whether the text is secular or sacred, from a myth derived from the oral tradition or a poem penned by a talented literary artist, the topic is mostly one mysterious, wonderful emotion: that of love. The presence or absence of love inspires much of creative, poetic thought. Myths and legends depict the involvement of gods and goddesses in their amorous affairs of human beings. Biblical writing praises the deity and laments humankind's imperfect adoration of it. In every language, singers worship the beloved from afar and denounce the pain of unrequited love. From ultimate joy to deepest despair, poetic texts center on the many manifestations of love.

What texts attract you most? Are you drawn to the ones that describe the ache of a loved one's temporary departure or even perhaps the agony of a permanent separation? Or would you prefer to sing about sharing the delight of an idyllic setting filled with natural beauty? Maybe you find the nostalgia of a former time especially appealing? Perhaps you exult in the surprises of a newly found attraction or in the triumphs of a long-awaited reunion? Based upon your personal experiences and literary background, some texts may be more understandable and relevant to you than others. Similarly, each culture has its own point of view regarding the essential elements required for a happy life. All cultures seem to agree that love, be it attainable or not, is one of the determining factors in the achievement of personal fulfillment.

In these pages, we deal exclusively with Western cultures, specifically English-, Italian-, German-, and French-speaking ones. Marriage, a dominant social and political institution in each of these cultures, has changed in its structures and importance from century to century and decade to decade. Love was not always the main incentive for marriage. In fact, until the mid-19th century, families controlled marital choices using money and property. It was assumed, in such marital arrangements that love would develop as a biproduct of the transactions between wise parents. Today we expect the couple to find one another through mutual attraction. Such agency on the part of the marital partners-to-be was unthinkable in earlier times. Negotiation for the hand of a bride depended upon strict rules of behavior. Fathers, brothers, and male relatives chaperoned unmarried young women in public settings. The education of most girls encouraged skill sets necessary for household and familial responsibilities. Etiquette required modesty, humility, and obedience from women of all ages. Social gatherings limited private contact between eligible partners. In our emancipated society, such restrictions are inconceivable, but as a singer, you must recognize the circumstances that trigger the texts you deliver in song. Unraveling the tangled path to love becomes part of the pleasure of singing.

Despite society's expectations, love has been known to "find its way," as the German poet Johann Gottfried von Herder (1744–1803) wrote. Johannes Brahms set the Herder texts as duets entitled "Weg der Liebe I and II," Op. 20. Much of world literature derives its plots from the intrigues designed to bend rules and trick heedless guardians. Here is a well-known example of such a plot: Ben Jonson (1572–1637) wrote two poems entitled "Song to Celia." (It should be noted that "Celia" is a common name for a female in pastoral poetry.) Jonson included both works in a group of miscellaneous poems under the heading *The Forest*, published in 1616. The second "Song to Celia" is best known in English-speaking circles by its first line, "Drink to me only with thine eyes." Set anonymously by an 18th-century composer, Roger Quilter (1877–1953) immortalized the setting by including it in the *Arnold Book of Songs* he published in 1950.

As you read this poem, keep in mind that a young woman in the 16th century, to avoid any semblance of flirtation, would have been trained to divert her gaze in the presence of an eligible young man. Yet this young man hopes to receive encouragement from his Celia. He suggests ways she could send him a signal with her eyes or by her behavior. The reader discovers in the second verse, that the poet recently sent a gift of flowers to Celia. Rather than simply accept them, Celia made the intimate gesture of breathing upon the bouquet before returning it to its sender. The return of the gift probably complied with the conventions of society. Celia, however, infused the flowers with her breath, a courageous move that surely pleased her suitor. It is possible, of course, that the standard bearers of societal norms in the 16th century may have frowned upon the manners of both young people. In the context of its time and culture, the poem depicts an episode rife with innocent intrigue. A modern reader of the text may find it nothing more than a charming tale of romance.

I

Drink to me only with thine eyes,

And I will pledge with mine;

Or leave a kiss but in the cup,

And I'll not look for wine.

The thirst that from the soul doth rise

Doth ask a drink divine:

But might I of Jove's nectar sup,

I would not change for thine.

II

I sent thee late a rosy wreath,

Not so much honoring thee,

As giving it a hope that there

It could not withered be.

But thou thereon didst only breathe,

And sent'st I back to me;

Since when it grows and smells, I swear,

Not of itself, but thee.

What is the poem's initial impact on you? Does it please you? Are you in agreement that the events of the second verse inspired the poem to be written? Did Celia's sign of approval invite the poet to request her glance? Can you imagine the scene? Have you considered how the poet knew that Celia breathed upon the bouquet before she returned it? How old do you think Celia and her suitor would have been? Is this a first love for them? Is the suitor more experienced in matters of the heart than Celia? Depending upon your interpretation, are there particular words or phrases you would wish to emphasize? What vowels or consonants provide opportunities for expression?

Poets often speak in symbolic language. This poet states that he would cherish one close encounter with Celia more than the chance to sip a fine wine, the "ambrosia of the gods" known as "Jove's nectar" (Greenblatt, Ed., 2012). Jove is also known as Zeus or Jupiter, the powerful god of sky and ruler of the Olympian gods. The wreath of roses he sends is symbolic of the beauty he observes in Celia and the depth of his passionate love.

Listen to the poem set to music by Quilter. Note all the poetic punctuation of the poem and the musical phrasing. The form of the song is "strophic," having two equal verses. The strophes or verses are framed by a prelude, interlude and postlude. Is there a sense of climax in each verse? Is one greater than another? Does the musical setting lend itself to the expression of those words you identified as most important?

Study the rhyme scheme for each verse. Note the differences from verse to verse. In both verses, there are archaic words such as *doth, thou,* and *sent'st.* To express clearly the meaning of the last two lines of the poem, acknowledge the commas carefully. The listener must understand that it is Celia's scent that emerges as the flowers open and ripen. The poet "swears" that this observation is true. To make the point perfectly clear to the listener, you must shape the closing words with convincing word inflection and clear articulation.

This example of a simple song setting shows the layers of meaning to be uncovered in history, culture, and literature. By immersing yourself in the poem as the composer did, you follow the compositional process and equip yourself to address issues of diction and interpretation more effectively. You will find that this process will empower your study and performance of all vocal music.

Where Were Songs Sung and Why?

Beginning in the late 19th century, music historians sought to codify repertoire by analyzing the historical circumstances of compositions. The information gleaned from these studies can be very useful to a singer. An awareness of the acoustic space, the age and the skill of the original performer can shed light on the intention and manner of performance.

In the 15th and 16th centuries, vocal literature was used to entertain and enlighten the royalty and their guest. Solo singing took place in elite, mostly small gatherings. The singer was often the poet, who accompanied himself on the lute or viol. In the 17th and early 18th centuries, nicknamed "the age of the *basso continuo*," the singer collaborated with a small accompanying group consisting of a sustaining bass instrument supported by a keyboard or string instrument capable of creating harmony. The development of the modern piano in the 19th century transformed music making into a collaborative art form in which pianists accompanied singers in performances in private homes or larger, public spaces. In the later 19th century, composers frequently orchestrated the songs that were originally performed with piano. An orchestrated song or aria heightens vocal demands upon a singer while offering new expressive possibilities. A thorough understanding of the original performing circumstance, its modern adaptation and its accompaniment will help you determine the challenges you face in bringing the music and text to life.

Why Do We Sing as We Do?

What is now called "classical singing" came to us from the liturgical practices of the early church in Italy. The secular application of those practices became known as *bel canto* or "beautiful singing," the singing style emulated later in early opera. The *Florentine Camerata*, a committee of poets, musicians, philosophers, rhetoricians, and politicians in 16th-century Florence, Italy, invented the genre known called "opera" or "work." The mission of the Camerata was to design an outlet that would feature all the artistic gifts of humankind. The Camerata chose to use the human voice to "elevate" the time-honored texts of Greek mythology and Roman legend in performances that included visual as well as musical art. Early opera composers were guided by the principles of "rhetoric," an expertise used to equate the quality of text with the grace of its delivery. The artist who was skilled in rhetoric used a broad palette of vocal colors, declarative nuances, and physical gestures to achieve a meaningful expression of the text. Diction was an essential skill for singers of early opera. They were trained to elongate pure vowels and to articulate crisp consonants in a flowing *legato* line. The timing of rests and fermatas was as important as proper pronunciation and enunciation. Shifts of body angle and musical mood were used to exploit every trace of dramatic content.

Early solo song was performed for an intimate gathering of guests, presumably friends. It was intended as intellectual amusement. After a singer presented a song, listeners were often expected to comment on the text and its relevance to societal mores and political views. Song functioned as a source for conversation, as an invitation to discuss the wit and symbolism contained within the texts. Clear diction, exact enunciation, and expression were the hallmarks of such performances. To "get the joke," the listener had to hear every syllable and punctuation mark. If you probe what made these songs humorous, ironic, or satirical to the ears and minds of their first audience, you will discover what words deserve special attention today.

The emergence of the middle class in 19th-century Europe brought new opportunities for solo singing. Guests invited to French salons or German *Hausmusiken* (musicales) anticipated that song performances would spawn deep, meaningful conversation. Those who composed songs sought inspiration from texts that probed aesthetic ideas worthy of further investigation. For example, it is common knowledge that Franz Schubert performed his earliest settings of Wilhelm Müller's poems for his closest friends when the ink was barely dry on the composer's manuscript. The opinion of his peers was invaluable to Schubert. Consider the scene of the composer amid the circle of his expectant friends. Imagine how attentive they would have been to every detail of word accent, expression, and dynamic contrast. Contemporary performances of these works require the same textual clarity. Later 19th-century composers such as Hugo Wolf, Gustav Mahler, Richard Strauss, and Hector Berlioz orchestrated their songs for use in public concerts. To be understood, singers of orchestrated song faced new vocal, interpretive, and diction challenges.

How Is Love Expressed in English?

To many, British society is perceived to be more cautious and formal than its American counterparts. The poetry set by 17th- and 18th-century composers such as Thomas Campion, Henry Purcell, George Frideric Handel, and their contemporaries demonstrate a restraint that complied with English manners of the time. In the 19th and 20th centuries, British composers Ivor Gurney, Benjamin Britten, Ralph Vaughan Williams, and Gerald Finzi created new settings of the time-honored texts from the Elizabethan era and experimented with the poetic sentiments of major contemporary British literary figures. W. B. Yeats, A. E. Housman, Robert Louis Stevenson, Gerald Manley Hopkins, and Thomas Hardy were among the poets whose works provided musical inspiration. These English song settings explore love as the source of great joy and fulfillment, though plenty of texts offer words of caution for the pain love's loss can inflict on the human heart. In comparison to the work of American poets, however, British poets and composers approach the passions evoked by love with a certain degree of restraint.

All English-speaking people recognize William Shakespeare as a formidable, foundational literary figure. According to the noted scholar Harold Bloom, it is William Shakespeare who taught us to be human. In describing Shakespeare's "universalism," Bloom in his book, *Shakespeare: The Invention of the Human*, states the following:

> . . . no Western writer, or any Eastern author I am able to read, is equal to Shakespeare as an intellect, and among writers I would include the principal philosophers, the religious sages, and the psychologists from Montaigne through Nietzsche to Freud. (Bloom, 1998)

From a literary standpoint, Shakespeare unites American and British traditions. For many decades, poets and musicians in America imitated their European role models. In the earliest song settings, American composers used works by British poets in equal measure with those of American poets. Arguably, the songs of Francis Hopkinson (1737–1791) are the first evidence of truly "American" song. American culture evolved much later as an adventurous, eclectic cultural "melting pot." In comparison to Europe, the United States is still a young country. The overall bounty of American vocal literature, though rich, is considerably smaller. To investigate the rich heritage of early American song, follow: https://www.loc.gov/creativity/hampson/. There you can explore "The Song of America Project," a collaboration between The Library of Congress and baritone Thomas Hampson that chronicles and promotes the creation and performance of American song.

Many American composers had a different influence than their British counterparts. Early in the 20th century, most aspiring American composers saw continental Europe as the "finishing school" for trained musicians. Most of the composers we consider the founders of the American vocal repertoire tradition had one famous French composition teacher in common, namely Nadia Boulanger (1887–1979). Beginning in 1921, Mademoiselle Boulanger was the cornerstone of the composition faculty at the American Conservatory at Fountainbleau in France. Aaron Copland, Leonard Bernstein, Virgil Thomson, and Ned Rorem, to name only a few American composers, attributed their compositional art and skill to Boulanger's tutelage. Boulanger's influence is seen in the melodic contours, harmonic variety and rhythmic drive to be found in the vocal and instrumental works of her students. The hallmark of Boulanger's teaching was her ability to guide each composer to his or her individual "voice." Under Boulanger's influence, students identified musical sounds and nuances that expressed their own unique, creative souls. To interpret the music of a Boulanger-trained composer, look for the unusual traits that define the composer's musical language or "voice."

Until recently, American art song served mainly to conclude a recital program, competing for recognition against familiar British master works. As you are already aware, the topic of love in American art song ranges from satire to seriousness and from frivolity to fairness. You may find that settings by some early 20th-century American song composers such as Ernest Charles and John Alden Carpenter are somewhat more nostalgic and sentimental than today's composers. Thomson, William Schuman, and Charles Ives were theoreticians who maintained an intellectual approach to songwriting. Samuel Barber, a linguist, singer, and pianist, created songs of literary and musical complexity. Bernstein brought a bit of Broadway flair to his composition of song. For American society, the 20th century presented diverse economic and political challenges. As you study the works of American composers, consider the current events that may have influenced both poet and composer. Through modern media, it is not difficult to ascertain significant details about literary and musical artists in the 20th century. For example, you may discover that a song or aria was created for a specific event to be broadcast on the radio or performed on an early television program. On the internet, you can readily find historical performances in which a composer premieres a new work as the collaborative pianist for a singer. It is easy to find interviews in which composers and performers offer commentary about their preparation for the first performance.

Contemporary composers such as Libby Larsen, Ricky Ian Gordon, and Jake Heggie have produced works that are utterly of our time. In the 21st century, through the efforts of the National Association of Teachers of Singing (NATS) and other initiatives, we are enjoying an explosion of interest in American art song composition, one that will enliven our culture. Visit the NATS website, https://www.nats.org/art-song-composition.html, to become acquainted with songs of the 21st century.

What Is the Italian View of Love?

Generally, in Italian literature and art, the word *love* or *amore* has life-giving power. To the Italian soul, being in love equates with being alive. God is love and love is a blessing. "Amore" or its apocopated version, "amor," is the spark that ignites human consciousness. Any confrontation with a love object brings invigorating sensations. If, as it was for Dante (1265–1321) and Petrarch (1304–1379), the beloved is unattainable, the desire to worship a person from a distance brings passions never known before. In poetry that celebrates love shared in equal measure, both hearts swell with joy and delight, sensing blessing and fulfillment. Should the love be physically absent, whether for a brief interval or forever, the presence of the beloved is felt. Even when love is not returned, unrequited love is a treasure to be cherished as a sign of personal growth. The poets and librettists of Italian vocal works speak of love as an opportunity for the exploration and expansion of human feeling. When a singer confronts the word *crudele* or *crudel* in a text, the level of cruelty is not necessarily equivalent to *cruel* in English. The circumstances might warrant a negative connotation, but the term can be used flirtatiously to say that "your presence in my life distracts me wonderfully from my work." Be aware that what would be an intellectual description of unacceptable, heartbreaking behavior in an English or German text might be a witty saying in Italian.

How Do Germans Interpret the Concept of Love?

The impact of the writings of Johann Wolfgang von Goethe (1749–1832) on literature, philosophy, and German culture is immeasurable. Beginning with *The Sufferings of the Young Werther* (1774), Goethe's investigations of the role of romantic love in human life have influenced generations of young people around the world. All of Goethe's literary work involve searches for fulfillment through human relationships. His thought permeates German culture. His writings suggest that the abundance or scarcity of love determines life's destiny. His works present happy outcomes for characters who find love to be available, perfectly timed and completely accepted. In Goethe's works, the characters who seek love but are thwarted in their pursuits live tainted, restless existences. *Faust*, a semiautobiographical tragic play completed in 1808, has been translated into numerous languages. Its themes and characters have spawned art works of many kinds. One of the major themes of *Faust* is the struggle between matters dictated by one's heart and those determined by reality and reasoning.

According to Goethe, "die Liebe" (German for "love") represents a colossal force that is capable of bestowing or withdrawing life energy. To understand and interpret German poetry, a singer must recognize that the smallest twist along love's path could bring ultimate delight or destruction for all parties concerned. In German poetry and song, love is a gravely decisive issue. Wickham Steed (1871–1956), British journalist and editor of *The Times*, once observed: "The Germans dive deeper—but they come up muddier" (Watson, 2010). His depiction applies especially to the issue of love in 19th-century German society. Goethe's poem, "Freudvoll und Leidvoll" ("Full of Joy and Full of Sorrow"), set to music by Schubert, Ludwig van Beethoven, and Franz Liszt, epitomizes this German love ideal. In the poem, Goethe juxtaposes extremes of feeling to express the overwhelming powers of love and passion. He writes that those in love may be simultaneously joyful and sorrowful, consumed by thought and longing. Love may cause anxious trembling, ecstasy or utter despair. Yet, Goethe concludes, only those who love are truly happy.

The musical language of 19th-century German Lieder is probing and complex. It is intended to emulate subtle sensitivity to the shifts of feeling and shades of thoughts that appear in the poetry. Often the text describes one single instant of recognition that determines the poet's fate. In Wilhelm Müller's well-known poem "Der Neugierge" ("The Curious One"), found in Schubert's timeless cycle, *Die Schöne Müllerin* (*The Beautiful Miller's Daughter*), the poet admits that his entire future depends on one of two short words: "yes" or "no." Either the miller's daughter loves him or she doesn't. If the answer is positive, he expects his life to be filled with purpose and prosperity. Should the response be negative, he faces years of longing and remorse.

Do the French Have Different Views of Love?

In French culture, the intellect rules over matters of the heart. Edith Wharton, expatriate American, observed in her book, *French Ways and Their Meaning:*

> The French are persuaded that the enjoyment of beauty and the exercise of critical intelligence are two of the things best worth living for; and the notion that art and knowledge could ever, in a civilized state, be regarded as negligible, or subordinated to merely material interests, would never occur to them. It does not follow that everything they create is beautiful, or that their ideas are always valuable or interesting; what matters is the esteem in which *the whole race* holds ideas and their noble expression. (Wharton, 1997)

For French poets, a romantic love that is desirable may not necessarily be essential. Love is a state of being that can be controlled by the mind. In 1878, Gabriel Fauré composed a song entitled "Adieu" ("Farewell") the third and last song in a cycle known as *Poemes du Jour* (*Poems of a Day*). At first reading, many singers are surprised by the wistful words of the poet, Charles Jean Grandmougin (1850–1930): "Mais hélas! Les plus longs amours sont court!" ("But alas, the best loves are short!"). The sentiment reflects Thomas Morley's observation in "It Was a Lover and his Lass" that " . . . love is crown'd in the prime." Brief love at its peak of perfection should be savored. Grandmougin suggests the mind can protect the heart from prolonged agony by intellectualizing the state of the affair. English, Italian, and German poets would likely find these ideas radical.

Love and the Seasons

English, German, and French poets frequently equate aspects of love with elements found in nature. Love is freshest in the springtime and may grow steamy in summer. Autumn is a season of transition, when leaves change color and drift to the ground from restless branches. The autumn of a love is an unsettling time when love is apt to wander. An autumnal season of love is often followed by a shift of affection, reminiscent of winter's chill. In Italian literature, where love tends to invigorate in any season, comparisons are drawn between love and landmarks such as mountains, sky, stars, and sea.

Singer's Diction: Poetry in Song

Singer's diction is more than the sum of pronunciation, articulation, and enunciation. In her excellent resource for singers of English, Kathryn LaBouff states that the absolute essentials of effective communication are to be heard and to be understood (LaBouff, 2008). It is also important to sing with vocal beauty and vigilant tuning. To be fully "in tune" with the music, a singing artist delves into the text's meaning in its context and examines the circumstances of the composer's encounter with it. A poet expresses emotion using words that are taken up into a musical embrace by a composer. With consonants and vowels, punctuation, and melodic phrasing, a singer creates an audible union of these thoughts and feelings. Through collaboration with a pianist or an instrumental ensemble, a singer is empowered to share with listeners the recollection of human experiences, exquisitely portrayed in words and music.

Since most poetry treats love as its topic, your song interpretations will investigate and comment on the role of love in human life. Jelaluddin Rumi, known as Rumi (1207–1273), was called by the Sufis the "pole of love" or "Quth," because his writings exclusively probed the heart's intersection with the human events. "Love is the way messengers from the mystery tell us things," says Rumi in his poem entitled "What Hurts the Soul?" (Banks, 2003).

Discussion Questions

1. Discuss how "the way of love" has been depicted by poets over the centuries.
2. What role do you think friends play in the creation of a composer's work?
3. What do you consider to be the American approach to love?
4. How does the American approach contrast with the British, Italian, German, and French concepts described?
5. When singing a poem, how important is it to be aware of the original circumstances?

Orpheus and His Lyre

Rainer Maria Rilke (1875–1926) began his "Sonnets to Orpheus" (Rilke, 1995) with the following words:

> Da steig ein Baum, O reine Übersteigung!
>
> O Orpheus singt! O hoher Baum im Ohr!
>
> Und alles schwieg. Doch selbst in der Verschweigung
>
> Ging neuer Anfang, Wink und Wandlung vor.

> A tree ascended there. O pure transcendence!
>
> Oh, Orpheus sings! O tall tree in the ear!
>
> And all things hushed. Yet even in that silence
>
> A new beginning, beckoning, change appeared.

Rilke, like many others, knew the "arrival of the muse" to be a reality. Inspiration sparks creativity in a startling moment known to artists of all kinds. Since ancient times, the name "Orpheus" has been considered a source of these experiences. First depicted on a Greek vase in the 6th century BC, Orpheus is seen dancing while playing a lyre. Greeks believed Orpheus to be the first singer of holy song and a mysterious enchanter. "Orpheus was called the first poet, of whom all poets since are echoes or incarnations; yet no poetry definitely survives from him," according to Wroe (2011). In Plato's *Dialogues*, the author frequently wrote " . . . as Orpheus says." In the 5th century BC, Herodotus mentions him in his travelogues. But was Orpheus really a person?

Throughout literature, Orpheus is included as a symbol of ingenuity through music. According to Shakespeare, Orpheus, son of Apollo and Calliope, had the power to calm the human spirit and bring peace to the physical world. In the world of early opera, Claudio Monteverdi believed that the story of Orpheus and his beloved, Eurydice, was particularly entrancing because it displayed passionate love and sacrifice with mortal tendencies. We hear this depth of distress in Monteverdi's "Orfeo" (1607), when the forsaken hero sings of his Eurydice in Act II: "Tu Sei Morta, Mia Vita, ed Io Respiro" ("You Are Dead, My Life, and I Breathe"). Compare it to the Act III aria "Che Farò Senz' Euridice" ("What Shall I Do Without Eurydice?") in Christoph Willibald von Gluck's 1762 version. The desolation and dissonance of Monteverdi illuminate the soulful agony of a sensitive spirit. Here the gods are called upon to respond without success. Though the harmonies are less jarring, Gluck's setting allows the singer to ornament and add personal touches of sadness in the process. Both operas deal with issues of human life, yet it is Orpheus' honest love of music and belief in its power that captivates the audience. Will music be the force that brings Eurydice back to Orfeo? Is music his only consolation? Is it yours?

In these renderings of Orpheus, whether mythological or historical, the fact remains that singing comes from within, from a hidden source of song. In the words of Rumi: "We are as the flute, and the music in us is from thee; we are as the mountain and the echo in us is from thee" (Banks, 1998). Singers sense what Orpheus knew, that singing is instinctive. You probably began to sing long before you read music or studied poems. Song sprang up within you as you walked and played. Perhaps, song slipped into your dreams or awakened you in the morning. Some would say that Orpheus, the muse was responsible for this sudden urge to sing. As a youngster, you may have sung to comfort yourself, to give yourself courage, or to celebrate success and happiness—just as Orpheus did. In an adaptation of the thought, Shakespeare quoted in Henry VIII the following words attributed to John Fletcher (1579–1625). The text describes the effect of Orpheus, when he sang and accompanied himself on the lute.

Orpheus with his lute made trees

And the mountain tops that freeze,

Bow themselves, when he did sing:

To his music plants and flowers

Ever sprung; as sun and showers

There had made a lasting spring.

Everything that heard him play,

Even the billows of the sea,

Hung their heads and lay by.

In sweet music is such art,

Killing care and grief of heart,

Fall asleep, or hearing, die.

There is such art in sweet music and with it, the power to ease pain and change moods. More than a dozen composers have been attracted to set the text "Orpheus with his Lute" to music. The most well-known British settings are by Gurney, Sir Arthur Sullivan, and Vaughn Williams. These songs could be sung with "Received Pronunciation," emphasizing the British origins of the poem. American composers Schuman and, more recently, Richard Hundley adapted the words to fit a more American approach to words and diction. The essence of the thought remains the same: Music masterfully and mysteriously impacts our daily lives.

Shakespeare's use of the text depicts Orpheus plucking a lute. We must not forget that the mythical Orpheus played the lyre, an instrument of great significance then and now. The adjective word *lyric* derives from it as does the noun *lyrics*. The lyre, a stringed instrument with a crossbar connecting two arms, is one of the symbols of music in Western civilization. The earliest evidence of the lyre shows a primitive stringing of twigs within a shell. Myths arose from spontaneous performances caused by breezes blowing through the strings. The flow of sound was believed to be a voice from beyond, be it a god or a departed soul. In every age, the lyre is a very personal instrument of musical expression, one that accompanies intimate thought and melody. Similarly, a lyric poet is a literary artist who expresses tender feelings through sensitive word choice. A lyric singer is one who easily emits spinning melodic lines that undulate like the air crossing the strings of a lyre. Art songs, operas, and oratorios are based upon preexisting texts. Art songs derive from poems while operas are based on a *libretto* (literally, *booklet*). Oratorios are based on libretti created from a variety of literary genres such as the Bible, hymns, and poetry. *Lyrics* are usually conceived with the melodic line by a lyricist and composer. In a few cases, the composer might be the poet, the librettist, or the lyricist. More often, the lyricist works as a team player with the composer. Gilbert and Sullivan, Rodgers and Hammerstein, and Sondheim and Bernstein represent three such important collaborative groups.

We should also keep in mind that Orpheus danced as well as sang. His whole body harmonized with his lyrical ways, causing him to feel rhythms pulsing from head to toe. As you learn to sing and express text, you too will become aware of sensations throughout your body. Singing technique is learned by the memorization and re-creation of those sensations. Resonance is felt through the phonation of vocal tone through pure and nasal vowels and through the articulation of consonants. Your heartbeat and sense of well-being reflect the pulse and pathos of the music. You sing with your whole being, as Orpheus did.

It should be noted that the story of Orpheus, Eurydice, and their encounter with the underworld has had far-reaching effects. Not only is it the source for a comic opera by Jacques Offenbach that premiered in Paris in 1858, but also a ballet by Igor Stravinsky in 1947. Stravinsky's "Orpheus" ballet was one of the composer's collaborations with the renowned choreographer George Balanchine (1904–1983). As a psychological tool, Carl Jung used the story of Orpheus and the underworld to suggest a life view in which hindsight is a potent tool. In the words and music of Lee Hoiby (1926–2011), we all want to be "where the music comes from." Orpheus symbolizes what each of us hopes to be: a performer who moves hearts and changes lives through song.

Can Poetry Be Defined?

What Is Poetry?

Poetry is not easy to define, though most human beings know when someone has said or written something "poetic." William Stafford (1914–1993), a poet and teacher, believes that poetry is something one sees from "the corner of one's eye":

> It's like a faint star. If you look straight at it you can't see it, but if you look a little to one side it is there. If people around you are in favor, that helps poetry to *be*, to exist. If you let your thoughts play, turn things this way and that, be ready for liveliness, alternatives, new views, the possibility of another world—you are in the area of poetry. (Stafford, 1978)

These excerpts come from Stafford's book entitled *Writing the Australian Crawl*. He equates the work of the poet to the efforts of a freelance swimmer who stretches out in the water and moves freely to achieve flotation and mobility. When reading a poem, Stafford asks the reader to open the mind and heart willingly; in other words, to "float out" upon the sea of language with the poet. In this way, the reader or singer can best grasp the concepts put forth by the poet. In the case of poetry set to music, the singer must track the composer's experiences to determine the composer's interpretation. In a song, the choice of key suggests the prevailing mood, while word or phrase repetitions indicate what the composer may have found most meaningful or indefinable among the poetic ideas. In searching the song for such clues, you, a singer, will become acquainted with the composer's thought processes and musical sensibilities. Certain aspects of melody and harmony seem instinctive to you, once you "embody" the composer's way of thinking and feeling.

Is poetry necessary to the human experience? In the anthology *The Handbook of Heartbreak*, the editor, Robert Pinsky (b. 1940), explains how human beings have the power through poetry to state and discuss intimate topics. Pinsky, the 1995 United States poet laureate and poetry consultant to the Library of Congress from 1997 to 2000, writes:

> Perhaps even more than drama or film, works that rely mainly on words produced by a voice, as in poetry or song, frequently seem to rely for their material on the unhappy parts of life, in order to give us the joy of art . . . The great answers to this mystery probably have, each of them, a measure of truth: by the artist's gift, we have our own unarticulated feeling to express: by catharsis we get the woe and the fear of woe out of our system; by sublimation we convert neediness into a possession; by recognition we feel companionship . . . all art is imitation, says Aristotle: poetry imitates speaking and being spoken to in response. (Pinsky, 1998)

Who Writes Poetry, When, and Why?

Note that Pinsky's book, mentioned above, references "heartbreak" in its title. It seems that what distresses or disappoints us is what sparks our creative process. The movements of the heart are many and varied, but those that trigger an ache seem to demand deeper reflection. Through exquisite word choice and careful use of linguistic tools such as rhyme, rhythm, and alliteration, a poet attempts to recreate the emotional circumstances of a moment, setting it apart for study and evaluation. Such poetic writing seals instances of human experience in time and in print. It is the rare mortal who would stop during an activity, be it pleasant or poignant, to gather the details into poetic verse. For this reason, most poems are written in the "gently past tense" and describe a completed act. The poetic heart and mind absorb the visceral, visual, and emotional content and process the results from a reflective distance. By taking the long view of the completed experience, the poet can explain and quantify the experience's overall impact. Through subtle arrangements of words and images, a poet hopes to make a reader feel, taste, see, smell, or hear what the poet did.

Take a moment to think about how a poet "receives" the seed that germinates into a finished poetic work. One of the most popular English poets of the 20th century, A. E. Housman (1859–1936), described the arrival of his poetic "muse" in the following way: "Experience has taught me, when I am shaving of a morning, to keep watch over my thoughts, because, if a line of poetry strays into my memory, my skin bristles so that the razor ceases to act. This particular symptom is accompanied by a shiver down the spine; there is another which consists in a constriction of the throat and a precipitation of water to the eyes" (Housman, 1933). Do not be surprised if you too have a visceral response. Allow a poem and its message to strike you with its full impact. Rhyme and rhythm are significant agents that drive a reader or a singer to a dramatic climax. Such tension promises the satisfaction of a resolution or an epiphany. Emily Dickinson's unorthodox use of punctuation heightened the visual aspects of the printed page. The presence of a momentary silence, whether it is created by dashes or other critical markings, changes the flow of thought for the reader or singer. For an interpreter of text, punctuation serves as stage directions that indicate a slight hesitation or a vocal color change. These poetic devices augment the communicative prospects for creator and interpreter alike.

How Should Poetry Be Read?

John Hollander (1929–2013), editor of *Committed to Memory: 100 Best Poems to Memorize*, celebrates the experience of reading a poem silently or listening to one being read by others as a human event that has existed through the millennia of written literature:

> . . . poetry retains its appeal to the ear as well as to the eye; to hear a poem read aloud by someone who understands it and who wishes to share that understanding with someone else, can be a crucial experience, instructing the silently reading eye ever thereafter to hear what it is seeing. Better yet is reading aloud that way oneself. (Hollander, 1996)

In the opening chapter of the book *How to Read a Poem and Fall in Love With Poetry*, Edward Hirsch compares a poem to a "message in a bottle"; thoughts tossed out upon the waters of life to be retrieved on a distant shore. Hirsch challenges the recipient to do the following:

Read these poems to yourself in the middle of the night. Turn on a single lamp and read them while you're alone in an otherwise dark room or while someone else sleeps next to you. Read them when you're wide awake in the early morning, fully alert. Say them over to yourself in a place where silence reigns and the din of the culture—the constant buzzing noise that surrounds us—has momentarily stopped. These poems have come from a great distance to find you. (Hirsch, 1999)

How Does a Singer Approach a Poem Set to Music?

Poetry set to music embodies a union of thought and feeling between a poet and a composer. A song setting presupposes a preexisting work of art as its creative foundation. Be it a poem or prose, lyrics or a libretto, the text has captivated the composer's senses. Maybe it is its rhythm or rhyme, its sensuality, or its sentiment; but somehow, the written word of a literary artist engages the sensibilities of a musical one. This encounter between composer and written work ignites a spark that may simmer slowly or burst instantaneously into an emerging melody. You, a singer, arrive on the scene long after the composer and text have become acquainted. You need evidence of what the composer loved about a text and what occasion prompted the composer's awareness of it.

- ◆ Did the composer know the poet?
- ◆ Was the work commissioned? If so, by whom and why?
- ◆ Is this the only poem by this poet that had such an impact upon the composer?
- ◆ Is this the only poem the composer has ever set?
- ◆ What is the cultural context of the poet's life? The composer's?

The role of culture is almost as important to a singer's interpretation as is the language of the text or the vocal technique required to sing it. With love as a universal theme, poetry generally explores love's origins, iterations, and various guises. Using words, poets shed light on how love is found, what happens when it is returned or unrequited, what happens when it changes form or disappears. Whether called by the name "Cupid," "Amor," or "Eros," the same feisty cherub wields an unlimited power to surprise, to confuse and to imprison human hearts. The topic of love and its proper expression evolves from century to century, differing by country and society. As part of the compositional process, a vocal composer analyzes the meaning and context of a poem. The resulting song reveals the composer's take on the poem. Poetry set to music layers many expressive morsels into an artistic whole. Singing is more a "re-creative" than a "creative" art, bringing to life a composer's setting of a poet's words. The singer who performs the song makes the composer's analysis audible to a listening audience.

You, the singer and your collaborative pianist begin with a printed musical score that contains melodic and harmonic guidelines to follow. Together you shape your performance based upon your collected knowledge of the literary and musical conventions that govern the given style period. You will speculate on the cultural beliefs and practices that may have influenced the poet and the composer. The sum of these elements determines your interpretative point of departure. There are times when delicacy is the appropriate delivery of a text. In other musical settings, the same words are best expressed by exploiting the meaning using a coarse declamation.

Let's begin with a poem in the English language: "Come Again, Sweet Love Doth Now Invite," set to music by John Dowland (1523–1626).

I

Come Again, Sweet Love doth now invite

Thy graces that refrain to do me due delight

To see, to hear, to touch, to kiss, to die with thee again

In sweetest sympathy.

II

Come again, that I may cease to mourn

Through thy unkind disdain for now, left and forlorn,

I sit, I sigh, I weep, I faint, I die, in deadly pain

And endless misery.

III

Gentle Love, draw forth thy wounding dart:

Though canst not pierce her heart; For I that do approve

By sighs and tears more hot than are thy shafts did tempt

while she for triumphs laughs.

In 1597, Dowland published this song in his *First Book of Ayres*. The text is anonymous, though many assume it to be Dowland's work. He was a lutenist and singer, whose songs had international meaning even in his own day. The term "ayre" or "air" referred to a song in which the melody was contained in the top voice. Dowland set most of his ayres for solo voice and for quartets of singers. The solo versions would have been performed with a greater sense of intimacy than the choral ones. An awareness of the existence of both versions informs the performance of either.

- ◆ Read the poem silently. Imagine yourself to be the poet who wrote it. What experience does the text recall? Does the poem evoke sensations? What are they? Did you feel a strong sense of rhyme? Of rhythm? How do rhyme and rhythm contribute to the overall dramatic effect of the text's meaning?

- ◆ Now read it aloud as poetry, taking care to stop at the end of each printed line. Do you hear a musical context within the poem itself? Can you imagine why the composer was captivated by its possibilities?

- ◆ Read the poem aloud again, but this time, ignore the confines of the printed page. Read the poem as if it were a work of prose. Move through the text from one punctuation mark to the next. Notice any effects of rhythm and rhyme within the text that may be different in the prose reading.

◆ Read the words as set by the composer, in rhythm and with any repetition that appears in the music. Allow your speaking voice to lilt and lower with the contours of the melody. Elongate the vowels and articulate the consonants crisply. Take time for interludes and sense any modulations. How is this reading different from the previous ones?

◆ Write the poem out, noting its punctuation marks carefully. Include commentary about what occurred for you during your silent and oral readings. Does this text relate to any experience in your own life? Is it foreign to you? Can you imagine how you might feel if you were the poet? The composer? When you sing the song in performance, you will be sharing not only the poem and the music, but also your insights into both. As a point of departure for your preparation, confirm for yourself in writing what you believe the text means in its musical context.

◆ Listen to recordings of performers from different time periods. Seek a performance by Alfred Deller (1912–1979), a British countertenor, as well as Barbara Bonney (b. 1956), an American soprano. How do the performances compare?

Next, compare two settings of "Fain Would I Change That Note" from two different historical time periods: that of Tobias Hume (ca. 1569–1645) and of Quilter (1877–1953). Both men are British. The text itself is attributed to Hume. Clearly, Quilter would have known of Hume's original setting of the text. Read the text closely as prescribed above.

I

Fain would I change that note to which fond love has charmed me

Long, long to sing by rote, fancying that that harmed me

Yet when this thought doth come: Love is the perfect sum of all delight,

I have no other choice, either by pen or voice to sing or write.

II

Oh Love, they wrong thee much, who claim Thy sweet is bitter

When Thy rich fruit is such that nothing can be sweeter

Fair House of Joy and Bliss where truest pleasure is, I do adore Thee

I know Thee what Thou art, I serve Thee with my heart and fall before Thee.

What is your initial impression of the text's meaning? Are there particular words or phrases that stand out to you as important or unusual? Consider the following information about the two settings. Hume's "Fain Would I Change That Note" was published in 1605 in a collection of "Musical Humors." The musical setting evokes an ironic tone expressed through cross rhythms and shifts of meter. Quilter chose the 16th-century text in 1907 for his sincere, stirring setting entitled "Fair House of Joy" (Op. 12. No. 7) and included it in *Seven Elizabethan Lyrics*, published in 1908. Quilter's title alerts you, the singer, to his compositional point of departure. He obviously found the phrase "Fair House of Joy and Bliss" as a characterization of love's presence that is worth pointing out from the very start. Hume's interpretation seems much more "tongue in cheek," acknowledging the power of love to surprise and entrap. Quilter's rhapsodic approach denotes genuineness.

Both settings pose situations that require specific diction strategies to ensure the listener's understanding of the text at first hearing. Note the phrase "long, long to sing by rote fancying that *that* harmed me." Listen to a performance of "Fain Would I Change That Note," performed by the Spanish duo of Montserrat Figueras (1942–2011) accompanied by viol player Jordi Savall (b. 1941). Contrast their performance of Hume's setting with Quilter's setting of the same text, entitled "Fair House of Joy," sung by Kathleen Ferrier (1912–1953), British contralto. In these two presentations, you will be hearing two different treatments of the text through form, rhythm, and key. You will also experience contrasting performance circumstances, that of a singer accompanied by a period instrument and one accompanied by the modern piano. Both performances should give you new insights into the text and its melodic and harmonic possibilities.

Consider two complementary versions of "Down by the Salley Gardens," one set by Britten and the other by Gurney. The arrangement by Britten may be more familiar to you. It is a strophic setting that uses the same music for both verses. The Britten arrangement exploits the folk song nature of the text. Gurney, English poet and composer, may be less well-known to you. In Gurney's setting of the text, you will find triplet figures that allow you to differentiate your interpretation of two very important, similar phrases: "but I, being young and foolish, with her did not agree" and "but I was young and foolish, and now am full of tears." Gurney presents the self-deprecating remark in a manner that permits you to acknowledge the comma in the first verse and thereby intensify the articulation of the words *young* and *foolish*. In the second verse, without the comma, you affirm the poet's recognition of his youth and foolishness. In the Gurney version, "full of tears" is repeated and has the effect of a coda to the song.

Down by the salley gardens

My love and I did meet;

She passed the salley gardens

With little snow-white feet.

She bid me take love easy,

As the leaves grow on the tree;

But I, being young and foolish,

With her would not agree.

In a field by the river

My love and I did stand,

And on my leaning shoulder

She laid her snow-white hand

She bid me take life easy,

As the grass grows on the weirs;

But I was young and foolish,

And now am full of tears.

Listen to Britten's version sung by tenor Peter Pears and Gurney's setting performed by tenor Anthony Rolfe Johnson. Note the interpretative nuances of these two British singers. As you listen to the two settings, be aware of the repetition of text in the Gurney setting. Compare it with Britten's simpler setting. Also, study the way punctuation is used to express the last phrase of each verse in both settings.

What do you need to know to sing this text with assurance? First, you need to know what "salley" gardens are. The word *salley* derives from the Latin for *willow*. The poet, William Butler Yeats (1865–1939), one of the most celebrated of 20th-century poets, visited a village where thatched roofed cottages each had a willow tree as a part of the garden landscape. The willow tree, prevalent in mythology and literature, symbolizes a living element that is capable of bending in extreme positions without breaking. The willow tree is used commonly to signify the moon, grief, weeping, healing, and ever-lasting life.

Where does the poem come from? Yeats published "Down by the Salley Gardens" in *The Wanderings of Oisin and Other Poems* in 1889. It is based on an Irish folk song. The poem has been set to music by others besides Britten and Gurney. If you wish to expand your understanding of the text, listen to its various settings for solo voice and for choir. You will find that the use of punctuation and the opportunities for expressive diction varies with each setting. The settings have been composed with slightly different approaches to Yeats' text.

Why Is Close Reading Important for Singing and Diction?

When studying any poem set to music, make it a practice to immerse yourself in the words the way the composer may have done. Read the poem many times and in various ways, both silently and aloud. Each time you read, honor every punctuation mark. Pause at each comma and note the finality of each period. Allow your voice to rise in the presence of question marks and exult with each exclamation point. Luxuriate in each element of sound.

Perhaps the following poem, written by Dickinson in 1862 (Johnson, 1951), will inspire you. Through her words, the poet assures you that you have a vast capacity to understand complicated structures.

The Brain—is wider than the Sky—

For—put them side by side—

The one the other will contain

With ease—and You—beside

The Brain is deeper than the sea—

For—hold them—Blue to Blue

The one the other will absorb—

As Sponges—Buckets—do

The Brain is just the weight of God—

For—Heft them—Pound for Pound—

And they will differ—if they do—

As Syllable from Sound—

Permit yourself to open your mind, heart, and voice to every syllable and every sound in a text, spoken and sung. Follow the poet's lead by acknowledging punctuation and nuance. Recognize the signals of meter, melody, and harmony provided by the composer. Your interpretation will reflect the artistry of both elements.

Discussion Questions

1. Who writes poetry? When? Why?
2. How does a single poem change its meaning from century to century?
3. Name the elements that make a poem endure from generation to generation.
4. Is the original context of a poem essential to its current meaning?
5. How does a singer's acquaintance with contrasting musical settings of a single poem increase interpretative skill?

The International Phonetic Alphabet: History and Use

Why do singers use the IPA as a pronunciation guide, you ask? The authors of the *Handbook of the International Phonetic Association: A Guide to the Use of the International Phonetic Alphabet* have written the following:

> From its foundation in 1886, the Association has been concerned to develop a set of symbols which would be convenient to use, but comprehensive enough to cope with the wide variety of sounds found in the languages of the world; and to encourage the use of this notation as widely as possible among those concerned with language. (International Phonetic Association, 2003)

The IPA provides you with a consistent way to record in written form the spoken or sung sounds you hear. The IPA is made up of symbols drawn from the Roman alphabet, the alphabet used in Western languages today. It also includes elements taken from other sources. The International Phonetic Association meets periodically for conventions to update IPA symbols and usage. At these events, experts add new symbols and revise or omit older ones. As you study resource materials for singer's diction, be aware that subtle differences exist in IPA usage based upon the judgement of the governing body of the International Phonetic Association. Check the date of the publication you are using to be certain that you are learning the most current information. Consult www.internationalphoneticalphabet. org: there you will find a full disclosure of the history and use of the symbols.

The IPA is divided into two basic phonetic types: those for vowels and those for consonants. Within these two groups, there are subsets. For example, vowels are categorized as monophthongs, diphthongs, and triphthongs. A monophthong is a vowel sound that contains only one sound. Diphthongs are formed when two sounds occur within one syllable, and triphthongs, when three sounds occur in a single syllable. The performance of each vowel sound category varies by language. Consonants appear in simple forms and in clusters. The IPA also has a set of symbols that bear no audible sound and indicate syllabic stress or separation. When you purchase dictionaries in the languages in which you will sing, choose editions that use the IPA as the pronunciation system. Be certain that dictionary you select in each case contains the symbols in the target foreign language. For example, if a German-English dictionary is published by a European publisher, it is intended for German speakers to learn English. In that case, you might find that the IPA symbols appear only in the English portion of the dictionary and not in your "target" language, or the language you seek to learn. The IPA is an important toolbox to distinguish color and purity of vowels and consonants in English and foreign languages. Using the IPA, we will study the sounds of the English language and the specific IPA symbols associated with those sounds.

Rules of the Road

The IPA is used to remember the "sound" of a word. You will use the IPA to record and remember the aural experience of a word or phrase. The IPA does not teach you to speak your language or foreign ones. It provides you with a series of symbols that help you relate the sounds you know in English to similar sounds in foreign words you do not know. Before assigning IPA symbols to sounds in foreign words, you will hear the words spoken or sung. Imagine someone wrote a word in Italian, German, or French on the blackboard and asked you to pronounce it. You might guess at the sound, but you would not be certain. If the foreign word is pronounced for you, you would have no difficulty repeating the proper pronunciation. Then, and only then, would you be able to write down how the word sounded. The IPA is a code to use for remembering sounds in new words. It will help you relate foreign sounds to sounds in English and recall the new sounds you encounter in foreign languages.

Essential Vocabulary

As a student of singing, you are seeking to develop a level of proficiency in English, Italian, German, and French to become competent and confident. Because the topics of love poetry are similar in each language, certain nouns appear frequently. You will discover that many of the words are cognates of English words you know. Your knowledge of these words will help you divide and conquer the texts you wish to sing.

Here is a partial list of words that commonly appear in poetry:

English	Italian	German	French
Love and Its Attributes			
Beauty (outer)	la beltà	die Schönheit	la beauté
Cupid	Cupido	Amor	Cupidon
Happiness	la gioja/gioia	die Freude	le bonheur
Heart	il core/cuore	das Herz	il coeur
Heartbeat	i palpiti	der Puls/der Schlag	la palpitation
Love	l'amore	die Liebe	l'amour
Sadness	la tristessa	die Traurigkeit	la tristesse
Soul	l'alma	die Seele	l'âme
Physical Aspects of Love			
Arm	il braccio	der Arm	le bras
Beloved	l'amante	das Liebchen	bien-aimée
Eyes	gli occhi	die Augen	les yeux
Face	la faccia	das Gesicht	le visage
Foot/Feet	il piede/i piedi	der Fuss	le pied
Friend	l'amica/l'amico	der Freund	l'amie
Hand	la mano	der Hand	la main
Laughing	ridente	das Lachen	rire
Lips/mouth	il labbro	die Lippen/der Mund	la lèvre/les levres
Smile	il sorriso	Lächeln	le sourire
Places and Activities			
Bells	le campane	die Glocken	les angelus
Cathedral	il duomo	der Dom	la cathédrale
Church	la chiesa	die Kirche	l'église
Dream	il sogno	der Traum	le songe/rêve
Footstep	il passo	der Schritt	le pas
House	la casa	das Haus/die Heimat	la maison
Pathway	la via	der Weg	le chemin
Serenade	la serenata	das Ständchen	la sérènade

English	Italian	German	French
Sleep	dorme	der Schlaf	le sommeil
Tear/s	la lacrima	die Tränen	les larmes
Walk/Stroll	la passeggiata	der Spaziergang	la promenade
Love and Spirituality			
Angel	l'angelo	der Engel	l'ange
Death	la morte	der Tod	la mort
God	Dio	Gott	Dieu
Love and the Seasons			
Autumn	l'autunno	der Herbst	l'automne
Spring	la primavera	der Frühling/Lenz	le printemps
Summer	l'estate	der Sommer	l'été
Winter	l'inverno	der Winter	l'hiver
Love and Music			
Harmony	harmonia	die Harmonie	harmonie/l'accord
Song/Melody	la canzone	das Lied/die Melodie	la chanson
Sound/Noise	il suono	der Klang	le bruit
Voice	la voce	die Stimme	la voix
Love and Nature			
Branch	il ramo	der Zweig	la branche
Cloud	la nube	der Wolke	le nuage
Heaven/Sky	il cielo	der Himmel	le ciel
Moon	la luna	der Mond	la lune
Stars	la stella/le stelle	der Stern/die Sterne	les étoiles
Sun	il sole	die Sonne	le soleil
Tree	l'albero	der Baum	l'arbre
Love and Family			
Aunt	la zia	die Tante	la tante
Baby	il bambino/ la bambina	das Baby	le bébé
Boy	il ragazzo	der Junge	le garçon

English	Italian	German	French
Brother	il fratello	der Bruder	il frere
Daughter	la figlia	die Tochter	la fille
Father	il padre	der Vater	le père
Girl	la ragazza	das Mädchen	la fille
Husband	il sposo	der Mann	l'homme
Mother	la madre	die Mutter	la mère
Sister	la sorella	die Schwester	la soeur
Son	il figlio	der Sohn	le fils
Uncle	lo zio	der Onkel	le oncle
Wife	la sposa	die Frau	la femme
Bodies of Water			
Lake	il lago	der See	le lac
River	il fiume	der Fluss	la rivière
Sea	il mare	der Ozean	la mer
Water	l'acqua	das Wasser	l'eau
Flowers and Trees			
Lilacs	il lillà	der Fliederbusch	le lilas
Lily	il giglio	die Lilie	le lis
Myrtle	il mirto	die Myrte	le myrte
Rose	la rose	die Rose	la rose
Love and the Weather			
Fog	la nebbia	der Nebel	le voile
Rain	la pioggia	der Regen	la pluie
Snow	la neve	der Schnee	la neige
Storm	la tempesta	der Sturm	la tempête
Wind	il vento	der Wind	le vent/le souffle
Temperatures			
Cold	freddo	kalt	froid
Frozen	congelato	frieren	glacé
Hot	caldo	heiss/warm	chaud

As you become familiar with these recurring words and their pronunciations, your confidence will grow, allowing you to express the meaning of the words in their musical contexts with authority and artistry.

Additional Tools

Terms from Greek Mythology and Roman Legend

In ancient times, humankind used characters in myth and legend to account for those events in history that lacked tangible evidence and defied reason. Gods, goddesses, and muses were imbued with powers that helped make sense of the world and its activities. These imagined deities appear in Western literature in every era. Below is a chart listing the names (Greek/Roman, respectively), lineage, and responsibilities of these characters:

Agamemnon	Legendary king of Mycenae, character in Homer's epic poems
Ares/Mars	God of war, son of Zeus with Hera
Apollo/Apollo	Son of Zeus/master of music/beauty and order Half-brother of Dionysus (wine and chaos) Tool: Lyre The sun (as twin to Artemis/Diana)
Artemis/Diana	Apollo's twin sister/daughter of Zeus The moon (as twin to Apollo)
Athena/Minerva	A daughter of Zeus who sprang from his head full grown and dressed in armor
Aphrodite/Venus	Daughter of Zeus, goddess of love and beauty
Clytemnestra	Wife of Agamemnon; opera plots involve her role in husband's murder
Cronus/Saturn	God of the sky/god of agriculture
Deter/Ceres	Goddess of grain
Dido	Legendary princess of Tyre
Dionysus/Bacchus	Half-brother of Apollo/god of wine and chaos
Eros/Cupid	God of love
Eumenides/Furies	Benevolent deities
Eurydice	Wife of Orpheus
Ganymede	Most beautiful of all mortals, cupbearer at the table of the gods

Hades/Pluto	Ruler of the underworld and the deceased, another brother of Zeus/Jupiter/Jove
	Tool: Helmet with the power to make its wearer invisible
Helen	Originally, a Greek goddess of vegetation; later, a heroine who appears in the epics *The Iliad* and *The Odyssey*
Hephaestus/Vulcan	Son of Hera/god of fire
Hera/Juno	One of Zeus/Jupiter/Jove's wives and sister; protector of marriage
Hercules/Hercales	Deeply beloved, legendary character, associated with Zeus
Hermes/Mercury	Son of Zeus
	Tool: Winged shoes and hat
Hero and Leander	Famous couple of Greek legend whose tragedy appears in Ovid and Schiller's work
Hestia/Vesta	Virgin goddess and goddess of the hearth, sister of Zeus/Jupiter/Jove
	Tool: Home
Homer	Thought to be the oldest, most significant epic poet; author of *The Iliad* and *The Odyssey*
Hope	Hope is what remained in Pandora's box after it was opened and every evil escaped into the world
Iliad	Homer's epic portraying 50 days in the 10-year Trojan War (its characters and situations are the plots of several operas).
Iphigenia	Legendary daughter of Agamemnon and Clytemnestra; sister of Orestes, Electra and Chrysothemis
Nike/Victoria	Goddess of victory
Orpheus	Son of Apollo, husband of Eurydice, muse of music
Orfeo/Eurydice	Myth of Orpheus' effort to retrieve Eurydice from the underworld
Pandora	First mortal woman fashioned by the gods
Poseidon/Neptune	Ruler of the sea, brother of Zeus/Jupiter/Jove
	Tool: Three-pronged spear called a "trident"
Zeus/Jupiter/Jove	Lord of the sky and ruler of all the other gods
	Tool: Lightning bolt

For a thorough understanding of Greek and Roman gods, goddesses, places, and events, consult *The Chiron Dictionary of Greek and Roman Mythology,* translated by Elizabeth Burr (2017).

Literary Symbols

Over many centuries, poets have used symbolism to expand the inner vision of the reader. Certain literary characters persist, appearing in many languages and cultures such as Dante's "Beatrice" and Petrarch's "Laura" as early examples of love worshipped from afar as an enrichment of life. "Elysium" or the Elysian fields represent a place for restful afterlife. Flowers like the rose, the lily, and the lilac bear significance related to specific seasons of love. The willow tree is used to depict states of sadness. Various birds, such as the dove, nightingale, and swan, have meaning beyond their gifts of song. Insects like the ladybug signal springtime. There are musical instruments that have been important in human history. The Aeolian harp or lyre, for example, is any harp suspended in the air, as noted in Psalm 137 where the Jewish exiles hung their harps by the waters of Babylon. The lyre or harp becomes a "wind instrument" evoking the expression of wordless feeling. We speak of a poet or singer as lyric when the flow of sound is easy and undulating.

Here is list of symbols frequently found in poetic texts set to music:

Apple often refers to the Garden of Eden's Tree of Knowledge and the tempting allure of a forbidden fruit.

April is a month when spring is at its peak in some cultures.

Arrow and *Bow* are the tools of Cupid, operating unexpectedly when targeting a heart.

Ash tree, *ash grove* refers to a strong, bountiful tree that has the power to mete out justice or make a person recognize a reality.

Autumn is a restless time between summer and winter, when harvest is gathered and cold weather anticipated.

Bees are valued for their honey and wax. They are very social, visiting flowers to sip nectar or to pollinate them. A single bee can provide society while a swarm of bees can be ominous.

Blue is the color of the sky on a sunlit day. *Azure* usually relates to the ocean waters, especially the Mediterranean.

Butterfly is a being with a brief, fragile life. It is often a symbol of the fragility of love. The butterfly does not wish to be touched or controlled as it flits by or rests on a flower petal. It is charming and hopes to be appreciated.

Clouds float in lofty places. They can also prevent a clear vision of the sky.

Cuckoo promises spring. The cuckoo often mocks the antics of lovestruck human beings.

Cypress is an evergreen tree that is associated with funerals or gravesites. It can also suggest eternal life.

Daffodil is one of the first flowers that appears in spring, jutting up through the snow to avail itself of the sun's warmth.

Dance implies ceremony, be it joyful and frivolous or ritualistic and somber. Courtship is sometimes described as a "dance."

Dawn represents "new" light and a fresh start. In some poetry, it marks sadly the conclusion of a night of love.

Death, in literary terms, may be physical or spiritual. It may be the end of a love or the sensual release into a deep affection.

Deer ("hart" or "stag"/male, "doe" or "fawn"/female) symbolize hunting. A lone deer implies a cruel fate. Deer live in herds and tend to reject a deer that is stricken by illness.

Dew brings freshness. It is a gift from nature. Dew responds to beautiful flowers and can be symbolic of tears that spring from a lovely encounter with love.

Dove or *turtledove* is the bird of love. The dove is a gentle, comforting spirit.

Dream symbolizes visions and suggests wisdom that is sought from other realms.

East/west can denote the travel of winds from one place to another. In poetry, the winds have been known to carry thoughts and feelings from one heart to another.

Evening implies rest after hard work. It invites quiet and inner peace.

Fire is essential to human life. It is present in the sun, the stars, lightning, candles, and warm hearths. Love can be the spark that kindles fire.

Flowers can represent young beauty, vulnerability, and innocence. Each individual flower type has its own characteristics.

Fly is an insect that delivers disease. It can bode ill. The word *fly* may simply mean a "winged" insect. In that case, the fly is a being with a short, busy life.

Forests can be places of danger or of solace. To be lost in a forest can be frightening, but to stroll through a forest with a companion can be a life-giving experience. To return to a forest without the companion can bring melancholy.

Fountains can be sacred, refreshing places. A fountain can be a celebratory site. To drink from a fountain is restorative.

Garden may refer to the Garden of Eden. A book of poetry or songs may be called a "garden" with the individual poems or songs the "flowers."

Green is the color of fresh, new growth. It suggests hope in the springtime. In some cases, it might be the color of an unripe fruit or an unhealthy person. In other cases, green can be a symbol of jealousy as in "green with envy."

Hair that flows can symbolize beauty, wealth, or sensuality. Blond hair can be a "golden crown."

Holly is evergreen and has "male" and "female" varieties. The plant has a red blossom and a prickly edge. It is symbolic of the Christmas season in combination with ivy and mistletoe.

Horse references are found in literature as a means of travel, either on horseback or in a horse-drawn carriage. *Pegasus*, the flying horse, was a favorite of the Muses. The Trojan horse suggests deception.

Hunting is the pastime of many characters in literature. The hunter is sometimes hunted. Beware of Cupid, who uses a bow and arrow to hunt for his prey.

Jasmine is a white, star-shaped flower depicting purity and innocence. It releases a sweet scent that makes an intoxicating, enveloping aura.

Lark is a popular bird that announces the early morning. Its presence symbolizes hope.

Laurel is a plant associated with victory or achievement.

Lightness/darkness relate to good versus evil, wisdom versus ignorance.

Lily is second only to the rose as a literary floral symbol. The lily is delicate and white. It can imply virginity.

Linden trees are appreciated for the shade they provide. In Europe, linden trees were planted in the town center to provide a place for strolling. Poets often depict lovers sitting together deep in conversation beneath linden trees.

Melancholy is a meditative state that frequently coincides with unrequited love or hopelessness.

Mill, particularly a water mill, is a symbol of power and productivity.

Mirror is a reflective item. It can be symbolic of vanity or narcissism. Mirrors also reflect truth and dispel illusions.

Moon is an important light; a silent strength and companion to both the lonely and the loved. Its silver glow at night contrasts with the golden rays of the day's sun. The moon is the eye of the evening, aware of lovers' secret meetings.

Mountains require climbing to heights. They can be the home of good or evil spirits, gods, or witches. The view of a mountain from below can be inspiring. People who live in the mountains may seem foreign to those who live in valleys below.

Music of the spheres is a phrase that represents a harmony among the moon, sun, stars, and earthly realms.

Myrtle is an evergreen plant that symbolizes love. Myrtle wreaths are worn by persons who are victorious in love. The plant suggests the possibility that life can triumph over death.

Nature is a maternal symbol, surrounding humankind with protective forces. It represents a degree of balance and harmony between living beings.

Night is the darkness that holds unseen danger. It can be a time of meditation and rest.

Nightingale is a bird that heralds spring and confirms the presence of love. It is a wakeful, solitary bird. Some poets suggest that the nightingale presses a thorn against its breast to stay alert to lament throughout the night. A nightingale is a shy, skittish bird whose song is heard only by those whose presence goes undetected. Such listeners must be at peace with one another to enjoy the sound of the nightingale's lament. In other words, the nightingale's song affirms the intimacy of confirmed lovers.

Olive trees grow slowly and yield precious fruit. Olive branches are symbols of peace and renewed trust.

Owl, a bird of wisdom, has a sharp, knowing gaze. The cry of an owl sounds ominous. The owl reigns over the darkness of the night.

Peacock, a bird with an expansive, colorful tail, struts proudly before spreading its tail's fan. It is a symbol of vanity, pride, and unrivaled beauty.

Pearl is an irregular, layered gem that develops in an oyster shell. There are pearls of wisdom and pearls of great price. It is a symbol of something worth protecting from harm.

Pelican, a bird that sacrifices its own well-being for the sake of its young, appears as a symbol of suffering.

Pipe, *reed*, and *flute* are rustic instruments played by pastoral characters who endure long hours watching flocks of animals.

Rain can symbolize inclement weather outwardly and inwardly. In more positive circumstances, rain cools and nourishes the earth.

Rainbow is a phenomenon that epitomizes the promise of a higher power. The rainbow is a Biblical reference to a covenant between the human and the divine.

Ravens and *crows* are prevalent in biblical and classical literature with negative connotations. In mythology, these birds have lives of tremendous longevity with prophetic powers.

Rings symbolize pledges of faith. Rings can be magical and therefore powerful. They can also be a sign of continuity.

Rivers have a variety of meanings. In poetry, the Jordan, the Rubicon, the Mississippi, the Rhine, the Arno, the Seine, the Ganges, and the Nile have been known to appear. A river can be a metaphor for a flow of language: "a river of words."

Roses are the most poetic of flowers, having many varieties and meanings. There are red ones that express passionate love. White roses are considered pure. Yellow ones indicate friendship and loyalty. The flower itself is made up of delicate, layered petals tightly wound around a fragrant center. Thorns protect the flower from harm. The rose can be a metaphor for a human heart made of layers of feeling and experience and anchored by a fervent soul.

Salamanders are cold-blooded amphibians that are capable of enduring fire. A salamander is a symbol of the unsuspecting mortal who falls into passionate flames of love and lives.

Seas or *oceans* are vast. We who live on land find the vastness of the sea or ocean to be an inviting danger, one that promises adventure as well as peril. Casting off toward the distant horizon can be a metaphor for a life span. Human beings depart from familiar settings to seek fortune by negotiating waves of favorable and unfavorable experiences.

Seasons are symbols of the phases of life and love. Spring offers hope and summer generates heat and closeness. Autumn is a season of restlessness and change. Winter is a time of cold and death.

Serpents, *snakes*, and *vipers* slither and cast spells. They can be very wise and crafty. A snake bite can change a destiny. Serpents or snakes gnawing on a heart represent guilt or remorse. Because serpents and snakes shed their skins, they can symbolize distrust and deceit.

Sewing, *quilting*, *spinning*, or *weaving* are symbols of women's work. Needlework can represent teamwork, endurance, and patience.

Sheep and *lambs* are integral parts of the pastoral scene. Sheep and lambs are harmless and innocent. They need the shepherd's protection and receive it. The enemy of the flock is the wolf and bad weather.

Ships are vessels that carry human beings and cargo across waterways. They can be metaphors for cradles in which babies are rocked to sleep.

Silver can be a symbol of coins. It is ranked second in importance to items made of gold.

Snow is a symbol of purity; a blanket that covers frozen earth. Snowstorms or blizzards can bewilder and confuse human beings.

Spleen is a term that relates to anger, melancholy, and bitterness. Literally, it is an organ of the human body that filters impurities in blood. The term "spleen" appears as the title of French poetry and song, symbolizing a state of mind fraught with unexplained anxiety.

Stars are the heavenly bodies that twinkle to the delight of lovers, lead wanderers across unfamiliar terrain, and illuminate the path of the lonely. The "dog star" is the brightest fixed star in the sky. The "evening star" and the "morning star," both of which are the planet Venus, are constant reassurances. The poet or singer can commune with a star to achieve many different purposes.

Sunflowers are flowers that long for the light of the sun. They symbolize the face of one who follows love wherever it may lead.

Swans are popular symbols in poetry and song. The tilt of the swan's head symbolizes modesty and grace. The layered, white feathers indicate purity. Swans symbolize suffering, mystery, and vulnerability. Swans glide effortlessly across the water, motivated by unseen motion beneath the surface. It is believed that swans make no audible sound until they approach the final moments of life. In the face of death, they release a last cry.

Trumpets announce ceremonies, festivities, or calls to arms. A trumpet can also be a symbol for fame.

Willow trees are found on the banks of rivers. The chartreuse vines of the tree bend into the water but do not break. This fact makes the willow a symbol of long suffering and patience.

Wine can symbolize celebration and release. It is often associated with high culture and nobility.

Yew, like cypress, is a plant that grows in graveyards. Yew is associated with death because yew berries and leaves are considered poisonous.

Zephyr is another word for "west wind."

Michael Ferber's *A Dictionary of Literary Symbols* (3rd ed.) is an excellent reference for literary symbols.

Translations: Literal, "Singable," and Poetic

According to Henry David Thoreau, "Books should be read as deliberately as they were written" (Cramer, 2012) and so it is with texts set to music. They should be studied with equal diligence. If the text is in English, the inner rhythms and rhymes, symbols, and expressivity of vowels and consonants contain clues to your interpretation. What is true in your own language will prove of value as you work with foreign language texts.

Rhythm

- As you read the foreign text for its literary content, try to respond viscerally to the pulse of the poetic rhythm.

- Repeat the text in the rhythm of the musical setting. Has the composer incorporated in the music the pulse you identified in your reading? Is the musical pulse a different one?

Rhyme

- The scheme of rhythm and rhyme of any text is most noticeable at the cadential points in a poem. Note the rhyming words and their frequency. Be sure that your phonetic transcription of the foreign text uses the same vowel symbol for the vowels of words that rhyme. In some cases, you may find that you must modify the vowel of a word to improve its power to rhyme and tune with its rhyming partner/s.

- Study the text for words that repeat. Be sure that those words are identified by the same phonetic symbols and are sung with the same vowel quality each time they occur.

Symbols

♦ Search for potential symbols in the foreign text that might reveal deeper meaning and may require special articulatory attention.

♦ Study the imagery within the poetry and note the composer's treatment of it in the musical setting.

Expressivity of Vowels and Consonants

♦ In English, alliteration is often used to color a poetic text. In foreign languages, there are similar devices that unify the sounds of poetry. In Italian poetry and libretti, the expressive power is generally carried by vowel sounds. The juxtaposition of vowels and consonants in German texts offer the speaker or singer an opportunity for articulatory expression. The use of elision and liaison in French creates a momentum toward a word or image of significance.

In foreign language texts, accessing the literal or "word-by-word" translation is an essential first step. In some editions, you will find a "singable" translation under the foreign language text. Many anthologies include a poetic equivalent as a supplement to the literal and singable translations. Within all these translations, there are hidden treasures you can use as keys to unlock vocal and poetic expression. If you search for these buried gems, you will prepare and perform your repertoire with greater confidence. Translation lifts the foreign words from the realm of mere pronunciation to the world of intellect and feeling. To sing without knowledge of the literal and poetic meanings of a text is an unrequited experience for singer and listener alike. If the singer does not thoroughly grasp the text, the singing will be a vocal sound event without pathos and artistry. To discern the exact meaning of individual words is to transform the text from a series of nonsense syllables into a potent expressive phrase. A series of nonsense syllables would be difficult to memorize, while a poetic thought abides securely in your mind and heart.

Literal or "Word-by-Word" Translations

Because the syntax of foreign languages differs from English word order, literal or word-by-word translations appear somewhat awkward at first. Your knowledge of the parts of speech in each language will be useful to you. It is vital that both singer and collaborative pianist embrace each word and its function in the poetic phrase. It is impossible to comprehend the composer's intentions, namely the union of text, melody, and harmony, without grasping what the word means and how it functions within the poetic and musical phrase.

The literal or word-by-word translation is not only the scaffolding upon which you build your interpretation of the music; it also serves as the framework for your memorization of the text. In the study of the true, literal meaning of a word, you will find many equivalent words in the foreign language dictionary. To facilitate your interpretation of a word, you will seek the exact meaning that is appropriate to the poetic and musical context. For the purpose of memorization, look for a word that is cognate of an English word.

Example I

Let's begin with an excerpt in Italian from "Alma del Core." The text and music were created by Antonio Caldara.

"Sarò contento nel mio tormento se quel bel labbro baciar potrò"

◆ Literal: I will be content in my torment if that beautiful lip to kiss I can

◆ Useful Cognates:

The word *baciar* begins with "b." One equivalent of "to kiss" is "to *buss.*" The word *potrò* means "to be able" or "to be *possible.*"

Example II

Here is an example in German from the Lied entitled "Heimliches Lieben" with a text by Karoline Louise von Klenke set to music by Franz Schubert:

"O du wenn Deine Lippen mich berühren, so will die Lust die Seele mir entführen"

◆ Literal: Oh you when your lips me touch/stir, so wants the desire the soul of me to abduct

◆ Useful Cognates:

The word *berühren* means *touch* or *be in contact with*. The root of *berühren* is *rühren*, which means to *stir, beat,* or *blend* as in cooking. As you practice, use a hand motion that imitates the act of blending ingredients to help you express the meaning of the verb.

The word *Lust* in German does not have the same meaning as its cognate *lust* in English, but the cognate would be an effective reminder. The German word *Lust* means *liking* or *willingness, delight* or *pleasure*. The word in English is charged with sensual connotations not expressed in the German equivalent.

The word *entführen* means *lead away, abduct,* or *kidnap*. It can also mean *elope* or *escape*. Either of these distant equivalents might be helpful as cognates that begin with the letter "e."

Example III

The following is an excerpt from the French mélodie "Mai," on a text by Victor Hugo set to music by Gabriel Fauré:

"Les larges clair de lune au bord des flots dormants . . . "

◆ Literal: The large moonlight on the bank of waves sleeping . . .

◆ Useful Cognates:

The word *larges* is an adjective meaning *broad*, *wide*, or *large*. It is obvious that *large* is the wisest choice as a cognate. In French, the word *moonlight* is expressed through the phrase "clair de lune." It occurs so frequently in French poetry that you will soon recognize it. At first use, however, *clear* and *lunar* are English words that spark an impulse for your memorization. Using the English words *border*, *floats*, and *dormant* might help you recall the French words *bord*, *flots*, and *dormants*. What matters is that you grasp the image of the golden glow of moonlight reflecting on the edge of moving water. Imagine the way the moon appears on the surfaces of the water as you express the words describing this scene.

Singable Translations

Song and Aria Anthologies

In many editions of vocal repertoire in foreign languages, we find an English equivalent printed directly under the original text. Such a translation is called a singable translation. It is not a literal or word-by-word equivalent, but a version of words that fit with the melody. The author of the singable text studied the intention, meter, and rhyme scheme of the original poem and adapted words that suit the music. A singable translation usually represents the general sense of the foreign language poem. It is, however, a new "equivalent" text, not a translation of the original. Because of its proximity in the printed score, the singable version appears, at first glance, to be a translation. The author of the singable text may be identified or may be assumed to be the editor of the printed edition. Singable translations are rarely performed. For your use, the singable translation may provide a sense of the overall meaning of the poem. It might also contain some useful cognates that will help you remember the foreign language words. A singable translation is never a substitute for a literal or word-by-word translation of a song or aria. You will always need to know the exact meaning of the words if you wish to develop a thorough understanding of a vocal work.

Oratorio and Opera Scores

In some oratorio and opera scores, English versions of the foreign text exist that can be sung. The author/s who create such translations have fulfilled a difficult assignment. The use the libretto of the original drama is used to invent an equally effective libretto in English. Henry S. Drinker (cantatas and oratorios of J. S. Bach) and the team of Ruth and Thomas Martin (operas of W. A. Mozart) are famous wordsmiths who have dealt successfully with the challenge. In the German language, there are worthy adaptations of English oratorios by Handel, F. J. Haydn, and Felix Mendelssohn, to name only few. Mozart's Italian operas are often heard in German translation as well. The translated version of these works may cause you, at times, to rework vocal technical issues such as breath marks, phrasing, and vowel choice. It is wise to sing the work with its original text as a means of understanding what is alike and what is different between the two languages set to the same music. Here again, the original language can provide insights into the translated version you sing.

Oratorio

It is not uncommon in the United States for choirs to sing oratorios in English rather than their original languages. With limited rehearsal time, choral conductors find it more feasible to sing a language the choristers speak. Clergy sometimes prefer choirs and soloists to perform in English as an enhancement of the congregation's worship experience. When engaged to perform an oratorio, it will be important for you to inquire about the specific edition of the work to be sung. Each edition will have its own English version of the text.

Opera

When operas in foreign languages are performed in English-speaking countries, supertitles are often used to project a version of the words for the audience to read. To engage the audience more directly in the drama of the plot, opera companies sometimes choose to perform such works in English translation. One good example is Engelbert Humperdinck's *Hansel and Gretel*, a popular work that appeals to the entire family as a holiday treat.

Performance Practice Using Bilingual Languages

In the United States, a performance practice of the most popular German oratorios of Johann Sebastian Bach (*Weihnachts-Oratorium* or *Christmas Oratorio, Johannes Passion* or *St. John Passion, Matthäus Passion* or *St. Matthew Passion*) has evolved using two languages for specific elements. The recitatives of the Evangelist and congregational hymns have been in English, while the arias and choruses are sung in German. In all three of these works, Bach derived the recitatives sung by the Evangelist directly from Biblical texts. Often, the hymns are familiar to American congregations in English translation. This mixed performance practice heightens the audience's involvement in the performance as an act of remembrance and response. The operetta *Die Fledermaus* by Johann Strauss is occasionally performed with dialogue in English and music in German to allow for "local color" references that keep the familiar story vital and up to date.

To sing works using two languages, you must be alert to various issues of diction and vocal technique. The situations described above involve German music that conforms perfectly to the German language. The segments sung in English will require special treatment to achieve intelligibility and vocal ease. The transition between spoken English dialogue and sung German arias or ensembles must be rehearsed with care. Though these circumstances sound unusual, they have proven satisfying to audiences who wish to engage more fully with the music and dramatic action. The purpose of this mixed method is clearly to achieve a compromise between musical expression and textual understanding.

Settings of Translated Texts

In 19th-century Germany, the translation of foreign literary texts to German was a means for the study of cultural differences between German citizens and their European and English counterparts. August Wilhelm Schlegel (1767–1845) and his brother, Friedrich

(1772–1829), were pioneers in comparative linguistics. Under their leadership, the major works of Shakespeare became available to German-speaking readers. The team of Emanuel Geibel and Paul Heyse gathered Spanish sacred and secular texts to translate. These works were set to music by Wolf in the *Spanisches Liederbuch*, completed in 1891. The texts for Wolf's *Italienisches Liederbuch* (Vol. I, 1892; Vol. 2, 1896) were collected and translated from the Italian folk tradition by Heyse. In both cases, the original Spanish and Italian poetry was transformed to new works of German literature. Imagine how the consonant-rich German syntax disrupted the lyric flow of these original Romance language texts. The translators created equivalents using words and meters that suited German poetic expectations. In both projects, the translations reflect universal human emotions such as religious fervor, youthful enthusiasm, passionate love, and despair. The translations are delightful to read and sing but are far from their original intentions. In the hands of Wolf, the translated texts of the *Spanisches Liederbuch* and *Italienisches Liederbuch* fueled miniature masterpieces of timeless beauty.

Poetic Translations/Equivalent

In his essay "Translation for Music," Joseph Kerman tackled the problems inherent in the translation of text for the purpose of singing. The translation in question is that of Mozart's *The Magic Flute*, translated by W. H. Auden and Chester Kallman. Kerman congratulated the literary quality of this highly valued translation, while lamenting the union of Mozart's music with a foreign text. He wrote: "The music can be 'interpreted,' but it can no more be translated than a cathedral" (Arrowsmith & Shattuck, 1964). Any poetic translation is a compromise between music and meaning. It will be your responsibility to provide your listeners with a poetic equivalent that unites the essence and beauty of the text. This book seeks to assist you in meeting the challenge.

Conclusion

The poet Thomas Lux (1946–2017) wrote that "the voice you hear when you read to yourself is the clearest voice" (Lux, 1997). The tools you have gathered will assist you in perfecting the sounds and perceiving the essential meaning of poems set to music in English, Italian, German, and French. With the IPA as your pronunciation guide, you will be able to deliver the text you hear with the clearest, most confident singing voice.

References

Banks, C. (Trans.). (1998). *Rumi: The book of love: Poems of ecstasy and longing*. New York, NY: Harper Collins.

Banks, C. (Trans.). (2003). *Rumi: The book of love: Poems of ecstasy and longing* (p. 89). New York, NY: Harper Collins.

Benjamin, W. (2000). *Introduction to a translation of Charles Baudelaire, 1923* (H. Zohn, Trans., 1968). Reprinted in L. Venuti (Ed.), (2012) *The translation studies reader* (3rd ed.). New York, NY: Routledge Press.

Bloom, H. (1998). *Shakespeare: The invention of the human* (pp. 1–2). New York, NY: Riverhead Books.

Burr, E. (Trans.). (2017). *The Chiron dictionary of Greek and Roman mythology*. Asheville, NC: Chiron Publications.

Cramer, J. (2012). "Reading" by Henry David Thoreau. In *The portable Thoreau* (p. 279). New York, NY: Penguin Books.

Ferber, M. (2017). *A dictionary of literary symbols* (3rd ed.). New York, NY: Cambridge University Press.

Greenblatt, S. (Ed.). (2012). *The Norton anthology of English literature* (9th ed., Vol. I, pp. 1548–1549). New York, NY: W. W. Norton.

Hirsch, E. (1999). *How to read a poem and fall in love with poetry* (p. 1). New York, NY: Harcourt.

Hollander, J. (Ed.). (1996). *Committed to memory: 100 best poems to memorize* (p. 1). New York, NY: Riverhead Books.

Housman, A. E. (1933). *The name and nature of poetry* (pp. 46–47). Cambridge, UK: Cambridge University Press.

International Phonetic Association. (2003). *Handbook of the International Phonetic Association: A guide to the use of the International Phonetic Alphabet* (p. 3). Cambridge, UK: Cambridge University Press.

Johnson, T. (Ed.). (1951). *The complete poems of Emily Dickinson* (pp. 312–313). Boston, MA: Little, Brown and Co.

Kerman, J. (1964). Translation for music. In W. Arrowsmith & R. Shattuck (Eds.), *The craft and context of translation* (p. 155). New York, NY: Anchor Books.

LaBouff, K. (2008). *Singing and communicating in English: A singer's guide to English diction* (p. 4). New York, NY: Oxford University Press.

Lux, T. (1997). *New and selected poems 1975–1995* (p. 15). New York, NY: Houghton Mifflin.

Pinsky, R. (1998). *The handbook of heartbreak* (pp. xiii–xv). New York, NY: William Morrow.

Rilke, R. M. (1995). *Ahead of all parting: Poetry and prose of Rainer Maria Rilke* (S. Mitchell, Trans., pp. 410–411). New York, NY: The Modern Library.

Rumi. *Masnavi-ye ma'navi* (Book I, pp. 599–607).

Sataloff, R. (2005). *Treatment of voice disorders* (pp. 27–28). San Diego, CA: Plural Publishing.

Smith, B., & Sataloff, R. (2013). *Choral pedagogy* (3rd ed., p. 28). San Diego, CA: Plural Publishing.

Stafford, W. (1978). *Writing the Australian crawl* (p. 3). Ann Arbor, MI: The University of Michigan Press.

Stemple, J., Glaze, L., & Klaben, B. G. (2010). *Clinical voice pathology* (4th ed., pp. 217–218). San Diego, CA: Plural Publishing.

Watson, P. (2010). *The German genius* (p. 845). New York, NY: HarperCollins.

Wharton, E. (1997). *French ways and their meaning* (p. 71). Lee, MA: Berkshire House Publishers.

Wroe, A. (2011). *Orpheus: The song of life* (p. 35). New York, NY: Overlook Press.

2

English

The Sounds of English

Singing in English: Why Is English Such a Challenge?

Diction study begins at home for every singer. Singers learn the International Phonetic Alphabet (IPA) in their native language and apply the IPA symbols as "points of departure for remembrance," tools for comparing sounds in every foreign language they sing. English diction poses challenges for all singers, no matter their native tongue, for a variety of reasons.

The prevalence of "unsingable" vowel sounds in English is one cause. "It is the colorless murmur of the *schwa*, represented by the symbol [ə] and appearing as one or more of the vowels in words without number," writes Bill Bryson in his popular book *The Mother Tongue: English and How It Got That Way* (1990). There are other vowel sounds such as those found in the words "learn" [ɜ] and "sun" [ʌ] that make the language less "lyric" or "singable."

Spoken in many regions of the world, the English language is subject to regional dialects or accents. Singers strive for a "neutral" English that is devoid of regional influences. Native speakers may not be aware of the dialectic tendencies in their local community. For example, some American Midwest residents would pronounce the word *roof* [rʌf] while in New England, one hears the word pronounced [ruːf]. Based on the word in its context, listeners understand the meaning intended by either pronunciation. As a student of singing, consider the sounds and their qualities with each iteration. Feel how different the tongue moves for the New England versus the Midwestern pronunciation. If you are native Midwesterner, you have developed aural and articulatory habits that reflect the sound of [ʌ] as in *up* as the central vowel. If you are assigned to sing a duet with someone who was born in New England, your duet partner is likely to associate a completely different central vowel for the word *roof*, namely [u]. More importantly, your duet partner will sing with puckered lips to create the sound and you will not. Suddenly, you two will be attempting to meld your voices from two quite different vocal production circumstances. Without some accommodation, the two of you will find it difficult to produce unified diction and well-tuned musical results. Stop for a moment to consider, as a native speaker, if you are aware of your regional pronunciation tendencies. Use the IPA as a tool for purifying your production of words in speech and singing and for blending your voice with the voices of others.

There are technical terms and slight aural differences that apply to the pronunciation of American and British English. The term "American Standard" (AS) is used for the pronunciation of vocal repertoire that derives from North America. "Received Pronunciation" (RP) refers to the pronunciation of repertoire written by composers from the British Isles. Pronunciation that melds the two to create a "neutral" English is called Mid-Atlantic or Transatlantic pronunciation. Your voice teacher or coach will help you understand the subtleties of these three approaches to English language pronunciation for singing.

This chapter includes study guides for English vowel and consonant sounds. The symbols for the diphthongs and triphthongs follow. Diphthongs and triphthongs are made from the building blocks of single sounds. After each symbol, there is a series of words that contain the vowels. For each IPA symbol, select one word that you are most likely to remember. You will use the associated word to relate to similar vowels and consonants in Italian, German, and French. Eventually, you may use the symbols to master a host of other sung languages such as Spanish, Portuguese, Russian, Czech, or maybe even the various languages of Scandinavia. It is not important which word you choose from the list associated with a symbol, but it is crucial that your choices make perfect sense to you. Say aloud each word you have chosen as you carefully transcribe its symbol. Be very accurate, so that you will develop perfectly legible IPA penmanship. Shape each symbol exactly as it appears in print. When you advance to foreign languages, you must be able to trust what you write or read in IPA transcriptions. Take care to master each associative word with its sound and symbol.

Singing in English: How Is Singing English Different From Speaking English?

As you begin your study of singer's diction, face the fact that, as a native English speaker, you may understand your language perfectly, but it is doubtful that your spoken pronunciation of it is devoid of negative habits. When you sing a text, you must seek not just an accurate pronunciation of each word, but also the most beautiful, expressive sound you can make. This requires a "clinical" look at the elements of English that lend themselves best to singing and those that require our attention.

The English language, a part of the Anglo-Saxon family of languages, has a heavy-light accent pattern replete with consonant combinations. Certain unaccented syllables contain vowel sounds that are not, by their very nature, elegant ones. There are consonants, such as "r," that must be minimized in length to retain the integrity of pitch and tuning. When reading poetry aloud, we strive for the most elegant manner of delivery. Call it "elevated" speech, if you will. The poet has chosen exquisite words to describe personal experiences. In poetry, rhythm, and rhyme, vowel and consonant qualities work together to achieve dramatic effects. Once set to music, the words will be pronounced in the rhythm and contours of the melody. Make it your practice to read the poetry first silently and then aloud. Next, read it as prose and finally, as it is set to music. In the process, your musical sense will guide you to "rhyme" the vowels, or seek the same vowel color as vowels repeat in the musical setting. Rhymed vowels tune more easily. Treat the consonants with equal care. Note how each consonant is created and work toward efficient, consistent articulation. Consonants must be crisp and clear. The articulation of a consonant sound should take as little time as possible from the flow of the vowels in a poetic phrase. As you master the poem, its meaning and each element of its delivery, you have in your power the tools to sing with lyrical beauty and communication.

The Sounds of English

English Vowel Sounds: The Cornerstones of Singer's Diction

Study the symbols and their shapes. Practice writing the symbols legibly. Select one word from each list that you will associate easily with the sound and symbol. You can check your memory by completing the quiz found in the appendix.

[i]   seem, seen, scene, mean, beam, dream, team, scream

[ɪ]   chin, fin, grin, sin, thin, brim, rim, Tim, quince

[e]   chaos or chaotic

(For the sound in English associated with the symbol [e] to be sounded purely, it must be followed by a vowel as in the two words given here as examples here. The closed [e] is uncommon in English, but will appear regularly in Italian, German, and French.)

[ɛ]   bed, bet, red, thread, Fred, wed, met, dread, bread

[æ]   add, past, can, bad, sad, can, plan, lamb, van

[ɑ]   father, bother, blossom, opt, Oscar, Oxford, October

[ɔ]   caught, cause, awe, moss, boss, cost

[o]   obey, obedient, oblation, omit

[ʊ]   book, hood, stood, look, brook, pull, full

[u]   fool, prove, shoe, spool, tool, rule, drool

[ɜ]   learn, burn, turn, word, yearn, bird, firm

(The symbols [ɜ], [ɝ], and [ɚ] represent very similar sounds that quantify the amount of "r" that will be heard before a consonant or at the end of a word in an English word.)

[ə]   abet, ahead, parade, jewel, funeral, little

(Known as the schwa, this is an unstressed/muted sound.)

[ʌ]   sun, hut, fun, blood, luck, ugly, punish

[ɨ]   lovely, pretty, country, happy, only

English Diphthongs

Diphthongs are defined as two vowel sounds in the same syllable. In English, the first vowel of a diphthong is called the *primary* or *principal* vowel. The second vowel of a diphthong is called the *vanish* or *slide*. The vanish or slide is a necessary element, but it receives less emphasis than the primary or principal vowel of the diphthong. Observe the list of symbols below. You will note that the primary or principal vowels are fundamental or "pure" vowel sounds: [a], [ɑ], [e] or [ɛ], [ɔ], and [o]. The second element in an English diphthong is a sound of lesser purity; namely, [ɪ] and [ʊ]. To sing an English diphthong, strive to maximize the time spent on the primary or principal vowel and minimize the second element. In other words, do not give the vanish or slide rhythmic integrity. This process ensures exquisite tuning and increases text intelligibility.

[aɪ] [ɑɪ]*	night, like, aisle, eyes, fly, tie, buy
[eɪ] [ɛɪ]*	day, daisy, break, sake, reign, main, play
[ɔɪ]	boy, voice, joy, soil, buoyant, moist, choice
[ɑʊ]	now, house, shout, about, doubt, mount, vow, thou
[oʊ]	know, no, roach, note, boat, slow, rose

English Diphthongs and The Letter "R"

Diphthongs formed with [ə] or [ɚ]

Below, you will find a list of English diphthongs created by a primary or principal vowel followed by the letter "r." In English, the letter "r" at the end of a word or before a pause requires extra care. The use of the schwa [ə] minimizes the "r" sound. The symbol [ɚ] acknowledges a slightly greater presence of "r." In each circumstance where such a diphthong appears, make a clear choice and be consistent in your use of it. Voice teachers and vocal coaches have specific preferences regarding the amount of "r" to be heard. Therefore, two possibilities are listed for each diphthong and triphthong with an "r." Consider beauty, intelligibility, and consistency when speaking and singing diphthongs and triphthongs in all languages.

[ɛə] [ɛɚ]*	air, ere, e'er, care, bear, fair, dare, hair, there, where
[ɪə] [ɪɚ]*	ear, dear, deer, here, tear, tier, sheer, sphere, mere
[ɔə] [ɔɚ]*	ore, or, o'er, restore, before, four, war, soar, tore, pour
[ʊə] [ʊɚ]*	poor, sure, tour, assure, azure, secure
[ɑə] [ɑɚ]*	are, garden, dark, mark, hard, marred, marvel

English Triphthongs

Triphthongs, in English, are defined as three vowel sounds in the same syllable; namely, a primary or principal vowel and an "r"-related diphthong.

[ɑɪə] [ɑɪɚ]*　fire, choir, admire, spire, entire, retire, aspire, desire

[ɑʊə] [ɑʊɚ]*　our, hour, tower, power, flower, sour, shower, devour

*indicates vowel choices applicable to the preferred sound ideal of singer, teacher, or vocal coach.

English Consonants

As we move from the study of English vowel sounds to consonants, one letter stands on either side of the aisle. It is the letter "y," a letter that can function in some situations as a vowel sound and in others, as a consonant. The letter "y" serves as a vowel sound in the middle of words like *rhyme* [aɪ] or [ɑɪ], and "rhythm" [I]. When it appears at the ends of words such as *pretty* or *lovely*, singers are encouraged to pronounce the letter "y" as the vowel [ɪ] or [ɨ]. Both symbols ([ɪ] and [ɨ]) represent the same sound. The former was used by diction authority Madeleine Marshall. The latter is in common use today. Spoken English does not necessarily demand the same level of care with unaccented syllables that sung English does. In fact, dictionaries indicate that the letter "y" at the end of a word should be pronounced [i]. In a musical context, the choice of [i] for the final syllable creates an unintended emphasis on an unaccented syllable and could invite a tuning discrepancy. The symbols [ɪ] and [ɨ] represent less intrusive vowels that do not detract from the stressed syllable/s of a word. The letter "y" can be used to spell a diphthong as in *by*, *bye*, or *buy* [baɪ], [bɑɪ]. The letter "y" presents as a consonant at the beginning of a word in the following words: *yes, youth, yield, yoke, yearn,* or *yule*. In the IPA, this sound is identified with the symbol [j]. (Note: The sound [j] can also be found in English words that are spelled with "u" as in *uniform, usual,* or *useful*. The sound [j] can be heard as a glide in the word *music* ['mjuz:ɪk].)

Examples in Context

Try speaking each of the following sentences. When the "y" is a consonant or glide, the tongue and the alveolar ridge make contact. Notice the point of contact and repeat the action as efficiently as possible. In the words where "y" appears in the unaccented, ending syllable, be sure to tune it toward [ɪ] or [ɨ].

[j]　　"Youth's a stuff, will not endure." ("O Mistress Mine," Shakespeare/Thomas Morley, Roger Quilter, and Gerald Finzi)

[ɪ], [ɨ]　"These pretty country folk did lie in the spring time." ("It Was a Lover and His Lass," Shakespeare/Morley, Quilter)

Study Guide: English Consonant Sounds

The following consonant sounds are represented in the IPA by lowercase letters:

b	d	f	g	h	k	l	m	n	p	s	t	z
[b]	[d]	[f]	[g]	[h]	[k]	[l]	[m]	[n]	[p]	[s]	[t]	[z]

Below are the symbols for consonant combinations. Study the symbols and their shapes. Practice writing the symbols legibly. Select one word from each list that you will associate easily with the sound and symbol. You can check your memory by completing the quiz found in the appendix.

[ŋ]   sing, song, strong, king, hang

[ŋk]   bank, ankle, sink, sank, tank, sunk

[ŋg]   finger, stronger, hunger, angle

[ʃ]   shade, sure, luscious, fashion, caution

[ʒ]   vision, casual, fusion, prestige

[ʧ]   chap, patch, ditch, chore, cheap, march

[ʤ]   hedge, budget, legend, ginger, jewel, jam

[ɹ]   wrong, wreath, rose, right, ev'ry

[θ]   earth, breath, think, width, breadth

[ð]   soothe, breathes, these, clothe

[j]   uniform, unite, useful, usual

[ʍ]*   when, where, whether, why

[w]   wander, way, weather, weigh, wonder

*[hw] is a symbol that was previously used for this sound. You may find it in an IPA transcription from an earlier time.

Practicing Vowel Spellings in English

Now that you are familiar with the IPA symbols for vowel sounds, identify and spell the vowel in each of the words given below. You will find that the words given below include examples of the symbols [a], [ɛ], [i], [ɔ], [u], [æ], [I], [ʊ], and [ʌ]; semiconsonants [j], [ʍ] or [hw], and [w]; the diphthong [oʊ]; and the "r-related diphthongs" [ɚ]. Note the musical context from which each word is taken. Soon you will be applying these symbols to all the texts of all repertoire you sing. Consider the difference, if any, between the vowel you would speak and the vowel you would sing.

Bank	[ ]	" . . . by yon bonnie banks . . . " ("Loch Lomond," traditional Scottish song)
Blue	[ ]	"I am Rose, my eyes are blue" ("I Am Rose," Gertrude Stein/Ned Rorem)
Bud	[ ]	" . . . the bud of the bud . . . " ("i carry your heart," e.e. cummings/John Duke)
Cheek	[ ]	" . . . on her damask cheek . . . " ("She Never Told Her Love," William Shakespeare/Franz Josef Haydn)
Damask	[ ] [ ]	" . . . on her damask . . . " ("She Never Told Her Love," Shakespeare/Haydn)
Dim	[ ]	" . . . that I my thoughts may dim" ("Heart, We Will Forget Him," Emily Dickinson/Aaron Copland)
Do	[ ]	" . . . to do me due delight" ("Come Again, Sweet Love," John Dowland)
Dress	[ ]	" . . . the black dress" ("The Black Dress," John Jacob Niles)
Due	[ ]	(ex. of the "liquid u") " . . . to do me due delight" (Dowland)
Eat	[ ]	" . . . and I did eat" ("Love Bade Me Welcome,"(George Herbert/Ralph Vaughan Williams)
False	[ ]	" . . . as my false love" ("O Waly, Waly," arr. Benjamin Britten)
Field	[ ]	"The fields are full . . . " ("The Fields Are Full," E. Shanks/Ivor Gurney)
Forsworn	[ ] [ ]	" . . . that so sweetly were forsworn" ("Take, O Take Those Lips Away," Shakespeare/ Quilter)
Full	[ ]	" . . . and now am full of tears" ("Down by the Salley Gardens," W. B. Yeats/Quilter, Gurney)
Gone	[ ]	"He's gone away . . . " ("He's Gone Away," folksong/John Jacob Niles)
Heed	[ ]	" . . . but he paid no heed" ("The Lass from the Low Countree," J. J. Niles)
Last	[ ]	" . . . tis the last rose of summer" (Irish folksong, arr. Benjamin Britten)
Look	[ ]	" . . . Look down, fair Moon" (Walt Whitman/ Rorem)
Lute	[ ]	("liquid u") "Orpheus with this lute" ("Orpheus With His Lute," Shakespeare/William Schuman, Sir Arthur Sullivan, Richard Hundley)

Mad	[ ]	"... in the mad spring weather" ("Song of the Blackbird," W. E. Henley/Quilter)
Meet	[ ]	"... we did meet" ("Down by the Salley Gardens," Yeats/Britten, Gurney)
Mid	[ ]	"... in the midnight hours" ("In the Mid-night," Thomas Moore/Britten)
Root	[ ]	"... the root of the root" ("i carry your heart," cummings/Duke)
Sit	[ ]	"... where you sit" ("Wher'er You Walk," [*Semele*] G. F. Handel)
Song	[ ]	"... twas the song of love" ("Silent Noon," Dante Gabriel Rossetti/ Vaughan Williams)
Tree	[ ]	"Under the Greenwood Tree" ("Under the Greenwood Tree," Shakespeare/Quilter, Douglas Moore, et al.)
Weep	[ ]	"I weep for wonder" ("Sure on This Shining Night," James Agee/Samuel Barber)
Whatever	[ ][ ][ ]	"... and whatever is done by only me" ("i carry your heart," cummings/Duke)
Wind	[ ]	"There came a wind" ("There Came a Wind Like a bugle," Dickinson/Copland)
You	[ ]	"O You whom I often"/"O You Whom I Often and Silently Come," Whitman/Rorem)

The Parts of Speech and Elements of Syntax in English

To understand, pronounce, and express a text accurately, you must comprehend the function of every word in each sentence or phrase. In every language, the parts of speech are arranged in an orderly way to provide textual meaning. The arrangement of these elements is called *syntax*. Each language has its own syntax. A study of the components of English syntax will help you to sing more expressively in English and to comprehend elements of foreign sentence structures.

Component Parts of English Sentences

A sentence is a complete thought. The simplest sentence consists of a subject and verb stating the action of someone or something. More complex sentences include a subject and a verb as well as an object (direct and indirect), words that describe the subject, the verb and/or the objects, and connecting phrases or clauses.

Nouns Name Beings (Human, Animal, Imaginary), Places, Things, Happenings, and Concepts

There are several categories of nouns, as you will see in the following sections:

Proper and Common Nouns

Nouns that name specific beings, places things, happenings, and concepts are called *proper nouns*. They are easy to identify because they are capitalized (e.g., Giuseppe Verdi, La Scala, Milan). Nouns called *common nouns* are not capitalized and refer to beings, places, things, happenings, and concepts in a general way (e.g., composer, opera house, city).

Concrete and Abstract

Nouns that name a tangible object are called *concrete nouns* (e.g., libretto, music stand, baton). Nouns that name an intangible idea or feeling are called *abstract nouns* (e.g., love, truth, revenge).

Collective

Nouns representing a unit of multiples are called *collective nouns* (e.g., choir, orchestra, quartet).

Pronouns Refer or Rename Nouns

There are several categories of pronouns, as you will see below:

◆ *Personal pronouns* are those that rename you and other persons in the following way:
   ◇ *Subject:* I, you, he, she, it, we, you, they
   ◇ *Object:* me, you, him, her, it, us, you, them
   ◇ *Possessive:* mine, yours, his, hers, ours, yours, theirs
   ◇ *Possessive Adjective:* my, your, his, her, its, our, yours, their
◆ *Relative pronouns* refer to previously stated nouns:
   ◇ *who* (subject), *whom* (object), *whose* (possessive) (e.g., The soprano *who* sang the role . . .)
   ◇ *that* (for persons and things)
◆ *Which* (for things) *interrogative pronouns* create direct or indirect questions: *Who? What? Which? Whatever? Whom?* ("*Who* is Sylvia? *What* is she?" Shakespeare).
◆ *Demonstrative pronouns* point out specifically a person, object or event: *that, those, these, that, this, such, so.* (Note that "such" and "so" function also as adjectives.)
   ◇ As a pronoun: ("Even *such* is time . . . " Sir Walter Raleigh)
   ◇ As an adjective: ("*Such* beauty as hurts to behold," Paul Goodman)
◆ *Indefinite pronouns* refer to an indefinite quantity of people, object, or event such as: *everybody, everyone, somebody, someone, anybody, anyone, nobody, no one.*
   Pronouns that refer to indefinite quantities are: *all, another, both, each, either, few, least, less, little, lots, many, most, much, other, plenty, several, some.*

◆ *Reflexive pronouns* reflect on the subject and refer to "self" or "selves." ("I celebrate *myself* and sing *myself* . . . " Walt Whitman)

Verbs Convey Action or Affirm States of Being

Here are points to remember:

1. A verb is an essential element in a sentence.
2. Verb forms change based upon gender and number.
3. Regular verbs follow consistent patterns. Irregular ones are "corrupted" due to frequent use. Irregular verbs in every language deserve careful study.
4. Tenses help verbs express when an action or a state of being occurs or occurred.

Verb Tenses

The tenses for current, past, and future events are, respectively: *present, past,* and *future* (e.g., I *sing.* I *sang.* I *will sing*).

The tenses used to express previous events are called *perfect.* A *past participle* is required when forming the perfect tenses. For events completed before the present, the tense is called *present perfect* (e.g., I *have sung*). For events completed before a past event, the tense is called *past perfect* (e.g., I *had sung*). For events completed before a future event, the tense is *future perfect* (e.g., I *will have sung*). All tenses have a *progressive* form, showing an action in progress. (e.g., I will be *singing*).

The *gerund* is a verb form that functions as a noun with one of two tenses:

◆ Present tense: *Singing* is a joyful act.
◆ Perfect tense: *Having sung* the role once, he was happy to sing it again.

The *infinitive,* the "stem" of the verb, may function as a noun, adjective, or adverb with one of two tenses:

◆ Present tense: I like *to sing* in the shower.
◆ Perfect tense: I was supposed *to have sung* the role last season.

The *participle,* ending generally in "-ing," "-ed," or "-en," appears as an adjective or an adverb in one of three tenses:

◆ Present participle: The mezzo soprano *singing* in the hallway is my friend.
◆ Past participle: The oratorio *sung* by the choir was Handel's "Messiah."
◆ Perfect participle: The work, *having been sung,* will not be repeated.

Adjectives and Adverbs Are Modifiers, Words That Describe Other Words

Adjectives modify nouns or pronouns (e.g., The *singing* child demonstrates his *budding* talent).

Adverbs modify verbs (e.g., He sings *well.* She sang *sweetly* and *accurately*).

Articles Are Words that Quantify Nouns or Pronouns, Either Specifically or Generally

- *Definite Article* = "the." It is pronounced [ði] before a vowel and [ðə] before a consonant.
  - ◇ *The* alto (pronounced [ði] before a vowel)
  - ◇ *The* bass (pronounced [ðə] before a consonant)

  Memory Tool: "<u>The</u> earth is <u>the</u> Lord's" (Psalm 24:1)

　　　　　　　[ði]　　　　　　[ðə]

- *Indefinite Articles* = "a" [a] before a consonant and "an" [æn] before a vowel.
  - ◇ *An* operatic ensemble (before a vowel)
  - ◇ *A* choral ensemble (before a consonant)

  Memory Tool: <u>An</u> open vowel is treated differently than <u>a</u> consonant.

Prepositions Are Connective Words that Show the Relationship Between Words

Prepositions introduce a phrase and the phrase functions as a noun, adjective, or adverb. In singing, prepositions should be sung with the phrase they introduce (e.g., " . . . <u>by</u> your charms . . . <u>in</u> your arms" ["If Music be the Food of Love," Purcell]).

Conjunctions Are Connective Words that Connect Words, Phrases, or Clauses

Word to Word: " . . . My love <u>and</u> I" ("Down by the Salley Gardens)

Phrase to Phrase: "Out of my dreams <u>and</u> into your arms . . . " (*Oklahoma*)

Clause to Clause: "She bid me take love easy as the leaves grow on the trees, <u>but</u> I was young and foolish, with her did not agree..." ("Down by the Salley Gardens")

"Figures of Speech" Are Creative Ways to Define Deeper Meaning

- *Simile* compares one thing to another using "like" or "as."

"My love is *like* a red, red Rose" (Robert Burns)

- *Metaphor* compares one thing to another without using "like" or "as."

"*Youth's a stuff* will not endure" (William Shakespeare)

- *Hyperbole* overstates an idea intentionally.

"I'll suffer death *ten thousand times* . . . " (John Jacob Niles)

- *Personification* attributes human traits to animals, things, or ideas.

"Pride, Ruin's *bride-to-be*, paced our property" (Todd Boss)

Keep these elements of grammar in mind as you investigate texts in Italian, German, and French. If you consider the individual elements of each phrase, word-by-word translations of foreign languages will be easier to understand. See three examples of phrases below that have been evaluated by grammatical function as well as literal translation to achieve a poetic equivalent.

Italian:	*Caro*	*mio*	*ben.*
	Adjective	Possessive Pronoun	Noun
	Dear	my	beloved

Poetic equivalent = "My dear beloved."
("Caro Mio Ben," text and musical setting by Giuseppe Giordani)

German:	*Du*	*bist*	*wie*	*eine*	*Blume.*
	Subject pronoun	Verb	Simile/ Preposition	Article	Noun
	You	are	like	a	flower.

Poetic equivalent = "You are like a flower/blossom."
("Du Bist wie Eine Blume," text by Heinrich Heine, set to music by Robert Schumann and by Franz Liszt)

French:	*L'ame*	*évaporée*	*et*	*souffrante*
	Definite Article+Subject	Adjective	Conjunction	Adjective
	The soul	evaporated	and	suffering

Poetic equivalent = "The transitory and suffering soul . . ."
("Romance," text by Paul Bourget, set to music by Claude Debussy)

William Shakespeare: The Place to Start in English

In speaking of the universality of Shakespeare's writings, Marjorie Garber writes: "Like a portrait whose eyes seem to follow you around the room, engaging your glance from every angle, the plays and their characters seem always to be "modern," always to be "us" (Garber, 2005). Since the Renaissance in England, Shakespeare's work has stood at the center of English literature. The characters in his plays have become symbolic of human behavior. Think of Othello's Iago, who is the very epitome of a jealous lover, or Romeo and his Juliet, timeless examples of youthful passion and innocence. Shakespeare has been called a "global poet;" a contributor to the literary life of cultures and languages everywhere (Wilson-Lee, 2016). During the 2012 Cultural Olympiad, all 37 of Shakespeare's plays were presented in languages other than English at London's Globe Theater. You too will find songs and arias set to Shakespeare's words in a wide variety of languages. Shakespeare's plots have been updated to fit many circumstances. Harold Bloom suggests in his book *Shakespeare: The Invention of the Human* (Bloom, 1999) that our culture has learned through the writings of Shakespeare how to deal with family drama, royal ambitions, personal and political intrigue, labors of love (lost and found), and matters of human greed and grace.

You may already have noticed that composers in every generation trust Shakespeare as a reliable source for musical settings. Excerpts from Shakespeare's plays and sonnets, translated into German, Italian, and French, represent some of the finest songs and libretti in the Western world. What makes Shakespeare's words, rhythms, and rhyme scheme so appealing to composers? What is so universal about his themes? Let's look at a few examples of plays by Shakespeare that contain poetic texts that have been particularly popular among song composers.

In Act 4, Scene 2 of Shakespeare's *Two Gentlemen From Verona*, we find a song sung by a musician to lift the spirit of Julia, the beloved of Proteus. The text of the song speaks of Sylvia, the beloved of Valentine. In its original context, the words of the song do not please its listener, Julia. As an excerpt from the play, the song has taken on a larger life. In the settings of "Who is Sylvia?" by Quilter (*Four Shakespeare Songs*) or by Finzi (*Let Us Garlands Bring*) or as "An Sylvia?" ("To Sylvia?"/D. 891, Op. 106, No. 4) by Franz Schubert, the text conveys the reality that the very presence of a human being can transform us and is worthy of praise.

One of the most famous passages from Shakespeare derives from *As You Like It*, Act 2, Scene 7 when Jacques, a gloomy traveler, states:

All the world's a stage,

And all the men and women merely players.

They have their exits and their entrances . . .

Shakespeare uses the theater to depict the world in which human beings live and move. The characters of *As You Like It* live to love in simple ways. In a setting where the beauties of nature complement human nature, the play concludes with four weddings. Three of five songs from the play have been frequently set to music. One of the songs, "Under the Greenwood Tree," is sung by Amiens, a lord who attends a duke in exile in Act 2, Scene 5, Amiens celebrates the easy life one lives when surrounded by nature. "Blow, Blow Thou Winter Wind" is a song performed for Duke Senior as a means of comparing the simplicity of country life with the stresses of the larger world. "It Was a Lover and His Lass" is perhaps best known in its strophic musical setting by Shakespeare's contemporary, Thomas Morley. The song appears in Act 5, Scene 3, performed by a page. When extracted, these songs hold new meaning. Outside of their theatrical context, the texts express a single truth regularly conveyed by Shakespeare: that human life includes both love and leisure.

Shakespeare's *Twelfth Night* is subtitled "What You Will." The English holiday called "Twelfth Night" is a traditional night of celebration during the Christmas season. The celebration takes place the night before January 6 and includes the feast of Epiphany. The feast itself entails the abundant consumption of food, drink, and entertainment. At this jovial event, guests are served a holiday cake into which a coin is baked. The recipient of the slice containing the coin is named Lord of Misrule. The play begins with the words: "If music be the food of love, play on!" It is from this opening passage that Henry Purcell later adapted his well-loved "If music be the food of love, sing on that I am filled with joy." In *Twelfth Night*, a clown named Feste sings a love song: "O mistress mine, where are you roaming, O stay and hear your true love's coming who can sing both high and low..." This song appears in Act 2, Scene 3 and celebrates the timeliness of youth. Best known in settings by Quilter and Finzi, "O Mistress Mine" is a strophic song that contains closing lines in both verses that create diction challenges; namely, "Every wise man's son doth know" and "Youth's a stuff will not endure."

In Act 2, Scene 4, Feste sings another song, "Come Away, Death." Its text has been set by Quilter, Finzi and, most recently, by Argento. Argento entitled his setting "Dirge," reminding us of the reality that in life we face elements of death. It can be found in the song cycle *Six Elizabethan Songs* (2015). "*Twelfth Night* is one of the most profound, lighthearted, delicate works of art ever created," according to Tina Packer (2016). At its conclusion, not all who love find love returned in equal measure. Life, like the winter wind, at times, can chill. It is the promise of spring's warmth that sustains hope.

You will find references to Shakespeare texts throughout your study of song. Take, for example, "Fair and True," a song by Peter Warlock (1894–1930) that quotes Shakespeare's Sonnet 105, (Vendler, 1997): "'Fair, kind, and true' is all my argument," concluding with the couplet "'Fair,' 'kind,' and 'true' have often lived alone, which three till now never kept seat in one." Compare this with the final words of Warlock's setting: "Sweet, fair, kind, true, where are all of these, but in *you?*"

Early English Song

Lute Songs and Their Lyrics Defined

According to Denis Stevens, "The English monarchy, with its frequently irksome French ties, preferred to regard secular music like wine: as a necessarily imported product" (Stevens, 1960). The lute song is the earliest English song you are likely to encounter for recital purposes. Lute songs date from the 16th century. Because solo song did not yet have a consistent role in societal life, composers frequently created a musical setting that could be performed by a single performer and also a version of the work for a small ensemble. In the solo version, the singer generally accompanied himself on the lute. (Though there were lute songs composed for women, most of the literature was composed for a tenor or baritone voice.)

Because of its limited acoustical properties, the lute is an instrument that demands an intimate setting. In the songs themselves, composers wed musical elements to poetry in a similarly fragile manner. The topics of lute song range from love lyrics to moral lessons. Because of the integral connection between poetry and music in a lute song, it is imperative that the singer savors the words, their meaning, and their expression. The songs are strophic in nature and often AAB in form. Like the Psalms of David, lute song poetry was conceived with its melodic potential in mind. The rhythm of a poetic text is the key that unlocks the rhythm of its song setting for you.

In Schmidt's *Lives of the Poets*, Thomas Campion (1567–1620) is quoted as having said, "The world is made of symmetry and proportion, and is in that respect compared to music, and music to poetry" (Schmidt, 1998). Campion was much loved at court for the poetry and songs he wrote. He studied medicine and may have practiced it. He is known to have been the friend of Philip Rosseter with whom he published *A Book of Ayres* in 1601. Little is known about Campion's life, but his musical and literary contributions are highly regarded for their sensitivity to audible beauty. You can easily listen to a performance of it sung by countertenor, Steven Rickards, accompanied by lutenist Dorothy Linnell (Naxos, 1998).

"When to Her Lute Corrina Sings"
Words and music by Thomas Campion (1601)

When to her lute Corrina sings,

Her voice revives the leaden strings,

And doth in highest notes appear

As any challenged echo clear.

But when she doth of mourning speak,

Ev'n with her sighs, the strings do break.

Notice how the first phrase leads to "sings" and the second to "strings." The next two phrases meld together with a sense of drive to "echo clear." These four phrases together create a *Stollen*, a German term, a closed unit with one melodic idea. Be certain to follow the rules for the liquid "u" when pronouncing the word *lute* [ljut]. The single phrase of the chorus is called the *Abgesang*, German for "singing out." The Abgesang unravels or comments upon the lines of first four phrases. In this case, *sings* and *strings*, and *appear* and *clear*, will rhyme perfectly. *Speak* and *break* create an "eye-rhyme" that will harmonize with one another based upon their mutual spelling, but not their sound. Feel the lilt of the Stollen section and the downward cascading of the Abgesang phrase.

In the second verse, notice the cadence of the spoken text in the first two lines: how "doth live or die" prepares you rhythmically for "so must I." It is likely you will feel a contrast in the next two phrases in which the response to "she doth sing" is "a sudden spring."

And as her lute doth live or die;

Led by her passion, so must I.

For when of pleasure she doth sing,

My thoughts enjoy a sudden spring.

But if she doth of sorrow speak,

Ev'n from my heart, the strings do break.

Campion's poetry and music form a beautiful unity of lyric expression.

An Exercise: Musical Settings of Early Texts

Below is a poem written in the 17th century by the poet Edmund Waller (1606–1687) and set to music by Quilter (1877–1953). The message of the poem is a universal one; however, the language may feel a little foreign to you. To express the text properly, you will sense the need to "elevate" your speech.

◆ First Reading: As you read silently, note the poet's core thoughts about beauty, shyness, and fleeting time.

◆ Second Reading: As you read aloud, follow the punctuation carefully. Strive for a heightened awareness of the vowels and consonants.

1. Notice the rhyme scheme. Shape your spoken lines with a sense of drive toward the climax of rhyming words. Release each rhyme and begin the next phrase.

2. Speak the "r" crisply when it appears before a vowel sound such as *rose*, *graces*, and *sprung*. Try to minimize the "r" before a consonant in words such as *deserts*, *worth*, *forth*, and *part*. Treat the "r" in *retired*, *desired*, and *admired* as well as *rare* and *share* in a comparable way.

"Go, Lovely Rose"

I

Go, lovely rose,

Tell her that wastes her time and me

That now she knows,

When I resemble her to thee,

How sweet and fair she seems to be.

II

Tell her that's young

And shuns to have her graces spied,

That hadst thou sprung

In deserts, where no men abide,

Thou must have uncommended died.

III

Small is the worth

Of beauty from the light retired;

Bid her come forth,

Suffer herself to be desired,

And not blush so to be admired.

IV

Then die! That she

The common fate of all things rare

May read in thee;

How small a part of time they share

That are so wondrous sweet and fair!

◆ Reflection: At your first reading, what did the poem convey to you? Why do you think the poet compared the object of his interest to a rose? What does a rose symbolize? How is it formed?

◆ Context for Discussion: A rose is a flower that blooms in nature once a year. A rose consists of delicate petals, tightly woven and protected by thorns. The essence of the rose lies deep within and its scent is often considered its "soul." Roses come in a variety of colors. Over the centuries, special significance has been assigned to the various colors. For example, pink roses are said to express gratitude and sweetness. Red ones are symbols of romance and intimacy. The yellow rose speaks of friendship. A white rose is thought to be a pure rose and, therefore, symbolizes secrecy.

◆ Discussion Questions:
1. To you, what color is the rose in the poem?
2. How will your color choice impact your poetic and musical interpretations?
3. What are the core issues addressed in this poem?
4. Does the archaic language pose a diction challenge?
5. What are the likely outcomes of the situation depicted in the poem?

Critical Listening

Listen to baritone Bryn Terfel sing "Go, Lovely Rose" ("Silent Noon," Bryn Terfel, Baritone, and Malcolm Martineau, Piano, *Deutsche Grammophon*, 2005). Below you will find discussion questions to guide your critical thinking:

◆ Discussion Questions:
1. What does the music add to the poetic expression of the words?
   a. Melody: Scalelike? Tuneful?
   b. Harmony: Major or minor key? Modulations?
   c. Form: Verses or "through-composed"?
   d. Structure: Role of introduction? Interlude? Postlude?
   e. Inflection of Text: Follows the poem?
   f. Interpretation: Composer's interpretation? Performer's interpretation?

2. What are the words in the poem that require specific attention?

   a. Which words rhyme? Follow down the right side of the text to identify rhymes such as *rose/knows, thee/me/be, young/sprung, spied/abide/died, retired/desired, she/thee,* and *rare/share/fair.*

   b. What about *worth* and *forth*? These words "rhyme" for the eye but not the ear. As you have learned, this is a common British poetic device. The vowels do not rhyme but your manner of speaking and singing must treat them as rhyming words.

   c. Which words, if any, repeat?

   d. Which words have expressive possibilities?

   e. Circle the words that invite expression such as *lovely, waste, sweet and fair, shuns, sprung, spied, uncommended, light retired, suffer herself to be desired,* and *how small a part.*

Comparative Performances

Compare Terfel's interpretation with that of tenor John Mark Ainsley, who is also accompanied by pianist Malcolm Martineau ("Songs of Roger Quilter," John Mark Ainsley, tenor, Malcolm Martineau, piano, Hyperion, 1996).

- ◆ Discussion Questions:

   1. How do the performances compare in timbre, key, and interpretation?

   2. Which performance do you prefer and why? (To this, there is no definitive answer.)

   3. Consider the diction of the two singers. Did they pronounce the text identically? Which words were pronounced the same? Which were different? Which words were given special emphasis or expression?

   4. Did the poem or music take on a different character based upon the voice classification of the singer? Did the poem or music seem different to you because it was sung by a tenor? By a baritone?

   5. If the song were sung by a female voice, how would the character of the poem and/or music be different? How would it be alike?

As you listen critically, you find that singers who are native speakers of a language may have great authority over the musical and poetic possibilities, but they may be less exact in matters of singer's diction, while non-native-speaking singers generally adhere closely to the rules.

Comparative Listening: Solo Settings of "Go, Lovely Rose"

Expand your comparisons by listening to other musical settings of the poem by composers of various times and cultures. Select one or more of the settings listed below for listening and comparison. As you see, "Go, Lovely Rose" is a popular text among song composers, including Samuel Adler (b. 1928) in *Three Songs about Love,* No. 1.; Thomas Arne

(1710–1778); Seymour Barab (1921–2014) in *Four Songs*, Op. 1.; John Alden Carpenter (1876–1951) in *Eight Songs*, Op. 5 (stanzas 1–2 and 4–5); Richard Cumming (1928–2009); John Duke (1899–1984) (the 1951 setting for baritone or tenor with piano is recommended); Humphrey Proctor-Gregg (1895–1980); Henry Lawes (1595–1662) (stanzas 1–4); Quilter in *5 English Love Lyrics*, Opus 24; Ned Rorem (b. 1923) in "Song" in *Nantucket Songs*, No. 4; and Malcolm Williamson (1931–2003) in *Six English Lyrics* (available for low voice with piano or string orchestra, also as a cappella Soprano/Alto/Tenor/Bass)(SATB choral work).

Comparative Listening: Choral Versions of "Go, Lovely Rose"

Using the following questions, compare the solo setting with a choral setting of the text. Z. Randall Stroope (b. 1953) has created choral versions for (SATB) and Tenor I/Tenor II/Baritone/Bass (TTBB) with piano. Eric Whitacre (b. 1970) included this text in *Three Flower Songs* for choir (SATB). The settings are Whitacre's first choral composition. Malcolm Williamson's a cappella arrangement of his own solo version provides a contrast in time period and tonality. Use your comparisons to reconsider your interpretation of the solo setting by Quilter with which you have become familiar.

Discussion Questions

1. Does the interplay of voices in the choral settings make a significant difference in your understanding of the text? If so, how?

2. Compare the form of each setting. Are there repetitions that provide insights into the meaning of specific words or phrases?

3. Which sections are chordal or "homophonic"? Which ones are imitative or "polyphonic"?

4. What is the overall effect of the choral versions?

5. How do the choral versions compare with the solo ones?

Diction in Context: Comparative Listening Exercises

In her essay "My Friend Walt Whitman," Mary Oliver (1935–2019) suggested that a poem is "a temple or a green field, a place to enter, and in which to feel" (Oliver, 2016). To sing a text with understanding and confidence, you must unlock its mysteries by entering in and feeling its meaning. The comparative listening exercises that follow offer the opportunity to listen critically to various performances of a text. In many cases, you have the possibility of hearing more than one composer's approach. As described in the previous chapter, begin your work by reading the poem silently and aloud. Read with an openness to nuance, symbol, and tone. Consider what the words convey. Investigate any words or symbols that are unfamiliar to you.

Before you listen, use the tools that you have gathered to identify the proper pronunciation of each word. Fill in the IPA for the words you already know, for the words that rhyme, and for those that repeat. The symbols of the IPA you have learned will help you codify the sounds you anticipate the performer will sing. Using the same symbols, you can note any modifications made by performers or necessitated by the music. As you prepare to listen, follow the rubric systematically. Each rubric suggests what is unique to the poem you are about to hear. Study the text for words or phrases that offer occasions for expression. Look for any diction challenges and consider how to address them. You will be able to access on the internet all the songs and arias presented in this text. In some cases, specific performers are suggested for your comparisons. As you use this book, you may wish to explore beyond the suggested performances to other historical presentations or contemporary ones. Ask your instructor to suggest examples that are especially valid and useful for your study. Take note of the performer and the accompanist or instrumental group. Keep a list of the performances you enjoy most.

English Ayres

John Dowland (1563–1626)

Lutenist, singer, and creator of the musical form called the *ayre*, Dowland served as a court musician in England, France, and Denmark. Many of his ayres are arranged as quartets for chamber use. Below is one of Dowland's most popular ayres.

"Weep You No More, Sad Fountains"

Before you listen, implement your dictation strategies:

1. IPA Spellings: This text has many words that begin with the letter "w" [w] such as *weep* and "wh" [ʍ] or [hw] in *what, when,* and *while.* Be careful to mark them with the proper IPA symbols.

2. Archaic Words: The text contains verb forms that are not in common usage such as *need you, doth,* and *e'en.* Take note of these words. Allow their presence in the text to influence the way you speak and read the words.

3. Rhyming Words: Follow down the right side of the text to identify rhymes such as *fountains/mountains, weeping/sleeping, reconciling/smiling,* and *begets/sets.* If they are to rhyme, you must use the same vowel symbol for each rhyming pair.

4. Repeating Words: Study the text for common words that repeat such as *sun, weeping, sleeping,* and *softly.* Be sure to use the same IPA symbols for each repetition.

5. Expressive Possibilities: Circle the words that invite expression such as *snowy, softly, heavenly, reconciling, fair, melt,* and *sad.*

6. Exception Words: In the first verse, the words *fast* and *waste* are rhymes of the eye but not the ear. Treat them carefully, so that your listener understands a relationship in their meaning. In the second verse, the word *rest* is used as a noun and as a verb. Be sure to inflect the words appropriately for each function.

I

Weep you no more, sad fountains;

What need you flow so fast?

Look how the snowy mountains

Heaven's sun doth gently waste.

But my sun's heavenly eyes

View not your weeping,

That now lies sleeping,

Softly, now softly lies sleeping.

II

Sleep is a reconciling,

A rest that Peace begets.

Doth not the sun rise smiling

When fair at e'en he sets?

Rest you then, rest, sad eyes,

Melt not in weeping

While she lies sleeping,

Softly, now softly lies sleeping.

Comparative Settings

"Weep you no more, sad fountains" was also set by Quilter as the first song in his Opus 12, *Seven Elizabethan Lyrics*. The American composer Barab and British composers Rebecca Clarke (1886–1979), Gurney, and Gustav Holst (1874–1934) also set this text. Listen to more than one setting of the text and use the following questions to focus your comparisons.

Discussion Questions

1. Why do you think this text attracted the attention of so many composers?

2. How does Dowland's lute song setting contrast with the later versions?

3. Do you hear any evidence of Dowland's musical ideas in the later settings by any of the text? Did the composer borrow harmony from Dowland? Melodic shapes? Repetitions?

4. The Gurney setting is entitled "Tears." How is that title fitting for his musical setting of the text?

5. What is your favorite phrase from the poem? From any of the song settings? Why?

Philip Rosseter (1568–1623)

A contemporary and friend of Campion and Dowland, Rosseter served as the court lutenist to James I of England. Here is the text from one of Rosseter's best-known lute songs. Read it and create a phonetic transcription.

"When Laura Smiles"

Before you listen, implement your dictation strategies:

1. Spellings: Look for IPA spellings you already know such as article *the*; conjunction *and*; prepositions *with, of, in, for,* and *from*; and pronouns *her, she,* and *he*.

2. Define Unfamiliar Words: Be sure you understand the meaning of these archaic words: *wanton* (extravagant or luxuriant), *tressèd* (long hair braided around the head), and *Muse* (inspirational spirit).

3. Repeating Words: The words *beauty, power,* and *Laura* recur throughout the poem. Be certain that you use the same IPA symbols for each repeated word and pronounce the words consistently each time they occur.

4. Rhyming Words: Follow down the right side of the text to identify rhymes such as *day/play, repair/despair, air/hair, shine/divine, eyes/lies,* and *subdues/Muse*.

5. Words That Do Not Rhyme: Study the third verse, where *power/lure* and *appear/there* relate but do not rhyme. Treat the words carefully to ensure tuning and intelligibility.

6. Expressive Possibilities: Circle the words that invite expression such as *cruel wounds of sorrow, untwine her tressèd hair, sweet Aurora, Morning queen, chiefest grace of beauty,* and *fills with heavenly spirits my humble Muse*.

7. Exceptional Words: "Laura" is a symbol from Italian literary history. "Aurora" and "Diana" come from Roman legend. "Laura" refers to an ideal woman who is worshipped from afar. "Aurora" is another word for "dawn." "Diana" is the goddess of the hunt.

I

When Laura smiles her sight revives both night and day;

The earth and heaven views with delight her wanton play;

And her speech with everflowing music doth repair

The cruel wounds of sorrow and untam'd despair.

II

The wanton spirits that remain in fleeting air

Affect for pastime to untwine her tressèd hair;

And the birds think sweet Aurora, Morning queen, doth shine

from her bright sphere, when Laura shows her looks divine.

III

Diana's eyes are not adorn'd with greater power

Than Laura's when she lifts awhile for sport to lure.

But when she her eyes encloseth, blindness doth appear

The chiefest grace of beauty sweetly seated there.

IV

Love hath no fire but what he steals from her bright eyes.

Time hath no power but that which in her pleasure lies.

For she with her divine beauty all the world subdues

And fills with heavenly spirits my humble Muse.

Comparative Performances

Listen to a performance of the song in which the singer is accompanied by a lute or other early instrument group and one in which the singer performs with a collaborative pianist. Use the questions listed below to delve into the differences and similarities between the historical and modern performances.

Discussion Questions

1. In which setting did the performer make the text seem most vivid?
2. Are there elements in the text that are more easily understood with the lute or early music group? With the modern piano? Which ones and why?
3. In songs of this nature, it is possible to omit a verse or to ornament one. Is there a verse you would wish to eliminate? If so, why? Does any word or phrase invite ornamentation?
4. In a strophic song of this nature, it is acceptable to vary the tempo from verse to verse. Is there a verse you would wish to sing more quickly or more slowly? If so, why?
5. How would you vary the dynamics from verse to verse?

Thomas Morley (1557–1602)

A chorister and organist, Morley wrote the music for Shakespeare's play, *As You Like It*. Below is the text of the strophic song "It was a lover and his lass," a lighthearted description of love in the springtime. Morley's use of cross rhythm gives the refrain a playful character, one that demands crisp diction. It is a song that has caught the fascination of many English-speaking composers.

"It Was a Lover and His Lass"

Before you listen, implement your dictation strategies:

1. Nonsense Syllables: The refrain "With a Hey and a Ho, and a Hey Nonni-No!" is comparable in meaning to "Fa-La-La" or "Tra-La-La" in other songs. You must decide what vowels you will use. Be consistent in your use of the IPA to ensure intelligibility, consistency and accurate tuning.

2. The letter "r": This text is a good study in the many ways the letter "r" is pronounced in English. Study *lover, hour,* and *flow'r* to be sure you treat the "r"s with the same r-diphthong choice. It is common practice to use the "r" in *springtime* and *ring* to emphasize the cross rhythms in the music. The "r" before a consonant in *cornfield, birds,* and *therefore* require extra care. Try to treat the "r" in *pretty* and *prime* in a consistent manner. The "r" in *rye* and *carol* must be understood without intruding on the quality of the vowel that follows it. Using the different types of IPA symbols for "r," mark each situation according to the rules for "r." Listen carefully to the way qualified singers perform the words.

3. Rhyming Words: Follow down the right side of the text to identify rhymes such as *lass/pass, ding/spring, rye/lie, hour/flow'r,* and *time/prime.* Use the same vowel symbol for each pair of rhymes.

4. Repeating Words: Study the text for common words that repeat such *as springtime, pretty ring time* as well as *when birds do sing, hey ding-a-ding, Sweet lovers love the spring.* Be sure that you use the same IPA symbols for each repetition and sing them with equal care and consistency.

5. Expressive Possibilities: Circle the words that help the refrain have a dancelike character such as *only* and *pretty ring time.* Note which consonants drive the rhythmic flow and which vowels deserve an extended length.

I

It was a lover and his lass

With a Hey and a Ho and a Hey Nonni-No!

That o'er the green cornfield did pass

In the springtime, the only pretty ring time

When birds do sing, hey, ding-a-ding-ding!

Sweet lovers love the spring.

II

Beneath the acres of the rye

With a Hey and a Ho and a Hey Nonni-No!

These pretty country folk did lie

In the Spring time, the only pretty ring time

When birds do sing . . .

III

This carol they began that hour

With a Hey and a Ho . . .

How that love is but a flow'r

In the spring time, the only pretty ring time

When birds do sing . . .

IV

So therefore, take the present time

With a hey and a ho . . .

Love is crownèd in the prime

In the spring time, the only pretty ring time

When birds do sing . . .

Comparative Settings

There are several settings of "It was a lover and his lass" by British composers. Listen to at least one, if not two or more, of the following settings for the sake of comparison with Morley's original setting. Select from settings by Frederick Delius (1862–1934) in *Four Old English Lyrics*; Finzi (1901–1956) in the cycle entitled *Let Us Garlands Bring*, Opus 18, #5; Quilter, Opus 3, #3; and "Pretty Ring Time" by Warlock.

Discussion Questions

1. Do you hear similarities between the settings?
2. Is there a setting in which the composer has a distinctly different approach to the text?
3. Has a composer facilitated crisp, clear diction by using melodic or rhythmic elements?
4. Is one of the settings more appealing to you than the others? How and why?
5. What harmonic factors influence the interpretation of the text in the settings? If there are modulations, how do they assist in text expression? If there is no modulation, what aspect of the harmony drives the overall shape of the setting?

Early Opera, Oratorios, and Airs

At the English court in the early 17th century, the main theatrical form was called the *masque*, a series of dances interspersed with short segments of song. By midcentury, the songs were written in "recitative" style to deliver the action of a plot. The topics of these early attempts at opera were derived from mythology and historical events.

Henry Purcell (1659–1695)

Purcell's work represented the consummation of divergent forces in dramatic vocal music. Himself a chorister of the Chapel Royal, Purcell composed anthems, secular and sacred vocal music, stage works, and instrumental music. His opera *Dido and Aeneas* (1689) is considered the first enduring English operatic work. It was written to be performed by amateur singers at a boarding school for girls. He created songs and arias that were inserted into plays such as *King Arthur* and *The Indian Queen*. His adaptations of works by Shakespeare include *The Fairy Queen* based on *A Midsummer Night's Dream* and *The Tempest*. Below is a text inspired by a line from Shakespeare's *As You Like It*. Read it and create a phonetic transcription.

"If Music Be the Food of Love"

Before you listen, implement your dictation strategies:

1. IPA Spellings: This text has many words that are spelled with the letter "r." Be careful to treat the words gracefully. The words with "r" are the following: *for, pleasures, never, declare, ev'rywhere, ear, transports, are, fierce, treat, perish, charms,* and *arms*.

2. Familiar Words: Look for words you recognize such as *music, food, love, I am,* and *you are*.

3. Rhyming Words: Follow down the right side of the text to identify rhymes such as *joy/ cloy, declare/everywhere,* and *charms/arms*. Be sure they receive the same vowel spellings.

4. Nonrhyming Words: In the second verse, the words *wound/sound* form an "eye" rhyme. Were they to be sung as rhyming words, the textual meaning would be obscure. Treat the words carefully. In this context, the word *wound* would be pronounced [wu:nd]; while *sound* would be pronounced [saʊnd] or [saʊnd].

5. Repeating Words: Study the text for common words that repeat such as *pleasure/pleasures* and *your*. Be sure that you use the same IPA symbols for each repetition.

6. Expressive Possibilities: Circle the words that invite expression such as *eyes, mien, tongue, music everywhere, invade, fierce, transports, wound, treat, sound, perish, charms, save me,* and *arms*.

7. Archaic Words or Expressions: In the first verse, the word *cloy* is not a common term. *Cloy* means to sate or satisfy. "To pleasures that will never stop giving delight" would be a paraphrase of the meaning. The concluding lines of the second verse contain the phrase *"Sure I must perish by your charms,"* which would be expressed today as *"Surely I would perish because of your charms."*

I

If Music be the food of love, sing on

That I am filled with joy

For then my list'ning soul you move

To pleasures that will never cloy.

Your eyes, your mien, your tongue declare

That you are music ev'rywhere.

II

Pleasures invade both eye and ear

So fierce the transports are, they wound

Though yet the treat is only sound

Sure I must perish by your charms

Unless you save me in your arms.

Poetic Context

The text is adapted from the first line of Shakespeare's *Twelfth Night*. The first verse explains the poet's admiration for someone whose affection would be gladly received. The text has also been set by Cecil Armstrong Gibbs (1889–1960).

George Frideric Handel (1685–1759)

Born in Germany and trained as a harpsichordist, organist, and violinist, Handel spent much of his professional career in London, where he composed in many genres. For voice, Handel composed operas in Italian and oratorios, a large-scale work for soloists, choir, and orchestra depicting historical or Biblical events, in English. The oratorio *Alexander Balus*, composed by Handel in 1747 on a text by Thomas Morell, is loosely based on a biblical tale from the Book of the Maccabeus. Read the text and create a phonetic transcription.

"Here Amid the Shady Woods"

Before you listen, implement your dictation strategies:

1. IPA Spellings: Because the text is repeated in a variety of ways throughout the aria, be sure that you use the same IPA symbols for each repetition. Should you sing this aria, transfer the symbols to your score to help you maintain the integrity of each syllable.

2. Familiar Words: Look for words you recognize such as *here, my soul, love,* and *calm.*

3. Rhyming Words: Follow down the right side of the text to identify the true rhyme of *seat/retreat* and the "eye" rhyme of *woods/floods*. Mark the vowels with care.

4. Expressive Possibilities: Circle the words that invite expression such as *shady, fragrant flow'rs, crystal floods, charming seat,* and *calm retreat.* Consider where

the composer has given emphasis to nouns, to words that modify the nouns and to the verb. Each element has its special moment of recognition, musically speaking.

5. Exceptional Words: Study the contractions *flow'rs* and *glory's* to be certain you articulate the letter "r" in appropriate, meaningful ways.

> Here amid the shady woods
>
> Fragrant flow'rs and crystal floods
>
> Taste, my soul, this charming seat
>
> Love and glory's calm retreat.

Poetic Context

Alexander Balus, King of Syria, was given in marriage to the innocent young princess, Cleopatra Thea, daughter of Egyptian King Ptolemy. Cleopatra Thea is abducted by "ruffians." The aria "Here amid the shady woods" is sung in the third act, when Cleopatra Thea anticipates the return of her husband.

Thomas Arne (1710–1778)

Himself a singer, Arne composed operas, masques, and songs. A self-taught musician, Arne played the lute and the violin. During his career, he was associated with Drury Lane Theatre and Covent Garden in London. The words of the following song come from Shakespeare's *Love's Labour Lost*. Read it and create a phonetic transcription.

"When Daisies Pied"

Before you listen, implement your dictation strategies:

1. IPA Spellings: This text is full of enumerations connected by "and." Decide what vowel you will use consistently for the word. The choices are [ɑ] or [æ].

2. Familiar Words: Look for words you recognize such as *when, of,* and *the*.

3. Rhyming Words: Follow down the right side of the text to identify rhymes such as *blue/hue, white/delight, tree/me, fear/ear, straws/daws,* and *clocks/frocks*.

4. Repeating Words: The word *cuckoo* in its various guises should have the same IPA symbols and maintain its integrity during each repetition. Note the alliteration in *pipes* and *ploughman,* and *merry* and *maidens*.

5. Expressive Possibilities: Circle the words that invite expression such as *mocks married men* and *oh, word of fear, unpleasing to a married ear!*

6. Unusual Words: The word *pied* [paɪːd] means "when daisies opened with patches of color." *Larks, rooks,* and *daws* are types of birds.

I

When daisies pied, and violets blue,

And lady smocks all silver white,

And cuckoo buds of yellow hue,

Do paint the meadows with delight:

The cuckoo then, on ev'ry tree,

Mocks married men; for thus sings he:

Cuckoo! O word of fear,

Unpleasing to a married ear.

II

When shepherds pipe on oaten straws,

And merry larks are ploughman's clocks,

And turtles tread, and rooks, and daws,

And maidens bleach their summer frocks:

The cuckoo then, on ev'ry tree . . .

Poetic Context

Also known as "The Cuckoo Song," the text mocks the amorous enthusiasms of young people during the early spring.

George Munro (1685–1731)

In his lifetime, George Munro was best known as a keyboard player and a composer of popular song, of which "My Lovely Celia" is a notable example. Read the composer's text and create a phonetic transcription.

"My Lovely Celia"

Before you listen, implement your dictation strategies:

1. IPA Spellings: Make clear choices about the type of "r" you will sing in the following two pairs: *fair/air* and *charms/arms*. Look also at the words *your* and *heart's*. Treat the letter "r" appropriately in each case. Mark your choices with the IPA symbols consistent with the rules for the letter "r." Note the choices made by the performers to whom you listen. Ask your teacher's advice about what choices are best for you.

2. Familiar Words: Look for familiar words such as *my*, *me*, and *but*. Choose vowel sounds that foster beautiful tone and word integrity.

3. Rhyming Words: Follow down the right side of the text to identify rhymes such as *fair/air*, *kind/mind*, *eyes/arise*, and *charms/arms*. Be sure to use the same IPA symbols for each rhyming pair.

4. Repeating Words: Study the text for common words that repeat such as and *o!* Be sure that you use the same IPA symbols for each repetition.

5. Expressive Possibilities: Circle the words that invite expression such as *heav'nly fair*, *lilies sweet*, *soft as air*, *melting beams*, *enchanted by your charms*, *o take me*, and *dying to your arms*. The poetic phrase containing "your bright eyes" requires a clear separation between *bright* and *eyes* to avoid any misunderstanding such as "bright ties."

6. Exceptional Opportunity: Munro set only the first and third verses of this poem. Were you to wish to sing the second verse, give extra expression to the unusual word *Ambrosia*, meaning "food of the gods." The rhyming words are *kiss/bliss* and *thine/divine*.

I

My lovely Celia, heav'nly fair,

As lilies sweet, as soft as air,

No more then torment me, but be kind,

And with thy love ease my troubled mind.

II

Give me Ambrosia in a kiss,

That I may rival love in bliss,

That I may mix my soul with thine,

And make the pleasure all divine.

III

O, let me gaze on your bright eyes,

Where melting beams so oft arise;

My heart's enchanted with thy charms.

O, take me, dying to your arms.

Discussion Questions

1. Archaic language appears in each of the early English song examples given above. What would you do to make the text intelligible to your listener?

2. What vowels and consonants required special treatment in these early ayres and songs?

3. What are the difficulties of singing a contraction such as *ev'ry, e'en,* or *heav'nly*? What are your strategies in each case?

4. How is singing the aria by Handel "Here Amid the Shady Woods" different than singing the songs by Purcell, Arne, and Munro?

5. After hearing comparative settings of texts, did your original concept of the text change? Stay the same? Why? How?

English Diction First Presentations

Below is a list of early English ayres, lute songs, and arias for class presentations. To prepare for your presentation, type or write legibly the text for your assigned selection. Allow enough space between the poetic lines that you can write in an IPA transcription of the text. Use and cite the printed and/or online resources available, where appropriate. Submit the text, your IPA transcription, and poetic equivalent to your diction instructor for correction and duplication for class use during your presentation.

In creating your IPA transcription, identify the proper pronunciation of each word as it would be spoken. Ask your studio teacher if there are any vowel modifications that should be made for the sung version of the text. Notate in your transcription any modifications your teacher has suggested. Write your IPA transcription into your musical score as a ready reference when you sing. At your presentation, the class will read the text aloud with you. This "choral" reading of the text gives your classmates the opportunity to grasp the poem and to recognize its diction challenges. After the group recitation, you will speak the text as you intend to sing it, acknowledging punctuation and giving attention to the rhyme scheme and expressive words. It is wise to rehearse this step with your studio teacher. Your performance will contribute to the language and repertoire learning of the entire class. Your diction instructor will offer information about the poet, composer, and cultural context of your selection. This presentation is evaluated pass/fail and serves as a "rehearsal" for the final, graded presentation you will make at the conclusion of the English Diction section of the course.

Repertoire Suggestions

Have You Seen but a White Lily Grow?	Anonymous/attr. B. Jonson
Sally in Our Alley*	Anonymous/attr. H. Carey
The Willow Song	Anonymous
When Daisies Pied	Thomas Arne
When to Her Lute Corinna Sings	Thomas Campion
Come Again, Sweet Love	John Dowland

Flow My Tears	John Dowland
Flow Not So Fast	John Dowland
Now, O Now I Needs Must Part	John Dowland
Weep You No More Sad Fountains*	John Dowland
The Silver Swan	Orlando Gibbons
Here Amid the Shady Wood	George Frideric Handel
Where'r You Walk	George Frideric Handel
Fain Would I Change That Note*	Tobias Hume
Tobacco	Tobias Hume
Drink to Me Only With Thine Eyes*	Ben Jonson
It Was a Lover and His Lass*	Thomas Morley
My Lovely Celia	George Munro
Underneath the Cypress Tree	Francis Pilkington
I Attempt From Love's Sickness	Henry Purcell
If Music Be the Food of Love (first version)	Henry Purcell
I'll Sail Upon the Dog Star	Henry Purcell
Music for a While	Henry Purcell
When Laura Smiles	Phillip Rosseter

*Indicates comparative setting with works to be presented in final presentations.

Duet Settings

Turn, Turn Thine Eyes	George Frideric Handel
Shepherd, Shepherd Leave Decoying	Henry Purcell
Sound the Trumpet	Henry Purcell

Poetry and Song in 19th- and 20th-Century England

The development of the modern piano occurred simultaneously with the Romantic movement in poetry. The art song flourished as a means of exploiting the piano's capacity to collaborate as an equal partner. "Though the singer obviously maintained the key role in declamation of the text, the piano acted as a running commentary," according to Hold (2002). The compositional ideas of early 19th-century German-speaking composers such as Schubert (1797–1828), Robert Schumann (1810–1856), Johannes Brahms (1833–1897), and Wolf (1860–1903) spread to France and, eventually, to the British Isles. In his early compositional career, Gabriel Fauré (1845–1924) was characterized as "the French Robert Schumann." Schumann was the German Lieder composer who melded the poetic text perfectly into the rhythm and inflection of the music. Henri Duparc (1848–1933) and Claude Debussy (1862–1918) were also strongly influenced by German models. The Norwegian composer Edvard Grieg (1842–1907) and Russian composers Modest Mussorgsky (1839–1881) and Peter Tchaikovsky (1840–1893) created songs that translated the Germanic ideals into their respective national traditions.

In England, the art song flourished a little later than on the European continent. The composers whose works are addressed below are those of Ralph Vaughan Williams (1872–1958), Quilter, George Butterworth (1885–1916), Gurney (1890–1937), Warlock, and Finzi. This circle of men does not represent a single school of thought. Many of them were well-acquainted with one another. Most were aware of the compositional output of the others. Because of their proximity and common training, these composers were enticed to set the same poems to music. The comparison of their approaches to the same poem or poet offers you the opportunity to extend the horizon of your interpretative world. You will notice that composers sometimes treat important words with melismatic melodic material that "paints" or depicts the meaning of the word. Such a text treatment gives the word emphasis through extension. A composer may alter the poet's work by repeating certain words or phrases. Composers have been known to omit or change a word or phrase. The accompaniment may be a simple, harmonic support or it may be an elaboration upon the text and music through any number of devices. The accompaniment might emulate the scene described in the poem. It may comment on the text through some form of imitative writing. One composer may "frame" the poem with an introduction and postlude, keeping the text together as a unit, while another may intersperse measures of musical interest that distribute individual poetic phrases over a larger musical landscape. No matter what devices are used, a successful song unites a shapely melodic line with an accommodating harmonic structure that together reflect the deeper meaning of the poetic text.

As was described above, 17th- and 18th-century composers often wrote the texts they set to music. In the 19th and 20th century British song, Gurney, like Campion, is the wordsmith who was also an outstanding song composer. In the 17th and 18th centuries, some composers added words to preexisting melodies to create new works. In the 19th and 20th centuries, composers concentrated their efforts on setting a preexisting literary work—a poetic text—to music. Most of the works you will study here were intended to be sung exclusively with piano accompaniment. A few songs were conceived to be performed with a string quartet or with an orchestra.

As you have already learned, English-speaking composers frequently select the texts of Shakespeare as the basis for song. Below you will encounter other poets whose works attracted 19th- and 20th-century song composers.

William Blake (1757–1823): Poet, Painter, and Printmaker

William Blake's creative output incorporates literary and visual artistry. During his lifetime, Blake was best known for engraving designs to illustrate the books of other authors. It is said that Blake had visions that inspired his poetry. The illustrated publications of Blake's own poetry reveal the essences of these visions. If you wish to perform one of Blake's many poems that have been set to music, you will find this visual evidence inspirational and informative.

Perhaps the most popular of Blake's poems are those entitled *Songs of Innocence*, written to be read aloud to young children. The *Songs of Innocence*, a collection of 23 short poems, were published in 1789. They later appeared with *Songs of Experience*, a set of poems depicting the grim realities of human life. Blake and his wife, Catherine, were a childless couple, who shared a profound sympathy for children. Blake was acutely aware of social injustice and its impact on the most vulnerable, especially the young and the poor. Among beautiful images intended to comfort a child listener, Blake often wove a stark message directed to the adult reader (Damrosch, 2015).

As you read Blake's poem called "The Lamb," you may sense a simplicity that is mingled with larger significance. For the illustrated publication of "The Lamb," Blake placed the poem in the center, surrounded by a protective set of arching branches from trees that are positioned on either side. At the base of the tree is a young shepherd boy with his small flock of sheep nestled at the door of a small thatched cottage. In some copies, the bottom of the picture shows a small stream of blue water that flows past the boy and his flock. In others, the bottom is a verdant green lawn. These elements imply a pastoral, idyllic setting. Visualize the scene as you read the poem silently and then aloud.

There are several musical settings of this poem for you to consider, both for solo voice and for choir. As you listen, consider the text from the viewpoint of the adult reader and the child recipient. Read the text and create a phonetic transcription.

"Little Lamb"

Before you listen, implement your dictation strategies:

1. IPA Spellings for Archaic Words: Observe the words not in common usage such as *dost*, *Thee*, and *Thou*. What choices would you make for your singing?

2. Thematic Words: Innocence is the theme of the text, as exemplified in phrases such as *Little Lamb*, *I a child*, and *God bless Thee!* How might a singer interpret the poet's words? What is the singer's point of view? What is the singer's responsibility as an interpreter?

3. Rhyming Words: Follow down the right side of the text of the first verse to identify rhymes such as *Thee/Thee*, *feed/mead*, and *voice/rejoice*. In the second verse, you will find two "eye" rhymes; namely, *name/lamb* and *lamb/name* with the authentic rhyme *mild/child* nestled between. Treat the "eye" rhymes carefully so that your listener hears the significance of the words.

4. Repeating Phrases: Study the form of the poem. The first verse opens and concludes with the questions, "Little Lamb, who made Thee? Dost Thou know who made Thee?" Mark the IPA accordingly. If you sing a setting of the text, you may wish to vary the inflection of the questions, but the words would be pronounced the same. The second verse contains repeated phrases. "Little Lamb, I'll tell Thee?" and "Little Lamb, God bless Thee!" The diction remains the same though the emphasis may change.

5. Expressive Possibilities: Circle the words that invite expression such as *by the stream and o'er the mead, tender voice, He is* <u>meek</u> *and he is* <u>mild</u>, and the repeated phrase *God bless Thee!*

I

Little Lamb, who made Thee?

Dost Thou know who made Thee?

Gave Thee life and bid Thee feed

By the stream and o'er the mead,

Gave Thee such a tender voice

Making all the vales rejoice.

Little Lamb, who made Thee?

Dost Thou know who made Thee?

II

Little Lamb, I'll tell Thee.

Little Lamb, I'll tell Thee.

He is callèd by Thy name,

For He called himself a lamb,

He is meek and he is mild.

He became a little child.

I a child and Thou a Lamb

We are callèd by His name.

Little Lamb, God bless Thee,

Little Lamb, God bless Thee!

Comparative Solo and Choral Settings

Compare any of the solo settings listed below. Consider what the similarities and differences are between the settings you hear. The British composers who set "The Lamb" by Blake were Sir Arthur Somervell (1863–1937), Vaughn Williams, and Maude Valérie White (1855–1937). The American composers who set "The Lamb" by Blake are Ernst Bacon (1898–1991), William Bolcom (b. 1938), Theodore Chanler (1902–1961), Celius Dougherty (1902–1986), and Lee Hoiby (1926–2011); and *Song of Innocence* was set by Paul Nordorff (1909–1977). Compare the choral settings by British composer John Tavener (1944–2012) with that of American composers James Erb (1926–2014), John Ferguson (b. 1941), and Donald McCullough (b. 1957). Consider the differences between the choral settings and compare them with your impressions of the solo settings of the text.

Discussion Questions

1. What does Blake's visual image add to a singer's interpretation of a text?
2. How does the social justice context of this poem impact your thinking about the song?
3. How can diction tools be used to express the deeper meaning of this text?
4. What is the role of punctuation and how will you use it? Do the composers of the comparative settings maintain the original punctuation? If not, does it matter?
5. How do the comparative settings deal with the concepts of innocence and experience? Do you notice differences in key, melodic contour and/or harmonic devices?

The Brownings: Elizabeth Barrett Browning (1806–1861) and Robert Browning (1812–1889)

The mere mention of the name "Browning" conjures up the famous first lines of Sonnet 43; namely, "How do I love thee? Let me count the ways . . . " The relationship between Elizabeth Barrett Browning (1806–1861) and Robert Browning (1812–1889) began as a correspondence, one in which Robert expressed his deepest affection for Elizabeth's verse. Their elopement and subsequent marriage have been interpreted thoroughly in books, plays, and film. Both Brownings published works early in life, though Elizabeth's publications were the more successful early works of the two. A book of her poems published in 1844 prompted Robert Browning's initial letter. The Brownings settled at Casa Guidi in Florence, Italy. There she wrote a verse novel entitled *Aurora Leigh* and *The Casa Guidi Windows*. Even Elizabeth Barrett Browning's letters were lyrical. Argento's song cycle for mezzo soprano called "Casa Guidi" is based upon personal letters written by Elizabeth Barrett Browning while she was living in Italy. It was premiered in 1983 by Frederica von Stade and the Minnesota Orchestra.

The *Sonnets From the Portuguese*, written between 1845 and 1846, dedicated to her husband, were first published in 1850. Elizabeth Barrett Browning's choice of the sonnet form was considered a courageous one, because sonnet had been the domain of male authors. Her sonnets continue to be beloved love lyrics, filled with tonalities of vowel and consonant that beg for melodic expression. The following sonnet is perhaps the most well known.

Comparative Listening

Elizabeth Barrett Browning wrote the sonnet "How do I love thee? Let me count the ways" in 1854, as the 43rd in the collection entitled *Sonnets From the Portuguese*. "The Portuguese" was a nickname Robert Browning coined for his wife. There are four versions, three solo settings, and one choral setting. Listen to all four and compare in detail what you hear in each version. Note the text underlay and syllabification. Consider the potential challenges of tessitura, articulation of consonants, vowel purity, and tuning. Circle the words that seem to present challenges. For example: The unvoiced "th" sound [θ] at the end of the words such as " . . . to the *breadth* and *depth* . . . with the *faith* I seemed to lose with my lost saints . . . I shall but love thee better after *death*" requires careful articulation. As you listen, create a phonetic reading of the sonnet text.

"How Do I Love Thee?"

<u>Before you listen, implement your dictation strategies:</u>

1. Spellings: Look for IPA spellings you already know such as article *the*; conjunctions *with* and *and*; prepositions *to, of, for, from, in*; and pronouns *I, thee*, and *me*.

2. Familiar Words: Look for words in common usage such as *count, soul, Being, men*, and *life*. Treat the "ly" ending of *freely* and *purely* with the same unaccented ending [lɨ] or [lɪ]. Be alert to forms of "r" such as *breadth, Grace, griefs, Praise*, and *strive* [ɹ] or [r] compared to *turn* [ɝ] or [ɜ], [ɾ] for *every*, and [ʁ] for *better*.

3. Rhyming Words: Follow down the right side of the text to identify rhymes such as *ways/day's, height/sight, candlelight/Right, lose/choose*, and *breath/death*. Note that *Grace, Praise, faith*, and *use* do not rhyme exactly with their paired equivalent. Treat the situation carefully to ensure intelligibility.

4. Repeating Words: Study the text for common words that repeat such as *I, love*, and *thee*. To ensure exquisite tuning, be certain they receive the same IPA symbols. Be aware of the lateral consonant [l] in *love-level* and *love-love-lose-lost*. Treat the letter "l" similarly with each repetition.

5. Expressive Possibilities: Circle the words that invite expression such as *depth, breadth, height, ideal Grace, quiet need, sun and candlelight, smiles, tears*, and *better after death*.

How do I love thee? Let me count the ways.

I love thee to the depth and breadth and height

My soul can reach, when feeling out of sight

For the ends of Being and ideal Grace.

I love thee to the level of every day's

Most quiet need, by sun and candlelight.

I love thee freely, as men strive for Right;

I love thee purely, as they turn from Praise.

I love thee with the passion put to use

In my old griefs, and with my childhood's faith.

I love thee with a love I seemed to lose

With my lost saints, —I love thee with the breath,

Smiles, tears, of all my life! and, if God choose,

I shall but love thee better after death.

—Sonnet XLIII (43)

Solo and Choral Settings

Compare one or more solo settings of this text, such as "How Do I Love Thee?" by Edouard Lippé (1884–1956), "Let Me Count the Ways" by Norman Dello Joio (1913–2008), and "How Do I Love Thee?" by Libby Larsen (b. 1950). You may be interested in a choral setting of the text entitled "How Do I Love Thee?" by Eric Nelson, performed by the Atlanta Sacred Chorale, conducted by the composer, and published by Galaxy Music Corp.

Comparative Listening

Let us turn to the poetry of Robert Browning. It is significant to note that Robert Browning's writings were popular in the United States before they won mass acclaim in his native England.

The poem is known by the title "Pippa Passes." You may recognize it by it first line: "The year's at the Spring." It appears in a verse drama entitled *Bells and Pomegranates*, published by Robert Browning in 1841. Read the text and create a phonetic transcription.

"Pippa Passes"

Before you listen, implement your dictation strategies:

1. Spellings: Look for IPA spellings you already know such as *the, at, year,* and *day*.

2. Familiar Words: Look for common words you know such as *spring, wing, heaven,* and *world*.

3. Rhyming Words: Follow down the right side of the text to identify rhymes such as *spring/wing, morn/thorn, dew-pearled/world,* and *seven/heaven*. Be sure to use the same IPA symbols for the vowels in the rhyming pairs.

4. Repeating Words: Study the text for common words that repeat such as *year's/day's, spring,* and *morn*. Choose the same phonetic spelling for each repetition and listen to hear if the musical setting demands any modifications that would help the repeated words "rhyme" and tune properly.

5. Diction Issues: Consider the difficulty of speaking and singing clearly the words that are apostrophized such as *year's/day's/morning's/hillside's/lark's/snail's* and *God's/All's*.

6. Expressive Possibilities: Circle the words that invite expression such as *Morning's at seven, hillside's dew-pearled,* and *All's right with the world!* Take note of the last word, *world*. Plan how you would articulate the word clearly in each setting.

The year's at the spring,

And day's at the morn;

Morning's at seven;

The hillside's dew-pearled;

The year's at the spring,

And day's at the morn;

> The lark's on the wing;
>
> The snail's on the thorn;
>
> God's in His heaven,
>
> All's right with the world!

Comparative Settings

"Pippa Passes," published in Robert Browning's *Bells and Pomegranates* (1841), has been set for solo voice by two American composers. One setting is called "The Year's at the Spring" by Amy H. H. Beach (1867–1944), *Three Browning Songs*, Op. 44; and the other, "Pippa's Song" by Rorem. Listen to these contrasting approaches to Robert Browning's text. What do you find most appealing? Are there similarities in the two settings? What are the primary differences?

Discussion Questions

1. How is the poetic language of Elizabeth Barrett Browning comparable to that of Robert Browning? How are their poetic styles different from one another?
2. Compare the two poetic forms of the sonnet and the rhymed strophes. Do you prefer one form over the other as a reader? As a singer?
3. What are the vocal challenges of each setting?
4. What are the diction challenges? How will you address the challenges?
5. Compare the singing of a poem by a solo singer to the choral setting you heard. How are the expressive possibilities the same? How are they different?

The Rossettis: Christina Rossetti (1830–1894) and Dante Gabriel Rossetti (1828–1882)

The Pre-Raphaelites

According to Michael Schmidt, "English critics tend to set Christina Rossetti in the frame alongside Emily Dickinson" (Schmidt, 1998). Arguably, Rossetti's writing evokes emotion over thought, while Dickinson's poems generate ideas from which feeling evolves. Unlike Dickinson, Rossetti was a deeply, overtly religious woman. Two of her best-known poems, "In the Bleak Midwinter" and "Love Came Down at Christmas," may be familiar to you in hymn, solo, and/or choral settings. Her poetry has attracted the attention of British and American composers alike.

Christina Georgina Rossetti and her brother Dante Gabriel Rossetti grew up in an Italian/English household. Their father, Gabriele, was a poet and translator. Their mother, Frances, was a deeply Christian woman. The letters between the siblings reveal the lifelong reverence they shared for their mother as a devoted teacher and friend. All the Rossetti children were active in artistic and scholarly endeavors. The oldest sister, Maria Francesca (b. 1827), was a commentator on the works of Dante Alighieri, while brother William Michael (b. 1829), became a critic, biographer, and editor.

For Dante Gabriel Rossetti, painting was of great significance. His artwork is deemed central to the founding of a group called the Pre-Raphaelite Brotherhood. The Brotherhood members were young English artists, who united to protest the prevailing academic, formal approach to English painting in London 1848. Inspired by the work of Italian painter and architect Raphael, the Pre-Raphaelites hoped to return art to the depiction of nature as it literally appeared. Raphael relied on careful drawings to capture vivid images that he later painted in realistic detail and perspective. Pre-Raphaelite artists used photography as a basis for their work, a technique that enabled the study of intricate detail previously unavailable. Their works encourage dialogue between nature and human experience. Other artists included Sir John Everett Millais (1829–1896) and Edward Burne-Jones (1833–1898). Christina Rossetti served as a model for several of Dante Gabriel Rossetti's paintings.

In 1850, the Brotherhood movement established a journal called *The Germ: Thoughts toward Nature in Poetry, Literature and Art* to rekindle interest in the poetic work of Romantics such as John Keats, Blake, Edgar Allen Poe, and Whitman. The writings of Dante Alighieri and Geoffrey Chaucer (1343–1400) were also strong influences. The poems of the Pre-Raphaelites display a distinct musicality, religious flair and dreamy atmosphere. The texts have been readily set in song. Though not a member of the Pre-Raphaelite Brotherhood, Christina Rossetti maintained an interest in their ideals. As you listen to the following setting of Christina Rossetti's work, consider what factors have made her poetry so inspiring to composers. Read the poem and create a phonetic transcription.

Comparative Listening

"A Birthday" is the original title of a poem by Christina Rossetti. You may be familiar with it as a song entitled "My Heart Is Like a Singing Bird." The text contains descriptive words that may seem obscure to you. The use of elevated, archaic language was common among the Pre-Raphaelite literary artists.

"The Birthday"

Before you listen, implement your dictation strategies:

1. Spellings: Look for IPA spellings you already know such as articles *a* and *an*; conjunctions *with* and *and*; prepositions *to*, *of*, and *in*; the comparative *like a*; possessives *my* and *whose*; and the pronoun *me*.

2. Familiar Words: Look for colorful words you know such as *nest*, *apple*, *boughs*, and *rainbow*. As you read, allow these nouns to create an imaginary atmosphere for you.

3. Rhyming Words: Follow down the right side of the text to identify the rhymes of *tree/sea/me*, *dyes/eyes*, and *fleur-de-lys/me*. Note that the French pronunciation of "lys" would express the "s," but the English version would not. Therefore, in this text, the word *lys* should rhyme with the word *me*. The word would be pronounced [flœːr də ˈli].

4. Repeating Words: Study the text for the phrase: "my heart is like . . . " that occurs three times. Will you read and sing them as an enumeration or as a thought with increasing intensity?

5. Expressive Possibilities: Circle the words that invite expression such as *singing bird*, *watered shoot*, *thickset fruit*, *rainbow shell*, and *halcyon sea*. What diction challenges do you anticipate when expressing the word *gladder*?

6. Exceptional Words: *dais* [d'eɪːɪs; 'dɛɪs, 'daɪːɪs], *vair* [vɛr] meaning *fur, doves and pomegranates, peacocks with a hundred eyes, gold and silver grapes*, and *fleur-de-lys*. Be sure you understand how to pronounce and define these words.

My heart is like a singing bird

Whose nest is in a watered shoot;

My heart is like an apple tree

Whose bough are bent with thickset fruit;

My heart is like a rainbow shell

That paddles in a halcyon sea;

My heart is gladder than all these

Because my love is come to me.

Raise me a dais of silk and down'

Hang it with vair and purple dyes;

Carve it in doves and pomegranates,

And peacocks with a hundred eyes;

Work it in gold and silver grapes,

In leaves and silver fleur-de-lys;

Because the birthday of my life

Is come, my love is come to me.

Comparative Settings

There are several settings of this poem for your comparative listening. Compare one or more by any one of these composers: H. T. Burleigh (1866–1949), Samuel Coleridge-Taylor (1875–1912), Richard Faith (b. 1926), Gibbs, Samuel Liddle (1864–1951), Darius Milhaud (1892–1974) from *Trois Poèmes*, Rorem from *Women's Voices* #2, and Cyril Scott (1879–1970). Notice the composer's choice for a title. Does it influence your interpretation of the text? Do you find similarities between your listening examples? Does one composer cope more successfully with the diction challenges than the others?

Comparative Listening

Those attracted to the poetry of Christina Rossetti also embrace the written work of her brother, Dante Gabriel Rossetti (1828–1882). Dante Gabriel Rossetti's poem "Silent Noon" may already be familiar to you in its setting by Vaughn Williams. It is one of six sonnets Vaughan Williams included in a song cycle for voice and piano entitled *The House of Life*.

"Silent Noon"

Before you listen, implement your dictation strategies:

1. IPA Spellings: Look for IPA spellings you already know such as articles *the* and *a*; conjunction *and*; prepositions *in through, from, to,* and *of*; and pronouns *your* and *we*.

2. Familiar Words: Look for the descriptive words that deserve emphasis such as *long fresh* grass, *rosy* blooms, *visible* silence, *still* as the *hourglass, blue* thread *loosened, winged* hour, and *song of love*.

3. Rhyming Words: Follow down the right side of the text to identify rhymes such as *grass/amass/pass/hourglass, blooms/glooms, edge/hedge, dragon-fly/sky, above/love,* and *dower/hour*. Be certain that each rhyming word shares the IPA symbol of its partner/s. You may choose to pronounce the letter "a" in the rhyming sequence of *grass, amass, pass,* and *hourglass* using the British pronunciation of [ɑ] or the more American pronunciation of [æ]. Choose deliberately and be consistent in your diction.

4. Repeating Words: "Silence" is the only noun that appears twice in this text. Treat it carefully both times. The silence is "visible" and "twofold." It is the embodiment of the title in the poetic text.

5. Expressive Possibilities: Circle the words that invite expression such as the alliterative *kingcup, hawthorn hedge,* and *deathless dower*.

6. Exceptional Words: This text is rich with words that have been created for descriptive purposes. Treat the "invented" words with special care. They are *finger-points, sun-searched, close-companioned, deathless dower,* and *inarticulate hour*.

Your hands lie open in the long fresh grass,

The finger-points look through like rosy blooms:

Your eyes smile peace.

The pasture gleams and glooms

,Neath billowing clouds (skies) that scatter and amass.

All round our nest, far as the eye can pass,

Are golden kingcup fields with silver edge,

Where the cow-parsley skirts the hawthorn hedge.

'Tis visible silence, still as the hourglass.

Deep in the sun-searched growths the dragonfly

Hangs like a blue thread loosened from the sky:

So this winged hour is dropt to us from above.

Oh! Clasp we to our hearts, for deathless dower,

This close-companioned inarticulate hour

When twofold silence was the song of love.

Comparative Settings

The most familiar musical settings are "Silent Noon" by British composer Vaughn Williams. Compare it with one of the less well-known settings such as those by American composers Frederick Shepherd Converse (1871–1940) or Henry Clough-Leighter (1874–1956). The latter is from "The Day of Beauty." Other settings of poems by Dante Gabriel Rossetti that you might enjoy are "English May" (1912), "One Hope" (1926), and "During Music" (1928) set by John Ireland (1879–1962).

Discussion Questions

1. What are the diction challenges of "Pre-Raphaelite" poetic language? How will you address the challenges?
2. What are the similarities between the writing styles of Christina Rossetti and her brother Dante Gabriel Rossetti? What the differences?
3. Do the British composers set these poets differently than the American composers do? If so, how?
4. What do you learn from the titles of each of these poems?
5. In your opinion, why are these poets so beloved in English-speaking countries?

Ivor Gurney (1890–1937): Poet and Composer

Always a musical child, Gurney was a chorister and a student of organ at King's School in Gloucester, England. The composer Herbert Howells was one of his classmates. Gurney advanced to study music at the Royal College of Music from 1911 to 1914. There he studied with Charles Stanford and Vaughn Williams. Gurney enlisted as a soldier and served from 1915 to 1917 on the Western front, where it is believed he experienced mustard gas. Upon his return to England, Gurney continued his study of music. After a few productive seasons of composition, Gurney was confined to a mental institution for the remaining years of his life. Shortly after his death, Gurney's work was championed by his contemporaries.

Like Campion, Gurney's words were as artful as his musical setting of them. In his 1917 setting of his own poem "Severn Meadows," written during his war ordeal in France, poetry and music are considered by many to be in perfect union. At least as much a poet as song composer, Gurney published two volumes of poems, "Severn and

Somme" (1917) and "War's Embers" (1919) and saw many of his poems appear in various periodicals.

At a time when the name "Gurney" was little more than a bibliographic reference, one of my mentors related an experience that caused me to reconsider not only "Gurney" but the history of 20th-century British song. During the proceedings of the 1989 Hans-Pfitzner Song Competition held in Hamburg, Germany, the members of the judging panel were challenged to name which British composer would be considered the most significant creator of song in the waning 20th century. To the great surprise of many, the name "Ivor Gurney" rose above all the somewhat more obvious choices including Britten, Vaughn Williams, and Finzi.

Here are some reasons why Gurney's songs Gurney are particularly appealing. The key and accompaniment of Gurney songs provide a sense of ambience, a perfect place for the poem to reside. The text settings unite punctuation with musical phrasing, giving the singer abundant chances to enhance the diction while expressing the text. Read the text and create a phonetic transcription.

Comparative Listening

Read the following text by Edward Shanks and create a phonetic transcription.

"The Fields Are Full"

<u>Before you listen, implement your dictation strategies:</u>

1. Spellings: Look for IPA spellings you already know such as article *the*; conjunction *and*; and prepositions *of, upon, from,* and *in with.*

2. Familiar Words: Look for the descriptive words that deserve emphasis such *full, still,* and *beautiful.*

3. Rhyming Words: Follow down the right side of the text to identify rhymes such as *still/hill, air/bear, youth/truth,* and *full/beautiful.* Be certain that each rhyming word shares the IPA symbol of its partner/s. Choose deliberately and be consistent in your diction.

4. Diction Challenges: In this text, the words *full* and *filled* are crucial to the listener's understanding of the poem. Finding just the right vowel that will tune perfectly is a challenge. The words *youth, strength,* and *truth* require extra attention so that the unvoiced "th" [θ] has enough length to be understood.

5. Expressive Possibilities: Circle the words that invite expression such as the alliterative pairs *breathe/brown, hedge/hill, sweetness/sense,* and the descriptive words *still, sweetness,* and the modified nouns *old couple/heavy age.*

The fields are full of summer still

And breathe again upon the air

From brown dry side of hedge and hill

More sweetness than the sense can bear.

So some old couple who in youth

With love were filled and over full,

And loved with strength and loved with truth,

In heavy age are beautiful.

Comparative Settings

Compare the setting by Gurney with that of Gibbs and/or the setting entitled "Late Summer" by Warlock.

Comparative Listening

The following text by W. B. Yeats has attracted British and American composers. Read it and create a phonetic transcription.

"The Cloths of Heaven"

Before you listen, implement your dictation strategies:

1. Spellings: Look for IPA spellings you already know such as article *the;* conjunctions *and* and *but;* prepositions *with, of, under,* and *on;* the possessives *yours* and *my;* and pronouns *I* and *you.*

2. Familiar Words: Look for the descriptive words that deserve emphasis such as the colors: *golden, silver, blue, light,* and *half-light.*

3. Repeating Words: The text is unified by the repetition of *cloths, light, feet,* and *dreams.* Be sure to note carefully the vowel choices in each case.

4. Expressive Possibilities: Circle the words that invite expression such as the alliterative use of *embroidered/enwrought, dim and dark, night-light-half-light,* and the use of *spread* and *tread* to indicate the spirit of the poet and his love.

5. Diction Challenges: This text is rich with words that have been created for descriptive purposes. Several words present diction challenges. The word *cloths* with its unvoiced "th" followed by the plural "s" [θːz] requires extra care. *Enwrought* [ɛnˈrɔt], meaning *adorned,* is an important but unfamiliar descriptive word.

Had I the heavens embroidered cloths,

Enwrought with golden and silver light,

The blue and the dim and the dark cloths

Of night and light and the half-light,

I would spread the cloths under your feet:

But I, being poor, have only my dreams;

I have spread my dreams under your feet;

Tread softly because you tread on my dreams.

Comparative Settings

Rebecca Clarke and Warlock are among those who have contributed significant musical settings of this text to vocal repertoire. Compare the setting by Gurney with either or both solo settings. There are also significant choral versions of the text by Z. Randall Stroope (b. 1953) and Stephen Lange (b. 1977) for your consideration, too.

Discussion Questions

1. Do you find the harmonic language of Ivor Gurney different or the same as that of the British composers of his time?

2. What role do the introduction and interludes in Gurney's settings play? Will they have an impact on your interpretation of a Gurney song?

3. Would you recognize that Gurney, the song composer, is a wordsmith? If so, how?

4. What other poems of Yeats do you know? Are any of them set to music?

5. Would you agree that Gurney might be considered the most significant creator of British song in the 20th century? Do you prefer another 20th-century British composer? If so, who and why?

A. E. Housman (1859–1936): Poet Whose Words Sparked British and American Song

Alfred Edward Housman (1859–1936) studied St. John's College Oxford but did not receive a degree. He proved to be an excellent Latin and Greek scholar. In 1911, he became professor of Latin at Cambridge University. As a poet, Housman published two collections of poems, one entitled *A Shropshire Lad* (1896) that depicts his remembrances of Shropshire and Worchestershire, in West Midlands, England, where he was born and the other, *Last Poems* (1922). Posthumously, two volumes were published by his brother, Laurence, entitled *More Poems* and *Additional Poems*. One of the best loved poets of his time, Housman was a gifted amateur, evidenced by his use of rhyme. The regularity of his rhyme may be the reason his work is so often set to music. Housman seems most moved by themes of the rural countryside, patriotism, doomed love and a certain sense of doubt regarding religious matters. The proximity of the Severn River, the U.K.'s longest river covering over 180 miles and crossing Shropshire, inspires much of the poetic references.

In 1933, Housman was invited to give the Leslie Stephen Lecture at Cambridge. To understand the significance of this honor, you should know that Leslie Stephen (1832–1904) was a 19th-century philosopher/critic and the first editor of England's *National Dictionary of Biography*. (His daughter, Virginia Stephen Woolf, became one of the most noted novelists of her time.) In the lecture, entitled "The Name and Nature of Poetry," Housman describes how he developed his poetic ideas by saying " . . . I would go out for a walk of two or three hours. As I went along thinking of nothing in particular, only looking at things around me and following the progress of the seasons, there would flow into my mind, with sudden and unaccountable emotion, sometimes a line or two of verse, sometimes a whole stanza at once, accompanied, not preceded, by a vague notion of the poem which they were destined to form part of" (Housman, 1933). Housman's poetry would seem to be a dialogue with himself. His themes are issues relating to the end of life and the lessons hindsight offer. The following text considers one's responsibility to classmates and colleagues. Read the text and create a phonetic transcription.

Comparative Listening

Read the following text from *A Shropshire Lad* (1896) by A. E. Housman and create a phonetic transcription.

"With Rue My Heart Is Laden"

Before you listen, implement your dictation strategies:

1. Spellings: Look for IPA spellings you already know such as articles *a* and *the*; conjunctions *with* and *and*; prepositions *for, by* and *in*; and the pronoun *I*.

2. Familiar and Unfamiliar Words: Look for the descriptive words that deserve emphasis such *golden friends* and unfamiliar words such as *roselipt maiden* and *lightfoot lad*.

3. Rhyming Words: Follow down the right side of the text to identify rhymes such as *laden/maiden, had/lad, leaping/sleeping,* and *laid/fade*. Be certain that each rhyming word shares the IPA symbol of its partner/s. Choose deliberately and be consistent in your diction.

4. Repeating and Alliterative Words: Notice the phrases *for many/and many* that equate the two genders described. Give attention to the repetition of the letter "b" in *by brooks too broad* and the letter "f" in *fields where roses fade*.

5. Expressive Possibilities: Circle the words that invite expression such as the word *rue*, meaning *regret, remorse,* or *the desire to return and atone*.

6. Exceptional Words: The words *roselipt* and *lightfoot* were created by the poet and function as terms of endearment and descriptions of the innocent boys and girls, maidens and lads.

> With rue my heart is laden
>
> For golden friends I had,
>
> For many a roselipt maiden
>
> And many a lightfoot lad.
>
> By brooks too broad for leaping
>
> The lightfoot boys are laid;
>
> The roselipt girls are sleeping
>
> In fields where roses fade.

Comparative Settings

The poem has been set by Samuel Barber (1910–1981), Butterworth, Vernon Duke (1903–1969), and Gurney (1890–1937). A comparison of the settings will help you expand your interpretative ideas.

Comparative Performances

Listen to the Barber setting sung by baritone Sir Thomas Allen and the George Butterworth version sung by baritone Benjamin Luxon for an edifying, interesting listening experience. Reflect on the level of sorrow expressed in the two settings and compare the treatment of the "invented" words *roselipt* and *lightfoot*. Do you prefer one setting over the other? If so, why?

Comparative Listening

Housman's love of nature is apparent in the following text. Read it and create a phonetic transcription.

"Loveliest of Trees"

Before you listen, implement your dictation strategies:

1. Spellings: Look for IPA spellings you already know such as article *the*; conjunctions *with* and *and*; prepositions *of, along, about, for,* and *from*; the possessive *my*; and the pronoun *I*.

2. Familiar Words: Look for the descriptive words that deserve emphasis such as *trees, seventy,* and *fifty*.

3. Rhyming Words: Follow down the right side of the text to identify rhymes such as *now/bough, ride/Eastertide, ten/again, score/more, bloom/room,* and *go/snow*. Choose deliberately and be consistent in your diction.

4. Diction Challenges: A few of the rhyming pairs you have identified contain diphthongs such as *now/bough, ride/tide, ten/again, score/more,* and *go/snow*.

5. Repeating Words: The following words repeat within the poem: *woodland/ woodlands, cherry, fifty,* and *bloom*. Be sure to mark the same IPA symbols for the vowels in the words.

6. Expressive Possibilities: Circle the words that invite expression such as the descriptive, opening word *loveliest*. It is a word that deserves very special care as do the alliterative phrases *bloom along the bough, woodland ride wearing white,* and *seventy springs a score*.

7. Exceptional Reference: To fully understand the poem, note the reference to "three score years and ten." This is a Biblical reference to the general life expectancy of human beings. Twenty years will not come again to the poet. This only leaves him 50 more years to savor the world in which he lives.

Loveliest of Trees, the Cherry now

Is hung with bloom along the bough,

And stands about the woodland ride,

Wearing white for Eastertide.

Now, of my three score years and ten,

Twenty will not come again,

And take from seventy springs a score,

It only leaves me fifty more.

And since to look at things in bloom

Fifty springs are little room,

Among the woodlands I will go

To see the cherry hung with snow.

Comparative Settings

This poem has been set by John Duke, Butterworth, Vernon Duke, and Gurney (1890–1937). In America, the setting by John Duke is well-known. Compare it to other versions. Can you recognize any differences between the British and the American approach to the text and its meaning?

Discussion Questions

1. Housman was an amateur poet who revered nature. Discuss the role of nature in his poetry.

2. Have you experienced a situation in which your heart has been laden "with rue"? How common is this human experience?

3. Is there a central lesson in the text of "Loveliest of Trees"? If so, what it is?

4. As you listen to the American and British settings of words by Housman, do you notice cultural differences or similarities regarding the issue of friendship? Love of nature?

5. Many poems by Housman offer advice from an older to a younger person. In a performance situation, consider how to deliver the advice in the two songs discussed here. What role would singer's diction play?

The 19th- and 20th-Century American Song

American art song is a somewhat youthful form. It is believed that "My Days Have Been So Wondrous Free" by Francis Hopkinson (1737–1791) was the first song composed on the American continent. It took many decades, however, before American-born composers were able to develop compositional styles that did not imitate European models. Even today, American art represents a blending of cultures, beliefs, and styles.

Composers such as Copland, Leonard Bernstein, Virgil Thomson, David Diamond, and Rorem, were highly influenced by Nadia Boulanger (1887–1979), their composition teacher at the Conservatoire Américain at Fountainebleau outside Paris. A student and protegé of Gabriel Fauré, Boulanger first gained a reputation as a teacher in the 1920s. It was at this time that Paris attracted American literary, musical, and visual artists. Boulanger's pedagogical methods encouraged each student to find his or her unique "voice" as a composer. Boulanger, an organist and choral conductor, based her teaching on the architectural and harmonic rigor found in the works of Johann Sebastian Bach (1685–1750). She was also inspired by the inventive vocal works of the Italian masters Claudio Monteverdi (1567–1643) and Carlo Gesualdo (1566–1613). Boulanger taught in the United States during World War II. Many of her students became the composition teachers of other great American art song composers.

On the American continent, Charles Ives (1874–1954) created his own approach to composition, setting texts and translations of texts in a purely "American" way. During the 1930s and 1940s, European émigrés such as Paul Hindemith, Ernst Bloch, and Arnold Schoenberg brought German and Austrian influences to American culture. Spirituals, hymns, jazz and popular music contribute to the way American composers set poetry to song. In his 1959 essay "Writing Songs," Rorem states: "The poem's rightness and the success of the resulting song come only with a sense of style and taste in determining the kind of music used with the kind of poem chosen" (Rorem, 1983). American song is a merger of words and music from many cultures into a living art form.

The American Approach to Poetic Thought

Emily Dickinson (1830–1886) and Walt Whitman (1819–1892)

Dickinson (1830–1886) and Whitman (1819–1892) are the most desired of poetic sources for the composition of American song. Arguably, Dickinson's words are set more frequently to song than any other American poet's. Almost completely unknown until after her death, Dickinson produced 1,775 poems and countless letters. From portraits that she displayed in her home, we know Dickinson was an avid admirer of Thomas Carlyle, Elizabeth Barrett Browning, and George Eliot. Though resistant to an affiliation with any single denomination, she was well-versed in hymns, the King James version of the Bible, and the *Book of Common Prayer*. Dickinson found great solace in Emily Brontë's poem "No Coward Soul Is Mine." The poem was read at Dickinson's funeral. Its opening stanza reads:

No coward soul is mine

No trembler in the world's storm-troubled sphere

I see Heaven's glories shine

And Faith shines equal arming me from Fear.

Dickinson has been characterized as a recluse. In an article entitled "Vesuvius at Home," Adrienne Rich writes, "Probably no poet ever lived so much and so purposefully in one house; even in one room" (Rich, 1976).

Whitman's *Leaves of Grass* and *Song of Myself* (1892) represent the quintessential coming of age ideas that inspired young intellectuals like Rorem and others in the development of the American art song. A devoted reader, Whitman was a close observer of human life, especially in urban settings. In his work as a journalist, Whitman opposed slavery and encouraged civil behavior between all humankind. His poetic output is known for its use of the first person to produce an honest, intimate discourse between poet and reader.

Comparative Listening

Here is one example of a text by Emily Dickinson that has been set to song. Read the poem and create a phonetic transcription.

"Out of the Morning"

Before you listen, implement your dictation strategies:

1. Spellings: Look for IPA spellings you already know such as articles *a* and *the*; preposition *from*; comparatives *like* and *as*; and pronouns *I* and *they*.

2. Familiar Words: Look for the descriptive words that deserve emphasis such as *morning*, *day*, *mountains*, *bird*, *countries*, and *skies*.

3. Rhyming Words: Follow down the right side of the text to identify rhymes such as *day/they*, *bird/heard*, and *skies/lies*. Choose the vowel sounds for each pair deliberately to ensure exquisite tuning and rhyme.

4. Diction Challenges: In the opening line, "really" must sound like [riːlɨ] and not [rɪːlɨ]. The tessitura of the melodic line will play a role. If vowel modification is needed to achieve a beautiful result, the word must not be distorted. The word *pilgrim* is crucial to the understanding of this text. Strive for a central vowel in both syllables [ɪ] that will be beautiful and intelligible. Equally important are the words *scholar* and *sailor*. Both should sound as natural as possible without a trace of affectation.

5. Expressive Possibilities: Circle the words that invite expression such as the alliterative words *feet*, *feathers*, and *famous*; *some scholar*, *some sailor*, and *some . . . skies*; and *please*, *pilgrim*, and *place*.

6. Exceptional Reference: In analyzing the text, consider the double meaning of "morning" as a place. To what is the poet referring? Morning? Heaven? Eternity? Your choice will determine your interpretation.

Will there really be a morning?

Is there such a thing as day?

Could I see it from the mountains

If I were as tall as they?

Has it feet like water-lilies?

Has it feathers like a bird?

Is it brought from famous countries

Of which I have never heard?

> Oh, some scholar! Oh, some sailor!
>
> Oh, some wise man from the skies!
>
> Please do tell a little pilgrim
>
> Where the place called morning lies!

Comparative Settings

This poem has been set by several composers. Compare the settings by Vincent Persichetti (1915–1987) and Richard Hundley (1931–2018). Notice the role of the accompaniment and the musical expression of the many punctuation marks.

Comparative Listening

Dickinson engages in a dialogue with the reader in the following poem. As you read and create a phonetic transcription, imagine how you will deliver the questions and responses.

"I'm Nobody"

Before you listen, implement your dictation strategies:

1. Spellings: Look for IPA spellings you already know such as articles *a* and *the*; preposition *of* and *to*; and pronouns *I, you, us,* and *they*.

2. Familiar Words: Look for the questions that deserve emphasis such as *Who are you? Are you nobody, too?*

3. Rhyming Words: Follow down the right side of the text to identify rhymes such as *you/too* and *frog/bog.* Choose the vowel sounds for each pair deliberately to ensure exquisite tuning and rhyme.

4. Diction Challenges: It will be important to make clear delineations of meaning between *nobody* and *somebody*. Notice how the word *how* gives energy to the beginning of the fourth and fifth phrase.

5. Expressive Possibilities: Circle the words that invite expression such as the action verbs *don't tell, banish,* and *tell your name* and the descriptive words *dreary, livelong,* and *admiring.*

6. Exceptional Reference: In analyzing the text, who do you think belongs to the "admiring bog"? Your interpretation of the poem and its song setting will depend upon your thought.

> I'm Nobody! Who are you?
>
> Are you nobody, too?
>
> Then there's a pair of us – don't tell!
>
> They'd banish us, you know.
>
> How dreary to be somebody!

> How public, like a frog
>
> To tell your name the livelong day
>
> To an admiring bog!

Comparative Settings

Compare the musical settings by Bacon and Persichetti. How do the composers express the punctuation through music and phrasing? Do you find one version more effective than the other? If so, why?

Comparative Listening

Walt Whitman in song—read the following poem and create a phonetic transcription.

"Look Down, Fair Moon"

<u>Before you listen, implement your dictation strategies:</u>

1. Spellings: Look for IPA spellings you already know such as article *the*; prepositions *on* and *with*; and possessives *their* and *your*.

2. Repeating Words: Compare the use of the word *pour* in *pour softly down night's nimbus floods* with *pour down your unstinted nimbus*.

3. Diction Challenges: The text is replete with difficult images and pronunciations such as *nimbus floods*, *faces ghastly, swollen, purple; your unstinted nimbus, sacred moon*. The articulation and timing of consonants are as significant as the choice of vowels.

4. Expressive Possibilities: Circle the words that invite expression such as <u>fair</u> *moon, bathe this scene, ghastly, swollen, purple; arms toss'd wide*; and <u>sacred</u> *moon*. Note how the prepositional phrases *on faces, on the dead, on their back* give unity to the poem and music.

> Look down, fair moon and bathe this scene,
>
> Pour softly down night's nimbus floods,
>
> On faces ghastly, swollen, purple;
>
> On the dead, on their backs, with their arms toss'd wide,
>
> Pour down your unstinted nimbus, sacred moon.

Comparative Performances

Listen to recorded performances of Rorem's setting sung Susan Graham, mezzo soprano and Donald Gramm, baritone. Both singers consulted the composer in the preparation of their respective recordings. Consider the similarities and differences in their respective approaches to the text. What difference do you hear in the timbre of the two voices, the use of consonants, and expression of vowel sounds?

Comparative Listening

Read the following poem by Whitman and create a phonetic transcription.

"O You Whom I Often and Silently Come"

Before you listen, implement your dictation strategies:

1. Spellings: Look for IPA spellings you already know such as article *the*; conjunctions *and* and *with*; prepositions *by*, *in*, and *within*; possessive *your*; and pronouns *you*, *I*, and *me*.

2. Repeating words: Consider the repetitions of the word *you*. Each statement has a slightly different meaning and deserves special treatment.

3. Diction Challenges: The word *often* offers the choice of a silent "t" or a spoken one. To maintain the grammatical sense of the poem, there must be clarity in the articulation of the "m" in *whom*. The word *subtle* must be sung clearly, if it is to be intelligible.

4. Expressive Possibilities: Circle the words that invite expression such as the descriptive words *silently*, *subtle electric fire*, and *for your sake*. Note also the progression of thought from *seeing you*, *walking with you*, *sitting near you* to *remaining with you* and the spark of electricity that occurs within. The poet provides stage directions through the sequence of verb; namely, *come*, *are*, *walk*, *sit*, *remain*, and *is playing*.

> O you whom I often and silently come
>
> Where you are that I may be with you,
>
> As I walk by your side or sit near,
>
> Or remain in the same room with you,
>
> Little you know the subtle electric fire
>
> That for your sake is playing within me.

Comparative Performances

The best-known musical setting of "O You Whom I Often and Silently Come" is by Rorem. Listen to the recordings of soprano Carole Farley and mezzo soprano Susan Graham singing it. Farley is accompanied by the composer. Both recordings demonstrate exquisite diction choices. Do you have a preference? Why?

James Joyce (1882–1941) and James Stephens (1880–1950)

The Portrait of an Artist as a Young Man and *Ulysses*, the masterworks of Irish novelist James Joyce (1882–1941), made strong impressions on many American composers. James Stephens (1880–1950) was another very popular, influential Irish poet who inspired American song compositions.

Comparative Listening

As you read the following text by Joyce and create a phonetic transcription. Consider the challenge of articulating the word *sleep* with clarity and expression.

"Sleep Now, O Sleep Now"

Before you listen, implement your dictation strategies:

1. Spellings: Look for IPA spellings you already know such as the articles *a* and *the*; conjunction *and*; prepositions *in*, *at*, *for*, and *to*; the possessive *your*; and pronouns *you* and *my*.

2. Repeating Words: Consider the repetitions of the exclamation "O." Each statement has a slightly different meaning and deserves special treatment.

3. Diction Challenges: The word *now* recurs throughout the poem. The diphthong must be spoken clearly in each instance. As noted above, the word *sleep* appears frequently with differing connotations. Strive for a clear, effective articulation of the consonants "s," "l," and "p."

4. Expressive Possibilities: Circle the words that invite expression such as the descriptive words *unquiet*, *voice crying*, *winter is crying*, and *in peace*. As you read and listen, note the progress of the poet from a disrupted heart to a peaceful one.

Sleep now, O sleep now,

O you unquiet heart!

A voice crying: Sleep now

Is heard in my heart.

The voice of the winter

Is heard at the door.

O sleep, for the winter

Is crying: Sleep no more.

My kiss will give peace now

And quiet to your heart.

Sleep on in peace now,

O you unquiet heart!

Comparative Settings

Compare the setting by Barber entitled "Sleep Now" with the musical setting by Persichetti entitled "Unquiet Heart." Do the composers confront this text from similar vantage points? Different ones?

Comparative Listening

As you read the following text by James Stephens and create a phonetic transcription, notice the charm to found in injection of "O!" Consider how you will sing it.

"The Daisies"

Before you listen, implement your dictation strategies:

1. Spellings: Look for IPA spellings you already know such as article *the*; conjunction *and*; prepositions *in* and *on*; and pronouns *I, she,* and *we.*

2. Familiar Words: Look for the descriptive words such as *up* and *down* and the phrase *hand in hand* that offer a sense of the naturalness of the situation.

3. Rhyming Words: Follow down the right side of the text to identify rhymes such as *far/are, speak/cheek, fro/O!* and *land/hand.* Be certain that each rhyming word shares the IPA symbol of its partner/s. Choose deliberately and be consistent in your diction.

4. Repeating Phrase: *In the bud of the morning, O!* occurs twice and requires careful enunciation of the punctuation to declare properly the exclamation "O!"

5. Expressive Possibilities: When the title of a song appears in a musical setting, it is common practice to express the title intentionally. In this song, the title appears twice, at the end of each verse: *"where the daisies are."* Consider how you would interpret those words in each repetition. Within the text, there are several opportunities for lyric emphasis such as *windy grass, rippling far, breezy land,* and *cloud afar.*

In the scented bud of the morning, O!

When the windy grass went rippling far!

I saw my dear one walking slow

In the field where the daisies are.

We did not laugh, and we did not speak,

As we wandered happ'ly, to and fro,

I kissed my dear on either cheek,

In the bud of the morning, O!

A lark sang up, from the breezy land;

A lark sang down, from a cloud afar;

As she and I went, hand in hand,

In the field where the daisies are.

Comparative Settings

Compare the musical settings by Barber with those of Barab and Quilter. What role do the accompaniment figures play in creating atmosphere in these song settings? Is there one you prefer? Why?

Discussion Questions

1. Why do you think American song composers favor Dickinson's and Whitman's poems?

2. American poets use punctuation and contraction as poetic devices. What diction challenges do these devices pose? What expressive opportunities do they offer?

3. What makes an American song quintessentially "American"?

4. Joyce and Stephens were Irish. What do you notice about their use of the English language that distinguishes them from American and British poets?

5. What differences do you notice between American and British composers of song?

English Diction Final Presentation Repertoire List

For the final, graded presentation, you will prepare the text, phonetic transcription, and poetic equivalent as you did for the first, ungraded one. You will use the resources listed in this book and those suggested by your instructor to investigate the poet and composer of your selection. Your class presentation will include a brief introduction to your song, its origins, and cultural context. You will be asked to submit a written version of the notes you gave orally. The assessment sheet for your presentation is provided in the appendix of this book.

Sure on This Shining Night	Samuel Barber
The Ash Grove	Benjamin Britten
Down by the Salley Gardens*	Benjamin Britten
Sally in Our Alley*	Benjamin Britten (tenor)
When I Have Sung My Songs	Ernest Charles
At the River	Aaron Copland
The Little Horses	Aaron Copland
Into the Night	Clara Edwards
O Mistress Mine*	Gerald Finzi

Who Is Sylvia?*	Gerald Finzi
Down by the Salley Gardens*	Ivor Gurney
Come Ready and See Me	R. Hundley
The Lass From the Low Countree	John Jacob Niles
Drink to Me Only With Thine Eyes*	Roger Quilter
Fair House of Joy*	Roger Quilter
It Was a Lover and His Lass*	Roger Quilter
Now Sleeps the Crimson Petal	Roger Quilter
O Mistress Mine*	Roger Quilter
Take, O Take Those Lips Away	Roger Quilter
Under the Greenwood Tree*	Roger Quilter
Weep You No More Sad Fountains*	Roger Quilter
Early in the Morning	Ned Rorem
Orpheus With His Lute	William Schuman
Bright Is the Ring of Words	Ralph Vaughan Williams
Hands, Eyes and Heart	Ralph Vaughan Williams
Fair and True	Peter Warlock

*Indicates comparative setting.

Conclusion

The American composer Charles Ives (1874–1954) described the publication of his *114 Songs* as a mere cleaning of his house. He claimed to have revealed himself to his neighbors through his lyrics and music (Ives, 1969). Song in English, be it British or American, reveals the thinking and feeling of English-speaking people through the centuries. The occasion for the composition and the manner of its performance give us clues to its interpretation. Literary symbols divulge layers of hidden connections between artistic and human experiences through the ages. The spark that causes song to be written and subsequently sung remains the same: a preexisting literary work of art demands musical expression. The singer breathes life into the composer's score, revealing mood and meaning. With the IPA in your toolbox, you have learned to notate similarities and differences in sounds. You have honed your listening skills through critical comparisons of solo and choral settings. A thorough understanding of English grammar and syntax will help you with your study of foreign languages. Your presentations of English and American song have set a standard for your work in other languages. You have created a context for your learning of singer's diction. May it serve you well with repertoire in Italian, German, and French!

References

Bloom, H. (1999). *Shakespeare: The invention of the human* (p. xix). New York, NY: Riverhead Books.

Bryson, B. (1990). *The mother tongue: English and how it got that way* (p. 84). New York, NY: Harper-Collins.

Damrosch, L. (2015). *Eternity's sunrise: The imaginative world of William Blake* (p. 66). New Haven, CT: Yale University Press.

Garber, M. (2005). *Shakespeare after all* (p. 3). New York, NY: Anchor Books.

Hold, T. (2002). *Parry to Finzi: Twenty English song-composers* (p. 7). Woodbridge, UK: The Boydell Press.

Housman, A. E. (1933). *The name and nature of poetry* (p. 255). New York, NY: Penguin Books.

Ives, C. (1969). In H. Boatwright (Ed.), *Essays after a sonata and other writings* (p. 131). London, UK: Calder and Boyars.

Oliver, M. (2016). *Upstream* (p. 22). New York, NY: Penguin Press.

Packer, T. (2016). *Women of will: The remarkable evolution of Shakespeare's female characters* (p. 213). New York, NY: Vintage Books.

Rich, A. (1976). Vesuvius at home. In *Parnassus poetry in review* (Vol. 5, No.1). New York, NY: Cadmus Press.

Rorem, N. (1983). *Setting the tone: Essays and a diary* (p. 301). New York, NY: Coward-McCann.

Schmidt, M. (1998). *The lives of poets* (p. 186). New York, NY: Random House.

Schmidt, M. (1998). *The lives of poets* (p. 478). New York, NY: Random House.

Stevens, D. (1960). *A history of song* (Rev. ed., p. 79). New York, NY: Norton.

Vendler, H. (1997). *The art of Shakespeare's sonnets* (p. 444). Cambridge, MA: Harvard University Press.

Wilson-Lee, E. (2016). *Shakespeare in Swahililand: In search of a global poet* (p. xii). New York, NY: Farrar, Straus, & Giroux.

The Sounds of Italian

The vowels of Italian are "pure" sounds. American singers must be careful to maintain the integrity of the vowels, never allowing the vowel sound to release into a diphthong "vanish" or "slide." The Italian language is spoken and sung fluidly. To achieve the lilting quality of the Italian language, vowels and consonants are articulated in an area of the mouth that is "in front of" the region used for the English language. Be careful not to use American or British vowel sounds as your guide when speaking or singing Italian, German, or French. Each language has its own "location" in your oral cavity. Notice the absence of the vowel [a] in the list below. The Italian language is a light, flowing, *legato* language. Each sound melds into the next one.

Italian Vowels

Here are the basic vowels of Italian:

[a]	a̲ma̲nte	[aˈmante]	*lover*
[e] (closed)	e̲sordir̲e	[ezorˈdire]	*to make one's debut*
[ɛ] (open)	e̲st	[ɛst]	*east*
[i]	innocente	[innoˈʧɛnte]	*innocent*
[o] (closed)	o̲mbra	[ˈombra]	*shadow*
[ɔ] (open)	o̲vest	[ˈɔv ɛst]	*west*
[u]	u̲tile	[ˈutile]	*useful*

Vowels combine to create diphthongs and triphthongs.

A diphthong occurs when two vowel sounds are adjacent in the same syllable. In English, we learned that the first vowel in a diphthong is the "primary" or "principal" sound we sing and the second one, a vanish or slide that is given little time and no rhythmic value. In Italian, both vowels in a diphthong are sung with beauty and integrity. In some words, both vowels are equally significant or equally insignificant. There are also diphthong combinations in which one vowel is more important than the other. Here is one example of each basic combination:

Both equally weak:	guidare	[gwi'dare]	*to guide*
Both equally strong:	poesia	[poe'zia]	*poetry*
The first vowel is strong:	aura	['aura]	*breeze*
The first vowel is weak:	piano	['pjano]	*softly*

A glide is a very short vowel that leads to a longer one. (Some books call them "semiconsonants" or "semivowels.") In Italian, the glides are [j] and [w].

A triphthong occurs when three *sounded* vowels occur in the same syllable. As with diphthongs, there is more than one combination.

Ex. In the word *miei* [mjɛːi] (*mine*), there is a glide plus two vowels.

Ex. In the word *gioja* ['dʒɔːja] (*joy*), because a glide appears between two vowels, the triphthong divides into two groups.

Often, the musical phrase will guide you to the proper pronunciation. If you wish to learn more about the rules for diphthongs and triphthongs, see the reference materials given at the conclusion of this book.

Italian Consonants

Consonants are important to the lyric flow of the Italian language. Be very careful to recognize the difference between a single consonant and a double one. Before a single consonant, the vowel sound is elongated. Before a double consonant, the vowel sound is shortened to accommodate the creation of the first consonant of the pair. In doing so, you will notice a shift in the rhythmic shape of the syllable in both speech and singing.

Fricative Consonants

The fricative consonants of the Italian language are:

[f]	finche	[fin'ke]	*until*		[ff]	affetto	[af'fɛtto]	*affection*
[v]	vivo	['vivo]	*alive*		[vv]	avverso	[av'vɛrso]	*adverse/hostile*
[ʃ]	scena	['ʃɛna]	*scene*		[ʃʃ]	lasciate	[laʃʃate]	*allow/leave*
[s]	sole	['sole]	*sun*		[ss]	rosso	['rosso]	*red*
[z]*	rosa	['rɔza]	*rose*					

*Note. The letter "z" does not carry the sound of [z] in Italian. Also, the letter "z" as a single letter or in a cluster ([ts] or [dz]) can be voiced or unvoiced. You will need to use a dictionary to ensure your accuracy.

The Letter "s" and the Letter "z"

The letter "s" can be pronounced as [s] or [z], depending upon the word.

- ◆ A single letter "s" at the beginning of a word is usually pronounced [s].
- ◆ When the "ss" is doubled or "geminated," the [s] sound is doubled in length.
- ◆ When the letter "s" appears between two vowels in Italian, it is pronounced [z].

Affricative Consonants

The affricative consonants of the Italian language are:

Voiced/Single and Doubled or Geminated

[dz]	romanza	[ro'mandza]	*song or ballad*
[dʒ]	gelo	['dʒɛlo]	*frost*
[ddz]	mezzo	['mɛddzo]	*medium*
[ddʒ]	struggimento	[struddʒi'mento]	*yearning*

Unvoiced/Single and Doubled or Geminated

| [tʃ] | certo | ['tʃɛrto] | *certain* | [ttʃ] | ghiaccio | ['gjattʃo] | *ice* |
| [ts] | senza | ['sɛntsa] | *without* | [tts] | bellezzatʃ | [bel'lettsa] | *beauty* |

Glides

The glides of the Italian language are:

| [j] | pieno | ['pjɛno] | *full* | [w] | uomini | ['wɔmini] | *men* |

Lateral Consonants

The lateral consonants of the Italian language are:

| [l] | lago | ['lago] | *lake* | [ll] | bella | ['bɛlla] | *lovely* |
| [ʎ] | gli | [ʎi] | *the* | [ʎʎ] | voglio | ['voʎʎo] | *I want* |

Nasal Consonants

The nasal consonants of the Italian language are:

[m]	lamento	[laˈmɛnto]	*groan*		[mm]	mamma	[ˈmamma]	*Mama*
[n]	pianto	[ˈpjanto]	*weeping*		[nn]	penna	[ˈpenna]	*feather*
[ŋ]	anche	[ˈaŋke]	*also*		[ɲɲ]	ogni	[ˈoɲɲi]	*every*
[ɲ]	gnomo	[ˈɲɔmo]	*gnome*					

Stop Plosive Consonants

The stop plosive consonants of the Italian language are:

Voiced/Single and Doubled or Geminated

[b]	bacio	[ˈbatʃo]	*kiss*		[bb]	babbo	[ˈbabbo]	*Daddy*
[d]	dormire	[dorˈmire]	*sleep*		[dd]	addio	[adˈdio]	*bye!*
[g]	largo	[ˈlargo]	*broad*		[gg]	struggo	[ˈstruggo]	*suffer*

Unvoiced/Single and Doubled or Geminated

[p]	pastore	[aasˈtore]	*shepherd*		[pp]	mappa	[ˈmappa]	*map*
[t]	fato	[ˈfato]	*fate*		[tt]	fatto	[ˈfatto]	*made*
[k]	caro	[ˈkaɾo]	*dear*		[kk]	bocca	[ˈbokka]	*mouth*

The Letter "r"

The letter "r" in the Italian language is pronounced as follows:

[ɾ] is the symbol for the letter "r" that is given a single "flip" or "tap." This occurs when the letter "r" appears between two vowels, as in *amore* [aˈmoːɾe], meaning *love*.

In all other situations, the letter "r" is "rolled" or "trilled," for which the symbol is [r]. Here are examples:

Single: ardore [arˈdore] (*ardor*)

Doubled or Geminated: marrone [marˈrone] (*brown*)

Diction in Context: Italian Vowels

The Letters "e" and "o"

In Italian, the letters "e" and "o" require special study. Singer's diction resources, in print and online, offer many lists of rules and their exceptions. The letter "e" in Italian has two possible pronunciations: [e] *closed* and [ɛ] *open*. Note: Both sounds ([e] or [ɛ]) are pure sounds with no glide or extraneous vowel sound following them. There are two ways to pronounce the letter "o" in Italian: [o] *closed* and [ɔ] *open*. You will always need a dictionary to determine if the vowels in a given word should be pronounced open or closed. In the act of singing, modifications to vowels commonly occur. Below is a summary of the general knowledge singers need to negotiate song texts in Italian.

More About the Letter "e"

When the letter "e" appears in a stressed syllable, verify in the dictionary whether the sound should be [e] *closed* or [ɛ] *open*. There are no rules identifying the right pronunciation. In fact, two words can be spelled the same way but have two different meanings based on the pronunciation. For example: The word *venti*, pronounced ['venti], means *twenty*, while the word *venti*, pronounced ['vɛnti], means *winds*. The letter "e" in an unstressed syllable, especially the final syllable of a word, is generally pronounced [e] *closed*. This is not only accurate, but it assists the tuning of a rhyming words such as *core* and *amore* ['kɔre] and 'a'more]. The letter "e" in a stressed syllable is generally pronounced [ɛ] *open* in spoken Italian. It is important to remember that exceptions exist. Your tools for determining the proper pronunciation will be your dictionary, your teacher, and your own ears as you listen to reliable performers. For a list of guidelines, consult the online resource associated with this textbook.

Antonio Caldara (1670–1736)

Listen to the aria "Selve Amiche" from Caldara's opera *La Constanza in Amor Vince L'inganno* (1710) sung by Cecilia Bartoli, a native speaker with collaborative pianist György Fischer. Next, listen to the aria sung by Korean countertenor David Dong Qyu Lee with collaborative pianist Yannick Nézet Séquin. Note how the performers treat the letter "e." Mark the letter "e" throughout the text below accordingly. Did both performers close every "e" in an unstressed syllable? Did they follow the rules given above regarding the letter "e" in stressed syllables? Were the performers consistent within their individual performances? To improve your understanding as you listen, a word-by-word translation and a poetic equivalent are provided.

Selve amiche, ombrose piante

Woods friendly, shadowy plants

Fido albergo del mio core,

Faithful shelter of (the) my heart

Chiede a voi quest'alma amante

Asks/seeks of you this soul loving

Qualche pace al suo dolore.

Some peace to his sadness/sorrow.

Poetic Equivalent

The amiable woods with its shady plants are a trusted shelter for my heart
That seeks some peaceful relief from sorrow for its loving soul.

More About the Letter "o"

When the letter "o" appears in a stressed syllable, verify in the dictionary whether the sound should be [o] *closed* or [ɔ] *open*. As with the letter "e," there are no rules identifying the right pronunciation. In fact, two words can be spelled the same way but have two different meanings based on the pronunciation. For example: The word *ora*, pronounced ['o:ra], means *now* while the word *ora*, pronounced ['ɔ:ra], commands one to "pray." As with the letter "e," the letter "o" in an unstressed syllable is usually closed [o]. When the letter "o" appears in a stressed syllable, it is generally an open vowel [ɔ]. The exceptions are comparable to those noted above for the letter "e." For a list of guidelines, consult the online resource associated with this textbook.

George Frideric Handel (1685–1759)

Listen to comparative performances of the aria "Ombra Mai Fu" from *Xerse* by Handel sung by mezzo sopranos Jennifer Larmore and Cecilia Bartoli. Notice how each performer expresses the opening word *ombra* (*shadows* or *shade*) using a *messa di voce* (consistent crescendo/decrescendo). Notice also the word *soave* (*soft*) in the final line. It is an example of an Italian diphthong containing two vowels of equal importance. The word-by-word translation and poetic equivalent for the text are provided.

Ombra mai fu

Shadows never made

di vegetabile

of vegetation/plant

cara ed amabile

dear and amiable/lovable

soave più.

soft/soothing more.

Poetic Equivalent

The shade from nature's plants has never had a more amiable, soothing effect.

Diction in Context: Consonants

More About the Letters "c," "g," and "sc"

The Letters "c" and "g"

Both letters "c" and "g" have two sounds: a "hard" sound and a "soft" sound.

The "hard" sound occurs when the letters "c" [k] and "g" [g] precede the letters "a," "o," and "u."

cantare [kan'tare] *to sing*   coda ['koda] *tail*   cura ['kura] *cure*

gatto ['gatto] *cat*   godere [go'dere] *to enjoy*   gusto ['gusto] *taste*

When hard "c" and hard "g" are doubled or geminated, the sounds are prolonged as usual.

bocca [bok:ka] *mouth*   agguantare [ag'gwan:tare] *to catch*

The "soft" sound occurs when the letters "c" [tʃ] and "g" [dʒ] precede the letters "e" and "I."

pace ['pa tʃe] *peace*   bacio ['ba tʃo] *kiss*

gentile [dʒen'tile] *kind*   girare [dʒi'rare] *to turn*

When soft "c" and soft "g" are doubled, the sounds are prolonged as usual:

faccia ['fattʃa] *face*   oggi ['ɔddʒi] *today*

When doubled, assume the tongue position for the first sound of the compound and delay sounding it.

The Cluster "sc"

When the letter "s" precedes a hard "c," it is unvoiced and sounds like [sk]:

Ex. scherzando [skɛr'tsando] (*playfully*)

When the letter "s" precedes a soft "c," a new combination is formed and sounds like [ʃ].

Ex. scendere ['ʃɛndere] (*to descend*)

Ex. lasciate [laʃʃa:te] (*let, allow*)

Here is a summary of the information given above.

Hard Spellings	Soft Spellings
c + a, o, u = [k]	c + e or i = [tʃ]
g + a, o, u = [g]	g + e or i = [dʒ]
sc + a, o, u = [sk]	sc + e or i = [ʃ]
che, chi = [k]	cia, cio, ciu = [tʃ]
ghe, ghi = [g]	gia, gio, giu = [dʒ]
sche, schi = [sk]	scia, scio, sciu = [ʃ]

Diction in Context Example

Here is another useful example from the operatic repertoire of George Frideric Handel. The text to the aria "Va tacito e nascosto" from *Giulio Cesare in Egitto* (1724) provides an opportunity for you to identify and hear in context the hard and soft sounds of the letters "c," "g," and "sc." Before you begin, study the text using the rules and the chart given above.

<u>Before you listen, implement your dictation strategies:</u>

1. Spellings: Look for IPA spellings you already know such as the auxiliary verb *è*, meaning *is*; the conjunction *e*, meaning *and*; the pronouns *chi* and *che*, meaning *who* and *what*, respectively; and the preposition *del*, meaning *of the*.
2. Familiar Words: Look for words you recognize such as *va* and *cor*.
3. Rhyming Words: Follow down the right side of the text to identify rhymes such as *nascosto/disposto*, *preda/veda*, and *cacciator/cor*. Be sure to mark each pair with the same IPA vowel symbols.
4. Expressive Possibilities: Circle the words that invite expression such as *tacito*, *nascosto*, and *cacciator*.

Va tacito e nascosto

(he) goes quietly and secretly

Quand' avido è di preda

When eager (he) is for prey

L'astuto cacciator.

The astute hunter.

E chi è malfar disposto,

And who is to evil (acts) disposed,

Non brama che si veda

Not longs that it might be seen

L'inganno del suo cor.

The deceit of his heart.

Va tacito e nascosto . . .

Poetic Equivalent

As the crafty huntsman who, in pursuit of his prey, stalks along in silence, unseen, so he who is intent on wrongdoing takes care to conceal the treachery in his heart.

Critical Listening

Listen to the aria sung by countertenor, Andreas Scholl and also by the baritone, Bryn Terfel. Note the proper pronunciation of the letters "c," "g," and "sc." The aria is in the *da capo* form (A-B-A). Listen critically to the melodic material of the A section. Expect ornamentation when the singer returns to the A section. Be aware of the diction challenges involved in the addition of agile notes. Expect a change of character in the B section. What role does the B section play? Does it add interest? Does it contribute to your understanding of the plot? When the A section returns, does it have the same meaning for you, the listener? Compare and contrast the performances.

Double Consonants and Consonant Clusters

Here is a brief summary of tips for successfully singing Italian doubled or geminated consonants and consonant clusters:

◆ Be certain to distinguish between single and double consonants. Sing single consonants as late and quickly as possible. Give double consonants length. They will generally make the preceding vowel a little shorter. In your IPA transcriptions, be sure that both consonants appear, such as [ʎʎ].

◆ Italian consonants "b," "p," "d," and "t" are sung without "aspiration." Produce them efficiently and gently. The bilabial consonants "b" and "p" should be articulated using the middle portion of the lips. For "d" and "t," the tip of the tongue intersects with the alveolar ridge. To avoid the intrusion of a neutral vowel [ə] after the consonants, use no extraneous pressure in the articulation of them. (Remember: There is no *schwa* [ə] in the Italian language.)

◆ The Italian consonant cluster "gn" [ɲ] or [ɲɲ] is pronounced similarly to "ni" or "ny"[nj] in the English words *onion* or *canyon*.

◆ The Italian consonant cluster "gli" [ʎ] or [ʎʎ] is pronounced close to but *not* identical to the glide [j] in the English word *valiant*. The sound of "gli" has little to do with its spelling and can be visually confusing. To achieve the exact articulation, you will need to imitate the proper pronunciation given to you by a qualified singer or speaker. Common words pronounced with "gli" are *gli* [ʎi] (*the*) and *voglio* ['vɔʎʎo] (*I want*).

◆ The Italian consonant clusters "nc"[nk], "nq" [ŋk], "ng," [ŋg] or [ŋ] are comparable to sounds in English, namely "sink" and "sing" respectively.

  Ex. bianco ['bjaŋko] (*white*) dunque ['duŋkwe] (*therefore*)
    sangue ['saŋgwe] (*blood*)

◆ The Italian consonant cluster "qu" [kw] is pronounced similarly to "qu" in English as in *quasi* ['kwɑzi] meaning *pseudo* or *semi*. In Italian, the word *quasi* is pronounced ['kwazi]. Note the difference in the vowel sounds. The English language uses "darker" vowel sounds than Italian.

◆ In Italian, double consonant are categorized in one of two ways: "stop" or "continuing."

◆ The stop doubled consonants are [b], [d], [k], [g], [p], and [t], because their presence will "stop" the flow the text for an instance as the two consonants are articulated.

◆ The continuing doubled consonants are [f], [l], [ʎ], [m], [n], [ɲ], [r], [s], [ʃ], and [v], because the doubling of the consonants is achieved by lengthening them.

Single and Double Consonant Practice

Use the following words to practice the articulation of single and double consonants by reading left to right, top to bottom, and bottom to top in each row. Note the differences carefully.

accenti	[at'tʃenti]	braccio	['brattʃo]	bacio	['batʃo]	bocca	['bokka]
avanti	[a'vanti]	avverso	[av'vɛrso]	batti	['batti]	bizzaro	[bid'dzarro]
babbo	['babbo]	labbro	['labbro]	grazie	['grattsje]	gatto	['gatto]
canta	['kanta]	cura	['kura]	certo	['tʃɛrto]	dolce	['doltʃe]
eco	['ɛko]	ecco	[ɛk:ko]	Puccini	[put'tʃini]	faccio	[fat'tʃo]
chiamo	[kja'mo]	chi	['ki]	occhi	['ɔkki]	acqua	['akkwa]
diva	['diva]	padre	['padre]	addio	[ad'dio]	freddo	['freddo]
infelice	[infe'litʃe]	figlia	['fiʎʎa]	affani	[af'fanni]	affetto	[af'fɛtto]
figura	[fi'gura]	gala	['gala]	fugga	['fugga]	caffè	[kaf'fe]
giorno	['dʒorno]	Gesu	[dʒe'zu]	maggio	['maddʒo]	raggio	['raddʒo]
guardo	['gwardo]	uguale	[u'gwale]	vaghi	['vagi]	Respighi	[rɛ'spigi]
Pagliacci	[paʎ'ʎattʃi]	Zerlina	[dzer'lina]	Masetto	[ma'zɛtto]	Susanna	[su'zanna]
fedele	[fe'dele]	dolore	[do'lore]	bello	['bɛllo]	gelo	['dʒelo]
tema	['tɛma]	dorma	['dorma]	mamma	['mamma]	gemma	['dʒemma]
nozze	['nɔttse]	domani	[do'mani]	donna	['dɔnna]	nono	['nono]
pensare	[pen'sare]	persona	[per'sona]	sposo	['spozo]	tesoro	[te'zɔro]
vissi	['vissi]	oppresso	[op'prɛsso]	tanto	['tanto]	punto	['punto]

Diction in Context

Take turns reading aloud the texts sung by the characters, Don Giovanni and Zerlina. Note the single and double consonants. Be careful to distinguish between them as you read. Next listen to a recording of the duet sung by qualified singers. For your convenience, a poetic equivalent follows the printed text. As you listen, create a phonetic transcription.

Duettino: "Là ci darem la mano" from Don Giovanni
Music by Wolfgang Amadeus Mozart (1756–1791)
Text by Lorenzo da Ponte (1749–1838)

(Don Giovanni)   Là ci darem la mano, Là mi dirai di sì.

Vedi, non è lontano; Partiam, ben mio, da qui.

(Zerlina)   Vorrei e non vorrei, Mi trema un poco il cor.

Felice, è ver, sarei, Ma può burlarmi ancor.

(Don Giovanni)	Vieni mio bel diletto!
(Zerlina)	Mi fa pietà Masetto.
(Don Giovanni)	Io cangierò tua sorte.
(Zerlina)	Presto non son più forte.
(Don Giovanni)	Andiam!
(Zerlina)	Andiam!
(Both)	Andiam, andiam, mio bene, A ristorar le pene
	D'un innocente amor.

Poetic Equivalent

DG: We take hands as a sign of "yes." See, it is not far; let's depart from here, my dear.

Z: (I would like to and yet, I don't want to. My heart trembles a bit. This might make me happy, it is true, but then again, he could be mocking me.)

DG: Come, my beloved!

Z: (I pity Masetto.)   DG: I will change your fate.

Z: I can't be strong any longer.   DG: Let's go!   Z: Let's go!

DG & Z: Let's go, my dearest, to comfort the pains of innocent love!

Parts of Speech and Elements of Grammar

Elements of Sentences

Here are some general principles regarding Italian sentence structure. Compare what you find below with the parts of speech learned in the English language portion of this textbook. A good Italian dictionary, preferably an Italian-English one, will always be needed to ensure a thorough understanding of any text you sing. Because scores and phonetic readings contain typographical or content errors, it is important that you familiarize yourself with the general principles given below.

Nouns

Nouns name animals, people, and things, real or invented. In Italian, each noun has a gender, either masculine or feminine. The gender of a noun is not necessarily linked to the word's meaning. There are endings that "signal" gender. Most nouns ending in "-o" are masculine words and those with "-a" are generally feminine ones, such as *il violino* [il vioˈlino] (*violin*, masculine) and *la musica* [la ˈmuzika] (*music*, feminine). Exceptions exist in which words are masculine in gender, but end in "-a," such as *il poeta* [il poˈɛta] (*poet*). Nouns ending in "-ma" come from Greek and are masculine in gender as in *schema* [ˈskema] (*scheme, plan*). Similarly, some words are feminine in gender, but end in "-o," like *la mano* [la ˈmano] (*hand*).

Nouns that end in "-ore," "-tore," "-ere," "-iere," "-ame," and "-ale" are generally masculine, such as *il dottore* [dot'tore] (*doctor*), *il canzoniere* [kantso'njiere] (*songbook*), *il legname* [leɲ'ɲame] (*lumber*), and *il ufficale* [uffi'ʧale] (*official*).

Nouns that end in "-ione," "-udine," "-igine," "-ice," "-tà," "-tù," and "-" are generally feminine, such as *la stagione* [sta'ʤone] (*season*), *la solitudine* [soli'tudine] (*solitude*), *la immagine* [im'maʤine] (*image*), *l'attrice* [at'triʧe] (*actress*), *la beltà* [bɛl'ta] (*beauty*), *la gioventù* [ʤoven'tu] (*youth*), and *la crisi* ['krizi] (*crisis*).

Many nouns adjust to the gender of the person:

l/la cantante [kan'tante] *singer*   Il/la pianista [pja'nista] *pianist*

Nouns referring to animals frequently have only one gender:

Il pesce ['peʃʃe] *fish*   La tigre ['tigre] *tiger*

Be aware that some nouns have two meanings, recognizable only by gender:

Il caso ['kaso] *case*   La casa ['kaza] *house*

Il modo ['mɔdo] *manner*   La moda ['mɔda] *fashion*

Days of the week (except Sunday), months of the year, names of trees, compass points, and geographic locations are generally masculine:

lunedì [lune'di] *Monday*   aprile [a'prile] *April*

Il pino ['pino] *pine*   il nord ['nɔrd] *north*

Fruits, names for cities, and school subjects are generally feminine:

la mela ['mela] *apple*   Roma ['roma] *Rome*   la storia ['stɔrja] *history*

Nouns that end with "-e" can be either masculine or feminine:

il consorte [kon'sɔrte] *husband*   la consorte [kon'sɔrte] *wife*

Here are some common nouns that end in "-e" that appear frequently in repertoire:

Masculine			**Feminine**		
il fiore	['fjore]	*flower*	la canzone	[kan'tsone]	*song*
il fiume	['fjume]	*river*	la chiave	['kjave]	*key*
il mare	['mare]	*sea*	la fame	['fame]	*hunger*
il nome	['nome]	*name*	la fine	['fine]	*end*
il ponte	['ponte]	*bridge*	la gente	['ʤɛnte]	*people*

Proper names and first words of sentences are capitalized. Plural nouns can be identified by a change in the article and generally a change in the spelling of the noun.

il libro	['libro]	i libri	['libri]	*book/books*	
la casa	['kaza]	le case	['kaze]	*house/houses*	
il nome	['nome]	i nomi	['nomi]	*name/names*	

◆ The plural form of masculine and feminine nouns that end in "-ca/-co" or "-ga/-go" change their spellings to accommodate the hard sound of the letter "c" [k] and "g" [g].

l'amica	[a'mika]	le amiche	[a'mike]	*female friend/friends*
il fungo	['fungo]	i funghi	['fungi]	*mushroom/mushrooms*

Here are important exceptions to these regular forms:

il amico	[a'miko]	i amici	[a'mitʃi]	*male friend/friends*
l'uomo	['wɔmo]	gli uomini	[ʎʎ'wɔmini]	*man/men*

Suffixes and Meaning

Diminutive endings portray an animal, person, thing or idea to be small and/or precious. Diminutive endings for masculine nouns: "-ino," "-icino," "-etto," "-ello," "-erello," "-etto;" and for feminine nouns: "-ina," "-icina," "-etta," "-ella," "-erella," and "-otta."

il cuore	['kwɔre]	il cuoricino	[kwori'tʃino]	*heart/tiny, dear heart*
la casa	['kaza]	la casina	[ka'zina]	*house/beloved little home*

Nouns derived from adjectives:

◆ As in English, the use of a definite article with an adjective describes a group by its characteristics.

i buoni	['bwɔni]	*the good folk*	i cattivi	[kat'tivi]	*the bad folk*
i nobili	['nɔbili]	*the noble*	i poveri	['pɔveri]	*the poor*

Pronouns

Pronouns are used in place of nouns. As in English, there are many kinds of pronouns in Italian. Being familiar with the types of pronouns and their functions will help you to grasp more clearly the action or intention of a poetic phrase. In English, the personal pronoun is required for every verb form except the imperative. In Italian, the verb form does not always include the personal pronoun. The inflected ending of the verb indicates the subject of the verb. You will also discern the meaning from the context of the phrase. It is significant to note that the use of the personal pronoun with an Italian verb usually implies emphasis.

◆ Subject pronouns refer to the subject of the sentence or clause.

io	['io]	*I*
tu	[tu]	*you, singular/informal*
lui/egli	['lui/'eʎʎi]	*he*
lei/ella	['lei/'ella]	*she*
noi	['noi]	*we*
voi	['voi]	*you/plural*
loro	['loro]	*they*
Lei	['lei]	*you, singular/formal; masc. or fem.*
Loro	['loro]	*you, plural/formal; masc. or fem.*

Note. "Lei" and "Loro" are formal pronouns that are used in conversational Italian for addressing persons of respect or strangers. These forms are rarely in poetry or libretti.

◆ Direct object pronouns receive the action of the verb in the sentence or clause.

mi	[mi]	*me*
ti	[ti]	*you, singular/informal*
lo	[lo]	*it/him*
la	[la]	*her*
ci	[tʃi]	*us*
vi	[vi]	*you/plural*
li	[li]	*them, plural; masc.*
le	[le]	*them, plural; fem.*

◆ Indirect object pronouns reply to "for whom?" or "to whom?" In Italian, that would be "per chi?" [per ki] or "a chi?" [a ki]

mi	[mi]	*for/to me*
ti	[ti]	*for/to you (singular/informal)*
gli	[ʎi]	*for/to him*
le	[le]	*for/to her*
ci	[tʃi]	*for/to us*
vi	[vi]	*for/to you (plural/informal)*
loro	['loro]	*for/to them*

| Le | [le] | *for/to you (singular/formal)* |
| Loro | ['loro] | *for/to you (plural/formal)* |

Note. See above regarding the purpose and use of formal forms of pronouns.

◆ Possessive pronouns replace nouns modified by possessive adjectives and agree in gender and number with the nouns the pronouns replace. Possessive pronouns are preceded by definite articles.

il mio	la mia	i miei	le mie	*mine*
[il 'mio]	[la 'mia]	[i miɛi]	[le miɛ]	
il tuo	la tua	i tuoi	le tue	*yours (informal)*
[il 'tuo]	[la 'tua]	[i tuɔi]	[le 'tue]	
il suo	la sua	i suoi	le sue	*his, hers*
[il 'suo]	[la 'sua]	[i suɔi]	[le sue]	
il nostro	la nostra	i nostri	le nostre	*ours*
[il 'nɔstro]	[la 'nɔstra]	[i 'nɔstri]	[le 'nɔstre]	
il vostro	la vostra	i vostri	le vostre	*yours*
[il 'vɔstro]	[la 'vɔstra]	[i 'vɔstri]	[le 'vɔstre]	
il loro	la loro	i loro	le loro	*theirs*
[il 'loro]	[la 'loro]	[i 'loro]	[le 'loro]	

◆ Singular Possessive Pronouns and Diction:

Perhaps more than any other part of speech, the possessive pronouns present a challenge when set to music. The singular first-, second-, and third-person forms of the possessive pronoun are either diphthongs (e.g., *mio, mia, mie, tuo, tua, suo, sua*) or triphthongs (e.g., *miei, tuoi, suoi*) that require multiple vowels to be sung on a single note. The penultimate vowel is the main vowel to be expressed in each case and never the last vowel of these words. To achieve the right result, isolate the pronoun. Say it in its proper rhythm until it flows easily. Next, sing it in its proper rhythm on one pitch. Place the word in its musical context.

◆ Relative pronouns link a noun to the relative clauses that modify it. Relative pronouns give additional information about the noun by indicating *whom, whose, which,* or *that*. In Italian, the relative pronouns are *che* [ke] and *cui* ['kui]. Unlike in English, these words can never be omitted in Italian.

Che (that, which, who, whom) replaces a person or thing and does not need to agree in gender or number.

La musica che ho canto   The music *that* I sing

Cui (of which, which, whom) often follows a preposition or article.

La cantante di cui parlo   The singer *of whom* I am speaking

Words that replace *che* and *cui* are *il quale, la quale, i quali,* and *le quali,* meaning *that* or *which,* and can only be used as the subject of a sentence. *Quale* in all its forms agrees with the noun for which it substitutes.

These words are pronounced:

il quale	[il 'kwale]	i quali	[i 'kwali]	*masculine, singular/plural*
la quale	[la 'kwale]	le quali	[le 'kwali]	*feminine, singular/plural*

It is also possible to substitute *chi (who)* for unspecified persons.

Chi cerca trova.   *He who seeks, finds.*

◆ Interrogative pronouns are used to ask questions. Unlike in English, sentence order in Italian is not always changed to create a question. It is possible to use the tone of your voice to turn a statement into an inquiry. Here are the words that invite an answer or express doubt. It would be wise to memorize them. They appear regularly in the texts you will sing.

Chi?	[ki]	*Who?*
Di chi?	[di ki]	*Whose?*
Che cosa?	[ke 'koza]	*What?*
Quale/quali?	['kwale/'kwali]	*Which?*
Quanto/quanti?	['kwanto/'kwanti]	*How much? How many?*

◆ Demonstrative pronouns provide contrast between specific nouns and agree in gender and number with the noun they replace.

Demonstrative pronouns denoting masculine nouns:

questo	['kwesto]	*this one*	questi	['kwesti]	*these . . .*
quello	['kwel:lo]	*that one*	quelli	['kwel:li]	*those . . .*

Demonstrative pronouns denoting feminine nouns:

questa	['kwesta]	*this one*	queste	['kweste]	*these . . .*
quella	['kwella]	*that one*	quelle	['kwelle]	*those . . .*

Demonstrative pronouns denoting singular and plural:

colui	[ko'lui]	*he who*	coloro	[ko'loro]	*they who . . .*
costui	[kos'tui]	*that male*	costei	[kos'tei]	*that female*
costoro	[kos'toro]	*those people*			

◆ Indefinite pronouns express indefinite quantities of people or objects, as in English. Below is a list of the indefinite pronouns most frequently appearing in texts for singing:

	Masculine	Feminine	
alcuni, alcune	[al'kuni]	[al'kune]	*some, any, few*
gli altri, le altre	[ʎʎaltri]	[le altre]	*the others*
molti, molte	['molti]	['molte]	*many*
molto, molta	['molto]	['molta]	*much*
nessuno, nessuna	[nes'suno]	[nes'suna]	*no one, nobody*
ognuno, ognuna	[oɲ'ɲuno]	[oɲ'ɲuna]	*each, everyone*
pochi, poche	['pɔki]	['pɔke]	*a little, few*
poco, poca	['pɔko]	['pɔka]	*a little*
qualcosa	[kwal'koza]		*something, anything*
qualcuno	[kwal'kuno]		*someone, somebody*
tanti, tante	['tanti]	['tante]	*many*
troppi, troppe	['trɔppi]	['trɔppe]	*so many*
troppo, troppa	['trɔppo]	['trɔppa]	*so much*
tutti, tutte	['tutti]	['tutte]	*everyone*
tutto, tutta	['tutto]	['tutta]	*everything*
un altro, un'altra	[un 'altro]	[un 'altra]	*another*
uno, una	['uno]	['una]	*a/any person*

Uno and *una* (a/any person) are used only in the singular and refers only to people, not to things or ideas. *Ognuno* and *ognuna* (each/everyone) are also used only in the singular to refer to people or things, agreeing in gender with the referenced noun.

◆ Reflexive pronouns relate action done and received by the subject. Unlike in English, reflexive pronouns appear frequently in Italian prose and poetry.

io – mi	*myself*	noi – ci	*ourselves/one another*
tu – ti	*yourself*	voi – vi	*yourselves/each other*
lui – si	*himself*	lei – si	*herself*
loro – si	*themselves*		

Ci [ʧi] and *ne* [ne] refer to nouns that have been previously mentioned. The word *ci* means *there* and refers to objects or places. It replaces a prepositional phrase. As in English, the word *ci* can also be used with the verb *to be* (essere ['essere]) in the singular or plural to mean *there is* (c'e) or *there are* (ci sono). The word *ne* refers to people, places, and things and can mean *some, any of, it, of them, from it, from her/him,* or *from there*. There is not necessarily an English equivalent to this pronoun. Because it functions like a direct or indirect object pronoun, the word *ne* is placed similarly within the sentence.

Verbs

Verbs express action, states of mind and being. Verbs have "moods" or "tenses." The basic stem of a verb is found in its infinitive or unconjugated form. The infinitive states the action of a verb in its simplest form. Verb forms appear in the dictionary listed as follows:

Present tense	Infinitive	Past participle
parlo ['parlo]	parlare [par'lare]	parlato [par'lato]
I speak	*to speak*	*spoken*

In Italian, there are three conjugation forms, known as first, second, and third conjugations. Below is an example of common regular verb infinitives in each of the three conjugations:

First Conjugation:	parl<u>are</u> [par'lare]	*to speak*
Second Conjugation:	ved<u>ere</u> [ve'dere]	*to see*
Third Conjugation:	part<u>ire</u> [par'tire]	*to leave/depart*

Common Verbs and Their Conjugations

Here are some verbs you are likely to encounter in singing, listed by their conjugation.

First Conjugation		Second Conjugation		Third Conjugation	
arrivare	*arrive*	accendere	*light/kindle*	aprire	*open*
ascoltare	*listen*	apprendere	*learn*	divertire	*enjoy*
aspettare	*wait*	chiedere	*ask*	fuggire	*escape*
ballare	*dance*	chiudere	*close*	inseguire	*follow*
cantare	*sing*	confondere	*confuse*	mentire	*lie/deceive*
giocare	*play*	credere	*believe*	offrire	*offer*
girare	*turn*	decidere	*decide*	seguire	*follow*
lasciare	*leave/allow*	godere	*enjoy*	sentire	*hear*
pensare	*think*	leggere	*read*	soffirere	*serve*

First Conjugation		Second Conjugation		Third Conjugation	
portare	*carry*	mettere	*put*	vestire	*dress*
provare	*try/prove*	nascondere	*hide*	*capire	*understand*
ricordare	*remember*	perdere	*lose*	*finire	*finish*
spiegare	*explain*	piangere	*weep*	*riunire	*meet*
suonare	*sound/play*	prendere	*take*	*spedire	*send*
trovare	*find*	ridere	*laugh*	*tradire	*betray*
volare	*fly*	temere	*fear*	*ubbidire	*obey*

*These third-conjugation verbs include "-isc" in the spelling of present indicative first-, second-, and third-person singular and third-person plural forms. For example: *capisco, capisci, capisce, capiscono*. For diction purposes, [ka'pisko], [ka'piʃi], [ka'piʃe], and [ka'piskono].

Here are sample conjugations of a verb in each category. Memorize the endings and use them as "signals" for the present tense form of each conjugation. The infinitives are mentioned with the auxiliary verb form that accompanies each conjugation. In general, verbs that refer to a stationary action use *avere*, while verbs that involve physical motion use *essere*. Consult references to assure yourself.

Present Indicative

First Conjugation

Endings: -o; -i; -a; -iamo; -ate; -ano

Infinitive:	parlare	[par'lare]	(conjugates with *avere*)
Past Participle:	parlato	[par'lato]	*spoken*
(io) parl<u>o</u>	['parlo]	*I speak*	
(tu) parl<u>i</u>	['parli]	*you speak (singular/informal)*	
(lui/lei) parl<u>a</u>	['parla]	*he/she speaks*	
(noi) parl<u>iamo</u>	[par'ljamo]	*we speak*	
(voi) parl<u>ate</u>	[par'late]	*you speak (plural)*	
(loro) parl<u>ano</u>	['parlano]	*they speak*	

Second Conjugation

Endings: -o; -i; -e; -iamo; -ete; -ono

Infinitive:	vedere	[ve'dere]	(conjugates with *avere*)
Past Participle:	veduto (visto)	[ve'duto]	*seen*
(io) ved<u>o</u>	['vedo]	*I see*	

(tu) ved<u>i</u>	['vedi]	*you see (singular/informal)*
(lui/lei) ved<u>e</u>	['vede]	*he/she sees*
(noi) ved<u>iamo</u>	[ve'djamo]	*we see*
(voi) ved<u>ete</u>	[ve'dete]	*you see (plural)*
(loro) ved<u>ono</u>	['vedono]	*they see*

Third Conjugation

Endings: -o; -i; -e; -iamo; -ite; -ono

<u>Infinitive:</u>	partire	[par'tire]	(conjugates with *essere*)
<u>Past Participle:</u>	partito/i	[par'tito/i]	*departed*
(io) part<u>o</u>	['parto]	*I depart/leave*
(tu) part<u>i</u>	['parti]	*you depart (singular/informal)*
(lui/lei) part<u>e</u>	['parte]	*he/she departs*
(noi) part<u>iamo</u>	[par'tjamo]	*we depart*
(voi) part<u>ite</u>	[par'tite]	*you depart (plural)*
(loro) part<u>ono</u>	['partono]	*they depart*

Remember, in Italian, the subject pronoun is not necessary for expressing the verb. Knowing the endings for these conjugations will help you discern who is performing what action. Take note of the signals provided by the endings in each conjugation.

Irregular verbs are verbs that because of their common use become "corrupted." Here is an example of the present tense of three irregular verbs from the first conjugation. "To go," "to give," and "to do or to make" represent daily activities.

<u>Infinitive:</u>	andare	[an'dare]	*to go*
<u>Participle:</u>	andato	[an'dato]	*gone* (with *essere*)
Present Indicative:			
	vado	['vado]	*I go*
	vai	['vai]	*you go (singular/informal)*
	va	['va]	*he/she goes*
	andiamo	[an'djamo]	*we go*
	andate	[an'date]	*you go (plural)*
	vanno	['vanno]	*they go*

| Infinitive: | dare | ['dare] | *to give* |
| Participle: | date | ['date] | *given* (with *avere*) |

Present Indicative:

	do	['dɔ]	*I give*
	dai	['dai]	*you give (singular/informal)*
	dà	['da]	*he/she gives*
	diamo	['djamo]	*we give*
	date	['date]	*you give (plural)*
	danno	['danno]	*they give*

| Infinitive: | fare | ['fare] | *to do, to make* |
| Participle: | fatto | ['fatto] | *made* (with *avere*) |

Diction Note. Not to be confused with *fato*/noun meaning *fate*

Present Indicative:

	faccio	['fattʃo]	*I make/do*
	fai	['fai]	*you make/do (singular/informal)*
	fa	['fa]	*he/she makes/does*
	facciamo	[fat'tʃjamo]	*we make/do*
	fate	['fate]	*you make/do (plural)*
	fanno	['fanno]	*they make/do*

Diction Note. Take care in expressing the second-person plural *fate*. It is easy to double or "geminate" the "t" unintentionally.

◆ Modal verbs are second-conjugation verbs that help you understand the intention or attitude of the speaker. They are:

| *dovere* (to have to . . .) | [do'vere] | *potere* (to be able to . . .) [po'tere] |
| *sapere* (to know how to . . .) [sa'pere] | | *volere* (to want to . . .) [vo'lere] |

◆ Auxiliary verbs (sometimes called "helper" verbs in English) are the most commonly used verbs in the Italian language and are irregular in their form. The auxiliary verbs are *essere* ['ɛssere] (*to be*) (past participle: *stato* ['stato], meaning *been*) and avere [a'vere] (*to have*) (past participle: *avuto* [a'vuto], meaning *had*). With each language you sing, it is very important to grasp the present tense forms of the auxiliary verbs, because the past and future tenses are built upon these verbs.

◆ Present Tense

sono	[sono]	*I am*	ho	[ɔ]	*I have*
sei	[sɛi]	*you are (sing. fam.)*	hai	[ai]	*you have (sing. fam.)*
è	[ɛ]	*he/she/it is*	ha	[a]	*he/she/it has*
siamo	['sjamo]	*we are*	abbiamo	[ab'bjamo]	*we have*
siete	[s'jete]	*you are (pl.)*	avete	[a'vete]	*you have (pl.)*
sono	[sono]	*they are*	hanno	['anno]	*they have*

◆ Imperfect Tense

ero	['ɛro]	*I was*	avevo	[a'vevo]	*I had*
eri	['ɛri]	*you were (sing. fam.)*	avevi	[a'vevi]	*you had (sing. fam.)*
era	['ɛra]	*he/she/it was*	aveva	[a'veva]	*he/she/it had*
eravamo	[ɛra'vamo]	*we were*	avevamo	[ave'vamo]	*we had*
eravate	[ɛra'vate]	*you were (pl.)*	avevate	[ave'vate]	*you had (pl.)*
erano	['ɛrano]	*they were*	avevano	[a'vevano]	*they had*

◆ Future Tense

sarò	[sa'rɔ]	*I shall be*	avrò	[a'vrɔ]	*I shall have*
sarai	[sa'rai]	*you will be (sing. fam.)*	avrai	[a'vrai]	*you will have (sing. fam.)*
sarà	[sa'ra]	*he/she/it will be*	avrà	[a'vra]	*he/she/it will have*
saremo	[sa'rɛmo]	*we shall be*	avremo	[a'vrɛmo]	*we shall have*
sarete	[sa'rete]	*you will be (pl.)*	avrete	[a'vrete]	*you will have (pl.)*
saranno	['saranno]	*they will be*	avranno	['avranno]	*they will have*

◆ *Passato prossimo* or perfect tense is used to express something that happened in the past. It is formed using the present tense of *avere* or *essere* + a past participle.

parlare *to speak/parlato spoken*

io	ho parlato	*I have spoken*	noi	abbiamo parlato	*we have spoken*
tu	hai parlato	*you have spoken*	voi	avete parlato	*you have spoken (pl.)*
lui/lei	ha parlato	*he/she has spoken*	loro	hanno parlato	*they have spoken*

partire *to leave, depart*/partito, a *left, departed*

io	sono partito/a	*I have left*	noi	siamo partiti/e	*we have left*
tu	sei partito/a	*you have left (sing. fam.)*	voi	siete partiti/e	*you have left (pl.)*
lui/lei	è partito/a	*he/she has left*	loro	sono partiti/e	*they have left*

◆ *Essere* is used mainly (but not always) with verbs of motion or those that describe changes in condition. Common ones are:

andare/andato	*to go*	venire/venuto	*to come*
arrivare/arrivato	*to arrive*	scendere/sceso	*to descend, go down*
salire/salito	*to go up, climb*	nascere/nato	*to be born*
morire/morto	*to die*	correre/corso	*to run*
ritornare/ritornato	*to return*	uscire/uscito	*to exit, go out*
diventare/diventato	*to become*	rimanere/rimasto	*to remain*

With verbs that use *essere*, the past participles must agree in gender and number with the subject.

Laura è partit̲a̲ ieri. *Laura left yesterday.*   Francesco è uscit̲o̲. *Frank has gone out.*

Paulo e Laura e Dante sono partit̲i̲ ieri.   *Paul, Laura and Dante left yesterday.*

With verbs that use *avere*, the past participle does not need to agree in gender and number except in rare cases.

Adjectives

Adjectives agree in gender and number with the noun or pronoun they modify.

◆ Descriptive adjectives describe the noun or pronoun, such as size, shape, color, or state of being and are generally, but not always, found behind the noun or pronoun.

◆ Demonstrative adjectives specify the noun and agree in gender and number with it. In Italian, as in English, the words mean *this/these* and *that/those*.

The demonstrative adjectives for masculine nouns are:

questo	['kwesto]	*this*	questi	['kwesti]	*these*
quell'	['kwel]	*that*	quei	['kwei]	*those*
quello	['kwello]	*that*	quegli	['kweʎʎi]	*those*

The demonstrative adjectives for feminine nouns are:

questa	['kwesta]	*this*	queste	['kweste]	*these*
quella	['kwella]	*that*	quelle	['kwelle]	*those*

◆ Indefinite adjectives refer to unidentified quantities of animals, objects or people. As in English, some are used with singular nouns and others with plural ones.

   ogni ['ɔɲi] (*each/every*) is always used with a singular noun.

   qualche ['kwalke] (*a few, any, some*) always used with a singular noun, sometimes has a plural meaning.

   tutto (-a) or tutti (-e) ['tutto] ['tutta] ['tutti] ['tutte] (*all the*) agrees in gender and number with the noun it identifies and is followed by a definite article and a noun.

   tanto ['tanto] (*a lot of*), molto ['molto] (*many*), troppo ['trɔppo] (*too many, too much*), and poco ['pɔko] (*a little*) agree in gender and number with the noun they identify.

◆ It would be useful to memorize the following indefinite adjectives and their meanings. They appear regularly in Italian texts and identify quantities that may demand your attention as an interpreter.

alcuno (-a, -i, -e) or qualche ['kwalke]	*some, any, few*		
altro (-a, -i, -e)	*other*	molto (-a, -i, -e)	*a lot, many, much*
ogni	*each, every*	poco (-a, -chi, -che)	*a few, a little*
troppo (-a, -i, -e)	*so much*	tutto (-a, -i, -e)	*all*

◆ Interrogative adjectives introduce questions. They appear before a noun. *Quale* (*which? what?*) has two forms, singular and plural, while the interrogative adjectives *quanto* (*how much? how many?*) have two singular and two plural forms, one each for masculine and feminine nouns, respectively.

Singular:	Quale	['kwale]	Plural:	Quali	['kwali]
Singular/masculine:	Quanto	['kwanto]	Plural/masculine:	Quanti	['kwanti]
Singular/feminine:	Quanta	['kwanta]	Plural/feminine:	Quante	['kwante]

◆ Possessive adjectives indicate ownership of the noun and agree in gender and number with it. *Note.* Possessive adjectives are pronounced the same as possessive pronouns.

il mio, la mia, i miei, le mie	*my*
it tuo, la tua, i tuoi, le tue	*your (singular)*

il suo, la sua, i suoi, le sue	*his/her/its*
il nostro, la nostra, i nostri, le nostre	*our*
il vostro, la vostra, i vostri, le vostre	*your (plural)*
il loro, la loro, i loro, le loro	*their*

Adverbs

Adverbs are words that modify verbs, adjectives or other adverbs, explaining to what extent or how an action is done. Some are formed by adding the ending "-mente" to an adjective in the feminine case and others differ from the adjective completely. There are also some exceptions. Look for the "-mente" ending as a signal for many adverbial forms.

Ex.	Adjective			Adverb		
	certa	['tʃɛrta]	*certain*	certamente	[tʃɛrta'mɛnte]	*certainly*
	dolce	['doltʃe]	*sweet*	dolcemente	[doltʃe'mɛnte]	*sweetly*
	lenta	['lɛnta]	*slow*	lentamente	[lɛnta'mɛnte]	*slowly*
	sincera	[sin'tʃɛra]	*sincere*	sinceramente	[sintʃɛra'mɛnte]	*sincerely*
	buono	['buono]	*good*	bene	['bɛne]	*well*
	cattivo	[kat'tivo]	*bad*	male	['male]	*bad*

Some adjectives and adverbs have the exact same forms. The sentence structure will tell you how the word is being used. Note that many of these words are used as indications of a composer's performance intentions for a song or aria.

Ex.	abbastanza	[abba'stantsa]	*enough; quite*
	affatto	[af'fatto]	*at all*
	assai	[as'sai]	*very much*
	così	[ko'zi]	*this way; so*
	meno	['meno]	*less*
	molto	['mɔlto]	*much, a lot*
	poco	['poko]	*a little*
	quasi	['kwazi]	*almost*
	tanto	['tanto]	*so much*
	troppo	['trɔppo]	*too much*

Adverbs are also used to express time. Below is a list of some adverbs you will see often in the texts you sing.

adesso	[a'dɛsso]	*now*	allora	[al'lɔra]	*then*
ancora	[aŋ'kɔra]	*yet, still*	appena	[ap'pɛna]	*as soon as*
domani	[do'mani]	*tomorrow*	dopo	['dopo]	*after*
fino a	['fino a]	*until*	finora	[fi'nora]	*until now*
già	[ʤa]	*already*	mai	['mai]	*never*
oggi	['ɔdʤi]	*today*	ora	['ɔra]	*now*
poi	['poi]	*next, then*	presto	['prɛsto]	*quickly, soon*
sempre	['sɛmpre]	*always*	spesso	['spɛsso]	*often*
tardi	['tardi]	*late*			

Adverbs express location or provide other important information about how action is taking place. Because these words express subtle gradations of meaning, you will find them throughout the texts you sing.

davanti	[da'vanti]	*in front*	dietro	[d'jetro]	*behind*
dove	['dove]	*where*	fuori	[fu'ori]	*out, beyond*
giù	['ʤu]	*down*	indietro	[in'djetro]	*behind*
lì, là	[li], [la]	*here/there*	lontano	[lɔn'tano]	*far*
sotto	['sɔtto]	*under*	su	[su]	*up*
vicino	[vi'tʃino]	*near*	anche	['aŋke]	*also*
appena	[ap'pena]	*as soon as*	come	['kɔme]	*how*
forse	['fɔrse]	*maybe, perhaps*	infatti	[in'fatti]	*in fact*
infine	[in'fine]	*at last*	insieme	[in'sjɛme]	*together*
nemmeno	[nem'meno]	*not even*	piuttosto	[pjut'tosto]	*rather*
proprio	['proprio]	*exactly, really*	pure	['pure]	*also*
soprattutto	[soprat'tutto]	*above all, especially*			

The words listed above are essential to your proper understanding of texts in Italian. Learn to recognize them in a sentence. Perhaps you will want to make flashcards to help you memorize the adverbs you expect to use most frequently.

◆ Comparative and superlative forms of adjectives and adverbs express levels of comparison and preference. As in English, the Italian language allows for comparing equal, superior, and inferior qualities. Below are examples of each form.

1. Equality can be expressed in Italian by using three forms. The forms are: *così . . . come* [ko'si] . . . ['kome], meaning *as . . . as*; *tanto . . . quanto* ['tanto] . . . ['kwanto], meaning *as much . . . as*; and *tanti . . . quanto* ['tanti] . . . ['kwanto] meaning *as many . . . as*.

2. Superiority can be expressed in Italian in three forms. The English equivalent is *more . . . than* that or *more than*. The forms are *più . . . di* ['pju] [di], used to compare to objects or subjects, as in English *more . . . than*; and *più . . . che* ['pju] [ke] used to compare to aspects within one subject.

3. Inferiority meaning *less than* is expressed in Italian using one of two forms. The forms are *meno . . . di* ['meno] [di] or *meno . . . che* ['meno] [ke].

Watch for the "signal words" of *così . . . come, tanto . . . quanto, tanti . . . quanto, più . . . di, più . . . che, meno . . . di,* and *meno . . . che*. They will help you determine levels of comparison, quality, and preference in a descriptive text.

The Articles

The articles appear in two forms in Italian. As in English, there are definite and indefinite ones. Though the definite article in Italian is translated as *the* in English, it is used much more frequently in Italian than in English sentence structure. The indefinite the articles (in English, *a/an* and *one*) refer to nonspecific people or things. All the articles agree in gender and number with the word to which they refer.

◆ The definite articles used with masculine nouns are:

il	[il]	translated "the"	singular
lo	[lo]	before "gn," "ps," "s" + a consonant, or "z"	singular
l'	[l]	before a vowel	singular
i	[i]	before most consonants	plural
gli	[ʎi]	before "s" + a consonant, "z," or a vowel	plural

◆ The definite articles used with feminine nouns are:

la	[la]	translated "the"	singular
l'	[l]	before a vowel	singular
le	[le]	before a consonant	plural

◆ The partitive article *di* is used with a definite article to express *some* or *any*. The endings follow the same patterns as the definite articles listed above.

del pane	[del 'pane]	*some bread*	masculine singular + "p"
dello zucchero	[dello 'tsukkero]	*some sugar*	masculine singular + "z"
della frutta	[della 'frutta]	*some fruit*	feminine singular

◆ The indefinite articles are used before singular nouns and agree in gender and number with them. The indefinite articles used with masculine nouns are:

un   [un]   uno   ['uno]   before "gn," "ps," "s" + a consonant, or "z"

The indefinite articles used with feminine nouns are:

una   [una]   un'   [un]   before words that begin with vowels

Prepositions

Prepositions link a noun or pronoun to other words to express cause, location, manner, ownership, purpose, or time. Master this short list of simple prepositions:

a	[a]	*at, in, to*	con	[kon]	*with*
da	[da]	*at, by, from*	di	[di]	*from, of*
dopo	['dopo]	*after*	in	[in]	*at, in, into, to*
per	[per]	*for*	su	[su]	*on, onto*
tra/fra	[tra]/[fra]	*among, between*	vicino	[vi'tʃino]	*near*

Prepositions locate in position or time a person/object in relation to another person/object. In English, they are words like *with, at, to, by, from, of, about*, etc. More information regarding specific uses of prepositions can be found on the online resource associated with this book.

Here is list of other prepositions you should learn to recognize:

accanto	*near*	al posto di	*instead of*	assieme a	*together*
a causa di	*because of*	a dispetto di	*despite*	a seconda di	*according to*
attraverso	*through/ across*	circa	*about*	contro	*against*
davanti a	*in front of*	dentro	*inside*	dietro	*behind*
di fronte a	*opposite*	dopo	*after*	durante	*during*
fino a	*as far as/ until*	fuori di	*outside/out of*	in cima	*at the top of*

in fondo a	*at the bottom of*	in mezzo a	*in the middle of*	insieme con	*together with*
intorno a	*around*	invece di	*instead of*	lontano da	*far from*
lungo	*along*	nel mezzo di	*in the middle of*	nonostante	*notwithstanding*
per mezzo di	*by means of/through*	prima di	*before*	presso	*near/not far from*
riguardo a	*regarding*	rispetto	*with respect to/as to*	salvo	*except for*
secondo	*according to*	senza	*without*	sino a	*as far as/until*
sopra	*above*	sotto	*under/ beneath*	verso	*towards*
vicino a	*near/next to*				

As you see, several prepositions have identical definitions. They are used differently for specific levels of meaning. You will know which usage is appropriate based on the context in which it is used.

Conjunctions

Conjunctions connect large groups of words (clauses). Memorize these words. Though they are small ones, they are very powerful. The coordinating conjunctions unite two thoughts. The subordinate ones qualify the information conveyed in the clause to which they are linked. You will find these words frequently in the Italian texts you read and sing.

◆ Conjunctions that "coordinate" two clauses are as follows:

anche	['aŋke]	*also*	e	[e]	*and*
ma	[ma]	*but*	o	[ɔ]	*or*
oppure	[ɔp'pure]	*or*	però	[pe'rɔ]	*but, however*

◆ Subordinating conjunctions are those that could not stand on their own without a clause that expresses a full thought.

benché	[bɛŋ'ke]	*although*	giacché	[ʤa'ke]	*since*
perché	[pɛr'ke]	*because/why*	prima che	['prima ke]	*before*
purché	[pur'ke]	*provided that*	se	[se]	*if, unless*

Interjections

Interjections are words that are inserted to express emotion such as *ahimè!* [ai'mɛ] meaning *alas!* or *coraggio!* [ko'radʤo] meaning *have courage!*

Word Order in Italian

In Italian, the subject can be placed almost anywhere in the sentence. Its location determines much about the meaning of the words. The verb must be adjacent to the subject, either before or after. Subject pronouns are omitted except when required for emphasis. If you wish to form a question, the word order need <u>not</u> be altered. To form a negative, you need only to place the word *non* before the verb. Modifying words such as adjectives generally follow the noun but need not. Adverbs are usually before the adjective. Adverbs of time (e.g., *sempre* ['sɛmpre], meaning *always*) are placed between the auxiliary verb and the past participle as in English.

The Italian Alphabet

The Italian alphabet has 21 letters: a, b, c, d, e, f, g, h, i, l, m, n, o, p, q, r, s, t, u, v, and z.

Accents: Types and Use

In Italian, two kinds of accents exist. They are the grave accent ` and the acute accent ´. Grave and acute accents change the sound of "e" vowels. In the case of *è* [ɛ], the grave accent opens the vowel, while the acute accent of *é* [e] closes it. In all other cases, grave and acute accents shift the accented syllable in a word without altering the pronunciation of the vowel sound.

Discussion Questions

1. Search your current repertoire to find one example of a verb from each of the three conjugations. Where is the verb placed in the sentence or phrase? Does the verb have modifiers? Are they adverbs or adjectives?
2. Compare the English and the Italian alphabets. Which letters do not appear in Italian?
3. How does the word order for an Italian sentence differ from a sentence in English?
4. Make a chart or flashcards of the most common Italian prepositions and conjunctions. Look for examples in your current repertoire.
5. Search for accents in the Italian texts you are studying. Note the ones that have an impact on the sound of the vowel and the ones that shift the syllabic accent.

Italian Language and Thought

Dante and Beatrice

In his *Life of Dante*, Giovanni Boccaccio recounts a life-changing encounter between two preteens, a story that serves as the foundation for the Italian culture's fascination with love as an enduring power. We learn that Dante Alighieri (1265–1321), at the age of 9, accompanied his father to a festival at the home of Folco Portinari. Here the young Dante saw the host's fine-looking daughter, Beatrice, a girl of comparable age and incomparable magnetism: "And although a mere boy, he received her beautiful image into his heart with such great affection that from that day forward it never departed while he lived." In this manner began, for Dante, a lifelong worship of his ideal love, an affection that required no physical consummation. Dante's expression of his love for the unattainable Beatrice is first documented in a semiautobiographical book entitled *Vita Nuova* or *New Life*, (1293–1294) published shortly after Beatrice's untimely death. Begun spontaneously, Dante's love of Beatrice produced vital artistic and spiritual energy for decades to come.

Dante had two models as guides. Guido Cavalcanti (1250–1300), a prominent figure in Florentine society, was the poet to whom Dante dedicated his *Vita Nuova*. Guido Cavalcanti (1255–1300), a love poet, is best known for a rather pessimistic analysis of the pangs and perils of love in a work entitled "Donna Me Prega" or "A Lady Asks Me." It was Guido Guinizzelli (1230–1276), a Bolognese poet from an earlier generation, who influenced Dante's approach to the topics of love and language. In his poem "Al Cor Gentil" or "To a Gentle Heart," Guinizzelli celebrated the positive force of love. His sensitive manner of expression came to be called the "dolce stile nuovo" or "sweet new style." It has been said that "The ethos known as courtly love, with its central conviction that love enables the lover, is presented by Guinizzelli in a version of extreme refinement and sensibility" (Shaw, 2015). Guinizzelli's philosophy of love and loving resonated deeply with Dante, who expanded both the ideal and literary method. In *Vita Nuova*, Dante wrote, "Amor e il cor gentil sono una cosa" or "Love and a noble heart are one thing" (Mortimer, 2013).

It became Dante's calling to love another, be it a human, an aspect of nature, or a deity. He saw Beatrice only twice, barely speaking either time; yet her presence in the world made his existence an elevated, enlightened one. After her death, Dante continued to write about the world around him. His treatise called *Il Convivio* (The Banquet) and an unfinished work entitled *De Monarchia* (About the Monarchy) earned displeasure in Florentine political circles. "It was the function of Dante, or so he thought, to be political," according to Williams (1943). He was accused of disturbing the peace and other misdemeanors, one of which related to the response of a young woman who peered at him through a window. Rather than resist the charges, Dante spent 19 years in exile, moving from town to town until his death in 1321 in Ravenna, Italy, at the age of 56. The years in exile were those in which he produced the three-part work now known as *The Divine Comedy*.

Writing his *Divine Comedy* in vernacular, Dante created what is known as the Italian language written and spoken today. Guided by Virgil, the literary sage of Rome, Dante embarks on a trip through Hell and Purgatory in search of the noblest city of all, Paradise. Why is Virgil significant as a fictional guide to Dante's journey? Virgil's masterwork, *The Aeneid*, was an epic poem which was said to have had prophetic powers. "Its author, after all, was the greatest and the most influential of all Roman poets. A friend and confidant of Augustus, Rome's first emperor, Virgil was already considered a classic in his own lifetime: revered, quoted, imitated, and occasionally parodied by other writers, taught in schools, and devoured by the general public. Later generations of Romans considered his works a font of human knowledge, from rhetoric to ethics to agriculture; by the Middle Ages, the poet had come to be regarded as a wizard whose powers included the ability to control Vesuvius's eruptions and to cure blindness in sheep," according to Mendelsohn (2018).

Along the road, Virgil and Dante meet people—some alive, others long dead, and a few imaginary—all of whom are struggling to cope with their vices. The most notable love triangle is that of Paolo and his sister-in-law, Francesca, who have been condemned for a meaningful glance exchanged while reading a book. (Their dilemma is the source of inspiration for numerous works of visual art, a play by Gabriele d'Annunzio, an opera by Riccardo Zandonai, and a symphonic work by Piotr Tchaikovsky, to name only a few.)

Few literary works have been as successful and influential as Dante's *The Divine Comedy*. With its famous opening "Nel mezzo del cammin di nostra vita" or "In the middle of our life journey," it has served as a guidebook in Western culture since its first appearance in 1321. The work continues to inspire, partly because of Dante's ability to invite a reader onto life's path with him. At each stop along the way, the reader learns more about what life has to offer and how its gifts should be worshipped and valued. Human love is the starting and ending point. The lessons of love give knowledge that enriches the soul. "In Dante's view, love is the key to understanding the way the universe functions. It causes the circling motion of the heavenly bodies. It drives all human behavior," writes Shaw (2015).

In Canto XVII of "Purgatory" in Dante's *The Divine Comedy*, he proclaims: "Thus you may understand that love alone is the true seed of every merit in you, and of all acts for which you must atone" (Ciardi, 2003). As interpreters of Italian texts through music, we can expect to find references to Beatrice and Dante, to the ennobling of a life through a single, shared gaze. We discover a philosophy suggesting that any nudge toward or away from love is positive. Love disrupts and repairs us. If the pain love inflicts is acute, we will savor more richly the grace that heals it. Should the beloved depart, each memory of times gone by will enliven us anew. If love remains, we must be alert to every nuance in honor of love's nobility. Love is to be cherished, not controlled. Love should always bring a smile, even through tears.

Petrarch and Laura

In the Renaissance, Francesco Petracco, known as Petrarch (1304–1374), brought the Italian literary art to new heights in the creation of sonnets honoring his "Laura." As a member of the family with the same political affiliation as Dante, Petrarch was born in exile. He was the son of a notary. At that time, a notary was a secular, well-educated trusted member of society who took care to transcribe documents that could impress and persuade. The papacy, which had devolved into an administrative, financial, and judicial body, was exiled in 1309 to Avignon, France. In 1312, Petrarch's father was engaged as a notary to the exiled pope and took his wife and sons with him. Avignon, at that time, represented a much larger world culturally and politically than Rome. In recalling the movement of his boyhood mind, Petrarch wrote: "I was noting the substance of thought—the pettiness of this life, its brevity, haste, tumbling course, its hidden cheats, time's irrecoverability, the flower of life soon wasted, the fugitive beauty of a blooming face, the flight of youth, the trickeries of age, the wrinkles, illnesses, sadness, and pain, and the implacable cruelty of indomitable death" (Bishop, 2001).

At the behest of his father, Petrarch studied law first at Montpellier, France, and later in Bologna, Italy. In 1326, Petrarch's father died. Petrarch abandoned Bologna, the law, and the large fortune he would likely have accumulated from such work. Instead, he returned to Avignon. On Good Friday, April 6, 1327, he entered the Church of St. Claire and saw Laura from afar. She became his muse, a being who inspired 366 sonnets of adoration in 366 days. Though there are numerous artistic representations of Petrarch's Laura, there are those who doubt her existence.

Like Dante, Petrarch used his poetic writing to understand himself. He felt driven by love and desire. His encounter with Laura on April 6, 1327, led to his discovery of love and inspired in him a new way to write. Laura represented the perfection of all the virtues: beautiful, chaste, silent. In all the art work depicting Petrarch's Laura, she appears as someone who has a rich interior life. Petrarch writes of her in Latin and in Italian, choosing the language that affords him the best opportunity to describe her traits exquisitely. See below how Petrarch describes his first experiences of "love at first sight." Note the intricate rhyme scheme and tight sonnet form. Notice the sense of surrender to love's power without any expectation of love returned. Petrarch's writings form the basis for the Italian reverence for human beauty and love. Written in 1327, the sonnets are called *Rime in Vita e Morta di Madonna Laura* or "Rhymes on the Life and Death of Lady Laura."

Below you will find a Petrarch sonnet that has been set to music by Franz Liszt (1811–1886) in the cycle *Tre Sonetti di Petrarca* and by Norman Dello Joio (1913–2008).

Benedetto sia 'l giorno, e'l mese, e l'ano	Blessed be the day, month, and year
E la stagione, e 'l tempo, e l'ora, e 'l punto	and the season, time, hour, and moment,
D 'l bel paese e 'l loco ov'io fui giunto	the lovely country and place, where I met
Da' duo begli occhi che legato m'ànno;	the two beautiful eyes that bind me.
E Benedetto il primo dolce affanno	and blessed be the first sweet affection
Ch'l ebbi ad esser con Amor congiunto	that I felt as I was conquered by love,
E l'arco e le saette ond 'i' fui punto	and the bow and arrows which pierced me,
E le piaghe, ch'infino al cor mi vanno.	And wounds that went deeply in my heart.
Benedette le voci tante, ch'io	Blessed be the verses which I
Chiamando il nome di Laura ho sparte	have scattered calling out Laura's name
E I sospiri, e le lagrime, e 'l desio	and the sighs, tears, and fervent desire
E benedette sian tutte le carte	and blessed be all the pieces of paper
Ov'io fama le acquisto, e il pensier mio,	from which I get fame for my thoughts,
Ch'e sol di lei, si ch'altra non v'ha parte.	That are only of her, their only origin.

Because of Petrarch's writings, the name Laura becomes deeply embedded in Italian literary history. Her name derives from *Lauro* or *laurel*, as in the laurel tree, a symbol from the myth of Daphne and Apollo in Ovid's *Metamorphoses*. In the myth, Daphne, the daughter of the river god, is a happily unmarried virgin. Apollo, son of Jove (Latin for Jupiter in Roman/Zeus in Greek), having offended Cupid, is shot with a hopeless love arrow. When Apollo sees Daphne, he chases her through the woods. Daphne recognizes Apollo's divine power. She hurries to her father for help. He saves his daughter by transforming her into a laurel tree, saving her virginity and protecting her from love's all-consuming force. Out of affection for her, Apollo chooses the laurel tree as his own symbol of love, victory, and distinguished artistry. You will discover that this myth of Daphne and Apollo permeates Petrarch's work. In Petrarch's time, myths were used to deal with issues of social practice. The myth described here contributed to the concept of arranged marriages. Marriage was an institution that created relationships between people and property in which love was not a requirement. (It should also be noted that the word *Lauro* may be used to refer to poetic success. *L'aura* means *breeze, breath,* or *aura*. Also, *l'aura/l'auro* can mean "gold.")

According to Morris Bishop, "Long, hopeless fidelity is the poet's best theme" (Bishop, 2001). Had Laura, in his opinion, ever yielded to Petrarch's advances, our poet would have escaped, convinced that his writing career would be ended. His writings about her were called "sonnets" by form but are referred to as "conceits," meaning works that were fanciful or on the edge of the absurd. Petrarch's work has been criticized for its simplicity. It is exactly that trait that has appealed to many—the honesty of his description and sentiments. From depictions of Petrarch in artwork, we assume that he was rather tall, with keen eyes and reddish-brown hair. His hair turned prematurely gray. He was known to be vain about his looks. In his "Letter to Posterity," Petrarch wrote, "youth deceived me, early adulthood seized me, but old age corrected me" (Celenza, 2017).

Arguably, Petrarch is considered the first "modern" man, because his writings in Italian reveal the analysis of his own most intimate thoughts and feelings. For similar reasons, Petrarch has been called the "Father of Humanism." He loved nature, especially flowers and the countryside. He loved the inventions and creations of humankind. Regarding music, he is thought to have felt that "a good concert made him cease to envy the gods their privilege of listening to the music of the spheres" (Bishop, 2001).

Petrarch maintained an interest in Cicero and Virgil, commissioning a frontispiece for the Ambrosian Virgil housed in the Ambrosian library in Milan and containing more than 2,500 annotations. He said, "I have ingested these things in such an intimate way that they have become fixed not only in my memory but in my marrow, having become as one with my own intellect. The result is that, even if I never read them again for the rest of my life, they would certainly stick, having taken deep root in the deepest part of my spirit" (Celenza, 2017). With these words, he admits to such close reading that he is unable to recognize the origin of his thought at times. In these notes, we learn that Petrarch believed in a supreme being. He felt that "gods" caused chaos and, therefore, could not be divine.

In need of patronage, Petrarch served as a family chaplain and notary. In 1337, he returned to Vaucluse, France, near Avignon, where he wrote his major work, *On Illustrious Men,* for which he was crowned poet laureate in both Paris and Rome. In receiving the award, Petrarch gave an oration on April 8, 1341, based on his original ideas regarding the power of art and poetry. He began with words of Virgil from *Georgics:* "It is love that compels me upwards, over the lonely slopes of Parnassus" (Johnson, 2011).

Throughout his life, Petrarch worked on *Canzoniere* (*Songs*). He continued to reorder the poems until he felt they were in the right sequence. He also wrote *Secretum* (*The Secret*), a semibiographical dialogue between himself and St. Augustine. The latter serves as a good introduction to the former. It is in the *Secretum* that we discern that Laura was a real woman, not an illusion.

The *Canzoniere* interest us because of their musical adaptations by Liszt and others. The "canzone" is a 13th-century northern Italian form, adopted to create "versi sciolti" or blank verse. Petrarch brought significance to the form by developing a uniformity in its syllabic shape and rhyme scheme. The sonnet of today bears close resemblance to the *canzone* of Petrarch. Celenza writes, " . . . the sonnet must be held to have been an unspeakable blessing for Italian poetry. The clearness and beauty of its structure, the invitation it gave to elevate the thought in the second and more rapidly moving half, and the ease with which it could be learned by heart, made it a valued event by the greatest masters" (2017). Petrarch died on July 19, 1374, at his writing desk.

Lorenzo da Ponte (1749–1838), one of Mozart's librettists, attributed his facility with the Italian language to the fact that da Ponte's tutor insisted that Dante and Petrarch were as worthy of study as the Latin masters Virgil and Horace. "Lorenzo set himself to studying Italian poetry with such ferocity that he barely stopped to eat, and within six months he knew Dante's *Inferno* by heart, as well as most of Petrarch's sonnets, and the choices passages from Tasso and Ariosto," according to Bolt (2006).

You will encounter the name "Laura" again and again in song literature. You are already familiar with the lute song by Philip Rosseter entitled "When Laura Smiles." Mozart's "Abendempfindung an Laura" ("Evening Sentiment about Laura") uses the image. The name "Laura" appears in two songs by Franz Schubert, "Seligkeit" and "Apollo Lebet Noch" (Sonett I, D628). Liszt wrote four settings on excerpts of Petrarch's words relating to Laura. They are "Oh! Quand Je Dors" and *3 Sonetti del Petrarca* (*Three Petrarch Sonnets*) that include Sonnet 47: "Benedetto Sia L'giorno" (given above), Sonnet 104: "Pace Non Trovo," and Sonnet 123: "I' Vivi in Terra Angelici." Liszt composed a piano sonata in b minor called the *"Dante" Sonata*, S. 161, No. 7, and a work for orchestra called the *"Dante" Symphony*, S. 109.

Early Italian Song

The basic concepts of *bel canto* singing evolved as a liturgical performance practice in the early Roman Church. It is a mode of expression that is based in the recitation of text. The method was later adapted as a style of singing in early operatic works. The roots of the *bel canto* singing technique can be found in the training of the papal choir during the earliest days of the established church in Rome. Based upon the practices used in ancient Greek and Roman theater and other pre-Christian rites, early "Catholic" or universal church leaders adopted the practice of spoken and sung texts for their sacred ceremonies. The texts, drawn from holy scriptures, hymns, and poetry, were combined to form the rituals or "liturgy" of the early church. The liturgy was performed by the monastics who led the worship services.

Initially, worship spaces were modest in size. In time, the church grew as an institution of religious and political power. To accommodate an increasing number of followers, church leaders called for the design and construction of large, imposing facilities. To be heard in such buildings, the monks were forced to change their method of text delivery. They began to "call out" the patterns of text, elongating the vowel sounds and delaying the articulation of consonants. This invented method of performance required significant breath energy. The resulting phrases arched and undulated through the worship spaces. The congregants and clergy considered the experience to be spiritually meaningful as well as beautiful.

You might say that singing, as we know it in the Western world, began as a coincidence of acoustics. As the monks chanted through the vaulted architecture, their voices reverberated, amplified by the acoustics of the space. The "elevation" of the sacred texts, delivered on steady streams of breath, enveloped the listener with tone and text. The monks delivered these arching phrases using a vocal means now known as "legato" or connected singing. Schools were formed to teach young men the skills required to chant or "sing" the liturgy. The basic training of legato singing formed the foundation for the vocal technique later as the *bel canto* technique.

During the Italian Renaissance period in Florence, a group of artists, musicians, philosophers, and politicians, later known as the Florentine Camerata (ca. 1580), met to conceive an art form that would make artistic use of the myriad gifts of human creativity and invention. The result of their work was the development of what we now call "opera," literally defined as "action" or "work." (A related word in common usage is "opus," meaning a composition or set of works composed at the same time.) The Camerata sought to examine the human condition through an interdisciplinary use of visual, literary, and musical arts. Early opera was based upon texts that had stood the test of time; namely, Roman legend and Greek mythology. In these narratives, moral virtues such as truth and honor are confronted by circumstances of jealousy, hatred, or revenge. (Even today, musical theater and operatic plots treat issues of societal or political frailty and offer moral solutions.) In the depiction of legendary and mythological characters, the earliest opera composers wrote melodies that could serve to exploit the timbres of a human voice. By elevating the text, the human voice conveyed the action of the plot and the emotional response to it.

Due to the predominance of the church and its practices, the earliest operatic singing style was based upon the traditions of the papal choir. Therefore, early opera represented a secular use of text-centered, legato singing, also called *bel canto* principles. Because morality and human virtue were the principal themes of early opera, the young men who had abandoned the monastic life were drawn to participate in this secular art form, one that demanded an evocative delivery of text. Some members of the Florentine Camerata were trained singers and singing teachers, particularly Emilio de' Cavalieri (1550–1602), Giulio Caccini (1551–1618), and Jacopo Peri (1561–1633). These men advanced their own ideas about singing along with concepts presented by the training and performance art of the papal choir. With vocal maturity, the earliest operatic singers eagerly investigated and expanded the capabilities of their voices through ornamentation and poetic nuance.

The Camerata agreed upon a template for the newly invented form called "opera." The plot was adapted into a *libretto* or "little book" of monologues, dialogues and ensemble responses as is done today when scriptwriters create the screenplay version of a short story or novel for a film. The three basic musical forms used to dramatize the plot were called recitative, aria, and ensemble. The passages that carried the details of plot action were to be sung on a recited tone or "recitative." Early composers of opera wrote recitatives within a limited vocal range to be chanted or recited on pitch to insure the audibility of the text. Recitatives followed closely the rhythm of spoken language, inviting the singer to "lift" the text from the parameters of simple utterance to that of dramatic expression. The emotional response to the action was "aired" by the character through an "aria," a lyric vocal composition based on a poetic text. The aria offered the singer a chance to express human feelings through vocal and musical flights of melody and ornamentation. The arias were designed with florid passages that showcased the abilities and sensitivities of the young vocal performers. Based on the ideals of Greek and Roman drama, opera included ensembles where appropriate. Choruses sang as a response to the action or an expression of the plot's moral lesson. Verbal exchanges between characters in the form of duets, trios, quartets, and small ensembles as well as dances served to present a musico-dramatic realization of the *libretto*.

Giulio Caccini (1546–1618)

Giulio Caccini was a singer, a member of the Florentine Camerata, and a voice teacher. His philosophy of teaching was summarized in a treatise entitled *Le Nuove Musiche* (1602). As you listen, create a phonetic transcription of the text.

Comparative Listening

"Amarilli"
(Text and music by Giulio Caccini.)

Before you listen, implement your dictation strategies:

1. Spellings: Look for IPA spellings you already know such as the article *il*; conjunction *e*; preposition *in*; and pronouns *mia, mio, tu,* and *mio*. Be careful to note the difference between the pronunciation of *e* [e], meaning *and*, and *è*, [ε] meaning *is*.
2. Familiar Words: Look for words you recognize such as *bella, cor/core, dolce, desio, amor/amore,* and *petto*.
3. Rhyming Words: Follow down the right side of the text to identify rhymes such as *desio/mio, t'assale/vale,* and *core/amore*. Be sure you use the same IPA spellings for the vowels of each rhyming pair.
4. Repeating Words: Study the text for common words that repeat such as *Amarilli, credi/credilo,* and *mio*.
5. Expressive Possibilities: Circle the words that invite expression such as *bella, dolce desio, timor t'assale, vedrai scritto,* and the closing cadence: *Amarilli è il mio amore*.

Amarilli, mia bella
Amarilli, my beautiful (one)

Non credi, o del mio cor dolce desio,
You do not believe, oh, of my heart sweet desire,

D'esser tu l'amor mio?

That to be you the love of me?

Credilo pur, e se timor t'assale

Believe it purely (completely) and let no fear you assail.

Dubitar non ti vale,

To doubt not you assert (claim)

Prendi questo mio strale.

Take this my arrow.

Aprimi il petto e vedrai scritto in core:

Open of me the breast and you will see written on my heart

Amarilli è il mio amore.

"Amarilli is (the) my love."

Poetic Equivalent

Amarilli, my beautiful, can you not believe that you are the sweet desire of my heart? Believe it and do not fear harm. If you have any doubt, take an arrow and pierce my heart. There you will find written: "Amarilli is my beloved."

Comparative Performances

Listen to performances by native Italian artists such as mezzo soprano Cecilia Bartoli or tenor Luciano Pavarotti. Compare the diction and interpretations of non-native-speaking Italian artists such as mezzo soprano Joyce DiDonato and bass Dmitri Hvorostovsky. What are the similarities? What are the differences?

Marco Antonio (Pietro) Cesti (1620–1669)

A choirboy and member of the Franciscan order, Antonio Cesti is said to have composed more than 100 operas. "Intorno Al'idol Mio" became one of Cesti's most successful operas entitled *Ornotea*, which premiered in 1649. Listen and create a phonetic transcription.

Comparative Listening

"Intorno Al'idol Mio"

Before you listen, implement your dictation strategies:

1. Spellings: Look for IPA spellings you already know such as the article *il*; the conjunction *e*; prepositions *all'/al*, *su*, and *per*; and pronouns *mio* and *me*. Mark them with the IPA symbols you expect the singer to use.

2. Familiar Words: Mark the words you may already have encountered in your study of Italian song such as *idol, spirate, aure, soave, grate, ben, riposa, sogni, ardore, amore*.

3. Rhyming Words: Follow down the right side of the text to identify rhymes such as *spirate/grate, elette/aurette*, and *ardore/amore*. If they are to rhyme, you must use the same vowel symbol for each rhyming pair.

4. Repeating Words: Study the text for common words that repeat such as *spirate, aura/aurette*, and *grate/grati*. Be sure that you use the same IPA symbols for each repetition.

5. Expressive Possibilities: Circle the words that invite expression such as *all'idol mio, spirate pur spirate, soavi e grate, cortesi aurette, riposa su l'ali della quiete, racchiuso ardore*, and *larve d'amore*.

Intorno al'idol mio
Around the beloved mine

Spirate pur, spirate,
Breathe again, breathe,

Aure soave e grate;
Breezes soft and gracious

E nelle guanci elette
And on the cheeks elite

Baciatelo per me, cortesi aurette!
Kiss it for me, courteous little breezes!

Al mio ben, che riposa
To my beloved, who reposes

Sull'ali della quiete,
On wings of quiet (peace)

Grati sogni assistete,
Pleasant dreams assist,

E il mio racchiuso ardore
And (the) my hidden ardor

Svelategli per me, o larve d'amore!
Reveal to him for me, o spirits of love!

Poetic Equivalent

Gentle breezes, blow around my beloved and mild winds, kiss his dear cheeks for me!

Send graceful dreams to my love while he sleeps and reveal to him the ardor of my love for him, o angels of love!

Comparative Performances

Listen to historical performances by Spanish mezzo soprano Teresa Berganza (b. 1935) and Italian tenor Beniamino Gigli (1890–1957). Compare them with modern performances by mezzo sopranos Cecilia Bartoli and Joyce DiDonato. What differences do you notice between the performances from contrasting time periods? What do you notice about vowel choices in the Italian diction of each performer?

Alessandro Scarlatti (1660–1725)

Born in Palermo, Italy, and trained in Rome, Alessandro Scarlatti spent most of his career in service to the leadership of Naples. Scarlatti composed prolifically, creating more than 30 operas and numerous solo cantatas. Listen and create a phonetic transcription.

Comparative Listening

"Toglietemi la Vita Ancor"
(From the opera *Il Pompeo* [1683].)

Before you listen, implement your dictation strategies:

1. Spellings: Look for IPA spellings you already know such as the articles *la, il,* and *i*; preposition *del*; and pronouns *mi* and *mio.* Mark them with the IPA symbols you expect the singer to use.
2. Familiar Words: Mark the words you may already have encountered in your study of Italian such as *vita, cieli, cor, ancor,* and *dolor.*
3. Rhyming Words: Follow down the right side of the text to identify rhymes such as *ancor/cor/dolor* and *cieli/dì.* If they are to rhyme, you must use the same vowel symbol for each rhyming pair.
4. Repeating Words: Note the phrase that appears three times: *toglietemi la vita ancor.* Be sure that you use the same IPA symbols for each repetition.
5. Expressive Possibilities: Circle the words that invite expression such as *vita ancor, crudeli cieli, i rai del dì,* and *severe sfere.*

Toglietemi la vita ancor
Take (from) me the life (still/now),

Crudeli cieli,
Cruel heavens,

Se mi volete rapir il cor.
If me you want to steal the (my) heart.

Toglietemi la vita ancor
Take (from) me the life (still/now),

Negatemi i rai del dì,
Deny (to) me the rays of day,

Severe sfere,
severe sphere,

Se vaghe siete del mio dolor,
If vague are (the) my sadnesses,

Toglietemi la vita ancor.
Take (from) me the life (still/now).

Poetic Equivalent

Take away my life, cruel skies. If you must steal my heart, take my life. Deny me the light of day, pitiless realms. If you are glad to see my sadness, take away my life.

Comparative Performances

Listen to the historical recordings of Italian tenor Carlo Bergonzi (1924–2014) and Canadian tenor Jon Vickers (1925–2015). Compare these performances with two modern performances by qualified singers. What are the differences in the sound ideal of the performances? Do you hear differences in the approach to diction by any of the singers?

Alessandro Parisotti (1853–1913)

Giovanni Battista Pergolesi (1710–1730) was a choirboy, violinist, and student of Francesco Durante at the Naples Conservatory. He wrote a comic intermezzo entitled *La Serva Padrona* that remains popular today. His sacred work for female voices, "Stabat Mater," continues in the choral repertory. For many decades, the aria "Se Tu M'ami" was thought to have been his work. In recent years, the work has been attributed to Alessando Parisotti (1853–1913), an Italian composer and music editor. Listen and create a phonetic transcription of the text.

Comparative Listening

"Se Tu M'ami"

Before you listen, implement your dictation strategies:

1. Spellings: Look for IPA spelling you already know such as the articles *la, il,* and *gli*; auxiliary verb *sei*; conjunction *con*; prepositions *de'/del/della/degli, per,* and *a*; and pronouns *tu, me, tuoi, tuo, ti, io,* and *mi.* Mark them with the IPA symbols you expect the singer to use.

2. Familiar Words: Mark the words you may already have encountered in your study of Italian such as *gentil pastor, dolor, diletto, amor, soggetto, rosa, oggi, giglio,* and *fiori.*

3. Rhyming Words: Follow down the right side of the text to identify rhymes such as *sospiri/martiri*, *pastor/amor*, *soletto/soggetto*, *riamar/ingannar*, *porporina/spina*, *sceglierà/sprezzera*, *consiglio/giglio*, and *seguirò/spresserò*. If they are to rhyme, you must use the same vowel symbol for each rhyming pair.

4. Repeating Words: Study the text for common words that repeat such as *per me* and *pastor/pastorello*. Be sure that you use the same IPA symbols for each repetition.

5. Exceptional Words: Notice the apocopated (shortened for sake of rhyme and rhythm) words: *sol* (only), *dolor* (sadness), and *doman* (tomorrow).

Se tu m'ami, se tu sospiri
If you me love, if you sigh

Sol per me, gentil pastor:
Only for me, gentle shepherd,

Ho dolor de' tuoi martiri,
I have sadness for your martyrdom (torment)

Ho diletto del tuo amor:
I have delight in your love:

Ma se pensi che soletto
But if you think that only

Io ti debba riamar,
I you must only have,

Pastorello, sei soggetto
Little shepherd, you are (the) subject

Facilemente a t'ingannar.
Easily to yourself deceive.

Bella rosa porporina
(The) beautiful rose crimson

Oggi Silvia sceglierà,
Today Silvia will choose,

Con la scusa della spina
With the excuse of a thorn

Doman poi la sprezzerà.
Tomorrow, then, it she may despise.

Ma degli uomini il consiglio
But of the men's (the) advice (on the advice of men)

Io per me non seguirò,
I for me not will follow.

Non perché mi piace il giglio
Not because me pleases the lily

Gli altri fiori sprezzerò.
The other flowers I do not despise.

Se tu m'ami . . .

Poetic Equivalent

If you love me, sigh only for me, gentle shepherd, you have my sympathy for your torment. I am delighted that you love me, but please do not think that you are the only subject of my interest. Upon the advice of wise men, I will follow what pleases me. What one likes one day can be distasteful another. Because one likes lilies, it does not mean that one dislikes all other flowers.

Comparative Performances

Listen to performances by men and women such as the historical performance of tenor Tito Schipa (1939) and soprano Angela Gheorghiu (2004). You might find it insightful to experience the performance of mezzo soprano Joyce DiDonato singing the aria in an arrangement for jazz ensemble created by Craig Terry. Is the work more effective in the voice of one gender or the other in your opinion?

Stefano Donaudy (1879–1925)

If Enrico Caruso, a world-famous tenor, had not performed one of the arias written by Stefano Donaudy on texts by his brother, Alberto, the singing world might never have known of the *36 Arie in Stile Antiche* (*36 Arias in the Old Style*). The Donaudy brothers were Sicilian, born of a French father and an Italian mother. Stefano Donaudy was educated at the conservatory in Palermo, Italy. He wrote operatic works on libretti created by his brother and a symphonic poem. Below you will find an aria by Stefano Donaudy on an anonymous text entitled "Sento nel Core" ("I Feel in My Heart"). The text was set by another Sicilian composer of an earlier time, Alessandro Scarlatti (1660–1725). The Scarlatti and Donaudy settings are very different in key, sentiment, and musical gesture. Use your strategies to conquer the text. Listen critically to the contrasting musical settings by Scarlatti and Donaudy.

Comparative Listening

"Sento nel Core"

Before you listen, implement your dictation strategies:

1. Spellings: Look for IPA spellings you already know such as the article *una*; auxiliary verbs *è* and *sarà*; preposition *nel*; and pronoun *mia*.

2. Familiar Words: Look for words you recognize such as *core, certo, dolore, pace, alma*, and *amore*.

3. Rhyming Words: Follow down the right side of the text to identify rhymes such as *core/dolore*, *pace/face*, *splende/accende*, and *va/sarà*.

4. Expressive Possibilities: Circle the words that invite expression such as *splende*, *l'alma accende*, *non è amore*, and *amor sarà*.

Sento nel core certo dolore,

I feel in my heart (a) certain/kind of distress/pain

Che la mia pace turbando va.

That (the) my peace disturbing goes (makes),

Splende una face che l'alma accende,

Shines a torch which the soul fires up/inflames,

Se non è amore, amor sarà.

If not (it) is love, love it will be.

Poetic Equivalent

I feel in my heart a sensation that disturbs my peace. My soul is aflame as by a torch. If this is not yet love, it will become (love).

Comparative Settings

Listen to recordings of "Sento nel Core" by Scarlatti and "Sento nel Core" by Stefano Donaudy. Study the differences. There are contrasts to note in key, form, melodic contour, and harmonic treatment.

Discussion Questions

1. What is the mood of the setting by Scarlatti?
2. What is the mood of the setting by Stefano Donaudy?
3. From listening to the Donaudy setting, do you believe the composer was aware of the earlier setting by Scarlatti? If so, why? If not, why not?
4. Which setting do you prefer? Why?
5. How does the key help you understand the composer's point of view? What do you learn from the melodic contours?

Italian Diction First Presentation Repertoire List

Below is a list of works to be assigned for the first presentations in Italian diction. The word-by-word translations and poetic equivalents of the works given below are readily available in anthologies and online. Using the resources, each student will create a phonetic transcription of the assigned aria, a word-by-word translation, and a poetic equivalent.

Per la Gloria D'adororavi	Giovanni Battista Bononcini
Alma del Core	Antonio Caldara
Comme Raggio di Sole	Antonio Caldara
Sebben, Crudele	Antonio Caldara
Vittoria Mio Core	Giacomo Carissimi
Non Posso Disperar	Salvatore DeLuca
Danza, Danza	Francesco Durante
Vergin Tutto Amor	Francesco Durante
Caro Mio Ben	Giuseppe Giordani
O del Mio Dolce	Christoph Willibald von Gluck
Che Fiero Costume	Giovanni Legrenzi
Pur Dicesti, o Bocca	Antonio Lotti
Il Mio Bel Foco	Benedetto Marcello
Lasciatemi Morire	Claudio Monteverdi
Nel Cor Piu Non Mi Sento	Giovanni Paisiello
Nina	attr. Giovanni Battista Pergolesi
Gia il Sole	Alessandro Scarlatti
Le Violette	Alessandro Scarlatti
O Cessate di Piargarmi	Alessandro Scarlatti
Se Florindo e Fedele	Alessandro Scarlatti
Sento nel Core	Alessandro Scarlatti
Pieta, Signore!	Alessandro Stradella
Tu lo Sai	Giuseppe Torelli
Star Vicino	Anonymous

Italian Vocal Music in the Nineteenth Century

In the Italian culture, the opera holds a central place. For use in chamber music, the *canzone* (song) and its diminutive, the *canzonetta*, the *romanza* (ballad) and the *arietta* (little aria) were works of a smaller scale. Neapolitan songs (*canzoni napolitane*) are the popular form perpetuated by singer and teacher Francesco Paolo Tosti (1846–1916).

As opera grew, there were clear delineations between the *opera seria*, the opera with a serious or tragic plot, and the *opera buffa*, its comic neighbor. Vocal technique was also growing at a rapid pace. Teachers of the *bel canto* singing styles developed useful skills for instilling the vocal "fireworks" necessary to meet compositional demands. Gioacchino Antonio Rossini (1792–1868), Gaetano Donizetti (1797–1848), and Vincenzo Bellini (1801–1835) were instrumental in designing an operatic form called the "*bel canto* opera," meaning operatic writing that featured opportunities for singers to display their technical agility. Giuseppe Verdi (1813–1901), a very powerful force in Italian political as well as artistic life, called for a "*verismo*" or "honesty" in the operatic idiom. He believed that the skilled singer should also act the role convincingly. Verdi's expectations for a singer-actor transformed the world of opera, placing some repertoire out of the reach of younger singers. Included here is a *romanza* (ballad) for you to enjoy.

Gioachino Antonio Rossini (1792–1868)

A singer, Rossini composed opera from an early age. His comic opera *Il Barbiere di Siviglia* (The Barber of Seville) brought him fame very early. He married a talented mezzo soprano named Isabella Colbran, who served as his muse and advisor. You may also be interested in Colbran's compositions. Ornamented phrases from her pen are likely to remind you of similar passages in Rossini's work. Rossini created multiple settings using the following text by Pietro Metastasio (1698–1782). Listen to three of them and create a phonetic transcription.

Comparative Listening

"Aragonese," "Il Risentimento," and "Bolero"

Before you listen, implement your dictation strategies:

1. Spellings: Look for IPA spellings you already know such as the articles *il*, and *la*; prepositions *del*, *in*, *per*, and *al*; and pronouns *mi*, *mia*, *io*, *lo*, *me*, and *mio*.
2. Familiar Words: Look for words you may recognize such as *sorte*, *cara*, *crudel*, *amor*, *bramo*, and *ancor*.
3. Rhyming Words: Follow down the right side of the text to identify rhymes such as *me/fede* and *ancor/amor*.
4. Repeating Words: Study the text for words that repeat such as *t'ami/t'amo*, *così*, and *ancor*.
5. Expressive Possibilities: Circle the words that invite expression such as *sorte amara*, *offesi farmi penar*, *ingrate*, *sincero amor*, *vindici*, *sdegno*, and *si*.

Mi lagnerò tacendo della mia sorte amara,

Me will languish silently in my situation bitter,

Ma ch'io non t'ami, o cara, non lo sperar da me.

But that I not you love, oh dear (one), not it to hope for me.

Crudel! in che t'offesi farmi penar così.

Cruel (one)! In that you are offended makes me to suffer so.

Come potesti ingrate mancar cosi di fede
How can you ungrateful lack such of faith

È questa la mercede al mio sincero amor.
Is this the reward of my sincere love.

Crudel in che t'offesi farmi penar così.
Cruel (one)! In that you are offended makes me to suffer so.

Ah eppur de' torti miei vindici i dei non bramo
Ah! Yet of the wrongs for my vindication of the gods not I yearn

sento che ancor io t'amo che non mi sdegno ancor.
I feel that still I you love who not me scorn still.

Crudel t'amo ancor, io t'amo ancor, si.
Cruel one! I love you, I love you still, yes!

Poetic Equivalent

I will languish in silence over my bitter situation. If only I did not love you, oh cruel one! There is clearly no hope for me. What have I done that has so offended you? Why do you make me suffer? I don't believe that I could win you back, even if the gods themselves were to forgive me. I shall love you still, even though you scorn me. Yes, I shall love you still.

Comparative Settings

Rossini set this text several times, each with a different title. Compare the settings titled "Aragonese" and "Il Risentimento" with the one entitled "Bolero." Consider what might have attracted Rossini to set this text many different ways. What does he express differently from one setting to another?

Gaetano Donizetti (1797–1848)

Born in Bergamo, Italy, Gaetano Donizetti grew up in poverty. With the generosity of a German mentor, Donizetti was able to realize his talent. His operas such as *L'elisir D'amore*, *Lucia di Lammermoor*, *La Fille du Régiment*, and *Don Pasquale* continue to be standard repertoire throughout the operatic world. Listen and create a phonetic transcription of the text.

Comparative Listening

"Me Voglio fà 'na Casa"

Before you listen, implement your dictation strategies:

1. Spellings: Because this *canzone napoletana* is in Neapolitan dialect, you will need to note the deviations from the normal sounds of Italian with which you have become accustomed. You will find the use of the schwa [ə] where you might expect a closed e [e]. Listen carefully and note the sounds you hear.

2. Familiar Words: Look for words you may recognize such as *voglio, casa, mare, ognuno dice,* and *sole.*

3. Rhyming Words: Follow down the right side of the text to identify rhymes such as *mare/fare.* Be sure to use the same IPA symbols to insure a perfect rhyme.

4. Repeating Words: Study the text for words that repeat such as *Tralla la le la* and *tra la la la.*

Me voglio fà 'na casa miezo mare

Me wants to make a house surrounded (by) the sea

fravecata de penne de pavune. Tralla la le la, tra la la la.

Made of feathers of peacocks. Tra la . . .

D'oro e d'argiento li scaline fare

Of gold and silver the stairs to make

e de prete preziuse li barcune. Tralla la le la, tra la la la.

And of stones precious the balconies. Tra la . . . .

Quanno Nennella mia se va a affacciare

When my Nennella me comes to lean out

ognuno (lo) dice, mo' sponta lu sole. Tra la la le la, tra la la la.

Everyone says, it has come out the sun. Tra la . . . .

Poetic Equivalent

I want to build a house made of peacock feathers and surrounded by the sea. The stairs will be made of silver and gold with balconies of other precious stones. When my Nennella comes to lean out from the balcony, everyone will say that the sun itself has risen. Tra la la!

Comparative Recordings

Compare the performances of the Italian tenors Pavarotti and Enrico Caruso (1873–1921). Both performers sang this folk song as encores at the conclusion of recitals. Listen also to more recent performances by qualified singers. How are the listening experiences the same? How are they different? What are the diction challenges of singing in Neapolitan dialect?

Vincenzo Bellini (1801–1835)

Born in Catania, Sicily, to a family of professional musicians, Vincenzo Bellini received his first music lessons at age 3. He became a composer whose works are noted for their sensitive, lilting melodies. His most famous *bel canto* operas include *Norma, La Sonnambula, I Puritani,* and *I Capuleti ed i Montecchi.* Bellini's operas continue to delight audiences. Below is an *arietta* (little aria) that displays the beautiful melodic essence of Bellini's artistry and pathos. Listen and create a phonetic transcription.

Comparative Listening

"Dolente Immagine di Fille Mia"
(From *Tre Ariette*, #2.)

<u>Before you listen, implement your dictation strategies:</u>

1. Spellings: Look for IPA spellings you already know such as the auxiliary verb *è*; prepositions *di, sul, de, ad,* and *in*; and pronouns *mia, mi,* and *io*.

2. Familiar Words: Look for words you may recognize such as *pianto, face, pace, ombra,* and *ardor*.

3. Rhyming Words: Follow down the right side of the text to identify rhymes such as *accanto/pianto, finor/ardor,* and *face/pace*. Be sure that each pair is given the same IPA spelling for the vowel sounds.

4. Repeating Words: Study the text for words that repeat such as *io* and *Fille/Fillide*.

5. Expressive Possibilities: Circle the words that invite expression such as *dolente, squallida, desideria, dirotto pianto, sacri giuri, riposa in pace, inestinguibile,* and *l'antico ardor*.

Dolente immagine di Fille mia

Sorrowful image of Phyllis mine

Perché si squallida mi siedi accanto?

Why so wretched me sit beside?

Che più desideri? Dirotto pianto

What more desire you? Streaming tears

Io sul tuo cenere versai finor.

I on your ashes poured so far.

Temi che immemore de' sacri giuri

Are you afraid that forgetting the sacred vows

Io posso accendermi ad altra face?

I can spark in me another flame?

Ombra di Fillide, riposa in pace;

Shadow of Phyllis, repose in peace;

È inestinguibile l'antico ardor.

It is inextinguishable, the old ardor (passion).

Poetic Equivalent

Sorrowful image of my Phyllis, why sit you so miserably at my side? What do you want? I have wept all my tears upon your ashes by now. Do you fear that I will forget our sacred vows? That I might someday love another? Spirit of Phyllis, you can rest in peace. Nothing can extinguish my passion for you. (Poet unknown)

Comparative Performances

It might be interesting to compare the performances of Renata Tebaldi (1922–2004), an Italian spinto, and the Italian mezzo soprano Bartoli. What differences do you hear in the Italian diction of these native speakers? Do you find their interpretations of the text different? In what ways are they similar?

Giuseppe Verdi (1813–1901)

From a simple background, Giuseppe Verdi grew to become the greatest Italian composer of his time. Fully active in political as well as cultural affairs, Verdi promoted the opera to new heights through his interest in a music drama that portrayed the action and the music on equal terms. Listen to this *romanza* (ballad) and create a phonetic transcription.

Comparative Listening

"In Solitaria Stanza"
(From *Sei Romanze*, # 3.)

Before you listen, implement your dictation strategies:

1. Spellings: Look for IPA spellings you already know such as the articles *il, le,* and *un'*; prepositions *in, per, alla,* and *dall,'*; and pronouns *io* and *voi.*
2. Familiar Words: Look for words you may recognize such as *labbro, voce, respiro, suon, beltà,* and *celeste.*
3. Rhyming Words: Follow down the right side of the text to identify rhymes such as *sen/svien, priva/estiva, rimote/puote,* and *intenerir/ordir.*
4. Expressive Possibilities: Circle the words that invite expression such as *solitaria stanza, senza voce/senza respire, deserta aiuola, mole narcisso svien, dall'affanno oppresso, vie rimote, rupi intenerir, beltà celeste,* and *un'altra Irene.*

In solitaria stanza langue per doglia atroce
In (a) solitary room (she) languishes in agony atrocious

Il labbro è senza voce, senz' respire il sen,
The lips are without voice, without breath the heart,

Come in deserta aiuola, che di rugiade è priva,
Like a deserted flowerbed, that of dew is deprived

Sotto alla vampa estiva molle narcisso svien.
Under the heat of summer (a) feeble narcissus fades

Io, dall'affanno oppresso, corro per vie rimote
I, with anxiety oppressed, run on paths remote

E grido in suon che puote le rupi intenerir
And scream in sounds that could the rocks soften

Salvate, o dei pietosi, quella beltà celeste;
Save, o gods merciful, this beauty celestial;

Voi forse non sapreste un'altra Irene ordir.
You perhaps may not know another Irene to create.

Poetic Equivalent

In a lonely room, she languishes in agony. She cannot speak or breathe, as a flower in an abandoned flower bed that fades in the heat of the summer sun. I run to her, screaming so loudly the very rocks should soften in response. Dear gods, be merciful to this celestial beauty. You may not know how to create another like Irene.

Comparative Performances

There are many opportunities for you to compare performances of this work. It might be interesting to listen to two dramatic voices, such as Sondra Radvanovsky (b. 1969) and Montserrat Caballè (1933–2018). Compare the diction and the interpretation of both sopranos. Does this experience help you define what *verismo* means?

Italian Diction Final Presentation Repertoire List

Below is a list of suggested works appropriate for the final presentation projects in Italian diction. Each student will prepare the text with its word-by-word translation, poetic equivalent, and a thorough program note. The program note should place the work in time and give its historical and musical context. Important biographical information regarding the librettist or poet and composer are to be included. These materials will be submitted to the instructor for correction and grading. The materials will be duplicated for class use during the presentations. *Note.* Repertoire assignments should be approved by the studio teacher, who may suggest other selections for this project.

Il Bacio	Luigi Arditi
Il Fervido Desiderio	Vincenzo Bellini
Il Zeffiro	Vincenzo Bellini
Malinconia, Ninfa Gentile	Vincenzo Bellini
Quando Verrà Quell Dì	Vincenzo Bellini
"Vaga Luna"	Vincenzo Bellini

Ah Mai Non Cessate	Stefano Donaudy
Amor Mi Fa Cantare	Stefano Donaudy
Amorosi	Stefano Donaudy
Come L'allodoletta	Stefano Donaudy
O del Mio Amato Ben	Stefano Donaudy
Sento nel Core	Stefano Donaudy
Spirate Pur	Stefano Donaudy
Berceuse ("Questo mio figlio")	Gaetano Donizetti
Il Giglio e la Rosa	Gaetano Donizetti
Leonora	Gaetano Donizetti
Se a Te D'intorno Scherzo	Gaetano Donizetti
Deh Vieni Non Tardar" (*Le Nozze di Figaro*)	Wolfgang Amadeus Mozart
"Porgi Amor" (*Le Nozze di Figaro*)	Wolfgang Amadeus Mozart
"Un Moto di Gioia" (*Le Nozze di Figaro*)	Wolfgang Amadeus Mozart
"Vedrai Carino" (*Don Giovanni*)	Wolfgang Amadeus Mozart
"Una Donna Quindici Anni" (*Così Fan Tutte*)	Wolfgang Amadeus Mozart
"Voi Che Sapete" (*Le Nozze di Figaro*)	Wolfgang Amadeus Mozart
"Non So Più" (*Le Nozze di Figaro*)	Wolfgang Amadeus Mozart
"È Amore un Ladroncello" (*Così Fan Tutte*)	Wolfgang Amadeus Mozart
"Deh Vieni alla Finestra" (*Don Giovanni*)	Wolfgang Amadeus Mozart
"Donna Mie, la Fate a Tanti" (*Così Fan Tutte*)	Wolfgang Amadeus Mozart
Dimenticar, Ben Mio	Amilcare Ponchielli
L'Eco	Amilcare Ponchielli
Sogno D'or	Giacomo Puccini
Sole e Amore	Giacomo Puccini
E L'uccellino	Giacomo Puccini
Chi M'ascolta il Canto Usato	Gioachino Rossini
Ch'io Mai Vi Possa	Gioachino Rossini
Al'aria Libera	Francesco Paolo Tosti
Canto Abruzzese	Francesco Paolo Tosti
Ideale	Francesco Paolo Tosti

Sogno	Francesco Paolo Tosti
Deh, Pietoso, o Addolorata	Giuseppe Verdi
Stornello	Giuseppe Verdi

Conclusion

In a letter written in 1766 to Francesco Giovanni di Chastellux, a member of the cultural elite, librettist Pietro Metastasio (1698–1782) wrote, "We are, then, unanimous in believing that music is an ingenious, marvelous, delectable, and enchanting art which, by itself, is capable of working miracles. But when it allies itself with poetry and makes good use of its enormous wealth, it is able not only to confirm and express all the changes of the human art but also to illumine and increase them with its imitations" (Weisstein, 1964). The art form we have inherited as singers comes from the traditions of the Italian Renaissance and its attempts to honor what human beings uniquely achieve through the union of text and music. The flowing legato line is the basis of the Italian language and its music. The purity of its vowel sounds and the ease of its consonants are hallmarks that make *bel canto* the beautiful singing style we hold as the standard for our art form.

References

Alighieri, D. (2003). *The divine comedy* (J. Ciardi, Trans., p. 162). New York, NY: New American Books.

Alighieri, D. (2013). *Vita nuova* (A. Mortimer, Trans., pp. 76–77). Surrey, UK: Alma Classics.

Bishop, M. (2001). Petrarch. In J. H. Plumb (Ed.), *The Italian renaissance* (p. 168). New York, NY: Mariner.

Bishop, M. (2001). Petrarch. In J. H. Plumb (Ed.), *The Italian renaissance* (p. 174). New York, NY: Mariner.

Boccaccio (2013). Life of Dante. In *Vita nuova* (A. Mortimer, Trans., App. II, p. 227). Surrey, UK: Alma Classics.

Bolt, R. (2006). *The librettist of Venice: The remarkable life of Lorenzo da Ponte, Mozart's poet, Casanova's friend and Italian opera's impresario in America* (pp. 11–12). New York, NY: Bloomsbury.

Celenza, C. (2017). *Petrarch: Everywhere a wanderer* (p. 19). London, UK: Reaktion Books.

Celenza, C. (2017). *Petrarch: Everywhere a wanderer* (p. 31). London, UK: Reaktion Books.

Johnson, K. (2011). *Georgics*, 3 (Virgil, Trans., p. 431, Lines 291–292). New York, NY: Penguin Classics Library.

Mendelsohn, D. (2018, October 15). Epic fail? *The New Yorker*, p. 87.

Shaw, P. (2015). *Reading Dante: From here to eternity* (p. 100). New York, NY: Liveright.

Shaw, P. (2015). *Reading Dante: From here to eternity* (p. 131). New York, NY: Liveright.

Weisstein, U. (1964). *The essence of opera* (p. 101). New York, NY: W. W. Norton.

Williams, C. (1943). *The figure of Beatrice* (p. 40). Berkeley, CA: Aprocryphile Press.

4

German

The Sounds of German

The vowels of the German language are more numerous than in Italian. The pure vowels appear in single and extended forms. The diphthongs give equal time to each of the two sounds. The German language includes vowel sounds that are present in English such as [ɪ], [ʊ], and [ə] but not in Italian. The German language also contains vowel sounds called "mixed" or "umlaut" sounds [y:], [ʏ], [ø], and [œ] that create new sounds for you to learn. As you develop skills to speak and sing the German language properly, you will notice that the sounds of German emanate "in front of" the Italian language. To speak German well, you use your articulators, namely, the lips, tongue, and palate, very actively. Classified as an Anglo-Saxon language, German words have heavy/light accentuation as English words do. Learning to give emphasis to the heavily accented elements is generally an easy task. Learning to resist an emphasis of the lighter elements is a greater challenge. German is a language rich in consonants that are juxtaposed with vowels. Concentrate on singing the vowels. Articulate the consonants as briskly as possible. This practice will free your tongue and lips for an easy production of the consonants, consonant clusters, and vowels of the German language. The following are the vowel sounds in German based upon the authorative text by Theodor Siebs, *Deutsche Aussprache* (German Pronuncation) and provided in the International Phonetic Alphabet (Siebs, 2011). Alternate phonetic spellings in common usage accompany a sample word for each sound.

Single Vowels or Monophthongs

The single vowels of the German language are:

[ɑ:]* [a:] *long, also called "dark"*

The letter "a" before "h"	B<u>a</u>hnen [bɑ:nen]	*roads, pathways*
The letter "a" doubled	S<u>aa</u>l [zɑ:l]	*hall, assembly room*
The letter "a" before a single consonant	S<u>a</u>ge [zɑ:gə]	*legend, myth*

[a] *short*

The letter "a" before two or more consonants	Gesang [gə'zaŋ]	*singing, song*

[e:] *long and closed*

The letter "e" before "h"	Sehnen [ze:nən]	*longing*
The letter "e" doubled	Seele [ze:lə]	*soul*
The letter "e" before a single consonant	Leben [le:bən]	*life*

[ɛ] *short and open*

The letter "e" before two or more consonants	Ende ['ɛndə]	*end*

[ɛ] *short and open*

The umlaut "ä" before two or more consonants	Nächte [nɛçtə]	*nights*
The letter "e" in prefixes	Erleben [ɛr'le:bən]	*experience*
	Vergeben [vɛr'ge:bən]	*forgive*

[ɛ:] *long and open*

The umlaut "ä" before "h"	ähnlich [ɛ:lɪç]	*similar, resembling*
The umlaut "ä" before a single consonant	Tränen [trɛ:nən]	*tears*

[i:] *long and closed*

The letter "i" before "h"	ihnen [i:nən]	*them, to them*
The letter "i" before a single consonant	Finale [fi:nalə]	*finale, ending*
The letter "i" before "e" in most situations	Siegen [zi:gən]	*triumph*

[ɪ] *short and open*

The letter "i" before two or more consonants	Singen [zɪŋən]	*singing, to sing*

[o:] *long and closed*

The letter "o" before "h"	Sohn [zo:n]	*son*
The letter "o" doubled	Boot [bo:t]	*boat*
The letter "o" before a single consonant	Bote ['bo:tə]	*message, messenger*

[ɔ] *short and open*

The letter "o" before two or more consonants	Wonne ['vɔnə]	*bliss*

[u:] *long and closed*

The letter "u" before "h"	Ruhe [ru:ə]	*rest, peace*
The letter "u" before a single consonant	rufen [ru:fən]	*call, call out*

[ʊ] *short and open*

The letter "u" before two or more consonants	Kunst [kʊnst]	*art*

[y:] *long and closed*

The umlaut "ü" before "h"	Mühe [my:ə]	*effort*
The umlaut "ü" before a single consonant	Süden [zy:dən]	*south*
The letter "y" in words derived from Greek	Mythe [my:tə]	*myth*

[Y] *short and open*

The umlaut "ü" before two or more consonants	künstlich [kYnstlıç]	*plastic, man-made*

[ø] *long and closed*

The umlaut "ö" before "h"	Söhnen ['zønən]	*sons*
The umlaut "ö" before one consonant	böse ['bøzə]	*angry*

[œ] *short and open*

The umlaut "ö" before two or more consonants	östlich [œstlıç]	*eastward*
[ə] The "schwa," unstressed final, some prefixes	Liebe ['li:bə]	*love*
	Gebet [gə'be:t]	*prayer*

*Indicates the pronunciation preferred by Siebs. In general, a vowel is long and closed before "h," a single consonant, or when doubled. It is short and open before two or more consonants. There are exceptions to these rules for closed and open vowels. See the online resources associated with the book for a complete list.

Diphthongs

The diphthongs of the German language are:

[ae] [ɑe]*	Stein [ʃtaen] or [ʃtɑen]	*stone*
	Mai [mae] or [mɑe]	*the month of May*
[ao]	Traum [trɑom]	*dream*
[ɔø]* or [ɔʏ]		
The sound of "äu"	Träume ['trɔømə] or ['trɔʏmə]	*dreams*
The sound of "eu"	Heute ['hɔøtə] or ['hɔʏtə]	*today*

*Indicates the pronunciation preferred by Siebs.

Glide

The German language contains one glide and it is:

[j]	ja ['ja]	*Yes!*

Fricative Consonants

The fricative consonants of the German language have similar sounds to their English equivalents:

Unvoiced [f]	fern [fɛrn]	*far*	Voiced [v]	Vase* ['vazə]	*vase*
Unvoiced [s]	dies' [dis]	*this*	Voiced [z]	Singen [zɪŋən]	*singing, to sing*
Unvoiced [ʃ]	Schale ['ʃalə]	*shell*	Aspirate [h]	Haus [haos]	*house*

*The word "Vase" in German represents a rare occasion when the letter "v" is spoken as [v]. The sound [f] is represented in German more frequently with the letters "f" or "v." The sound [v] is generally spelled with the letter "w." Words like wieviel [vi:'fi:l] (*how many?*) or Volkswagen [fɔlks'vagən] (*Volkswagen*) may help you remember that "f" and "v" are usually pronounced [f] and "w" is pronounced [v] in German.

The consonant cluster "ch" has two possible sounds.

◆ One is called the "ich-laut" and is noted in IPA with the symbol [ç]. The sound occurs when "ch" follows "ä," "e," "i," "ö," "ü," or a consonant. To create the unvoiced "ich-laut" [ç], whisper the English word *he*. The sound is named for the word *ich* [ɪç] (*I*).

◆ The other is called the "ach-laut" and is noted in IPA with the symbol [x]. The "ach-laut" [x] occurs after the letters "a," "o," and "u" and requires a gentle motion of the back of the tongue toward the velum. It gains its name from the exclamation *Ach!* [ax] (*Oh!*).

Affricative Consonants

The affricative consonant of the German language has a similar sound to its English equivalent:[ts], represented by the letter "z" as in z̲ehn [tseːn] (*ten*) but pronounced as in *tents.*

Lateral Consonant

As in English, the German language contains one lateral consonant. It is:

[l] L̲iebe ['liːbə] *love*

The nasal consonants of the German language have similar sounds to their English equivalents:

[m]	M̲usik [muˈziːk]	*music*		[mm]	Schlum̲m̲er [ˈʃlʊmər]	*slumber*
[n]	n̲ein! [naen]	*No!*		[ŋ]	Klan̲g [ˈklaŋ]	*sound*

The stop plosive and stop consonants of the German language have similar sounds to their English equivalents.

Unvoiced Stop Plosive Consonants

[p]	P̲appe [ˈpapə]	*cardboard*		[t]	T̲abak [ˈtabak]	*tobacco*
[k]	K̲ern [kɛrn]	*seed*				

Voiced Stop Consonants:

[b]	B̲oot [boːt]	*boat*		[d]	D̲ezember [deˈtsɛmbər]	*December*
[g]	g̲ehen [geːən]	*go*				

Note. At the ends of German words, the letters "b" and "d" change their pronounciation as follows: "b" becomes [p]. The word for *love*, *Liebe* [liːbə], in its apocopated form "Lieb" is pronounced [liːp]. The letter "d" at the end of a word is always pronounced [t] as in the word for *and*, *und* [ʊnt]. In certain circumstances, the letter "g" at the end of word is pronounced [k], as in the word for *day*, *Tag̲* [tak].

The letter "r" is always rolled in German, according to Siebs. There are situations in which the "r" appears at the end of a word or element (e.g., prefix, compound word) where little time is allowed. When this occurs, some references suggest [ʁ] as the appropriate symbol. It is important to acknowledge the "r" in all words. It contains expressive power and brings color to the sounds that follow.

Single "r"	Doubled "r"	Concluding "r"
[r] Herz ['hɛrts] *heart*	[rr] herrlich ['hɛrrlɪç] *glorious*	[ʁ] ihr [iːʁ] or [iːr] *her*

Note. When singing a word such as *besser,* pronounced ['bɛsər] (*better*), you may be asked to modify the schwa [ə] to the vowel [ɛ] and the "r" to [ʁ] to improve the tuning of the syllable. This would follow the suggestions for pronunciation found in Siebs.

Onset of Open Vowels

Because every word beginning with an open vowel requires a separation from the sound of the previous word, the following symbol is given: [ʔ].

Diction in context example: The title of a motet by Johannes Brahms, "Ich aber bin elend," would be pronounced: [ʔɪç ʔ abər bɪn ʔˈeːlɛnt].

Parts of Speech and Elements of Grammar

The structure of the German language developed as Indo-Europeans settled west of the Baltic Sea. Old High German and Saxon are early iterations of the language. Spoken Middle High German, dating from about 1050 to 1350, was a mingling of regional dialects. Throughout these early periods, Latin was the dominant written language. The period from 1350 to 1600 is notable because of the invention of the printing press by Johannes Gutenberg (ca. 1440). Soon there were four different "printer languages" that equated to specific German dialects such as Austro-Bavarian, Schwabien, Rhenisch, and Swiss. It was Martin Luther who standardized what is now thought of as High German. In 1522, Luther, a linguist and scholar, translated the New Testament from Hebrew and eventually translated the entire Bible, updating the German language as he edited his work. Luther's printed writings spread rapidly throughout what was known as the German-speaking world, solidifying the German language into a form known today called *Hochdeutsch* or High German.

German regional dialects appear in folksongs such as the arrangements for solo voice by Brahms. The best known are "Da Unten Im Tale" and "Och Mod'r Ich Well 'en Ding Han!" Be aware that during the reign of Louis XIV (1643–1715) in France, the German aristocracy took on the manners of French culture. We know that French was spoken at the court of Friedrich II of Prussia (1712–1786) in Potsdam. Do not be surprised to find a French word mingled amid German phrases or idioms from time to time.

The grammar of German is somewhat complex. Related to Latin, the nouns decline and the verbs conjugate through inflected endings. At first sight, the rules may be intimidating. You need not conquer the grammatical rules. Strive to recognize the "signals" for the parts of speech and syntactic elements. For the repertoire you are likely to sing, a word-by-word translation and a poetic equivalent will be readily available through printed and online sources. The information below is intended to help you see the building blocks that form the language you will sing.

Elements of Sentences

In German, the structure of sentences differs from English in important ways. The German language contains verbs that are "separable" or "inseparable." A separable verb is made up of a verb and its prefix such as *anfangen* [an'faŋən], meaning *begin*. "Fang an, fange wieder an" ("An eine Äolharfe"/Mörike, Brahms, and Wolf) means "begin, begin again." As you see, the parts of the verb are separated. An inseparable verb contains a prefix that cannot stand on its own such as *verlieben* [fɛr'liːbən] (*to be in love with*). "Ich bin verliebt, doch eben nicht in Dich!" (*Italienisches Liederbuch*/Heyse and Wolf) means "I am in love, just not with you!" Because the German language has nouns that "decline" or change their endings based on their use in a sentence, it is essential that you become familiar with sentence elements. The more you recognize the elements and the changes in spelling that indicate their various uses, the better you will understand what sentences in German mean.

Nouns

Nouns are easily identified in the German language, because nouns are *always* capitalized. German nouns have gender and number. There are three genders: masculine, feminine, and neuter. Gender does not always derive from the gender of a person or object. To divide and conquer German texts, it will help you to recognize the word endings that signal gender. Here is a list of characteristics that can be used to identify the gender of a noun.

The following endings <u>usually</u> indicate masculine nouns:

-en [ən]	der Wag<u>en</u>	*cart, wagon, car*	-er [ɛr] [ɛʁ]	der Säng<u>er</u>	*male singer*
-ich [ɪç]	der Tepp<u>ich</u>	*carpet*	-ling [ɪŋ]	der Früh<u>ling</u>	*springtime*
-iker [ɪkɛr]	der Musik<u>er</u>	*musician*	-ig [ɪç]	der Kön<u>ig</u>	*king*

The following endings <u>usually</u> indicate feminine nouns:

-e [ə]	die Lieb<u>e</u>	*love*	-heit [haet]	die Kind<u>heit</u>	*childhood*
-ie [iː]	die Melod<u>ie</u>	*melody*	-ik [iːk]	die Mus<u>ik</u>	*music*
-ei [ae]	die Kantor<u>ei</u>	*chamber choir*	-in [ɪn]	die Säger<u>in</u>	*female singer*
-ion [i'on]	die Relig<u>ion</u>	*religion*	-keit [kaet]	die Einsam<u>keit</u>	*loneliness*
-schaft [ʃaft]	die Leiden<u>schaft</u>	*passion*	-tät [tɛːt]	die Qualit<u>ät</u>	*quality*
-ung [ʊŋ]	die Wohn<u>ung</u>	*living quarters*	-ur [uːr]	die Nat<u>ur</u>	*nature*

The following endings <u>usually</u> indicate neuter nouns:

-chen [çən]	das Mädchen	*maiden*	-lein [laen]	das Blümelein	*little flower*
-ma [mɑ]	das Thema	*theme/topic*	-ment [mɛnt]	das Firmament	*firmament*
-o [o]	das Radio	*radio*	-um [uːm]	das Königtum	*monarchy*

Masculine Nouns

The general categories for nouns identified as masculine are (a) male persons such as *der Junge* (*boy*); (b) large animals such as *der Bär* (*bear*); (c) the days of the week, the months of the year, the seasons, and points of the compass; and (d) words that derive from infinitives, such as *der Besuch* (*the visit*) derived from *besuchen* (*to visit*).

Feminine Nouns

The general categories for nouns identified as feminine are (a) female persons such as *die Mutter* (*the mother*); (b) small animals such as *die Ente* (*the duck*); (c) flowers such as *die Rose* (*the rose*); (d) numerals such as *die Eins* (*one*); and (e) rivers such as *die Elbe* (*Elbe River*), with the exception of *Der Rhein* (*Rhine River*).

Masculine and Feminine Nouns

When indicating title, profession or nationality, the ending "–in" added to a masculine noun identifies the noun as a female person.

der Sänger (male)/die Sängerin (female)   *Singer*

Neuter Nouns

The general categories for nouns identified as neuter are (a) young persons such as *das Baby* (*the baby*); (b) continents and countries such as *das Europa* (*Europe*) and *das Deutschland* (*Germany*); and (c) metals and materials such as *das Gold* (*gold*) and *das Holz* (*wood*).

In English, most singular nouns become plural by adding an "s" to the end of the noun. In German, the article <u>and</u> the noun may change their spellings to indicate more than one. The nouns and their articles have specific spellings based upon number (singular or plural) and function in a sentence or clause. Familiarize yourself with the various ways to recognize gender and number. Knowledge of the endings and their significance will strengthen your ability to express the words appropriately.

Number

The plural form of a singular noun may be formed in one of several ways:

1. By changing the article and adding "-s" to the noun: das Baby/*die* Babys (*baby/babies*)

2. By changing the article only: der Wagen/*die* Wagen (*wagon* or *car/wagons* or *cars*)

3. By changing the article and the noun: der Vater/*die* Väter (*father/fathers*)

4. By changing the article and adding "-en" to the noun: das Herz/die Herzen (*heart/hearts*)

5. By adding "-n": die Lampe/die Lampen (*lamp/lamps*)

6. By changing the vowel to an umlaut and adding "-e": die Nacht/die Nächte (*night/nights*)

7. By changing the article from singular to plural, changing the vowel to an umlaut and adding "-r": der Wald/die Wälder (*forest/forests*)

In summary, plural forms of nouns are inconsistent. Some nouns add endings while others change their inner spelling. When in doubt, check the dictionary.

Compound Words

One of the most creative aspects of the German language is the capacity to expand or define meaning by combining words. This technique was used extensively during the fanciful time of the 19th century. Compound words use the gender of the last part of the word.

der Zauber + der Fluss = der Zauberfluss *magic river (of words)*
(Schubert/Goethe "Gretchen am Spinnrade")

die Liebe + das Weh = das Liebesweh *love's waves of pain*
(Robert Schumann/Heine "Die Lotosblume")

Pronouns

In German, pronouns have the same gender as the gender of the noun they replace. Because the gender of a noun is not necessarily the same as the person or object it represents, it is important that you keep in mind the gender of the noun a pronoun replaces.

Subject

ich [iç] *I*	du [du] *you*, singular/informal	er [eːr], sie, [ziː] es [ɛs] *he, she, it*
wir [wiːʁ] *we*	Ihr [iːʁ] *you*, plural	sie [ziː] *they*
	Sie [ziː] *You*, singular or plural/ formal	

Direct Object Pronouns

Masculine: ihn [iːn]   Feminine: sie [ziː]   Neuter: es [ɛs]

These pronouns represent respectively a masculine, feminine, or neuter person or thing that appears as the object of a verb.

Indirect Object Pronouns

Masculine: ihm [iːm]   Feminine: ihr [iːʁ] or [iːr]   Neuter: ihm [iːm]

These pronouns represent respectively a masculine, feminine or neuter person or thing that appears as the indirect object of a verb.

Possessive Pronouns

The possessive pronouns are:

mein [mɑen] *mine*   dein [dɑen] *yours*, singular/informal   sein [zɑen]   *his*

ihr [iːʁ]   *hers*   sein [zɑen] *its*   unser [ʊnzər] *our*

euer [ɔøər]   *yours*, plural/formal   ihr [iːʁ] or [iːr] *their*

Ihr [iːʁ]   *yours*, singular and plural formal

◆ Possessive pronouns are inflected in the following manner:

Case	Masculine	Feminine	Neuter	Plural
Nominative (Subject)	mein	meine	mein	meine
Accusative (Direct Object)	meinen	meine	mein	meine
Dative (Indirect Object)	meinem	meiner	meinem	meinen
Genitive (Possessive)	meines	meiner	meines	meiner

◆ Relative pronouns appear at the beginning of clauses to provide additional information about a person or thing mentioned earlier in the sentence. (Das Kind, das; meaning *the child, who*.)

◆ Interrogative pronouns are the equivalent of *who?* and *what?* in English. In German, *wer? wen?* and *wem?* are the interrogative pronouns that express *who?* as a subject, a direct object, or an indirect object, respectively. *Was?* meaning *what* has only one form. Interrogative pronouns do not change to express number or gender.

◆ Reflexive pronouns refer to a person connected to an action or topic. Reflexive pronouns function as direct objects, indirect objects, and objects of preposition. They inflect according to use. Reflexive pronouns "reflect" upon a person or thing the action of a verb. Reflexive pronouns are conjugated with verbs, such as *ich befinde mich* (literally, "I find myself") meaning "I am located."

Verbs

Present Indicative—Regular

In German, there is only one form of the present tense: Käthe singt = *Kathy sings* or *Kathy is singing*. Most infinitives end in "–en." The stem of the verb is the portion of the infinitive that appears before the "–en": singen = sing/en

ich singe	*I sing, I am singing*	wir singen	*we sing, we are singing*
du singst	*you sing (sing. informal)*	ihr singet	*you sing, you are singing (pl. informal)*
er, sie, es singt	*he, she, it sings, is singing*	sie singen	*they sing, they are singing*
Sie singen	*you sing, you are singing (formal, singular or plural)*		

Note. For an English speaker, the spelling of the word "singen" can be confusing. The word in German is pronounced [zɪŋːən] though it may be hyphenated in the music as "sin-gen."

Irregular Verbs

Irregular verbs change their stem or spelling in certain parts of the verb.

Examples: finden (*to find*), warten (*to wait*), regnen (*to rain*), heissen (*to be called*), reisen (*to travel*), tanzen (*to dance*), tragen (*to carry*), geben (*to give*), sehen (*to see*)

Auxiliary Verbs

Haben (*to have*)

ich habe [ɪç habə]	*I have*	wir haben [viːʁ habən]	*we have*
du hast [du hast]	*you have (sing. informal)*	ihr habt [iːʁ hapt]	*you have (pl. informal)*
er [eːr] sie [ziː] es [ɛs] hat [hat]	*he, she, it has*	sie haben [ziː habən]	*they have*
Sie haben [ziː habən]	*you have (formal, singular or plural)*		

Sein (*to be*)

ich bin [ɪç bɪn]	*I am*	wir sind [viːʁ zɪnt]	*we are*
du bist [du bɪst]	*you are (sing. informal)*	ihr seid [iːʁ zaet]	*you are (pl. informal)*
er, sie, es ist [eːr ˈɪst]	*he, she, it is*	sie sind [ziː zɪnt]	*they are*
Sie sind [ziː zɪnt]	*you are (formal, singular or plural)*		

◆ Simple Past Tense of Auxiliary Verbs

ich hatte ['hatə]	*I had*	wir hatten ['hatən]	*we had*
du hattest ['hatɛst]	*you had*	ihr hattet ['hatɛt]	*you had (pl. informal)*
er, sie, es hatte ['hatə]	*he, she, it had*	sie hatten ['hatən]	*they had*
Sie hatten ['hatən]	*you had (formal, singular or plural)*		
ich war ['var]	*I was*	wir waren ['varən]	*we were*
du warst ['varst]	*you were*	ihr wart ['vart]	*you were (pl. informal)*
er, sie, es war ['var]	*he, she, it was*	sie waren ['varən]	*they were*
Sie waren ['varən]	*you were (formal, singular or plural)*		

◆ Future Tense of Auxiliary Verbs

The future tense is formed by using the future of *werden* plus an infinitive.

Werden (*will* or *to become*)

ich werde ['ve:rdə]	*I will*	wir werden ['ve:rdən]	*we will*
du wirst ['vɪrst]	*you will (sing. informal)*	ihr werdet ['verdɛt]	*you will (pl. informal)*
er, sie, es wird ['vɪrt]	*he, she, it, will*	sie werden ['ve:rdən]	*they will*
Sie werden ['ve:rdən]	*you will (formal, singular or plural)*		

Modal Verbs

Modal verbs are a type of auxiliary verb that allows the speaker to express permission or capability. This verb form is used frequently to express poetic thought.

dürfen ['dʏrfən]	*be allowed to*	können [kœnən]	*be able to*
mögen [møgən]	*want to*	müssen [mʏsən]	*have to*
sollen [zɔlən]	*supposed to*	wollen [vɔlən]	*to want to*

Simple Past (Used for Storytelling)

Note the use of the letter "t" to indicate the simple past. Here are some verbs that appear frequently in poetry set to music:

◆ Simple Past of the Regular Verb:

Spielen (*to play*)

ich spielte [ʃpiːltə]	*I played*	wir spielten [ʃpiːltən]	*we played*
du spieltest [ʃpiːltəst]	*you played (sing. informal)*	ihr spieltet [ʃpiːltət]	*you played (pl. informal)*
er, sie, es spielte [ʃpiːltə]	*he, she, it played*	sie spielten[ʃpiːltən]	*they played*
Sie spielten [ʃpiːltən]	*you played (formal singular or plural)*		

◆ Simple Past of the Irregular Verb:

Gehen (*to go*)

ich ging [gɪŋ]	*I went*	wir gingen ['gɪŋən]	*we went*
du gingst ['gɪŋst]	*you went (sing.)*	ihr ginget ['gɪŋət]	*you went (pl.)*
er, sie, es ging [gɪŋ]	*he, she, it went*	sie gingen ['gɪŋən]	*they went*
Sie gingen ['gɪŋən]	*you played (formal, singular or plural)*		

Diction in Context Example of the Simple Past:

"Wir wandelten, wir zwei zusammen." *We strolled, the two of us together.*

(Brahms/text by Georg Friedrich Daumer, after a Hungarian text.)

Past Tense

The past tense is formed by using the appropriate helper verb (*haben* or *sein*) plus the past participle of the verb.

ich habe gesungen, gedacht, geschlafen	*I sang, I thought, I slept*
du bist gewandert, geflogen, geblieben	*you wandered, you flew, you remained*
sie hat gesehen, getragen, getanzt	*she saw, she carried, she danced*
er ist gestorben, gekommen, geboren	*he died* or *he is dead, he came, he was born*
es hat gefunden, geregnet, geschneit	*it found, it rained, it snowed*
wir sind gegangen, gefallen, geritten	*we went, we fell, we rode*
ihr habt gesehen, genommen, geholfen	*you have seen/saw, you have taken, you helped*
sie sind geschwommen, gelaufen, geworden	*they swam, they ran, they became*

Reflexive Verbs

Reflexive verbs consist of a main verb and a reflexive pronoun.

sich beeilen   *to hurry one's self*   sich freuen auf   *to look forward to*

Conditional and Subjunctive Verbs

These verbs express doubt, uncertainty or longing.

◆ Conditional: Wenn ich Geld hätte . . .   *If only I had money*
◆ Subjunctive: ich würde einen Ring kaufen   *I would buy a ring*

Adjectives

In English, adjectives do not change their form. In German, adjectives must agree in case, gender, and number with the noun they modify.

Descriptive adjectives in German are of two types: predicate or attributive.

◆ Predicate adjectives have the same form as given in the dictionary entry.
   Example: "Mein Liebster ist so <u>klein</u>" ("My beloved is so small") (H. Wolf/ *Italienisches Liederbuch*)

◆ The attributive ones change with the gender, case, and number of the noun they describe.
   Example: "Von <u>ewiger</u> Liebe" ("About eternal love") (J. Brahms)

Demonstrative Adjectives

In English, *this* and *that* are the singular demonstrative adjectives and *these* and *those* are the plural ones. In German, the stems are "dies-" meaning *this*, "jen-" meaning *that*, and "jed-" which means *every*.

Adverbs

Adverbs describe a verb, an adjective, or another adverb. In German, adverbs are invariable and should be memorized as vocabulary words.

Articles

Definite and indefinite articles are influenced by the gender of nouns. The article generally appears with the noun.

◆ Definite article: *the*

When used with subjects (nominative case):

der (masculine)	die (feminine)	das (neuter)
der Mann (*Man*)	*die* Frau (*Woman*)	*das* Kind (*Child*)

When used with direct objects (accusative case):

den Mann	*die* Frau	*das* Kind

When used with indirect objects (dative case):

dem Mann	*der* Frau	*dem* Kind

◆ Indefinite article: *a, an*

When used with subjects (nominative case):

ein	eine	ein
ein Mann	*eine* Frau	*ein* Kind

When used with direct objects (accusative case):

einen	eine	ein
einen Mann	*eine* Frau	*ein* Kind

When used with indirect objects (dative case):

einem Mann	*einer* Frau	*einem* Kind

When used to indicate possession (genitive case):

eines Mann	*einer* Frau	*eines/es* Kind

Comparatives and Superlatives

In German, comparative adjectives and adverbs are formed adding the suffix "-er." Superlatives are formed by adding the suffix "-st-" to the word. The "-st-" addition is pronounced [st], not [ʃt]. schön [ʃøn] *beautiful,* schöner ['ʃønər] *more beautiful,* schönste ['ʃønstə] *most beautiful*

Prepositions

Prepositions are used to describe relationships between people or things. In German, prepositions vary in form based upon grammatical use and meaning. Some prepositions call for the accusative case and others call for the dative case. There are also some prepositions that use one or the other for a specific purpose. See below examples of each.

◆ Prepositions requiring the accusative case:

bis	*until, as far as*	durch	*through*	für	*for*
entlang	*along*	gegen	*into, about*	ohne	*without*
um	*at, around*				

◆ Prepositions requiring the dative case:

aus	*from, out of*	bei	*at, near, with*	gegenüber	*opposite*
mit	*by, with*	nach	*to, after*	seit	*for (since)*
von	*from*	zu	*to*		

◆ Prepositions requiring the accusative or dative case for differing purposes:

an	*up to, over to, onto*	accusative	*on, at*	dative
auf	*onto*	accusative	*on, at*	dative
hinter	*(go)behind*	accusative	*behind*	dative
in	*into*	accusative	*in*	dative
neben	*(go) beside/next to*	accusative	*next to, near*	dative
über	*(go) over, across*	accusative	*over, above*	dative
unter	*(go) under*	accusative	*under*	dative
vor	*(go) in front of*	accusative	*in front of*	dative
zwischen	*(go) between*	accusative	*(be) between*	dative

Conjunctions

Conjunctions link two or more words or word groups, either coordinating or subordinating them.

◆ Coordinating Conjunctions:

aber ['a:bɐr]	*but*	denn ['dɛn]	*because*	oder ['o:dər]	*or*
sondern ['zɔndɛen]	*rather*	und ['ʊnt]	*and*		

◆ Subordinating Conjunctions:

als [als]	*when*	bevor [bə'fo:r]	*before*	bis [bɪs]	*until*
da [da]	*since*	damit [da'mɪt]	*so that*	dass [das]	*that*
ehe ['e:ə]	*before*	falls [fals]	*in case*	nachdem [na:x'de:m]	*after*

| ob [ɔp] | whether, if | seit [zaet] | since | sobald [zo'balt] | as soon as |
| soviel [zo'fi:l] | as far as | weil [vael] | because | wenn [vɛn] | whenever |

Question Words and Expressions of Time

◆ The following words introduce questions:

Wann?	When	Was?	What?	Was für?	What kind of?
Wo?	Where?	Wohin?	Where to?	Woher?	Where from?
Wozu?	What for?	Womit?	What with?		
Warum?	Why?	Wie?	How?	Wie lange?	How long?
Wie viel?	How much?	Wie viele?	How many?	Wer?	Who?

◆ The following words indicate time of day or frequency of an activity:

täglich	daily	jeden Morgen/Tag	every morning/day
einmal	one time, once	abends	in the evening
tausendmal	a thousand times	nie, niemals, nimmer	never
oft	oft, often	manchmal	sometimes
immer	always	immerdar/ewiglich	eternally

Goethe and Romanticism

Why is the work of Johann Wolfgang von Goethe (1749–1832) central to the understanding of German Lieder of the late 18th and early 19th centuries? According to John Armstrong, Goethe is one of the most famous names in literary and cultural history (Armstrong, 2006). With the publication in 1774 of *The Sorrows of Young Werther*, Goethe became a celebrity at the age of 25. His early work appealed to young readers because of its passion and honesty. By the time he completed his masterwork, *Faust*, in 1832, Goethe had become a household name in both Europe and America. He wrote studies in the theory of color, botany, philosophy, art, politics, and love. Because his works were translated and widely disseminated during his long lifetime, Goethe profoundly influenced not only his readers, but also the cultural thought of subsequent generations. The issues that interested him are still tantalizing today. Now as then, Goethe's writings provoke conversation about the role of fate in the achievement of a good life. His novels and plays are rife with characters who confront matters of the heart to be tackled through reason. These "coming of age" themes seem to have had their roots in Goethe's own life experiences. A quick perusal of his autobiography, *Dichtung und Wahrheit* (*Truth and Poetry*), affirms Goethe's attention to life's smallest details and their emotional significance.

Goethe was an enthusiastic music lover and a "scholar of life." An avid reader and gifted poet from an early age, Goethe assembled a body of work and a sphere of influence uncommon among human beings in any century. He was a student of languages including English, French, Italian, Latin, Greek, and Hebrew. It is said that Goethe read the Bible in Latin and Greek. In creating poetry, plays, and novels, Goethe used real-life experiences. The translator of Rüdiger Safranski's biography entitled *Goethe: Life as a Work of Art*, David Dollenmayer writes: " . . . from Goethe, we can learn how a healthy intellect and spirit function: how they complement the body" (Safranski, 2016).

In his book about Goethe and Schubert, Kenneth Whitton explains that Franz Schubert (1797–1828) set to music 80 texts by Goethe without once meeting or corresponding with the poet (Whitton, 1999). In 1814, at the age of 17, Schubert set his first Goethe text, the masterwork called "Gretchen am Spinnrade" from *Faust*. The young Schubert was well read and thoroughly qualified to understand the pathos of the passage from Part One of Goethe's masterwork, published in 1806. It is thought that Schubert may have sent Goethe several Lieder to approve. It is said that the parcels were returned unopened.

Goethe seems to have written the poetry that many composers wished to set. There are numerous musical settings of texts by Goethe that have been translated into English, Italian, and French. Many German literary scholars value Goethe's unique juxtaposition of vowels and consonants because they create a "harmonic road map" for the eye, tongue, and ear. Goethe's poetry and prose writing show his musicality. Take, for example, the monumental poem "Über allen Gipfeln ist Ruh," also known as "Wanderers Nachtlied II" (translated "Over every hilltop is rest" in the first line of Wanderer's Night Song II). It is frequently identified by Germanists as a perfect combination of sounds, evoking living and dying through the appearance and absence of a single consonant. The solitude of the scene is described as one in which "barely a breath of air can be felt" (" . . . spürest du kaum einen <u>H</u>auch"). Compare this image with the final phrase that depicts the rest one experiences after death when breath is not required ("ruhest du auch," "rest you also"). To articulate the word *Hauch*, meaning *hint, breeze,* or *touch*, the speaker must release a hint or touch of air for the "h." The poem concludes with a breathless *auch* (*also*) expressing the lifeless body resting in the peaceful setting. With an unprecedented economy of word, Goethe arrives at an exquisite depiction of life and its eventual end. Besides the setting by Schubert, this poem has been set to music by Fanny Mendelssohn Hensel ("Über allen Gipfeln ist Ruh"), Robert Schumann ("Nachtlied"), Franz Liszt ("Wanderers Nachtlied"), Max Reger ("Abendlied"), and Charles Ives ("Ilmenau"). The text appears below as the third comparative listening example.

To understand Goethe's artistic output, it is important for you to consider his love of folksong and folklore. As an assistant to the philologist Johann Gottfried Herder, Goethe helped gather folk poetry and song. Goethe seems to have cherished the simplicity of folk texts and melodies. In his correspondence to Carl Friedrich Zelter, director of the Berliner Singakademie (Berlin Singing Academy), Goethe encouraged uncomplicated musical settings of poetry that would focus fully on the poetic texts. There is speculation that the much-admired settings of Goethe texts by Ludwig van Beethoven, Wolfgang Amadeus Mozart, Franz Schubert, and Hugo Wolf, might not have been so cherished by the esteemed poet. It is believed that Goethe preferred modest works like those of Zelter and his contemporary, Johann Friedrich Reichardt.

Goethe believed in the theater as a cultural center for the development of artful political thought. It was a place for the citizenry to study human behaviors. In Weimar, Germany, he was briefly assisted by Friedrich Schiller, whose "Ode to Joy" Beethoven chose for the final movement of his 9th symphony. Goethe's love of nature and plant life is apparent in his descriptions of flowers and trees. As a botanist, Goethe actively studied cross-fertilization of plants, establishing a garden plot of vegetables and flowers. These activities complemented his belief in his own version of transcendentalism. A visit to his home on the Frauenplan in Weimar, Germany, will reveal to you his sense of proportion and his preference for an unusually meaningful color palette. Architecture and ambience mean as much in his writings as they did in his home décor. Goethe's written work is praised for its design, detail, and economy. Prolific though he was, Goethe chose words intentionally and repeated words rarely. When expressing a text by Goethe, explore every vowel and consonant for its dramatic or colorful potential.

Comparative Listening

"Heidenröslein" by Johann Wolfgang von Goethe epitomizes the poet's deep interest in folklore. Read the text and create a phonetic transcription.

Before you listen, implement your dictation strategies:

1. Spellings: Look for IPA spellings you already know such as the articles *ein* and *der* the conjunction *und*; the prepositions *auf* and *mit*; and the pronouns *er, es, ich, mich, dich,* and *sich.*

2. Familiar Words: Look for words you may recognize such as *Knabe [knabə]* and its apocopated version, *Knab' [knap],* as well as *jung, morgen, schön,* and *Freuden.*

3. Rhyming Words: Follow down the right side of the text to identify rhymes such as *steh'n/seh'n, dich/mich, brach/stach/ach,* and *Heiden/leiden.* Be sure to use the same IPA symbols for each pair to ensure a perfect rhyme.

4. Repeating Words: Study the text for words that repeat such as *Röslein, Röslein, Röslein rot, Röslein auf der Heide.*

5. Expressive Possibilities: Circle the words that invite expression such as *morgenschön, brach, stach, ewig,* and *leiden.*

Sah ein Knab' ein Röslein stehn,
Saw a boy a little rose standing

Röslein auf der Heiden,
Little rose on the hedge,

War so jung und morgenschön,
(the rose) was so young and morning lovely (fresh),

Lief er schnell es nah zu sehn,
Ran he quickly it nearer to see,

Sah's mit vielen Freuden.
Saw it with much joy/pleasure.

Röslein, Röslein, Röslein rot,
Little rose, little rose, little rose red,

Röslein auf der Heiden.
Little rose on the hedge.

Knabe sprach: Ich breche dich
(The) boy spoke: I will break you

Röslein auf der Heiden.
Little rose on the hedge.

Röslein sprach: ich steche dich,
(The) little Rose spoke: I will stick you,

Dass du ewig denkst an mich,
(So) that you always think of me,

Und ich will's nicht leiden.
And I will it not suffer.

Röslein, Röslein Röslein rot . . . .
Little rose, little rose, little rose red . . .

Und der wilde Knabe brach
And the wild boy broke

's Röslein auf der Heiden;
it—the little rose on the hedge;

Röslein wehrte sich und stach,
(The) little rose defended herself and stuck (him)

Half ihm doch kein Weh und Ach,
Helped him though no woe and Ah!

Musst es eben leiden.
Must it suffer/endure.

Röslein, Röslein Röslein rot . . . .
Little rose, little rose red . . . .

Poetic Equivalent

A little boy saw a lovely rose on a hedge early in the morning. He hurried to see it and was pleased with what he saw of the little rose. The boy said to the rose: I will break you.

She replied: I will stick you, so that you will never forget me. The wild boy broke the rose from the bush, and she pricked him. None of his complaining helped, he simply had to suffer.

Comparative Settings

Choose from this list of musical settings: Franz Schubert (1791–1828), Robert Schumann (1810–1856), Johannes Brahms (1833–1897), and Franz Léhar (1870–1948). After listening to more than one version, consider what you appreciate about each.

Comparative Listening

"Wanderers Nachtlied I" ("Wanderer's Night Song I") is a poetic gem. Read the text and create a phonetic transcription.

Before you listen, implement your dictation strategies:

1. Spellings: Look for IPA spellings you already know such as the articles *der* and *dem*; auxiliary verbs *bist* and *ist*; the conjunction *und*; prepositions *von* and *in*; and pronouns *du* and *ich*.
2. Familiar Words: Look for words you may recognize such as *Himmel*, *Alles*, *Leid*, *Schmerzen*, and *Ach!*
3. Rhyming Words: Follow down the right side of the text to identify rhymes *bist/ ist*, *stillest/fullest*, and *Lust/Brust*, are exact rhymes. The words *müde* and *Friede* have a relationship in meaning and form, though not as rhyming words. This combination is a German "eye" rhyme. Treat both words with special care.
4. Repeating Words: Notice the words that repeat such as *doppelt* and *komm*.
5. Expressive Possibilities: Circle the words that invite expression such as *elend*, *Erquickung*, *Treibens*, *Schmerz*, *Lust*, *süßer*, *Friede*, *komm*, and *Brust*.

Der du von dem Himmel bist,

Since/That you from the Heaven are,

Alles Leid und Schmerzen stillest,

All suffering and pain quiet/still/ease

Den, der doppelt elend ist,

(For) him, who doubly wretched/in despair is,

Doppelt mit Erquickung fullest,

Doubly with refreshment fills,

Ach! Ich bin des Treibens müde!

Ah, I am of the striving tired!

Was soll all der Schmerz und Lust?

What should (be done) with all the pain and desire?

Süsser Friede,

Sweet Peace,

Komm, ach komm in meine Brust!

Come, ah come into my heart!

Poetic Equivalent

Since you were sent to me from Heaven, all the pain and suffering has been eased.

I, who am doubly ailing, have been healed doubly by your remedy. Ah! I am tired of the strife! What is to be done with all the pain and desire? Sweet peace, ah, come into my heart!

Comparative Settings

Choose from this list of musical settings: Carl Loewe (1796–1869), Franz Schubert (1797–1828), Fanny Mendelssohn-Hensel (1805–1847), Franz Liszt (1811–1886), Hugo Wolf (1860–1903), and Alexander Zemlinsky (1871–1942). After listening to more than one version, consider what you appreciate about each.

Comparative Listening

With its economy of words and wealth of imagery, "Wanderers Nachtlied II" is best known in its setting by Franz Schubert (1792–1828). Choose below from among the many composers who found musical inspiration from this text. Each setting has its own point of view. Allow the range of possibilities to inspire your interpretation. Read the text and create a phonetic transcription.

Before you listen, implement your dictation strategies:

1. Spellings: Look for IPA spellings you already know such as *über, ist, allen, du,* and *auch.*

2. Familiar Words: Look for words you may recognize such as *Ruh, Walde, warte,* and *nur.*

3. Rhyming Words: Follow down the right side of the text to identify rhymes such as *Gipfeln/Wipfeln, Ruh/du, Walde/balde,* and *Hauch/auch.* Be sure to use the same vowel choices for each rhyming pair.

4. Expressive Possibilities: Circle the words that invite expression such as *allen, Ruh, spürest, kaum, Hauch, schweigen,* and *ruhest du auch.*

Über allen Gipfeln

Over all the peaks/summits

ist Ruh,

is peace/rest

in allen Wipfeln

in all the treetops

spürest du

feel/sense you

kaum einen Hauch'

barely/hardly a breath (of air)

die Vögelein schweigen im Walde,

the little birds are silent in the woods.

warte nur, balde

wait only/merely, soon

ruhest du auch!

rest you also!

Poetic Equivalent

Over the mountain tops is rest, above all the treetops you cannot sense the slightest breath of air: Even the birds are silent in the woods. Wait only a little while and you too will rest!

Comparative Settings

Select a few from this list of musical settings for comparison. Those who have set this text are Fanny Mendelssohn-Hensel (1805–1847), Robert Schumann (1810–1856), Franz Liszt (1811–1886), Max Reger (1873–1916) "Abendlied" ("Evening Song"), and Charles Ives (1874–1954) "Ilmenau."

Discussion Questions

1. Johann Wolfgang von Goethe is considered the Shakespeare of the German language, having created long works in perfect rhythm and rhyme. What is the impact of rhythm and rhyme in the Goethe poems you have studied?

2. What elements cause the poem "Heidenröslein" to be considered "folklike"?

3. How are the "Wanderers Nachtlied I" and "Wanderers Nachtlied II" alike? How are they different?

4. Knowing that Goethe studied architecture and colors, do you detect evidence of form and tone color in his poetry? Is it reflected in the song settings?

5. Goethe's writing is said to be timeless. How do his texts relate to your current world?

The Poets

Heinrich Heine (1797–1856): Lyric Poet

In the minds of many literary critics, Heinrich Heine stands second only to Goethe in importance as a master of German poetic expression. As intellectuals, Goethe and Heine responded to the political impulses of their day. Both men wrote travel diaries and extensive correspondence. The lives and output of these two literary giants took quite different courses. The evolution of Heine's literary thought has been said to have been influenced by Goethe, Byron, Wilhelm Müller, and the writings contained in the folklore collection *Des Knaben Wunderhorn* (*The Young Boy's Wonder Horn*). The lyricism of his earliest works gave way to an ironic and at times satirical tone. In response to the Revolution of 1830, Heine left Germany and settled in Paris, where he was introduced to Karl Marx and the concept of an egalitarian society. In the French capital, Heine associated regularly with the luminaries of French literature and music, such as George Sand, Honoré de Balzac, Giacomo Meyerbeer, and Victor Hugo. There he also met Franz Liszt, Frederic Chopin, and Hans Christian Andersen. Heine's writings in exile were met with mixed success. Throughout Heine's life, however, the *Buch der Lieder* (*Book of Songs*, 1827) was a popular, literary success. In the preface to its second edition (1837), Heinrich Heine wrote: " . . . and thus it was the German muse showed me all of her love and fidelity. She comforted me in domestic afflictions, followed me into exile, gladdened my heart in evil hours of despair, never left me in the lurch – even when my purse was empty, she knew how to help me, did the German muse, that excellent wench!" (Draper, 1982).

Many of the poems found in Heine's *Buch der Lieder* attracted early Romantic song composers such as Felix Mendelssohn-Bartholdy, Clara and Robert Schumann, and later Hugo Wolf. The volume contains the collections *Junge Leiden* (*Sorrows of Youth*), *Lyrische Intermezzo* (*Lyric Intermezzo*), and *Die Heimkehr* (*The Homecoming*). Poetic travelogues *Aus der Harzreise* (*From the Harz Journey*) and *Die Nordsee* (*The North Sea*) complete the volume. Note that the best-known Heine settings derive from the three earliest of his poetic offerings. Robert Schumann set individual poems and selected freely from Heine's *Buch der Lieder* to create the song cycles we know as *Liederkreis*, Op. 24 and *Dichterliebe*, Op. 48. Both cycles display a sense of wholeness that is based upon the composer's selection and positioning of the poet's texts. It could be that " . . . arguably Schumann misses the irony; yet his delicate near-sentimentality expresses the Heine his age chose to hear" (Rolleston, 1993). It is significant to note that Robert Schumann sent Heine a copy of *Liederkreis von Heine*, Op. 24 in 1840.

In 1844, Heine published a collection of new poems and *Deutschland. Ein Wintermärchen* (*Germany. A Winter Fairytale*) to great acclaim. His several volumes of travel prose entitled *Reisebilder* (*Travel Pictures*) were translated into French. Gérard de Nerval translated *Lyrisches Intermezzo* and *Die Nordsee* for an issue of *Revue des deux Mondes* in 1849. Several of Heine's writings were banned in Germany due to political content. By 1850, Heine's *Deutschland. Ein Wintermärchen* was already in its 12th printing. Heine spent the last 8 years of his life as an invalid, stricken with spinal tuberculosis. Heine is buried in the Montmartre cemetery in Paris.

Comparative Listening

Heinrich Heine's poem "Die Lotosblume" ("The Lotus Flower") comes from the collection called *Lyrisches Intermezzo* (*Lyric Intermezzo*). Read it and create a phonetic transcription.

"Die Lotosblume"

Before you listen, implement your dictation strategies:

1. Spellings: Look for IPA spellings you already know such as the articles *die* and *der*; and the pronouns *sie*, *sich*, *er*, *ihr*, and *ihm*.

2. Familiar Words: Look for words you may recognize such as *Sonne*, *Nacht*, *Mond*, *Licht* und *Liebe*.

3. Rhyming Words: Follow down the right side of the text to identify rhymes such as *Pracht/Nacht* and *Licht/Blumengesicht*.

4. Expressive Possibilities: Circle the words that invite expression or have special meaning such as *Sonne Pracht, träumend die Nacht, ihr Buhle, ihm entschleiert sie freundlich, blüht-glüht-leuchtet,* and *starret stumm*. Note the compound word *Liebesweh*, meaning *love's pain*. Schumann has given you two chances and ways to express meaning.

5. Diction Rules to Remember: Remember that "st" is only pronounced [ʃt] at the beginning of a word but not when it functions within a conjugating verb or declining noun. In the verb *ängstigt* the "st" is pronounced [st]. Remember also that the letter "g" before a "t" is pronounced [k].

Die Lotosblume ängstigt
The lotus flower is afraid

Sich vor der Sonne Pracht,
For herself in the sun's glory/presence,

Und mit gesenktem Haupte
And with lowered/sunken head

Erwartet sie träumend die Nacht.
Awaits she dreamily the night.

Der Mond, der ist ihr Buhle,
The moon, he is her lover/friend,

Er weckt sie mit seinem Licht,
He awakens her with his light,

Und ihm entschleiert sie freundlich
And to him unveils she kindly/friendly

Ihr frommes Blumengesicht.
Her holy flower-face.

Sie blüht und glüht und leuchtet,
She blooms and glows and lights up,

Und starret stumm in die Höh;
And stares dumbly/silently into the heights/Heavens;

Sie duftet und weinet und zittert
She smells releases her scent and weeps and shivers

Vor Liebe und Liebesweh.
Before/in the presence of love and love's pain.

Poetic Equivalent

The lotus flower is shy in the presence of the sun's radiance. She lowers her head and awaits the night. The moon is her companion. He awakens her with his light. She responds by revealing to him her beautiful, holy face. She blooms, glows, and radiates light as she stares straight up into the sky. She releases her perfume, weeps, and shivers at the thought of love and love's pain.

Comparative Settings

The best-known setting of "Die Lotosblume" is the one by Robert Schumann (1810–1856). The poem was set by Robert Franz (1815–1892), Carl Loewe (1796–1869), and Anton Rubinstein (1829–1894). Compare the Schumann setting with other settings mentioned.

Comparative Listening

A famous poem by Heinrich Heine, "Du bist wie eine Blume" ("You are Like a Flower"), is from the collection *Die Heimkehr* (*The Homecoming*). Read it and create a phonetic transcription.

"Du bist wie eine Blume"

<u>Before you listen, implement your dictation strategies:</u>

1. Spellings: Look for IPA spellings you already know such as the adverb *so*; the articles *eine* and *die*; conjunction *und*; prepositions *aufs* and *dass*; and pronouns *Du, ich, mir,* and *es*.

2. Familiar Words: Look for words you may recognize such as *Blume, schön, Herz, Hände,* and *Gott*.

3. Rhyming Words: Follow down the right side of the text to identify rhymes such as *rein/hinein* and *sollt/hold*. Be sure to choose the same IPA symbols for each pair.

4. Repeating Words: Study the text for common words that repeat such as *rein, schön,* and *hold*. (In this case, the reversed order of the words that repeat has an impact on their meaning. The poet describes the beloved as "dear and beautiful and pure." He hopes that she matures, she will remain "pure, beautiful and dear.")

5. Expressive Possibilities: Circle the words that invite expression such as *Blume, hold, schön, rein, Wehmut, schleicht,* and *Herz*. The pauses after *betend* and *erhaltet* offer opportunities for poetic expression. Throughout the poem, the word *so* deserves your special care.

Du bist wie eine Blume

You are like a flower/blossom/bloom

So hold und schön und rein;

So dear and beautiful and pure;

Ich schau dich an, und Wehmut
I look you on, and longing

Schleicht mir ins Herz hinein.
Slips/slithers to me in the heart into.

Mir ist, als ob ich die Hände
To me it is, as if I the (my) hands

Aufs Haupt dir legen sollt,
On the head of you lay should,

Betend, daß Gott dich erhalte
Praying that God you keeps

So rein und schön und hold.
So pure and beautiful and dear.

Poetic Equivalent

You are like a flower, so dear and beautiful and pure; I look at you and sense a longing creeping into my heart. It is as though I would like to place my hands on your head, praying that God will keep you so pure, beautiful, and so dear.

Comparative Settings

Compare the musical settings of this poem by Robert Schumann and Franz Liszt, noting the differences between the text treatments.

Comparative Listening

Another poem from Heine's *Lyrisches Intermezzo (Lyric Intermezzo)* is "Auf Flügeln des Gesanges" ("On Wings of Song"). Read it and create a phonetic transcription.

"Auf Flügeln des Gesanges"

Before you listen, implement your dictation strategies:

1. Spelling: Look for IPA spellings you already know such as articles *die, den,* and *ein*; the conjunction *und*; and prepositions *auf* and *nach*.

2. Familiar Words: Look for words you may recognize such as *Garten, Sternen, Rosen, Baum,* and *Traum.*

3. Rhyming Words: Follow down the right side of the text to identify rhymes such as *Gesanges/Ganges* (being careful to sing [ŋːəs] and not [ŋgːəs]), *fort/Ort, Garten/ erwarten, Mondenschein/Schwesterlein, kosen/Rosen, empor/Ohr, lauschen/rauschen, Gazelln/Welln, niedersinken/trinken,* and *Palmenbaum/Traum.*

4. Expressive Possibilities: Circle the expressive opportunities such as the musical picture of "waiting" created by *erwarten* and descriptive phrases: *rotblühender*

Garten/heimlich erzählen/duftende Märchen/frommen, klugen Gazellen/lauschen/ rauschen, heiligen Stromes Well'n/Liebe, and Ruh trinken/seligen Traum.

5. Form Considerations: Notice that the first two verses of the poem are set to the same music, the first verse fitting more closely than the second. The third verse is a musical variation with a coda.

I

Auf Flügeln des Gesanges,
On wings of song,

Herzliebchen, trag ich dich fort,
Heart's beloved, carry I you forth (away),

Fort nach den Fluren des Ganges,
Away to the plains of the Ganges (river),

Dort weiß ich den schönsten Ort.
There know I the most beautiful place.

Dort liegt ein rotblühender Garten
There lies a red-blooming garden

Im stillen Mondenschein;
In the still moonlight;

Die Lotosblumen erwarten
The lotus flowers await

Ihr trautes Schwesterlein.
Their trusted little sister.

II

Die Veilchen kichern und kosen,
The violets giggle and cuddle,

Und schaun nach den Sternen empor;
And look toward the stars above (on high);

Heimlich erzählen die Rosen
Secretly tell (whisper) the roses

Sich duftende Märchen ins Ohr.
One another scented fairytales in their ear.

Es hüpfen herbei und lauschen
There hop nearby and eavesdrop

Die frommen, klugen Gazelln;
The fervent (holy), smart gazelles;

Und in der Ferne rauschen
And in the distance rustles

Des heiligen Stromes Welln.
The holy stream's (Ganges River) waves.

III

Dort wollen wir niedersinken
There will (want) we downward sink

Unter dem Palmenbaum,
Under the palm tree

Und Liebe und Ruh trinken,
and love and rest drink,

Und träumen seligen Traum.
and dream (a) blessed dream.

Poetic Equivalent

On wings of song I would carry you to the banks of the mighty Ganges, my beloved.

There I know of the most beautiful place, where there is a garden rich with blossoms of red in the stillness of the moonlight. There are lotus flowers that are waiting for you, their trusted little sister. The violets are giggling and cuddling and gazing at the stars above, while secretly roses are whispering scented fairytales in one another's ears. There are gazelles springing through the landscape not far away, and in the distance, we can hear the rustling of the holy river's waves.

There we would want to sink down under a palm tree and drink love, peace, and blessed dreams.

Comparative Performances

Listen and compare performances by the German tenor Peter Schreier and American soprano Barbara Bonney. How are the performances the same? How do they differ?

Comparative Listening

The poem "Ich stand in dunklen Träumen" ("I Stood in Dark Dreams") by Heinrich Heine found in *Die Heimkehr* XXIII (*The Homecoming* No. 23) was set by Franz Schubert with the title "Ihr Bild" ("Her Picture") and appears in the posthumous collection known as *Schwanengesang* (*Swan Song*). Clara Schumann created two settings of the text, one entitled "Ihr Bildnis" ("Her Likeness") and another, "Ich Stand in Dunklen Träumen." Read it and create a phonetic transcription.

"Ich Stand in Dunklen Träumen"

<u>Before you listen, implement your dictation strategies:</u>

1. Spellings: Look for IPA spellings you already know such as the article *ihr*; conjunctions *und* and *auch*; prepositions *in*, *um*, *von*, and *daß*; pronouns *ich* and *es*; and the interjection *Ach!*

2. Familiar Words: Look for words you may recognize such as *Lippen* and *Tränen*.

3. Rhyming Words: Follow down the right side of the text to identify rhymes such as *an/began*, *wunderbar/Augenpaar*, and *herab/hab*. Be sure to use the same IPA symbols for each pair.

4. Expressive Possibilities: Circle the words that invite expression such as *dunklen Träumen*, *starrte*, *heimlich*, *wunderbar*, *erglänzte*, *Augenpaar*, and *verloren*.

I

Ich stand in dunkeln Träumen
I stood in dark dreams

Und starrte ihr Bildnis an,
And stared her portrait at,

Und das geliebte Antlitz
And the beloved countenance

Heimlich zu leben begann.
Secretly to live began.

Um ihre Lippen zog sich
Around her lips pulled itself

Ein Lächeln wunderbar,
A smile wonderful,

Und wie von Wehmutstränen
And as from melancholic tears

Erglänzte ihr Augenpaar.
Glistened her two eyes.

II

Auch meine Tränen flossen
And my tears flowed

Mir von den Wangen herab—
For me from the cheeks downward—

Und ach, ich kann es nicht glauben,
And ah! I can it not believe,

Daß ich dich verloren hab!
That I you lost have!

Poetic Equivalent

I stood in dark dreams and stared at your portrait and (it seemed to me) that her countenance became alive. An unusual smile rippled across her lips and teardrops of sadness glistened in her eyes. My tears also began to flow down my cheeks. Ah! I can hardly grasp that I have lost her!

Comparative Settings

Listen to "Ihr Bild" by Franz Schubert and at least one version of the text set by Clara Schumann. Compare the approach of each composer to this text. If possible, compare the two settings by Clara Schumann with one another. How are the endings different? What is the impact on the listener in each case?

Discussion Questions

1. How is the poetry of Heinrich Heine, a "lyric" poet, conducive to musical settings?

2. What is unusual about Heine's use of the German language? Alliteration? Description?

3. It is said that Robert Schumann set the German language in perfect rhythm with the spoken text. Read aloud Heine's "Die Lotosblume" in the rhythm of Schumann's setting to see if you agree. Does the rhythmic accuracy of the setting help you perform the Lied?

4. The song cycle *Dichterliebe* has long been considered repertoire for male voices. In recent years, it has been performed and recorded by female singers. Consider the obstacles and the advantages of singing the work as a male or as a female.

5. In reading "Ich Stand in Dunklen Träumen," what do you think has occurred? In what way has the poet "lost" his beloved? How would your choice determine your interpretation?

Friedrich Rückert (1788–1866)

The poetry of Friedrich Rückert inspired over fifty compositions by Robert Schumann, including the cycle of songs entitled *Myrthen*, Op. 25 that was dedicated to Clara Schumann and presented to her on her birthday in 1841. Robert Schumann shared a copy of the cycle with Rückert. The gift prompted a poetic response from Rückert, establishing a lifelong correspondence between the artists. Texts by Rückert were also set by Schubert, Clara Schumann, Brahms, Wolf, Gustav Mahler, Liszt, Hensel, and others.

A native of Schweinfurt, Germany, Rückert was a German poet and scholar of Asian cultures. He was educated at the universities of Würzburg and Heidelberg. He spent much of his professional career as a professor of Asian languages, first at the University of Erlangen and later at the University of Berlin. He was said to have mastered as many as 30 languages. Besides his poetic works and translations, Rückert published several dramatic works and a six-volume study entitled "The Wisdom of the Brahmins."

Comparative Listening

Here is a Rückert poem from *Bilder aus dem Osten* (*Pictures from the East or Orient*), set by Robert Schumann for the *Myrthen* (*Myrtles*) cycle. Read it and create a phonetic transcription.

"Aus den Östlichen Rosen" ("From the Eastern Roses")

Before you listen, implement your dictation strategies:

1. Spellings: Look for IPA spellings you already know such as the articles *ein/einen*; the preposition *aus*; and pronouns *ich, ihn, dich,* and *er*.

2. Familiar Words: Look for words you may recognize such as *Gruß, Duft, Rosen, Herz,* and *Himmel*.

3. Rhyming Words: Follow down the right side of the text to identify rhymes such as *Rosen/Frühlingskosen, durchtosen/Freudelosen, Rosenangesicht/Frühlingslicht,* and *nicht/Licht*. To ensure tuning, choose the same IPA symbols for each rhyming pair.

4. Repeating Words: Study the text for common words that repeat such as the phrase *Ich send'*.

5. Exceptional Words: The compound words *Rosenangesicht, Frühlingslicht,* and *Schmerzstosen* were created by the poet to express specific descriptive thoughts.

> Ich sende einen Gruss wie Duft der Rosen,
> *I send a greeting like the scent of roses,*
>
> ich send' ihn ein Rosenangesicht,
> *I send it (the greeting) to a rose-countenance*
>
> ich sende einen Gruss wie Frühlingskosen,
> *I send a greeting like Spring's teasing (endearment).*
>
> ich send' ihn ein Aug' voll Frühlingslicht.
> *I send it (the greeting) to an eye full of Spring's light.*
>
> Aus Schmerzenstürmen die mein Herz durchtosen,
> *Out of storms of pain that my heart toss about,*
>
> send' ich den Hauch, dich unsanft rühr' er nicht!
> *Send I the breeze/breath, you unsoft stir the greeting not!*
>
> Wenn du gedenkest an den Freudelosen
> *If you think (fondly) of the joyless (one)*
>
> so wird der Himmel meiner Nächte licht.
> *So will the sky (or Heaven) of my night brighten (light up).*

Poetic Equivalent

I send a greeting that is scented like roses to a rosy countenance. I send a greeting like Spring's caresses to an eye filled with Spring's light. Out of the storms of pain that my heart sustains, I send a breath of air that may stir your heart gently. If you should think of this joyless one, then the night's sky would light up for me.

Comparative Performances

Listen to a performance of an American singer, a British singer, and a German singer. Compare the nuances and diction choices of the singers. Whom do you prefer and why?

Comparative Listening

"Du Bist die Ruh" ("You Are Rest") is an endearing Rückert poem. Its Schubert setting is more familiar than Hensel's. Read the text and create a phonetic transcription.

"Du Bist die Ruh"

Before you listen, implement your dictation strategies:

1. Spellings: Look for IPA spellings you already know such as the articles *die, der, dieser,* and *deiner;* the conjunction *und;* prepositions *aus, von, hinter,* and *zur;* and the pronouns *du, sie, ich, dir, mein, mir, deiner, deinem,* and *es.*
2. Familiar Words: Look for words you may recognize from other poems such as *mild, Sehnsucht, voll, Lust, Schmerz, Herz, Brust,* and *Glanz.*
3. Rhyming Words: Follow down the right side of the text to identify rhymes such as *Ruh/du, mild/stillt, dir/hier, Schmerz/Herz, mir/dir, du/zu, Brust/Lust,* and *Glanz/ ganz.*
4. Expressive Possibilities: Circle the words that invite expression such as <u>R</u>uh, meaning physical peace or rest; *Friede*, meaning outward peace; *stillt, schließe du still, Augenzelt* (compound word for "desired closeness"), *a<u>ll</u>ein erhe<u>ll</u>t,* and *fü<u>ll</u> es ganz.*
5. Diction Challenges: *Pforten* can be difficult to pronounce. Divide and conquer the word by saying *orten* ['ɔrtən], *forten* ['fɔrtən], and finally *pforten* ['pfɔrtən].

Du bist die Ruh,

You are the rest,

Der Friede mild,

The peace mild,

Die Sehnsucht du

The longing you

Und was sie stillt.

And what it quiets.

Ich weihe dir
I dedicate to you

Voll Lust und Schmerz
Full desire and pain

Zur Wohnung hier
To a residence here

Mein Aug und Herz.
My eyes and heart.

Kehr ein bei mir,
Enter in with me,

Und schließe du
And close you

Still hinter dir
Quietly behind you

Die Pforten zu.
The gates closed

Treib andern Schmerz
Drive other pain

Aus dieser Brust!
From this breast/heart

Voll sei dies Herz
Full is this heart

Von deiner Lust.
From your desire (desire for you).

Dies Augenzelt
This tabernacle or temple

Von deinem Glanz
(made) from your gaze

Allein erhellt,
Alone lights it.

O füll es ganz!
O fill it completely!

Poetic Equivalent

You are rest, you bring peace. You are the longing I feel and what relieves it. I dedicate to you a place, my eyes and heart filled with desire and feeling. Come closer to me and close out the world. Drive out all other longing from this heart, a heart filled with love for you. Allow our closeness to be filled with the light from your gaze.

Comparative Settings

Comparison of the Schubert and Hensel settings reveals two contrasting approaches. There are numerous recordings of the Schubert setting of this text. Compare native speakers to non-native speakers to grasp the differences in their interpretation and diction. Here are a few suggested performances of the Schubert setting: Peter Schreier, tenor; Dietrich Fischer-Dieskau, baritone; Bryn Terfel, baritone; Elly Ameling, soprano; and Barbara Bonney, soprano. Compare with Susan Fritton's performance of the Hensel setting.

Comparative Listening

Clara Schumann and Mahler set the text "Liebst du um Schönheit" by Friedrich Rückert. Clara Schumann's Lied was composed to be sung with piano accompaniment, Gustav Mahler conceived his as an orchestrated song. Read the text and create a phonetic transcription.

"Liebst du um Schönheit" (If You Love for Beauty)

Before you listen, implement your dictation strategies:

1. Spellings: Look for IPA spellings you already know such as the articles *die* and *der*; the conjunction *und*; the preposition *um*; and the pronouns *du, sie, ich,* and *dich*.

2. Familiar Words: Look for words you may recognize from other poems such as *nicht, immer,* and *immerdar*.

3. Repeating Words: Study the text for common words that repeat such as *liebst du um, nicht mich liebe,* and *Liebe*.

4. Rhyming Words: Follow down the right side of the text to identify rhymes such as *Haar/Jahr/klar/immerdar*. Be sure to use the same IPA symbols for each rhyming vowel.

5. Expressive Possibilities: Circle the words that invite expression such as *Schönheit, Sonne, gold'nes,* the alliteration of *jung ist jedes Jahr, Meerfrau,* and *Perlen klar*.

Liebst Du um Schönheit,

Love you for beauty,

O, nicht mich liebe!

Oh, not me love!

Liebe die Sonne, sie trägt ein gold'nes Haar.
Love the sun, she wears golden Hair.

Liebst Du um Jugend,
Love you for youth,

O, nicht mich liebe!
Oh, not me love!

Liebe den Frühling, der jung ist jedes Jahr.
Love the Springtime, that young is every year.

Liebst Du um Schätze,
Love you for treasures,

O, nicht mich liebe!
Oh, not me love!

Liebe die Meerfrau, sie hat viel Perlen klar.
Love the Mermaid, she has many pearls clear.

Liebst Du um Liebe,
Love you for love,

O, ja mich liebe!
Oh, yes me love!

Liebe mich immer,
Love me always,

Dich lieb' ich immerdar!
You love I eternally!

Poetic Equivalent

If you love for beauty, don't love me! Love the sun, with its beautiful golden hair. If you love for youth, don't love me! Love the springtime, it returns young every year. If you love for treasures, don't love me! Love a mermaid, who has loads of pearls. If you love for love, oh yes, love me! I will love you forevermore!

Comparative Settings

Listen to the Clara Schumann setting performed by mezzo soprano Nathalie Stulzmann and compare it to performances of the Mahler setting with piano and with orchestra. The experience will broaden your understanding of the meaning of the text, its nuances, and its diction challenges.

Discussion Questions

1. "Aus den Östlichen Rosen" and "Du Bist die Ruh" contain words that were invented for the text. What effect, if any, does such a word have on you, the reader? How will you express this word to your audience when you sing it?

2. Compare the contrasting settings of "Du Bist die Ruh" by Franz Schubert and Fanny Mendelssohn Hensel. What elements of the text receive attention in the Schubert setting? In the Hensel setting? Might one setting have been inspired by the other? If so, discuss the hypothetical situation.

3. "Liebst du um Schönheit" is a text set by Clara Schumann and Gustav Mahler for two very different singing circumstances. What is different about learning a song composed for a piano accompaniment as opposed to a song intended for an orchestral accompaniment?

4. Friedrich Rückert's poetry inspired many musical settings during his lifetime. What do you think made Rückert's poetry so appealing to 19th- and early 20th-century composers?

5. How is the poetic style of Heinrich Heine different from that of Rückert? How are their poetic styles alike?

Joseph von Eichendorff (1788–1857)

Born into privilege, Joseph von Eichendorff received a Catholic, classical education by private tutors. Eichendorff enjoyed a happy-go-lucky childhood on his family's estate, where he immersed himself in the natural beauty of the woods. During his university years, Eichendorff was influenced by Clemens Brentano and Achim von Arnim, early leaders of the Romantic literary movement. After a period of military service, Eichendorff dedicated himself to a career as a writer of poetry and novels.

Comparative Listening

Several of Eichendorff's poems inspired some of the best-known Lieder by Schumann and Wolf, among others. Below is an example.

"Waldesgespräch" (Conversation in the Woods)

Before you listen, implement your dictation strategies:

1. Spellings: Look for IPA spellings you already know such as the pronouns *es, du, ich, dich,* and *mich*; the auxiliary verbs *ist, bist,* and *bin*; the articles *der, mein,* and *das*; and descriptive words *spät, kalt, lang, einsam, allein, wunderschön, tief,* and *nimmermehr*.

2. Familiar Words: Look for words you may recognize such as *Wald, Braut, Schmerz, Herz, Gott, Hexe, Stein,* and *Rhein*.

3. Rhyming Words: Follow down the right side of the text to identify rhymes such as *kalt/Wald, List/ist, hin/bin/ Weib/Leib, bei/Lorelei,* and *Stein/Rhein.* Be sure that all the vowels rhyme in each pair.

4. Repeating Words: Study the text for common words that repeat such as *schon spät, schon kalt,* and *Wald.*

5. Expressive Possibilities: Circle the words that invite expression such as *schon spät/schon kalt, Trug und List, Schmerz mein Herz, Wohl irrt das Waldhorn, reich geschmückt, wunderschön, Hexe Lorelei, and still mein Schloß tief in den Rhein.*

Es ist schon spät, es ist schon kalt,
It is already late, it is already cold,

Was reitest du einsam durch den Wald?
What (what is the reason) ride you lonely through the wood?

Der Wald ist lang, du bist allein,
The wood is long, you are alone,

Du schöne Braut! Ich führ dich heim!
You beautiful bride! I (will) lead you home!

"Groß ist der Männer Trug und List,
"Great is (the) men's deceit and cunning,

Vor Schmerz mein Herz gebrochen ist,
(Because of) in the presence of pain my heart broken was,

Wohl irrt das Waldhorn her und hin,
Fully wanders the hunting horn here and there,

O flieh! Du weißt nicht, wer ich bin."
O flee! You know not, who I am."

So reich geschmückt ist Roß und Weib,
So richly adorned is stallion and woman,

So wunderschön der junge Leib,
So wonderfully beautiful the young body,

Jetzt kenn ich dich—Gott steht mir bei!
Now recognize I you—God stand me by! (stand by me!)

Du bist die Hexe Lorelei.
You are the witch Lorelei.

"Du kennst mich wohl—vom hohen Stein
"You recognize me indeed—from the high stone

Schaut still mein Schloß tief in den Rhein.
Looks quietly my castle deeply into the Rhine (River).

Es ist schon spät, es ist schon kalt,
It is already late, it is already cold,

Kommst nimmermehr aus diesem Wald."
Come you nevermore out of these woods."

Poetic Equivalent

Man: It is already late; it is already cold. Why are you riding along lonely through the woods? The woods are long, you are alone, you, beautiful bride! Let me take you home!

Witch: The deceit and cunning of men is great, my heart is broken because of pain, Clearly the hunting horns are wailing here and there, Oh, flee! You don't know who I am.

Man: The stallion and the woman are so richly adorned, so wonderfully lovely is the young body. Now I recognize you—Oh God help me! You are the witch called Lorelei.

Witch: You recognize me, indeed—from the high rocks my castle gazes down deeply into the Rhine River. (Mockingly) It is already late; it is already cold . . . You will never leave this forest!

Comparative Settings

"Waldesgespräch" has been set to music by Hans Pfitzner (1869-1949) and Alexander Zemlinsky (1871-1942). Compare one of these with Schumann's *Liederkreis*, Op. 39 setting. Do you recognize influences of Schumann's style in the work of the later composers?

Comparative Listening

Eichendorff's "Mondnacht" depicts the unity of nature and humanity. Read the text and create a phonetic transcription.

"Mondnacht" ("Moon Night")

Before you listen, implement your dictation strategies:

1. Spellings: Look for IPA spellings you already know such as the articles *der* and *die*; auxiliary verbs *war* and *hätt'*; the conjunction *und*; prepositions *als, im, von, durch,* and *nach*; and the pronouns *es, sie, ihm,* and *ihre*.

2. Familiar Words: Look for words you may recognize such as *Himmel, Erde, Luft, Nacht, Seele, Lande,* and *Haus*.

3. Rhyming Words: Follow down the right side of the text to identify rhymes such as *geküsst/müsst, Felder/Wälder, sacht/Nacht,* and *aus/Haus*. Use the same IPA symbols for each rhyming pair.

4. Compound Words: Note *Blütenschimmer* (*blossom shimmer*) and *sternklar* (*star clear*).

5. Expressive Possibilities: Circle the words that invite expression such as *still geküsst/träumen müsst, wogten sacht, rauschten leis, meine Seele spannte, durch die stillen Lande,* and *nach Haus.*

Es war, als hätt' der Himmel

It was as had the Heaven

Die Erde still geküsst

The earth quietly kissed

Dass sie im Blütenschimmer

That it (the earth) in blossoms' shimmer

Von ihm nun träumen müsst

From him (the Heaven) only dream must.

Die Luft ging durch die Felder

The air went through the fields

Die Ähren wogten sacht

The grains waved gently

Es rauschten leis die Wälder

It rustles lightly the woods

So sternklar war die Nacht

So star-clear was the nicht

Und meine Seele spannte

And my soul expanded/spread

Weit ihre Flügel aus

Wide its wings out

Flog durch die stillen Lande

Flew through the still land

Als flöge sie nach Haus.

As if flew she (my soul) (to the house) toward home.

Poetic Equivalent

It was as if the Heavens had quietly kissed the Earth as if the Earth in her shimmer of blossoms had been dreaming of the Heavens. The breeze blew through the fields. The wheat swayed gently. There was a rustling in the woods. So starry-clear was the night. And my soul spread out its wings as if it could fly through this land of stillness to fly to its eternal home.

Comparative Settings

There are two well-known settings of this Eichendorff text. One is by Schumann and the other by Wolf. Listen to both of them and make comparisons.

Eduard Mörike (1804–1875)

Educated in seminaries, Eduard Mörike was a German poet and novelist whose lyric writings were considered among the best of their time. He served as a Lutheran pastor in the southwestern region of Germany called Swabia. On excursions from his parish service, Mörike developed a poetic language that followed classical models and included simple, fanciful imagery. His novella, *Mozart on the Journey to Prague* (1885), imagined the experiences of Mozart and Mozart's wife, Konstanze, en route from Vienna to the premiere of *Don Giovanni*. Many of his poetic works are set to music by Brahms, Schumann, and Wolf. The text below evokes intense emotions. Read it and create a phonetic transcription.

Comparative Listening

"Das Verlassene Mägdlein" ("The Forsaken Maiden")

Before you listen, implement your dictation strategies:

1. Spellings: Look for IPA spellings you already know such as the adjectives *früh* and *plötzlich*; adverbs *so*, *darein*, and *heran*; articles *die* and *der*; prepositions *wann*, *am*, *dass*, *von*, and *auf*; and pronouns *ich*, *es*, *dir*, and *er*.

2. Familiar Words: Look for words you may recognize such as *Feuer*, *schön*, *Schein*, *Nacht*, *Träne*, *Tag*, and *wieder*.

3. Rhyming Words: Follow down the right side of the text to identify rhymes such as *krähn/stehn*, *Funken/versunken*, *Knabe/habe*, and *hernieder/wieder*. Use the same IPA symbols for each pair.

4. Expressive Possibilities: Circle the words that invite expression such as <u>schwindet</u>, *Schein*, <u>springen</u>, <u>Funken</u>, <u>plötzlich</u>, <u>Träne auf Träne</u>, and <u>stürzet</u>.

Früh, wann die Hähne krähn,

Early, when the cocks are crowing,

Eh' die Sternlein schwindet,

Before the little stars disappear,

Muß ich am Herde stehn,

Must I at the hearth stand,

Muß Feuer zünden.

Must fire kindle.

Schön ist der Flammen Schein, Es springen die Funken;
Beautiful is the flame's glow, there spring the sparks;

Ich schaue so darein, in Leid versunken.
I look so therein, in sorrow sunk/downcast.

Plötzlich da kommt es mir, treulose Knabe,
Suddenly then comes it to me, untrue fellow,

dass ich die Nacht von dir geträumet habe.
That I the night from you dreamed have.

Träne auf Träne dann stürzet hernieder.
Tear upon tear than strumbles downward.

So kommt der Tag heran, O ging er wieder.
So comes the day on, o went it (away) again.

Poetic Equivalent

As the cock crows at early dawn before the little stars have disappeared, I must arise and prepare the hearth. The glow of the fire is beautiful. I stare into it full of sorrow. Suddenly, it comes to me, unfaithful fellow, that it was you I dreamt of. The tears stumble down my cheeks one after another. This is how the day begins. How I wish it were gone again.

Comparative Settings

Schumann and Wolf are good examples of this poem set to music. Compare performances of the two works.

Discussion Questions

1. "Waldesgespräch" by Joseph von Eichendorff is a poem that tells a story in two voices. What elements of diction will you use to bring these stories to life?

2. The poems "Mondnacht" by Eichendorff and "Das Verlassene Mägdlein" by Mörike are in the first person. How will you approach the intimate nature of these two situations?

3. Compare the imagery found in the texts by Eichendorff and Mörike.

4. How did the melodic and harmonic language differ in the two settings of "Das Verlassene Mägdlein"? Were there similarities? If so, what were they?

5. Did you prefer the Robert Schumann or the Hugo Wolf setting of Mörike's poem? Why?

The Composers

Fanny Mendelssohn Hensel (1805–1846) and Felix Mendelssohn-Bartholdy (1809–1847)

Fanny Mendelssohn and her younger brother, Felix, enjoyed the best musical education available at the time in Berlin, the city of their birth. As young adults, Fanny and Felix Mendelssohn attended the Berliner Singakademie under the tutelage of its director, Carl Friedrich Zelter. There they developed their musical skills, performed masterworks, and composed new works of their own. As a gift to her father on his birthday, Fanny Mendelssohn at age 12 is said to have performed the preludes and fugues from J. S. Bach's *Well-Tempered Clavier* by memory. Fanny Mendelssohn married August Wilhelm Hensel, a visual artist. During her lifetime, Fanny Mendelssohn was best known in Berlin for her "Sonntagsmusiken" ("Sunday Musicales"), where the finest musicians of the early Romantic period gathered to make music and discuss the artistic and literary news of the day. Near the end of her life, Fanny published several of her own compositions. In recent years, these works have been absorbed into the standard vocal recital repertoire.

Felix Mendelssohn-Bartholdy had a distinguished career as composer, performer, and conductor. A singer, pianist, and violinist, Felix Mendelssohn composed in many genres. His revival of Bach's *St. Matthew Passion* in 1829 was part of a larger effort to study the choral masterworks of earlier times. In his time, he was an internationally known artist. Two oratorios by Felix Mendelssohn, *Elijah* and *St. Paul*, were originally performed in London and later translated for performances in German-speaking countries. The city of Leipzig, Germany, remembers Felix Mendelssohn as one of its most successful conductors and teachers. Statues commemorating Mendelssohn can be seen at the Gewandhaus Orchestra and the St. Thomas Church. Leipzig's music conservatory is also named for him.

The Mendelssohn family maintained lively contact with Goethe. It is known that Felix Mendelssohn made at least two visits to Weimar to visit the aging poet. The earliest Lieder published by Felix Mendelssohn was a compilation of works composed by him and his sister, Fanny. It is interesting to compare the work of siblings, whose experiences, training, and interests were so similar. When setting the same poem, their unique gifts for musical expression are evident. Below is such a text for you to read and transcribe phonetically.

Comparative Listening

"Erster Verlust" (First Loss)
(Text by Johann Wolfgang von Goethe [1749–1832].)

Before you listen, implement your dictation strategies:

1. Spellings: Look for IPA spellings you already know such as the articles *die* and *der*; the conjunction *und*; and pronouns *wer* and *ich*.

2. Familiar Words: Look for words you may recognize such as *Ach*, *Tage*, *Liebe*, and *Zeit*.

3. Rhyming Words: If you follow down the right side of the text, you will identify a rhyme between *Stunde/Wunde*. Use the same IPA symbol for both vowels.

4. Repeating Words: Study the text for common words that repeat such as *die schönen Tage*, and *Zeit zurück*.

5. Expressive Possibilities: Circle the words that invite expression such as *schönen*, *einsam*, *traur' ich*, *verlorne Glück*, and *holde Zeit zurück!*

Ach, wer bringt die schönen Tage,

Ah, who brings the beautiful days [times] (Ah, if only one could bring back . . .)

Jene Tage der ersten Liebe,

Those days of (one's) first love,

Ach, wer bringt nur eine Stunde

Ah, who brings only one hour

Jener holden Zeit zurück?

Of such lovely time back?

Einsam nähr' ich meine Wunde,

Alone nourish/nurture I my wounds,

Und mit stets erneuter Klage

And with continual/constant renewed complaining

Traur' ich ums verlorne Glück,

Grieve I for the lost happiness,

Ach, wer bringt die schönen Tage,

Ah, who brings back the beautiful days

Jene holde Zeit zurück!

Such dear time back!

Poetic Equivalent

Ah, who could bring back those beautiful days of first love? Ah, who could deliver just one of those precious hours again? Alone, I nurture my wounds and continue to revisit the sadness, grieving over my lost happiness, Ah, if only I could bring back those dear, beautiful times!

Comparative Settings

Compare the settings of this text by Hensel, Mendelssohn, Schubert, Wolf, and Alban Berg, among others.

Robert Schumann (1810–1856) and Clara Wieck Schumann (1819–1896)

There is no absence of reliable information about this influential couple. The Schumanns embody the term *romantic* as a love match that inspired beautiful music. Robert and Clara Schumann encouraged the creative development of poets and composers. Robert Schumann founded a publication called the *Neue Zeitschrift für Musik* (*New Journal of Music*) that continues under a different title today. Each of us performs works by Robert Schumann that bear editorial markings from Clara Wieck Schumann, his champion and editor.

After an injury to his hand, Robert Schumann turned to composition as his creative outlet. The period of 1839 to 1840 is regarded by many as Robert Schumann's "Golden Year of Song," when he was inspired to write nearly 140 songs in honor of his approaching marriage to Clara Wieck. Robert Schumann contributed significantly to the development of the 19th-century German Lied. In his Lieder compositions, Robert Schumann adhered meticulously to the spoken rhythm of a poetic text. Robert Schumann sets the poem musically exactly as it would be read aloud with stressed syllables falling on important beats in a measure. Unstressed syllables in a Robert Schumann setting receive less musical emphasis. If you read the text of a Lied by Robert Schumann in rhythm, you will achieve the perfect prosody of the German language. The musical setting and the spoken version are identical in their rhythmic flow. Allow this principle to build your confidence as a singer of the German language.

Clara Wieck Schumann, a child prodigy known for her pianistic skill, premiered many of her husband's compositions. Her professional career included teaching, composing and music editing. In the latter role, Clara Schumann promoted the creative works of her talented but ailing husband, Robert. She collaborated as a performer and consultant with the most prominent musicians of her day including the singer Pauline Viardot-Garcia and the violinist Joseph Joachim. Clara Schumann was a longtime friend and compositional consultant to Brahms. Though her Lieder output is small, Clara Schumann's settings are appreciated for their intricate harmonies and expansive piano accompaniments.

You have already studied several musical settings by Clara Wieck Schumann and Robert Schumann in the comparative listening examples in this chapter. Use those experiences to help you evaluate the contributions of the Mendelssohns and the Schumanns to the development of the 19th-century German Lied.

Discussion Questions

1. Compare the settings by the siblings Fanny Mendelsssohn Hensel and Felix Mendelssohn. What similarities do you notice? What differences?

2. How do the compositions of Robert Schumann differ from those of Clara Schumann? How are they similar? Consider the text setting, the formal aspects, and the piano accompaniment in your discussion.

3. How are the compositional styles of Fanny Mendelssohn Hensel and Felix Mendelssohn different from those of Robert and Clara Schumanns? How are they similar?

4. One of Robert Schumann's contributions to the development of the German Lied was his perfecting the melding of text and musical rhythm. Choose a sample

phrase. Say it and then sing it. How does the spoken version compare with the musical setting?

5. What are the creative identity elements of the poets represented above? Do the words of Goethe or Heine inspire individual harmonic sounds or melodic contours? What about those of Rückert? Eichendorff? Mörike?

Johannes Brahms (1833–1897)

Unlike other composers of the German Romantic era, Johannes Brahms did not leave a memoir or a large amount of correspondence. Photographic evidence attests that Brahms lived modestly, despite a successful career as a performer, conductor, and composer. His vocal works demonstrate a strong love of folk song and poetry. Though he set texts by the great poets of his time, Brahms favored the simpler work of less well-known literary figures such as Klaus Groth (1819–1899), Hans Schmidt (1854–1923), and Josef Wenzig (1807–1876). Perhaps it was his early association with the prodigious Hungarian violinist Joachim (1831–1907) that caused Brahms to favor the flowing, lyric line in much of his work. His career was influenced significantly by the mentorship of Clara Wieck Schumann (1819–1896) and her husband, Robert Schumann (1810–1856). The Lied "Meine Liebe ist Grün" is one of three settings Brahms created from poetry by the Schumanns' son, Felix.

Born in Hamburg, Germany, Brahms spent most of his professional life in Vienna. From his youth, Brahms played the piano and composed vocal works. Brahms' musical language and form were highly influenced by his study of the works of Bach and George Frideric Handel. The interest Brahms maintained in Baroque compositional techniques is evident in the contrapuntal writing of vocal and piano lines and in his preference for theme and variations as a form.

One of Brahms' major vocal works was the masterpiece for choir, soloists, and orchestra called *Ein Deutsches Requiem (A German Requiem)*, written initially to honor the life of Robert Schumann. Brahms later added a movement in memory of his own mother. The use of German text instead of the traditional requiem liturgy parallels that of the *Musikalische Exequien (Funeral Music)*, written by early Baroque church musician Heinrich Schütz (1585–1672). Both *Ein Deutsches Requiem* and the *Musikalisches Exequien* present texts intended to comfort those who grieve a departed one. Other choral works by Brahms are "Nänie" (translated "Funeral Song," based on a text by Friedrich Schiller and honoring the death of Amseln Feuerbach), "Gesang der Parzen" ("Song of the Fates," text by Goethe), "Schicksalslied" ("Destiny's Song," text by Friedrich Hölderlin), and "Alto Rhapsody" (written as a wedding present to Julie Schumann on a text by Goethe).

Inspired by life in the Austro-Hungarian realm, Brahms created the *Zigeunerlieder (Gypsy Songs)* in choral and solo versions, both with piano accompaniment, and two sets of *Liebeslieder Walzer (Love Song Waltzes)* sung by four singers or larger choral groups with piano four hands. *Romanzen aus Ludwig Tiecks Magelone (Ballads from L. Tieck's "Magelone")* by Brahms is a song cycle depicting the saga of Magelone and her beloved Peter. Brahms set many German folksongs as solo songs and as choral works known as *Deutsche Volkslieder*. In the realm of chamber music, Brahms wrote many vocal duets and quartets. Among his last works, Brahms composed in 1896 a set of four "serious" songs or *Vier ernste Gesänge* based on Biblical texts. In total, Brahms created more than 200 works for solo voice and piano in addition to virtuoso piano works, a violin concerto, and orchestral compositions.

Comparative Listening

Listen and compare the melody of the Lied "Sapphische Ode" to the main theme of the 2nd movement in the Brahms *Violin Concerto*, Op. 77. The experience has proven its worth for many beginning singers. Brahms wrote the *Violin Concerto* for his virtuoso friend, Joachim. The theme of the second movement epitomizes the lyric line indicative of song melodies by Brahms. Comparisons of the performances of Anne Sofie Mutter (Berlin Philharmonic under the direction of Herbert von Karajan) with that of Rachel Barton Pine (Chicago Symphony under the direction of Carlos Kalmar) are recommended as excellent examples. Allow both performances to inform and inspire you. The latter is performed on an historic violin known as the "ex-Soldat." It is an instrument with a strong connection to both Brahms and Joachim. Information about Pine and her acquisition of the right to play this historic instrument is readily available on her website. Read the text of the poem and create a phonetic transcription.

"Sapphische Ode" ("Sapphic Ode")
(Poem by Hans Schmidt [1854–1923].)

Before you listen, implement your dictation strategies:

1. Spellings: Look for IPA spellings you already know such as the articles *die* and *der*; prepositions *am, vom,* and *im*; and pronouns *ich, mir, mich, sie,* and *dir*.

2. Familiar Words: Look for words you may recognize such as *Rosen, Duft, Tage, Küße,* and *Tränen*.

3. Rhyming Words: Follow down the right side of the text to identify rhymes such as *Hage/Tage, Äste/näßte, berückte/pflückte,* and *jenen/Tränen*. Use the same IPA symbols for the rhyming pairs, noting that *jenen* and *Tränen* are not exact rhymes. They will need special care to ensure exquisite tuning.

4. Repeating Words: Study the text for common words that repeat such as *Duft* and *doch*.

5. Expressive Possibilities: Circle the words that invite expression such as *dunkeln, Süßer, verstreuten reich, bewegten, näßte, Küsse, berückte, Strauch, Lippen, pflückte, Tauten,* and *Tränen*.

6. Exceptional Words: *Gemüt* [y] and *berückte* and *pflückte* [ʏ] follow the rules, but *Süßer* [y] is an exception.

Rosen brach ich nachts mir am dunkeln Hage;
Roses broke (plucked) I in the evening for myself from the dark hedge

Süßer hauchten Duft sie, als je am Tage;
Sweeter breathed scent they as ever during the day

Doch verstreuten reich die bewegten Äste
Yet distributed richly the moving branches

Tau, der mich näßte.
Dew, that me dampened.

Auch der Küsse Duft mich wie nie berückte,
Also the kisses' scent to me as such never before entranced

Die ich nachts vom Strauch deiner Lippen pflückte:
That I in the evening from the bouquet of your lips plucked

Doch auch dir, bewegt im Gemüt gleich jenen,
Yet also to you, moved in (your) spirit similarly as such

Tauten die Tränen!
Melted the tears

Poetic Equivalent

I plucked roses one night from the dark hedge; they exhaled a scent that was sweeter than by day; the moving twigs rustled and dampened me with dew. In the same way, the scent of your kisses entranced me when I plucked them at night from your lips, and you too were deeply moved when drops of tears fell like thawed dew.

Comparative Performances

Listen to performances by the two native-speaking German baritones Thomas Quasthoff and Dietrich Fischer-Dieskau. Compare their approach to the tempo, the punctuation, and the cadential figures in each verse. How did each performer use elements of diction to express the text?

Comparative Listening

Klaus Groth (1819–1899), a north German, maintained a long personal and professional acquaintance with Brahms. Read the text and create a phonetic transcription.

Heimweh II (Homesickness II) "O wüsst' ich doch . . . "

Before you listen, implement your dictation strategies:

1. Spellings: Look for IPA spellings you already know such as the articles *den*, *dem*, and *die*; the conjunction *und*; the prepositions *zu*, *nach*, *von*, and *zum*; and the pronouns *ich*, *mich*, and *mir*.

2. Familiar Words: Look for words you may recognize such as *O*, *Weg*, *Ach! den*, *wie*, *mich*, and *nichts*. Practice saying and speaking *nichts* [nɪçts]. Begin by saying the word you know: *ich* [ɪç]. Next, move to the end of the word and say "ts." Unite *ich* with "ts," and finally add the opening "n" to arrive at *nichts*.

3. Rhyming Words: Follow down the right side of the text to identify rhymes such as *Kinderland/Hand/Strand, auszuruh'n/zuzutun, aufgeweckt/bedeckt,* and *lind/Kind.* Choose the same IPA symbols for the rhyming vowels in each pair.

4. Repeating Words: Study the text for common words that repeat such as *Weg, Kind* and its derivative *Kinderland,* as well as *Glück.*

5. Expressive Possibilities: Circle the words that invite expression such as "keinem *Streben aufgeweckt,*" "von Liebe *sanft* bedeckt," "nichts zu *forschen,* nichts zu *späh'n,*" and "nur zu *träumen,*" "*leicht* und *lind,*" "*Vergebens* such' ich," and "*öder* Strand."

O wüsst' ich doch den Weg zurück, den lieben Weg zu Kinderland!
O knew I yet the way back the lovely way to children's land!

Ach, warum sucht' ich nach dem Glück und liess der Mutter Hand?
Ah, why sought I after the fortune/happiness and left the mother's hand?

O wie mich sehnet auszuruh'n, von keinem Streben aufgeweckt
O how me longs to rest up from no stress awakened

Die müden Augen zuzutun, von Liebe sanft bedeckt.
the tired eyes to close from love softly covered

Und nichts zu forschen, nichts zu späh'n, und nur zu träumen
and nothing to investigate, nothing to scout out, and only to dream

Leicht und lind, die Zeiten Wandel nicht zu seh'n,
lightly and mildly, the times' changing not to see,

Zum zweitenmal ein Kind.
for the second time a child.

O zeigt mir doch den Weg zurück, den lieben Weg zu Kinderland!
O show me yet the way back, the lovely way to children's land!

Vergebens such' ich nach dem Glück,
Vainly seek I after the fortune,

Ringsum ist öder Strand.
all around is odious beach.

Poetic Equivalent

If only I knew the way back to my lovely childhood! Why did I ever leave to search for my fortune and abandon my mother's hand? How I long to relax and be released from stress,

To close these tired eyes and be surrounded by love, not to notice the press of time, rather to be a child again. If only I knew how to go back to my lovely childhood! Without success I seek my fortune. Everything around me is worthless sand.

Comparative Performances

Compare the interpretation of soprano Elly Ameling with that of baritone Thomas Quasthoff. What are the similarities? What are the differences?

Discussion Questions

1. Are there musical similarities in songs by Johannes Brahms and Clara and Robert Schumann?

2. What is distinctive about the treatment of text in the songs among the three composers?

3. What are the diction challenges of singing texts by Heinrich Heine, Joseph von Eichendorff, Hans Schmidt, and Klaus Groth?

4. How are the settings of Fanny Mendelssohn Hensel and Felix Mendelssohn-Bartholdy different from those of the Schumanns and Brahms?

5. How important is the quality of a poem as literature in the creation of a musical setting of beauty and meaning? Consider the poets you have read in this chapter. Compare their words as spoken texts and as song settings.

German Diction First Presentation Repertoire List

The following is a list of suggested repertoire to be assigned for the first presentation in German diction. The student will prepare the text with its word-by-word translation and poetic equivalent. These materials will be submitted to the instructor for correction and duplication for class use.

Ich Liebe Dich	Ludwig van Beethoven
Sonntag	Johannes Brahms
Ständchen "Der Mond Steht"	Johannes Brahms
Vergebliches Ständchen	Johannes Brahms
Wie Melodien Zieht es Mir	Johannes Brahms
Widmung "O Danke Nicht . . . "	Robert Franz
Lob der Faulheit	Franz Josef Haydn
Die Stille Lotosblume	Fanny Mendelssohn Hensel
Du Bist die Ruh	Fanny Mendelssohn Hensel
Italien	Fanny Mendelssohn Hensel
Das Erste Veilchen	Felix Mendelssohn-Bartholdy
Der Mond	Felix Mendelssohn-Bartholdy
Der Zauberer	Wolfgang A. Mozart

Die Männer sind Mechant	Wolfgang A. Mozart
Trennungslied	Wolfgang A. Mozart
Das Fischermädchen	Franz Schubert
Die Forelle	Franz Schubert
Lachen und Weinen	Franz Schubert
Leise Flehen Meine Lieder	Franz Schubert
Morgengruss	Franz Schubert
Was ist Sylvia?	Franz Schubert
Der Nussbaum	Robert Schumann
Du Ring an Meinem Finger	Robert Schumann
Erstes Grün	Robert Schumann
Ich Grolle Nicht	Robert Schumann
Jasminenstrauch	Robert Schumann
Marienwürmchen	Robert Schumann
Schneeglöckchen	Robert Schumann
Seit Ich ihn Gesehen	Robert Schumann
Widmung	Robert Schumann

Later 19th-Century German Lied

Hugo Wolf (1860–1903) is considered to be the composer whose work concluded the development of the 19th-century German Lied and ushered in the concept of the orchestrated song. Wolf was an expert of the miniature, yet he held a master of large scale works as his ideal, namely, Richard Wagner (1813–1883). It would be instructive for you to hear the scope and harmonic language of Wagner's music. From an early age, Wolf was captivated and influenced by it. The text and translation to "Träume" ("Dreams"), the fifth song of the *Wesendonck Lieder*, a cycle of songs on poetry of Mathilde Wesendonck (1828–1902), Wagner's protegé and muse, is available for you to investigate through the online resource associated with this book.

Wolf incorporated Schubert's use of the leading tone to express emotion in music. Wolf followed Schumann's example by setting text perfectly to the rhythm of spoken German. He judiciously selected keys and chordal progressions that mirrored the atmosphere of the poem, as Brahms had done. Wolf honored the poetic form by making few if any repetitions of text not prescribed by the poet. It is said that Wolf immersed himself in the poetry of a single poet at a time, creating a unique harmonic language he felt reflected the poet's personality and intention. He called his Lieder "poems set to music." Below are examples from these events of "poetic immersion." We begin with settings by the German poet Mörike.

Hugo Wolf (1860–1903) and Eduard Mörike (1804–1875)

Comparative Listening

Wolf composed 53 musical settings on Mörike's poems, some on secular and others on sacred themes. The following is an example of a secular text by Mörike. Read the text and create a phonetic transcription.

"Er ist's" (It is here)

Before you listen, implement your dictation strategies:

1. Spellings: Look for IPA spellings you already know such as the articles *die*, *das*, and *ein*; prepositions *durch* and *von*; auxiliary verbs *bist*, *ist*, and *hab'*; and pronouns *du* and *dich*.

2. Familiar Words: Look for words you may recognize such as *sein*, *blaues*, *wieder*, *süße*, *schon*, *wollen*, *balde*, *kommen*, and *ja*.

3. Rhyming Words: Follow down the right side of the text to identify rhymes such as *Band/Land*, *Lüfte/Düfte*, *schon/Harfenton*, and *kommen/vernommen*. Be sure to use the same IPA symbols for the vowels of the rhyming pairs.

4. Repeating Words: Study the text for common words that repeat such as *Frühling* and the phrase *ja, du bist's*.

5. Expressive Possibilities: Circle the words that invite expression such as *flattern*, *streifen*, *ahnungsvoll*, *Veilchen träumen*, *von fern ein leiser Harfenton*, and *vernommen*. As you listen, notice how performers use the elements of diction to express the text.

6. Exceptional Words: Remember the rules for umlauts such as *süß*. Mark the compound words *wohlbekannte* and *Harfenton*. In the closing passage, the word *ja*, literally *yes*, or perhaps *indeed*, is an affirmation of spring's arrival.

Frühling läßt sein blaues Band
Spring lets his blue band (ribbon)

Wieder flattern durch die Lüfte;
Again flutter through the air;

Süße, wohlbekannte Düfte
Sweet, well-recognizable scents

Streifen ahnungsvoll das Land.
Stroke intuition-full the land.

Veilchen träumen schon,
violets dream already,

Wollen balde kommen.
Want soon to come/arrive.

Horch, von fern ein leiser Harfenton!
Hark! From afar a quiet harp-tone!

CHAPTER 4 ◆ GERMAN 211

Frühling, ja du bist's!

Spring, yes you are it!

Dich hab' ich vernommen!

You have I expected!

Poetic Equivalent

Spring unleashes its blue ribbon to flutter again across the air; sweet, familiar scents streams expectantly across the land. Violets are already dreaming of arriving soon. Hark! In the distance you can hear the lilting sound of a harp! Spring, indeed it is you! I have been sensing you were near.

Comparative Settings

Both Schumann and Wolf created Lieder from the text "Er Ist's." As you listen to the contrasting settings, notice the similarities in the setting of text by Schumann and Wolf. Note also the differences in the harmonic structures. Which setting do you prefer? Why?

Comparative Listening

This setting of a sacred text by Mörike demonstrates very clearly the influence of Wagner's harmonic language on Wolf's compositional style. Read the text and create a phonetic transcription.

"Gebet" (Prayer)

Before you listen, implement your dictation strategies:

1. Spellings: Look for IPA spellings you already know such as the definite articles *ein* and *dein*; the auxiliary verb *bin*; the conjunction *und*; prepositions *aus, in,* and *mit*; and pronouns *du* and *ich*.

2. Familiar Words: Look for words you may recognize such as *Händen, Liebes, Leides, Leiden, Freuden,* and *Mitten.*

3. Rhyming Words: Follow down the right side of the text to identify rhymes such as *willt/quilt* and *Leides/beides.* Mark the vowels of the rhyming pairs with the same IPA symbols.

4. Expressive Possibilities: Circle the words that invite expression such as *willt, vernügt, quillt, überschütten,* and *holdes Bescheiden.*

Herr, schicke, was du willt,

Lord, send (me), what you wish/will,

Ein Liebes oder Leides!

A (something) of love or of suffering!

Ich bin vergnügt, daß beides

I am satisfied, that both

Aus deinen Händen quillt.
From your hands originate.

Wollest mit Freuden
(Whether) want you with joy

Und wollst mit Leiden mich
And want you with suffering me

Nicht überschütten!
Not overwhelm!

Doch in der Mitten
Yet in the midst (of it)

Liegt holdes Bescheiden.
Lies dear humility.

Poetic Equivalent

Lord, send me what You will, be it desirable or dreaded! I am satisfied that both come directly from Your hands. Whether it brings joy or suffering to me, I will not be overwhelmed, for in the midst of it lies Your grace.

Comparative Performances

Listen to recordings of performances by soprano Elly Ameling and baritone Dietrich Fischer-Dieskau. Compare the prayerful atmosphere created by a high voice with that of a lower one.

Hugo Wolf and Johann Wolfgang von Goethe (1749–1832)

Between 1888 and 1889, Wolf set to music 51 poems by Goethe. The texts include incidental poems as well as excerpts from novels and plays. Below you will find "Anakreons Grab," a poem that describes a pilgrimage to the grave of the Greek lyric poet Anacreon (b. ca. 570 BC). The style of Anacreon's verse, called "Anacreontic verse," strongly influenced European poets of various time periods. Read and create a phonetic transcription.

Comparative Listening

"Anakreons Grab" ("Anacreon's Grave")

Before you listen, implement your dictation strategies:

1. Spellings: Look for IPA spellings you already know such as the articles *die, das, ein, der,* and *dem;* the conjunction *und;* prepositions *mit* and *vor;* and pronouns *sich, es,* and *ihn.*

2. **Familiar Words:** Look for words you may recognize such as *Rose, Grab, Leben, Ruh, Frühling, Sommer, Herbst, Winter, Dichter,* and *Hügel*.

3. **Repeating Words:** Note the words that repeat such as *wo* and *hier*. Be sure to mark them with the same IPA symbols.

4. **Expressive Possibilities:** Circle the words that invite expression such as *Reben um Lorbeer sich schlingen, Turtelchen lockt, Welch ein Grab, alle Götter, schön bepflanzt und geziert, der glückliche Dichter, endlich,* and *der Hügel geschützt*. Note also the alliterative words such as <u>G</u>rillchen, <u>G</u>rab, and <u>G</u>ötter and <u>w</u>o, <u>w</u>elch, and *vor dem* <u>W</u>inter.

5. **Exceptional Words:** The phrase "Es Ist Anakreons Ruh" offers an exceptional opportunity to build a poetic climax through careful pacing and articulation.

> Wo die Rose hier blüht,
> *Where the rose here blooms,*
>
> wo Reben und Lorbeer sich schlingen,
> *Where vines around laurel themselves twist/entwine*
>
> Wo das Turtelchen lockt,
> *Where the turtledove coos,*
>
> wo sich das Grillchen ergötzt,
> *where the crickets frolic,*
>
> Welch ein Grab ist hier,
> *Such a/which grave is here,*
>
> das alle Götter mit Leben schön bepflanzt
> *that all the gods with life beautifully planted*
>
> und geziert? Es ist Anakreons Ruh.
> *And adorned? It is Anacreon's resting (place).*
>
> Frühling, Sommer und Herbst genoß
> *Spring, Summer and Autumn enjoyed*
>
> der glückliche Dichter;
> *the happy poet,*
>
> vor dem Winter hat ihn
> *before the winter (of his life) has him*
>
> endlich der Hügel geschützt.
> *Finally the hill sheltered.*

Poetic Equivalent

Where the roses here bloom, where vines and laurels are interwoven, where the little dove coos, where the little cricket is gleeful, what a grave is here, that all the gods would plant so beautifully with life, decorated? It is Anacreon's resting place. Spring, summer, and autumn were enjoyed by the happy poet; at the end, he was protected from the winter by the hillside.

Comparative Performances

Compare a performance by soprano Elizabeth Schwarzkopf with that of baritone Fischer-Dieskau. How do they treat the text? Do you recognize differences?

Hugo Wolf and Joseph von Eichendorff (1788–1857)

Wolf set 20 poems by Eichendorff to music. Wolf's expansive harmonic color palette creates a sonorous atmosphere that captures the poet's reverence for nature. Read the text and create a phonetic transcription.

Comparative Listening

"Verschwiegene Liebe" ("Silent Love")

Before you listen, implement your dictation strategies:

1. Spellings: Look for IPA spellings you already know such as the articles *den, die, eine, sie,* and *der;* the conjunction *und;* prepositions *über, in, an, beim,* and *als;* and pronouns *sie, sich, es,* and *mein.*

2. Familiar Words: Look for words you may recognize such as *Nacht, Wolken,* and *Lieb'.*

3. Rhyming Words: Follow down the right side of the text to identify rhymes such as *Saaten/erraten, hinein/ein, wiegen/verschwiegen, gedacht/wacht/Nacht,* and *fliegen/verschwiegen.* Choose the same IPA symbols for the vowels of the rhymes.

4. Repeating Words: Study the text for common words that repeat such as *wer, Gedanken, Nacht,* and *verschwiegen.*

5. Expressive Possibilities: Circle the words that invite expression such as <u>*Wipfeln und Saaten,*</u> <u>*Glanz hinein,*</u> *Gedanken sich* <u>*wiegen,*</u> <u>*erraten/errät,*</u> <u>*Rauschen der Haine,*</u> and *fliegen/*<u>*verschwiegen/schön.*</u>

6. Exception Words: Remember the rules for umlauts.

Über Wipfeln und Saaten
Over treetops and fields

In den Glanz hinein—
In the glow therein—

Wer mag sie erraten,
Who could they (the thoughts) guess,

Wer holte sie ein?
Who gathers them (the thoughts) in?

Gedanken sich wiegen,
Thoughts themselves cradle,

Die Nacht is verschwiegen,
The night is silent,

Gedanken sind frei.
Thoughts are free.

Errät es nur eine,
Guess it only one,

Wer an sie gedacht
Who on/of her thought

Beim Rauschen der Haine
In the rustling groves,

Wenn niemand mehr wacht.
When no one anymore watches/wakes.

Als die Wolken, die fliegen—
As the clouds, that fly—

Mein Lieb' ist verschwiegen
My love is silent

Und schön wie die Nacht.
And beautiful like the night.

Poetic Equivalent

Illuminated above the treetops and fields, who can imagine what thoughts are being expressed? Who would gather them? Thoughts are floating in the night's silence. Is there any chance that she, of whom I am thinking out here in the rustling groves, senses my thoughts? No one else is watching except the clouds that pass by. My love is silent and as lovely as the night.

Comparative Performances

Listen to performances by Olaf Bär and Fischer-Dieskau. What are the similarities?

Hugo Wolf and *Italienisches Liederbuch*

In the 19th century, there was great interest in the literature of other cultures. Paul Heyse (1830–1914) translated a book of Italian folk poetry he titled *Italienisches Liederbuch* or

Italian Songbook. Wolf embraced these texts as German poems, setting 46 of them (23 for a female voice and 23 for a male voice) in a short period of time. As you listen, you may note a certain "Italianate" approach to the text setting. Read the following text and create a phonetic transcription.

Comparative Listening

"Auch Kleine Dinge Können uns Entzücken"
("Also Small Things Can Charm Us")

Before you listen, implement your dictation strategies:

1. Spellings: Look for IPA spellings you already know such as the article *die*; auxiliary verbs *ist, sein, werden,* and *wird*; the conjunction *und*; prepositions *mit, um,* and *an*; and pronouns *uns, wir, si , ihre,* and *ihr.*

2. Familiar Words: Look for words you may recognize such as *kleine/klein, Perlen,* and *Rose.*

3. Rhyming Words: Follow down the right side of the text to identify rhymes such as *entzücken/schmücken, sein/klein, Olivenfrucht/gesucht,* and *ist/wißt.* Use the same IPA symbols for the vowels of each rhyming pair.

4. Repeating Words: Study the text for common words that repeat such as *auch, wie, bedenkt/denkt,* and *kleine/klein.* Be sure to mark the same IPA symbols for each repetition.

5. Expressive Possibilities: This text is rich with words that invite expression through the combinations of consonants/vowels such as *kleine Dinge, entzücken, teuer, wie gern, schmücken, schwer bezahlt, ihre Güte, die Rose nur, duftet doch so lieblich,* and *wie ihr wißt.* Circle them as you listen.

6. Exceptional Words: The word *doch* is an addition to the syntax that is intended to give emphasis. In English, we might translate it as *indeed* or *yet.* In the German language, it is often called a "flavoring particle," a word that is tossed into the phrase to add "flavor" to it.

No. I, *Italienisches Liederbuch*

Auch kleine Dinge können uns entzücken,
Also (even) small things can us entice,

Auch kleine Dinge können teuer sein.
Also (even) small things can precious (to us) be.

Bedenkt, wie gern wir uns mit Perlen schmücken;
Ponder, how gladly we ourselves with pearls adorn;

Sie werden schwer bezahlt und sind nur klein.
They are difficult to pay for and are only small.

Bedenkt, wie klein ist die Olivenfrucht,
Ponder, how small is the fruit of the olive tree/olive-fruit,

Und wird um ihre Güte doch gesucht,
And will because of her goodness yet be sought,

Denkt an die Rose nur, wie klein sie ist,
Think of the rose only, how small she is,

Und duftet doch so lieblich, wie ihr wißt.
And releases scent yet so lovely, as you (all) know.

Poetic Equivalent

Even small things can charm us and be regarded as precious. Think about the pearls that adorn us. They are costly but are very small. Think about the olive that we savor for its taste, yet it too is quite small. Think only of the rose, small as it is, releases a scent that is so sweet—as you know.

Comparative Listening

Compare the performances of sopranos Elisabeth Schwarzkopf and Barbara Bonney. Contrast the approach of each singer to the text. Which words attract special attention? How does each singer shape the final cadential phrase?

Hugo Wolf and *Spanisches Liederbuch*

The *Spanisches Liederbuch* consists of 10 sacred Spanish texts and 34 secular ones translated by Heyse and Emanuel Geibel (1818–1884). Here is an example of one of the most popular songs from the secular portion of the collection. Notice how Wolf imitates the Spanish guitar in the accompaniment. Read the text and create a phonetic transcription.

Comparative Listening

"In dem Schatten Meiner Locken" ("In the Shadow of My Curls")

Before you listen, implement your dictation strategies:

1. Spellings: Look for IPA spellings you already know such as the articles *der*, *den*, and *diese*; the conjunction *und*; prepositions *in* and *bei*; and pronouns *mir*, *ich*, *ihn*, *meine*, *sie*, *er*, *ihm*, *mich*, and *mir*.

2. Familiar Words: Look for words you may recognize such as the injections *Ach nein!*

3. Rhyming Words: Follow down the right side of the text to identify rhymes such as *ein/nein*, *krausen/zerzausen/Windessausen*, *Frühe/Mühe*, and *Wange/Schlange*.

Each pair should have the same IPA symbols for the rhyming vowels. The pair *gräme/nehme* must be tuned to rhyme though they are not an identical match.

4. Repeating Words: Study the text for common words that repeat such as *weck' ich ihn* and *ach nein!* Note the repetitions in the inner dialogue: *Daß er/daß ihm* followed by *und er/und doch*. Each use of the repeated words will have a different vocal color but should be pronounced similarly.

5. Expressive Possibilities: Circle the words that invite expression such as *Schatten, Locken, sorglich strählt, meine Mühe, Winde sie zersausen, schläferten den Liebsten, gräme, schmachtet schon,* and *seine Schlange.*

6. Exceptional Words: *Lockenschatten/Windessausen* are compound words created to accommodate the translation. Both words deserve special care because they combine the images of the poem into single expressions.

In dem Schatten meiner Locken
In the shadow of my curls

Schlief mir mein Geliebter ein.
Asleep near me my beloved fell.

Weck ich ihn nun auf?—Ach, nein!
Wake I him now up?—Oh, no!

Sorglich strählte ich meine krausen Locken täglich in der Frühe,
Carefully combed I my curly curls daily in the early (morning),

Doch umsonst ist meine Mühe,
Yet for nothing is my effort,

Weil die Winde sie zerzausen.
While/since the winds they rustle around.

Lockenschatten, Windessausen,
Curl shadows, Wind rustlings,

Schläferten den Liebsten ein.
Asleep the beloved fell.

Weck ich ihn nun auf?—Ach, nein!
Wake I him now up?—Oh, no!

Hören muß ich wie ihn gräme,
Hear must I how he grieves,

Daß er schmachtet schon so lange,
That he suffers already so long,

Daß ihm Leben geb' und nehme
That him life gives and takes

Diese meine brauen Wange,
These my brown cheeks,

Und er nennt mich seine Schlange,
And he names me his snake,

Und doch schlief er bei mir ein.
And yet asleep he near me fell.

Weck ich ihn nun auf?—Ach, nein!
Wake I him now up?—Oh, no!

Poetic Equivalent

In the shadow of my curls, my beloved has fallen asleep. Should I wake him up yet? Oh, no! I brush my hair carefully every morning. Despite my effort, the wind tosses my curls around. It was the curls' shadow and the rustling wind that lulled my beloved to sleep. Should I wake him up yet? Oh, no! If I did, I would have to hear how I make him suffer, how he feels consumed by his love of the sight of me. Sometimes he even refers to me as if I were a flirtatious serpent. Should I wake him up yet? Oh, no!

Comparative Performances

"In dem Schatten Meiner Locken" has been recorded by many performers. As you compare performances, notice how each singer times the delivery of the question/answer sequence. How does the tempo impact a convincing delivery? How are the expressive words addressed?

Gustav Mahler (1860–1911)

Gustav Mahler composed more than 40 songs as well as orchestral works. He was also an international orchestral conductor. Though Mahler's song repertoire is published in piano-vocal score, the songs were intended to be performed with an orchestra in public concert halls. They require a vocal and diction approach that will accommodate the orchestral idiom.

Comparative Listening

Here is an example of one of Mahler's five songs on texts by Rückert, written in 1901 and 1902. The Lied was created as an orchestrated song but is often performed with piano accompaniment. Read the text and create a phonetic transcription.

"Ich Atmet eine Lindenduft" ("I Breathed the Scent of Lime")

Before you listen, implement your dictation strategies:

1. Spellings: Look for IPA spellings you already know such as the articles *einen, ein, der,* and *das;* prepositions *im* and *von;* and pronouns *ich* and *du.*

2. Familiar Words: Look for words you may recognize such as *Zimmer, Hand,* and *Liebe.*

3. Rhyming Words: Follow down the right side of the text to identify rhymes such as *Duft/Lindenduft/Duft* and *Linde/gelinde/Linde.* Mark each rhyming word with the same IPA symbols.

4. Repeating Words: Study the text for words that repeat such as *ich atmet'/ich atme,' linden,* and *Duft.*

5. Expressive Possibilities: Circle the words that invite expression such as the alliterative *Zimmer stand ein Zweig, lieblich war der Lindenduft, Lindenreis brachst du gelinde,* and *Liebe linden Duft.*

6. Exceptional Words: The German word *Linden* is translated in most dictionaries as *lime.* A linden tree on the European continent is not exactly analogous to a fruit-bearing lime tree. It is a tree that blossoms in early spring. In German folklore, the Lindenbaum (linden tree) is referred to as the "tree of lovers."

Ich atmet' einen Lindenduft

I breathed a linden scent

Im Zimmer stand ein Zweig der Linde,

In the room stood a twig from a linden tree,

Ein Angebinde von lieber Hand.

An offering from a dear/loved hand.

Wie lieblich war der Lindenduft!

How lovely was the linden scent!

Das Lindenreis brachst du gelinde:

The linden sprig broke you gently:

Ich atme leis im Duft der Linde

I breathe lightly in the scent of the linden (twig)

Der Liebe linden Duft.

Of love's linden scent.

Poetic Equivalent

I breathed the scent of a linden tree. In the room stood the twig from a linden tree that was given me by your loving hand. How lovely was the linden scent! The sprig of a linden tree you had gently broken off; I inhaled the scent lightly, the scent of love's linden tree.

Comparative Performances

This song has been performed by female and male singers with piano and with orchestra. Select performances that will help you study the diction challenges and interpretative possibilities.

Richard Strauss (1864–1949)

The German composer Richard Strauss composed more than 200 songs. He was a prolific and influential composer whose orchestral and opera works remain in the repertory. Like Mahler, Strauss created solo songs that could be performed with piano but were ultimately intended as orchestrated songs. His wife, Pauline de Ahna (1863–1950), was an operatic soprano, whose voice served as the model for Strauss' songwriting. You will face the vocal demands of singing with an orchestra later in your training. Allow this poem set to music by Strauss to inspire you to meet future challenges. Read the text and create a phonetic transcription.

Comparative Listening

"Die Nacht" ("The Night")
(Text by Hermann von Gilm zu Rosenegg [1812–1864].)

Before you listen, implement your dictation strategies:

1. Spellings: Look for IPA spellings you already know such as the articles *dem*, *die*, *den*, *dieser*, *des*, and *der*; the conjunction *und*; prepositions *aus*, *im*, and *vom*; and pronouns *sie*, *sich*, *mir*, and *dich*.

2. Familiar Words: Look for words you may recognize such as *Walde*, *Nacht*, *Bäume*, *Welt*, *Blumen*, *Silber*, and *Gold*.

3. Rhyming Words: Follow down the right side of the text to identify rhymes such as *Nacht/acht*, *leise/Kreise*, *Welt/Feld*, *Farben/Garben*, *hold/Gold*, *Stroms/Doms*, *Strauch/auch*, and *Seele/stehle*.

4. Repeating Words: Study the text for words that repeat such as *aus*, *alle* (*alles*), and *nimmt*.

5. Expressive Possibilities: Circle the words that invite expression such as <u>schleicht</u> <u>sie leise</u>, <u>schaut</u> <u>sich um</u>, <u>weitem</u> <u>Kreise</u>, <u>löscht</u>, <u>stiehlt</u>, <u>Silber weg des Stroms</u>, <u>Kupferdach</u> des <u>Doms</u>, <u>ausgeplündert</u>, <u>Seel</u> an <u>Seele</u>, *mir bangt*, and the final *auch*.

Aus dem Walde tritt die Nacht,

Out of the woods treads the night,

Aus dem Bäumen schleicht sie leise,

Out the trees slithers she lightly,

Schaut sich um im weite Kreise,

[She, the night] looks (herself) around in a wide circle,

Nun gib acht.

Now give attention.

Alle Lichter dieser Welt,

All the lights of the world,

Alle Blumen, alle Farben
All the flowers, all the colors

Löscht sie aus und schielt die Garben
Extinguishes she out and steals the grain stalks

Weg vom Feld.
Away from the field.

Alles nimmt sie, was nur hold,
Everything takes she, what (that) only dear (is),

Nimmt das Silber weg des Stroms,
Takes the silver away from the streams,

Nimmt vom Kupferdach des Doms
Takes from the copper roof of the cathedral

Weg das Gold.
Away the gold.

Ausgeplündert steht der Strauch,
Pilfered stands the shrubbery,

Rücke näher, Seel an Seele;
Cluster closer, soul on soul;

O die Nacht mir bangt, sie stehle
Oh, the night me frightens, she (the night) could steal

Dich mir auch.
You from me also.

Poetic Equivalent

The night steps out of the woods and slips gently through the trees, looking around in all directions. Pay attention! All the lights of the world, all the flowers and colors, the fields of grain are about to be lost in the night's darkness. The silver of the stream and the copper of the cathedral roof are dimmed. The shrubs have been plundered. O, the night makes me afraid. What if she were to steal you from me as well?

Comparative Performances

This song is a favorite of many performers. You will be able to compare singers of many eras performing it with piano and with orchestra. After listening to the orchestrated version, begin to imagine the instrumental colors as you listen to the piano accompaniment. Notice how each performer exploits the many vivid images through the tools of diction you have gathered.

Discussion Questions

1. What are the differences between the song settings by Hugo Wolf and Gustav Mahler?
2. Compare the similarities between songs by Richard Strauss, Wolf, and Mahler. How are they different?
3. Why are Wolf's songs considered the culmination of the early German Lied?
4. What are the diction challenges of translating texts such as those found in Wolf's *Italienisches Liederbuch* and *Spanisches Liederbuch*?
5. What is different about a Lied that was conceived for an orchestrated accompaniment?

German Diction Final Presentation Repertoire List

Below is a suggested works appropriate to be assigned for the final presentations in German diction. The works by Brahms and Schumann included here are those that require deeper acquaintance with German language and history. The Lieder by Wolf represent each of the collections. Each student will prepare the text with its word-by-word translation, poetic equivalent, and a thorough program note. The program note should place the work in time and give its historical and musical context. Important biographical information regarding the poet and composer must be included. These materials will be submitted to the instructor for correction and grading. The materials will be duplicated for class use during the presentations. *Note*. Repertoire assignments should be approved by the studio teacher, who may suggest other selections for this project.

An die Nachtigall	Johannes Brahms
Dein Blaues Auge	Johannes Brahms
Der Tod, das Ist die Kühle Nacht	Johannes Brahms
Die Mainacht	Johannes Brahms
Feldeinsamkeit	Johannes Brahms
Immer Leiser Wird Mein Schlummer	Johannes Brahms
In Waldeseinsamkeit	Johannes Brahms
Sommerabend	Johannes Brahms
Wie Bist du Meine Königin	Johannes Brahms
Wir Wandelten	Johannes Brahms
Es Muß ein Wunderbares Sein	Franz Liszt
Freudvoll und Leidvoll	Franz Liszt
Ihr Glocken von Marling	Franz Liszt

Erinnerung	Gustav Mahler
Frühlingsmorgen	Gustav Mahler
Hans und Grete	Gustav Mahler
Ich Ging mit Lust (*Des Knaben Wunderhorn*)	Gustav Mahler
Wer hat dies Liedlein Erdacht? (*Des Knaben Wunderhorn*)	Gustav Mahler
Die Beiden Grenadiere	Robert Schumann
Er, der Herrlichste von Allen (*Frauenliebe und Leben*)	Robert Schumann
Frühlingsnacht (*Liederkreis*, Op. 39)	Robert Schumann
Ich Grolle Nicht (*Dichterliebe*)	Robert Schumann
In Wunderschönen Monat Mai (*Dichterliebe*)	Robert Schumann
Meine Rose	Robert Schumann
Mit Myrthen und Rosen (*Myrthen*)	Robert Schumann
All Mein Gedanken	Richard Strauss
Allerseelen	Richard Strauss
Für Fünfzehn Pfennige	Richard Strauss
Hat Gesagt – Bleibt's Nicht Dabei	Richard Strauss
Ich Trage Meine Minne	Richard Strauss
Morgen	Richard Strauss
Traum Durch die Dämmerung	Richard Strauss
Zueignung	Richard Strauss
Blumengruß (Goethe)	Hugo Wolf
Der Gärtner (Mörike)	Hugo Wolf
Der Musikant (Eichendorff)	Hugo Wolf
Fussreise (Mörike)	Hugo Wolf
Gesang Weylas (Mörike)	Hugo Wolf
Heiss Mich Nicht Reden (Goethe)	Hugo Wolf
Mein Liebster Singt (*Italianienisches Liederbuch*)	Hugo Wolf
Morgentau (Miscellaneous)	Hugo Wolf
Nun Wandre, Maria (*Spanisches Liederbuch*)	Hugo Wolf
Verborgenheit (Mörike)	Hugo Wolf
Wie Lange Schon (*Italianienisches Liederbuch*)	Hugo Wolf

Conclusion

In March 1854, Brahms gave Marie Schumann, daughter of Clara and Robert Schumann, a small leather book of blank pages. He inscribed the second page with the following attribution: "Let who will and can pour forth melodies from ev'ry tree. There is room for many birds in the woods of poetry" (Schumann, 149). From folksong and sacred chorale, to *Singspiel*, opera, cantata, and Lied, German composers through the centuries have poured forth melodies inspired by poetic thought. From their output, we experience the myriad ways that unique "voices" can express the styles, nuances, and symbols of German culture and language in each historical period through song.

References

Armstrong, J. (2006). *Love, life, Goethe: Lessons of the imagination from the great German poet* (p. 3). New York, NY. Farrar, Straus and Giroux

Draper, H. (1982). *The complete poems of Heinrich Heine: A modern version* (p. 5). Boston, MA: Suhrkamp/Insel.

Reusch, F. (1971). *Der kleine hey: Die kunst des sprechens* (p. 16). Mainz, Germany: Schott.

Rolleston, J. L. (1993). German poetry. In A. Preminger & T. Brogen (Eds.), *The new Princeton encyclopedia of poetry and poetics* (p. 470). New York, NY: MJF Books.

Safranski, R. (2016). *Goethe: Life as a work of art* (D. Dollenmayer, Trans., p. xxvi). New York, NY: Norton.

Schumann, E. (1927). *The Schumanns and Johannes Brahms* (p. 149). Lawrence, MA: Music Book Society.

Siebs, T. (2011). In H. Boor (Ed.), *Deutsche aussprache* (19th ed., p. 3). Berlin, Germany: DeGruyter.

Whitton, K. S. (1999). *Goethe and Schubert: The unseen bond* (p. 151). Portland, OR: Amadeus Press.

5

French

The Sounds of French

In comparison to the English, German and Italian languages, French is less "phonetic" than the others. It may not feel as intuitive to you as English, German, and Italian did. To gain confidence in your pronunciation of French, imitate good models and memorize not just the sounds, but also the sensations of those sounds. In French, there are 15 vowel sounds, including the "schwa" [ə], and three "mixed" sounds. There are four nasal vowels that are distinctly "French." The mixed vowels of French resemble three comparable German umlauts you already know: [y:], [ø], and [œ]. The schwa and the mixed vowels will sound slightly different than in German because of the lip position you assume for French. Thomas Grubb explains that French is a frontal, highly placed language. He encourages a pursing of the lips to a round and forward articulatory pattern (Grubb, 1979).

The International Phonetic Alphabet (IPA) symbols for the nasal vowel sounds are [ã], [ɛ̃], [ɔ̃], and [œ̃]. The presence of these nasal sounds creates a lighter, brighter quality in the flow of the French language than any of the languages we have addressed. For a native French speaker, the language floats effortlessly. This is possible because of the practices of "liaison" and "elision" that meld word endings. Liaison is the practice of adding a final consonant from one word to the beginning of the next, the flow is maintained in certain circumstances. "Elision" is the omission of the final unaccented "e" [ə] to avoid interruption of sound. There are many rules that govern this practice in singing. You will wish to consult printed resources and your instructor to properly implement the compulsory, forbidden, and optional liaison practices. To achieve a sense of the forward flow essential to speaking and singing French, try rocking your body from side to side as you read your poetic readings, both aloud and silently.

Here is an introduction to the vowel sounds of French, identified by the following IPA symbols:

| [a] | voi<u>là</u> | [vwa'la] | *there* | "toi que voilà, de ta jeunesse . . . " ("Prison"/"D'une Prison," Verlaine/Fauré, Hahn) |
| [ɑ] | âme | [ɑm] | *soul* | "l'âme évaporée et souffrante . . . " ("Romance," Bourget/Debussy) |

[e] *closed*

bont<u>é</u>	[bõte]	*bounty,*	"je songe à ta bonté . . . "
		goodness	("Ta Bonté," Verhaeren/Pugno-Boulanger)

[ɛ] *open*

rêve	[rɛv]	*dreams*	"rêve e chers instants . . . "
			("Green" and "Offrande," Verlaine/Debussy, Fauré, Hahn)

[o] *closed*

beau	[bo]	*beautiful*	"triste et beau . . . "
			("En Sourdine," Verlaine/Debussy/Fauré)

[ɔ] *open*

robe	[rɔb]	*robe*	"robe des cieux . . . "
			("Mai," Hugo/Fauré)

[i]	lis	[lis]	*lily*	"des lys divins . . . "
				("Romance," Bourget/Debussy)
[u]	d<u>ou</u>x	[du]	*sweet*	"doux et frêles . . . "
				("Si mes vers avaient des ailes!" Hugo/Hahn)

Mute "e": [ə] or [œ]

The schwa symbol [ə] used in the French dictionary for the letter "e" often remains silent in spoken French. In sung French, the muted vowel will be sounded at times and avoided at others. For sustained word endings, your teacher or coach may suggest a vowel modification toward the mixed vowel [œ]. This rounded sound improves tuning and continuity of a musical phrase.

Glides

[j]	b<u>i</u>en	[bjɛ̃]	*good, well*	"que tu m'aimes bien . . . " (that you love me well)
				("À Chloris," de Viau/Hahn)
[w]	esp<u>oi</u>r	[es'pwar]	*hope*	"tout d'espoir . . . " (full of hope)
				("Les Cloches," Bourget/Debussy)
[ɥ]	l<u>ui</u>re	[lɥir]	*shine*	"luire dans son nid . . . " (shine on his nest)
				("Le Colibri," Leconte de Lisle/Chausson)

Mixed Vowels

A mixed vowel unites two pure vowels of different sounds. The French mixed vowels are more focused than their German counterparts. Compare the pronunciation of the German word *für* (*for*) to the French word *sûr* (*on the*). Note the "higher" focus of the French sounds.

[y]	[lyn]	lune	*moonlight*	("Clair de Lune," Verlaine/Debussy, Fauré)
[ø]*	[aˈdø]	adieu	*farewell*	("Adieu," Grandmougin/Fauré)
[œ]	[flœr]	fleur	*flower*	("Fleur Jetée," Silvestre/Fauré)

*In singer's diction, the vowels [e] and [ɛ] as well as [ø] and [œ] are occasionally rhymed to improve tuning. There are two circumstances for [e] and [ɛ]. They are:

1. If the vowel spelled "ai" [ɛ] is followed by vowels spelled with "é," "-er," or "-ez" [e], all the vowels are pronounced [e]. For example, *baiser* (*kiss*), pronounced spoken as [bɛze], is sung [beze].

2. If the article precedes a word that begins with the sound of [e], the vowels of the article and the noun will be rhymed, such as in *les étoiles* [lezeˈtwaːlə] (*the stars*).

3. If [ø] and [œ] appear in the same word, they will be rhymed to [ø]. This practice insures tuning without changing the meaning of the word, such as in *heureux* [øːrø] (*happy*).

Nasal Vowels

The nasal vowels of French are foreign sounds that you will learn to produce through imitation. Keep in mind that the written "signal" for a nasal vowel is the letter "m" or "n" that follows it. The signal consonants (i.e., "m," "n") must *never* be heard in speech or song. Below are the IPA symbols for each of the four nasal vowels with an example and its translation. For each nasal vowel, an English word is listed that you might nasalize as a reminder of its French nasal equivalent.

[ɑ̃]	<u>en</u>se<u>m</u>ble	*ensemble/ together*	Nasalize the words "honk" or "song" to find [ɑ̃].
[ɛ̃]	div<u>in</u>	*divine*	Nasalize the words "sank" or "tank" to find [ɛ̃].
[ɔ̃] [õ]*	col<u>om</u>be	*dove*	Nasalize the words "don't" or "won't" to find [ɔ̃].
[œ̃]	h<u>um</u>ble	*humble*	Nasalize the words "hunt" or "grunt" to find [œ̃].

*Both [ɔ̃] and [õ] are in common usage in published resources. In this text, [õ] will be used.

Nasal Vowels and Their Spellings

French nasal vowels can be identified by their spelling. There are two ways to identify a nasal vowel spelling. A vowel is a nasal vowel when it is followed by a single "m" or "n" *in the same syllable*. The "m" or "n" cannot be followed by another "m" or "n" respectively nor an "h." A nasal spelling (vowel plus "-m" or "-n") within a word will always be followed by a "sounded" consonant. The "m" or "n" in a nasal vowel spelling is always silent. It is the signal to you that you are to nasalize the vowel. A nasal spelling (vowel plus "-m" or "-n") will never be followed by a vowel. A nasal spelling (vowel plus "-m" or "-n") may conclude a word.

Four types:

[ã]   Hint: "song" or "honk"

Spellings: -am   le bambou [bã:'bu]   *the bamboo*

-an   balance [ba:'lã:s]   *balance*

-em   le temps [tã:]   *the time*

-en   immense [im'mã:s]   *immense*

Here are some common words in English usage: *embouchure* [ã:bu'ʃy:r] (*mouthpiece/opening*), *encore* [ã:'kɔ:r] (*again*), and *ensemble* [ã:'sã:bl] (*together/group*).

[ɔ̃]   Hint: "don't" or "won't"

Spellings: -om   colombe [kɔ'lõ:b]   *the dove*

-on   gazon [ga'zõ]   *grass*

[ɛ̃]   Hint: "sank" or "tank"

Spellings: -aim   essaim [ɛ's ɛ̃]   *swarm, crowd*

-ain   la main [mɛ̃:]   *the hand*

-im   simple [sɛ̃:pl]   *simple*

-in   jardin [ʒar'dɛ̃:]   *garden*

-ein   plein [plɛ̃:]   *full*

-ym   symphonie ['sɛ̃fɔ'ni]   *symphony*

-yn   syncope [sɛ̃'kɔp]   *syncopation* (musical term)

Words in common use: *refrain* [rœ'frɛ̃:] (*chorus* or *refrain*) and *timbre* ['tɛ̃:br] (*timbre* or *tone quality*)

[œ̃]   Hint: "hunt" or "grunt"

Spellings: -um   parfum [par' fœ̃]   *perfume*

-un   un [œ̃]   *a, an*

Diacritical Marks

The sounds of vowels can be altered through any one of four markings:

◆ Accent grave [ak'sã gra:v] *grave accent*

The accent grave (`) can occur with the following vowel sounds: "è," "à," and "où." The accent grave only affects the pronunciation of the letter "è." It opens the sound to [ɛ].

◆ Accent aigu [ak'sã e'gy] *acute accent*

The accent aigu (´) occurs with the following vowel sound: é. It closes the sound to [e].

◆ Accent circonflexe [ak'sã sirkõ'flɛks] *accent circumflex*

The circumflex (^) can occur with the following vowel sounds: "â," "ê," "î," "ô," "û," "aî," "oî," "aû," and "oû."

The accent circumflex has an impact on the pronunciation of only three of those vowels: "â," "ê," and "ô." The accent circumflex changes the pronunciation of the three vowels in the following ways:

> â [ɑ] The accent circumflex indicates that the vowel is the "dark ɑ." Ex. *âme* [ɑm] (*soul*)
>
> ê [ɛ] The accent circumflex "opens" the vowel [e]. Ex. *rêve* [rɛv] (*dream*)
>
> ô [o] The accent circumflex keeps the vowel [o] closed. Ex. *hôtel* [o'tɛl] (*hotel*)

◆ Diérèse or "dieresis"

The diérèse (¨) can occur only with the following vowel sounds: "ë," "ï," and "ÿ." The diérèse (dieresis) indicates a separation between two vowel sounds, causing both vowels to be pronounced, as in *naïve* [na'iv] (*naïve*) and *Noël* [nɔ'ɛl] (*Christmas*).

French Consonants

The fricative consonants of the French language are:

[f]	spelled "f," "ff," and "ph"	chef	['ʃɛf]	*chef*	effigie [efi'ʒi]	*effigy*	sphere ['sfɛr]	*sphere*
[s]	spelled "s," "ss," "ç"	lis	[lis]	*lily*	laissez [lese]	*leave*	ça [sa]	*that is*
[v]	villanelle	[vila'nɛl]	*pastoral poem*			[z] rose	[ro:z]	*rose*
[ʃ]	chose	[ʃoz]	*thing*			[ʒ] image	[i'ma:ʒ]	*image*

The lateral consonants of the French language are:

[l]	ciel	[sjɛl]	*sky, heavens*	[ll]	ville	[vil]	*village*

The nasal consonants of the French language are:

[m]	amour	[aˈmuːr]	*love*		[mm]	i<u>mm</u>ense	[imˈmãs]	*immense*
[n]	neige	[nɛːʒ]	*snow*		[nn]	e<u>nn</u>ui	[ãˈnɥi]	*boredom*
[ɲ]	cygne	[siɲ]	*swan*					

The plosive consonants of the French language are:

[b]	baiser	[beze]	*kiss*		[p]	papillon	[papiˈjõ]	*butterfly*
[d]	des	[dɛ]	*of the*		[t]	tarte	[tart]	*tart*
[g]	garçon	[garˈsõ]	*boy*		[k]	calme	[kalm]	*calm*

In elision and liaison, consonants turn from voiceless to voiced.

The letter "r" is pronounced:

[r]	brûler	[bryle]	*to burn*		[rr]	irriter	[irriˈte]	*to irritate*

Parts of Speech and Elements of Grammar

Elements of Sentences

There are a variety of ways a sentence can be constructed in French. Like Italian, French is a Romance language. It is based on Vulgar Latin, a form that lacked the grammatical complexity of Classical Latin. It has only two genders for nouns. Many grammatical elements in the French language vary by the gender and number of the noun. The definite article, translated as *the* in English, indicates the gender and number of a noun, be it feminine or masculine. As in Italian, the spelling of a definite article in French is influenced by whether the first consonant of the noun it identifies is a consonant or a vowel. Until you become familiar with the French language, the placement of pronouns between the subject and verb in any clause may cause confusion. The lyric flow of the language will be helpful to you as a singer in the achievement of a fluid legato line. Here are some general rules that will acquaint you with the sentence elements of French.

Nouns

A noun's gender and number can be identified by the definite article that precedes it. If a singular noun is masculine and begins with a consonant, the definite article will be *le* [lə].

le ballet [lə baˈlɛ]   *ballet*

If a singular noun is feminine and begins with a consonant, the definite article will be *la* [la].

la musique [la myːzik]   *music*

If the singular noun begins with a vowel or mute "h," the definite article will be *l* [l] regardless of the gender.

l'opéra	[ɔpe'ra]	*opera*	(masculine)
l' harmonie	[armɔ'ni]	*harmony*	(feminine)

The gender of nouns corresponds with the gender of the male or female subject.

le père	[pɛ:r]	*father*	la mère	[mɛ:r]	*mother*
le frère	[frɛ:r]	*brother*	la sœur	[sœ:r]	*sister*
l'acteur	[ak'tœr]	*actor*	l'actrice	[ak'tris]	*actress*

Words ending in "-e" or "-on" are usually feminine.

la danse	[dɑ̃:s]	*dance*	la chanson	[ʃɑ̃'sɔ̃]	*song*

Words ending in sounding consonants or the vowels -i or –u are usually masculine.

le ciel	[sjɛl]	*sky*	l'oubli	[u'bli]	*oblivion*

Pronouns

Subject Pronouns

Singular				Plural			
je	[ʒə]	*I*		nous	[nu]	*we*
tu	[ty]	*you (sing. familiar)*		vous	[vu]	*you (pl. or formal)*
il	[il]	*he, it*		ils	[il]	*they (masc.)*
elle	[ɛl]	*she, it*		elles	[ɛl]	*they (fem.)*
on	[ɔ̃:]	*one/it, we, people*				

In French, the gender of the noun the pronoun replaces matters.

Direct Object Pronouns

First and Second Person

me	[mə]	*me*		nous	[nu]	*us*
te	[tə]	*you*		vous	[vu]	*you*

Third Person

le	[lə]	*him, it*	la	[la]	*her, it*	les	[lɛ]	*them*

In French, the direct object pronoun is placed between the subject and the verb.

Indirect Object Pronouns

First and Second Person

me	[mə]	*to me*		nous	[nu]	*to us*
te	[tə]	*to you*		vous	[vu]	*to you*

Third Person: The forms differ when referring to a person or an idea or a tangible item.

Person

Singular: lui   [lɥi]   *to him* or *to her*   (masculine or feminine)

Plural: leur   [lœr]   *to them*   (masculine or feminine)

Idea or Tangible Item

Singular and Plural: y   [i]   *to it*

Plural: The forms are the same ones used for subject and object.

In French, the indirect direct object pronoun is usually located before the verb.

Possessive Pronouns

Singular Ownership

Masculine:	le	[lə]	le mien	[lə mjɛ̃:]	(masculine noun, *belonging to me*)
Feminine:	la	[la]	la mienne	[lə mjɛn]	(feminine noun, *belonging to me*)
Masculine/ Feminine:	les	[lɛ]	les miens	[lɛ mjɛ̃:]	(plural nouns, *belonging to me*)

Plural Ownership

nôtre [nɔtr] *ours*   vôtre [vɔtr] *yours*   leur [lœ:r] *theirs*

Relative Pronouns

Singular or Plural Subject (person/thing):	qui [ki]	*who* or *that*
Singular or Plural Direct Object (person or thing):	que or qu' [kə]	*who* or *that*
Singular or Plural Indirect Object:	à qui [a ki]	*to whom*
Possessive:	dont [dõ:]	*whose*

Interrogative or Question Words

Subject: qui? [ki]   *Who?*

Direct Object: qui est-ce que? [ki ɛsə kə]   *Whom?*

Indirect Object: The forms differ when referring to a person or an idea or a tangible item.

Person:	a qui est-ce que?	[a ki ɛsə kə]	*To whom?*
	avec qui est ce que?	[avɛk ki ɛsœ kə]	*With whom?*
Idea or Tangible Item:	a quoi est-ce que?	[a kwa ɛsœ kə]	*To what?*
	avec quoi est ce que?	[avɛk kwa ɛsœ kə]	*With what?*

Demonstrative Pronouns

Singular: Masculine

celui-ci	[səlɥi si]	*this one*	celui-là	[səlɥi la]	*that one*

Feminine

celle-ci	[sɛl si]	*this one*	celle-là	[sɛl la]	*that one*

Plural:	ceux-ci	[sø si]	*those*	celles-là	[sɛl la]	*those*

Reflexive Pronouns

Singular				Plural		
me	[mə]	*myself*		nous	[nu]	*ourselves*
te	[tə]	*yourself*		vous	[vu]	*yourselves*
se	[sə]	*himself, herself, itself, oneself*		se	[sə]	*themselves*

Reflexive verbs are listed in the dictionary by the infinitive of the verb. For example, the reflexive verb *se promener* [sə promɛne] (*to walk oneself* or *to take a walk*) would be found under *promener* in the dictionary.

Verbs

Regular Conjugations

Regular verbs in French are divided into three conjugations.

The signal for a conjugation is the ending of the infinitive.

First conjugation	-er	donner	[dɔne]	*to give*
Second conjugation	-ir	finir	[fini:r]	*to finish*
Third conjugation	-re	vendre	[vɑ̃:dr]	*to sell*

Present Indicative of First Conjugation:

je donne	[ʒə dɔn:]	*I give*	nous donnons	[nu dɔnõ]	*we give/let's give*
tu donnes	[ty dɔn:]	*you (sing.) give*	vous donnez	[vu dɔne]	*you (pl.) give*
il donne	[il dɔn]	*he gives*	ils donnent	[il dɔn]	*they give (masc.)*
elle donne	[ɛl dɔn]	*she gives*	elles donnent	[ɛl dɔn]	*they give (fem.)*

Present Indicative of Second Conjugation:

je finis	[ʒə fini:]	*I finish*	nous finissons	[nu fini'sõ]	*we finish*
tu finis	[ty fini:]	*you finish*	vous finissez	[vu fini'se]	*you finish (pl.)*
il finit	[il fini:]	*he finishes*	ils finissent	[il fi'nis]	*they finish (masc.)*
elle finit	[ɛl fini:]	*she finishes*	elles finissent	[ɛl fi'nis]	*they finish (fem.)*

Present Indicative of Third Conjugation:

je vends	[ʒə vã]	*I sell*	nous vendons	[nu vã'dõ]	*we sell*
tu vends	[ty vã]	*you sell*	vous vendez	[vu vã'de]	*you sell (pl.)*
il vend	[il vã]	*he sells*	ils vendent	[il 'vãdə]	*they sell (masc.)*
elle vend	[ɛl vã]	*she sells*	elles vendent	[ɛl 'vãdə]	*they sell (fem)*

Negation of Verbs

To negate a verb's meaning, place "ne" before the verb and "pas" after it.

Ex.	je *ne* donne *pas*	[ʒənədɔnpa]	*I do not give*
	je ne suis pas	[ʒənəsɥipa]	*I am not*
	je n'ai pas	[ʒənəpa]	*I do not have*

Irregular Verbs

As in every language, French has many irregular verbs. Consult references such as *501 French Verbs*, a textbook, or a dictionary for further details. Here are a few examples.

The verb *tenir* [təni :r] *to hold*   Participle: tenant [tənã]

Present Indicative of *tenir*

je tiens	[ʒə tjɛ̃]	*I hold*	nous tenons	[nu tənõ]	*we hold*
tu tiens	[ty tjɛ̃]	*you hold*	vous tenez	[vu təne]	*you hold (pl.)*
il tient	[il tjɛ̃]	*he holds*	ils tiennent	[il tjɛ̃]	*they hold (masc.)*
elle tient	[ɛl tjɛ̃]	*she holds*	elles tiennent	[ɛl tjɛ̃]	*they hold (fem.)*

Other common verbs that follow irregular conjugation patterns are:

apprendre	*to learn*	craindre	*to fear*	prendre	*to take*	comprendre	*to contain*
asseoir	*to sit*	savoir	*to know*	voir	*to see*	vouloir	*to want*
boire	*to drink*	dire	*to say*	écrire	*to write*	lire	*to read*
rire	*to smile*	conduire	*to lead*	courir	*to run*	couvrir	*to cover*
ouvrir	*to open*	faire	*to make*	plaire	*to please*	mettre	*to put*
permettre	*to permit*	mourir	*to die*	offrir	*to open*	recevoir	*to receive*
venir	*to come*	suivre	*to follow*	vivre	*to live*	connaître	*to be acquainted*

Modal Verbs

The modal verbs in French are:

devoir	[də'vwa :r]	*to owe, to obliged to, to be bound to, to have to, to must*
pouvoir	[pu'vwa :r]	*to be able, to have power, to be allowed, to be possible*
vouloir	[vu'lwa :r]	*to will, desire, wish, require, want*

The modal verbs are irregular verbs you will confront regularly in poetic texts.

Auxiliary Verbs

Also called "helper" verbs, the auxiliary verbs are irregular. They appear very often in poetic texts. You will want to memorize the auxiliary verbs in the list below. Future and past tense verb forms are built upon the auxiliary verbs. Be sure you understand their spellings, their phonetic pronunications, and their meanings. This knowledge will help you divide and conquer the texts that you study.

avoir	[a'vwa:r]	*to have*	être	['ɛtr]	*to be*
j'ai	[ʒe]	*I have*	je suis	[ʒə sɥi]	*I am*
tu as	[tya]	*you have*	tu es	[tyɛ]	*you are*
il a	[ila]	*he has*	il est	[ilɛ]	*he is*
elle a	[ɛla]	*she has*	elle est	[ɛlɛ]	*she is*
nous avons	[nuzavõ]	*we have*	nous sommes	[nusɔm]	*we are*
vous avez	[vuzave]	*you have (pl.)*	vous êtes	[vuzɛt]	*you are (pl.)*
ils ont	[ilzõ]	*they have (masc.)*	ils sont	[ilsõ]	*they are (masc.)*
elles ont	[ɛlzõ]	*they have (fem.)*	elles sont	[ɛlsõ]	*they are (fem.)*

Note. Often in poetry, you will find *ce* [sə] or *il* [il] as subjects of *être* or another verb, as in:

Ce as Subject: "C'est l'extase langoureuse/c'est la fatigue amoureuse" or "It is a languorous ecstasy, it is an amorous fatigue" (Verlaine/Debussy, Fauré).

Il as Subject: "Il pleure dans mon coeur . . . " or "It weeps in my heart" (poetic equivalent: "My heart weeps") (Verlaine/Debussy, Fauré).

Adjectives

In French, adjectives change their form to agree with the gender and number of the noun or pronoun they modify.

- ◆ Descriptive adjectives indicate the quality of a noun.

    Le ciel est bleu. *The sky is blue.* La robe est bleue. *The dress is blue.*

- ◆ Demonstrative adjectives point to a noun. In French, the demonstrative adjective *ce* [sə] stands for both *this* and *that*, and *these* and *those*.

    "Auprès de ce berceau . . . " *Close to this cradle* . . . ("Soir d' Hiver," N. Boulanger)

    "Cet" or "cette" before a vowel

    "Cette âme adorable" *This soul adorable* . . . ("Romance," Bourget/Debussy)

    "Ces" is the plural form

    "Ces cloches parlaient" *These bells tell* . . . ("Les Cloches," Bourget/Debussy)

- ◆ Interrogative adjectives ask questions of a noun. There is only one interrogative adjective in French. It is *quel* [kɛl], meaning *what?* or *which?* The form will change based upon the gender and number of the word it modifies. The forms are:

Masculine singular	quel [kɛl]	Masculine plural	quels [kɛl]
Feminine singular	quelle [kɛl]	Feminine plural	quelles [kɛl]

- ◆ Possessive adjectives indicate ownership of a noun. They agree in gender and number with the noun they modify.

    First Person:

Masculine singular	mon [mõ] *my*		plural	mes [mɛ]
Feminine singular	ma [ma]/mon [mõ] *my*		plural	mes [mɛ]

    Second Person:

Masculine singular	ton [tõ] *your*		plural	tes [tɛ]
Feminine singular	ta [ta]/ton [tõ] *your*		plural	tes [tɛ]

Third Person:

Masculine singular	son [sõ] *his*			plural	ses [sɛ]
Feminine singular	sa [sa]/son [sõ] *hers*			plural	ses [sɛ]

Plural Ownership

Singular	notre [nɔtr] *our*	votre [vɔtr] *your*	leur [lœr] *their*
Plural	nos [no] *our*	vos [vo] *your*	leurs [lœr] *their*

Adverbs

Adverbs describe verbs, adjectives, or another adverb. In French, adverbs can be recognized by their "-ment" endings. Unlike in English, the adverb is placed after the verb in most sentences.

Articles

◆ Definite Articles

le + masculine noun   la + feminine noun

l' + either if it begins with vowel/"h"   les = all plural nouns

◆ Indefinite Articles

un + masculine noun   une + feminine noun   des + all plural nouns = some

Comparatives and Superlatives

◆ Comparisons in French

Comparisons to a greater degree are formed with "plus" [ply], meaning *more*, an adjective, and *que* [kə], meaning *than*.

Comparisons to a lesser degree are formed with *moins* [mwɛ̃], meaning *less*, an adjective, and *que* [kə] meaning, *than*.

Comparison of equal degrees are formed with *aussi* [osi], meaning *as*, an adjective, and *que* [kə], meaning *than*.

◆ Superlatives in French

Superlatives of the greatest degree are formed with *le, la,* or *les* (*he, she, they*) (depending upon the gender and number of the noun being described) followed by *plus* [ply], meaning *most*, and an adjective.

Superlatives of the lowest degree are formed with *le, la,* or *les* (*he, she, they*) (depending upon the gender and number of the noun being described) followed by *moins* [mwɛ̃], meaning *less,* and an adjective.

bon/bonne [bõ:] [bɔn] *good*		meilleur/meilleure [mɛˈjœ:r] [mɛˈjœ:r] *better*		
le meilleur/la meilleure *the best*		bien [bjɛ̃] *well*		
mieux [mjø] *better*				

Prepositions

Prepositions situate a noun or verb in single words or phrases.

à	[a]	*at, in, to*	à cause de	[a ko:z də]	*because of*
à côté de	[a kote də]	*next to*	à propos de	[a propo də]	*regarding*
après	[aprɛ]	*after*	au centre de	[o sãtrədə]	*in the center of*
au lieu de	[o ljø də]	*instead of*	au milieu de	[o miljø də]	*in the midst of*
au sujet de	[o syˈʒɛ də]	*concerning*	au-dessous de	[odəˈsu də]	*underneath*
au-dessus de	[odəˈsy də]	*above, over*	avant	[avã :]	*before*
dans	[dã:]	*in*	de	[də]	*of, from*
de la part de	[də la par:də]	*from*	de peur de	[də pœr də]	*in fear of*
en	[ã:]	*in, of, on*	en face de	[ã:fas də]	*across from*
entre	[ãtr]	*between*	grâce à	[gras:a]	*thanks to*
jusque	[ʒysk]	*until*	loin de	[lwɛ̃ də]	*far from*
malgré	[malˈgre]	*in spite of*	pendant	[pã:dã]	*during*
pour	[pu :r]	*for*	près de	[prɛ də]	*near*
sans	[sã:]	*without*			

Conjunctions

Conjunctions connect ideas from one element of a sentence to another.

Coordinating Conjunctions

ainsi	[ɛ̃ˈsi]	*thus*	donc	[dõ :k]	*so/then*
et	[e]	*and*	mais	[mɛ]	*but*
ou	[u]	*or*	par contre	[par kõtr]	*on the other hand*
pourtant	[purˈtã:]	*however*	surtout	[syrˈtu:]	*especially*

Subordinating Conjunctions

alors que	[a'lɔr kə]	*while/when*	aussitôt que	[osi'to]	*as soon as*
bien que	[bjɛ̃ kə]	*although*	car	[kar]	*for*
comme	[kɔm]	*like/as*	dès que	[dɛ kə]	*as soon as*
lorsque	['lɔrskə]	*when*	malgré que	[mal'gre kə]	*although*
parce que	[parsə 'kə]	*because*	pendant que	[pɑ̃:dɑ̃ kə]	*while*
puisque	[pɥiskə]	*since*	quand	[kɑ̃:]	*when*
quoique	['kwakə]	*whatever*	tandis que	[tɑ̃'di kə]	*while*

The Early French Art Song

The French art song or *mélodie* developed after the German Lied and is grounded in the harmonic language of Robert Schumann and Richard Wagner. Arguably, the program music of Hector Berlioz (1803–1869) heralded the arrival of the idea of "romanticism" or literary-based art in France. The premiere of *Symphonie Fantastique*, Op. 14 took place in Paris on Dec. 9, 1830. "Fantastic Symphony: An Episode in the Life of an Artist in Five Parts" depicted five imaginary situations. The literary basis for these five events was invented by Berlioz as a "skeleton" he would "dress" through orchestral means. He won the coveted *Prix de Rome* on his fourth attempt. Berlioz was not only a composer and conductor; he was also a man of letters. His opinions and experiences are well-documented in his musical reviews, essays, and memoir. Through his travels, Berlioz became an international figure whose opinions and practices influenced musicians and philosophers in London, throughout Europe, and Russia. Berlioz studied at the Paris Conservatory. Berlioz' operas maintain their place in modern repertory. His song cycle, *Les Nuits d'été* on poems by Théophile Gautier, is frequently performed in recital with piano or in the concert setting with orchestral accompaniment.

Hector Berlioz (1803–1869)

Here is a selection from *Les Nuits d'Été*. Use the strategies you have learned to divide and conquer these texts. Read the text and create a phonetic transcription.

Comparative Listening

"Villanelle" ("Pastoral Poem")
(from *Les Nuits d'Été*, #1.)

Before you listen, implement your dictation strategies:

1. Spellings: Look for IPA spellings you already know such as articles *la, les, le, de,* and *des*; the auxiliary verb *est*; conjunctions *quand* and *et*; possessive adjectives

ma, nos, son, and *ta;* prepositions *aux, sous, au, du,* and *en;* and pronouns *on, nous,* and *moi.*

2. Familiar Words: Look for words you may recognize such as *saison, deux, belle, pieds, matin, printemps, amants, oiseau, amours, bien, loin,* and *bois.*

3. Rhyming Words: Follow down the right side of the text to identify rhymes such as *nouvelle/belle, froids/bois, trembler/siffler, belle/aile, béni/nid, mousse/douce, amours/toujours, courses/sources, caché/penché/aisés,* and *doigts/bois.* Be sure to use the same vowel choices for each of the rhyming pairs.

4. Repeating Words: Study the text for common words that repeat such as *quand ma belle/bois* and *loin.* Mark them with the same IPA spelling in each repetition.

Quand viendra la saison nouvelle,
When comes the season new,

Quand auront disparu les froids,
When departs the cold (frost)

Tous les deux nous irons, ma belle,
Both two of us shall go, my beauty,

Pour cueillir le muguet aux bois.
To gather lily of the valley in the woods.

Sous nos pieds égrenant les perles
Under our feet treading on the pearls

Que l'on voit au matin trembler.
That one sees in the morning trembling.

Nous irons écouter les merles: siffler!
We will listen to the blackbirds: let's whistle!

Le printemps est venu, ma belle,
The spring has come, my beauty,

C'est le mois des amants béni;
This is the month of lovers blessed;

Et l'oiseau satinant son aile,
And the bird preening his wing,

Dit ses vers au rebord du nid.
Says his verses from the edge of the nest.

Oh! Viens donc, sur ce banc de mousse
Oh! Come then to this bank of moss

Pour parler de nos beaux amours,
To speak of our beautiful love,

Et dis-moi de ta voix si douce,
And say to me with your voice so sweet,

Toujours!
Always!

Loin, bien loin, égarant nos courses,
Far, very far, straying from our course,

Faisant fuir le lapins caché,
Making us flee the rabbits hidden,

Et le daim, au miroir des sources
And the deer on the mirror of the brook

Admirant son grand bois penché;
Admiring his grand antlers tilted;

Puis chez nous, tout heureux, tout aisés,
Then to our home, so happily, so at ease,

En paniers enlaçant nos doigts,
In baskets intertwining our fingers,

Revenons, rapportant des fraises des bois.
Dreaming, bringing back the strawberries from the woods.

Poetic Equivalent

When the seasons change and the cold departs, let's go, my dear, to gather lily of the valley in the woods. We will stroll on the trembling pearls that one sees in the early morning and hear blackbirds singing. Whistle at them! The spring is coming, my dear. It is the month for lovers who are blessed. A bird is preening his wings and singing from the edge of his nest. Oh, come to the mossy bank. We will settle down and talk of our love. In your sweet voice say "Always!" Let's stray far off the path and cause the rabbits to flee their hiding places. We might see a deer who is tilting his antlers, admiring himself in the clear brook. Then, let's go home, very happy, very relaxed, hand in hand, carrying our baskets filled with strawberries fresh from the woods.

Comparative Performances

Listen to a performance of this song with a piano accompaniment. Compare it to an orchestrated version of the song. What are the similarities? What are the differences? What diction challenges do you anticipate with the orchestrated version?

Cesar Franck (1822–1890)

Though born in Belgium, Cesar Franck spent most of his career as an organist and professor at the Paris Conservatory. To understand how Franck expanded the musical language of French music, one need only to hear the chromaticism that pervades his beloved *Prelude, Chorale, and Fugue* for piano or the *Violin Sonata in A Major*. Franck trained many significant composers of his time. His devoted students called themselves "Franckists" and include Ernst Chausson, Henri Duparc, Gabriel Fauré, Camille Saint-Saëns, and Vincent D'Indy. As you listen, observe Franck's harmonic language. Read the text and create a phonetic transcription.

Comparative Listening

"La Procession" ("The Procession")
(Text by August Brizeux [1803–1858].)

Before you listen, implement your dictation strategies:

1. Spellings: Look for IPA spellings you already know such as the articles *les* and *la*; the conjunction *et*; prepositions *du, par, aux, sous, sur, avec,* and *à*; possessives *vos* and *votre*; and pronouns *on* and *vous*.

2. Familiar Words: Look for words you may recognize such as *cantiques, l'homme, oiseaux, soleil, fleurs,* and *champs*.

3. Rhyming Words: Follow down the right side of the text to identify rhymes such as *hêtres/prêtres, chants/couchants/chants/champs,* and *antique/mystique*. Be sure to treat each rhyming pair with the same IPA spellings.

4. Repeating Words: Study the text for common words that repeat such as *dieu s'avance, travers les champs,* and *mêlez vos chants*. Be sure to treat each repetition with the same IPA spellings.

5. Expressive Possibilities: Circle the words that invite expression.

Dieu s'avance à travers les champs!
God himself advances across the fields!

Par les landes, les prés, les verts taillis de hêtres.
Through the land, the meadow, the green copse of beech.

Il vient, suivi du peuple et porté par les prêtres:
He comes, followed by people and carried by the priests:

Aux cantiques de l'homme, oiseaux, mêlez vos chants!
With the songs of the men, birds, mingle your songs!

On s'arrête. La foule autour d'un chêne antique
They halt themselves. The crowd around an oak ancient

S'incline, en adorant, sous l'ostensoir mystique:
Bowing, in adoration, under the monstrance mystic:

Soleil! Darde sur lui tes longs rayons couchants!
Sun! Beam on it your long rays setting!

Aux cantiques de l'homme, oiseaux, mêlez vos chants!
With the songs of the men, birds, mingle your songs!

Vous, fleurs, avec l'encens exhalez votre arôme!
You, flowers, with the incense inhale your aroma!

Ô fête! Tout reluit, tout prie et tout embaume!
O festival! All is relit, everything is prayer and everything fragrant!

Dieu s'avance à travers les champs.
God himself advances across the land.

Poetic Equivalent

God moves across the fields! By the heath, meadows, and beech groves so green, He comes, borne by the priests and faithful people. The crowd stops and bows in adoration as the mystic incense is dispensed. Sunbeams, send forth rays of light! Birds, blend your songs with the hymns of the people! Flowers, release your scent! It is a celebration. All is renewed through prayer and incense. God himself moves across the fields.

Comparative Performances

Compare performances of this song sung by soprano Elly Ameling and baritone Bruno LaPlante. Consider how each singer creates the atmosphere of the "procession." What words seem to be used expressively. Do you prefer one interpretation? If so, why?

Charles Gounod (1818–1893)

Considered by many to have created the mélodie as a French art form, Charles Gounod was a multifaceted artist. A winner of the coveted 1839 Prix de Rome, Gounod attracted the attention of the artist Jean-Auguste-Dominique Ingres, the director of the Villa Medici. Ingres offered Gounod a scholarship to study visual art. While in Rome, Gounod became acquainted with Fanny Mendelssohn Hensel, who shared with him the world of German music and literature. Later Gounod composed an opera on Johann Wolfgang von Goethe's masterwork, *Faust*. Gounod published approximately 120 songs, known for their singable melodies. Below are two examples of Gounod's contribution to the development of the mélodie. Read the texts and create phonetic transcriptions.

Comparative Listening

"Le Soir" ("The Night")
(Text by Alphonse de Lamartine [1790–1869].)

Before you listen, implement your dictation strategies:

1. Spellings: Look for IPA spellings you already know such as the articles *le, ces, les, des, la,* and *le;* the auxiliary verb *es-tu;* possessive adjectives *mes, sa, mon, mes,* and *mon;* prepositions *sur, dans, à,* and *pour;* and pronouns *je, tu, me,* and *te.*

2. Familiar Words: Look for words you may recognize such as *soir, silence, horizon, étoile, cieux, rayon, mes yeux, âme, mondes, divin, mystère, secrets, sphere, jour, coeur,* and *aurore.*

3. Rhyming Words: Follow down the right side of the text to identify rhymes such as *silence/s'avance, deserts/des airs, l'horizon/gazon, amoureuse/mystérieuse, cieux/yeux, nocturne/taciturne, flame/âme, veux-tu/abattu, révéler/rappeler, mystère/sphere, avenir/finir,* and *t'implore/aurore.*

4. Expressive Possibilities: Circle the words that invite expression such as *silence, amoureuse, mystérieuse, charmant rayon,* and *le divin mystère.*

I

Le soir ramène le silence.
The evening brings the silence.

Assis sur ces rochers déserts,
Seated on these rocks deserted,

Je suis dans la vague des airs
I am in the vagueness of the air

Le char de la nuit qui s'avance.
The chariot of the night which itself advances.

II

Vénus se lève à l'horizon;
Venus herself lifts to the horizon;

A mes pieds l'étoile amoureuse
At my feet the star of love

De sa lueur mystérieuse
With its light mysterious

Blanchit les tapis de gazon.
Bleaches the carpets of grass.

III

Tout à coup détaché des cieux,
All at once detached from the skies,

Un rayon de l'astre nocturne,
A ray of the star nocturnal,

Glissant sur mon front taciturne,
Glistening on my face solemn,

Vient mollement toucher mes yeux.
Comes softly to touch my eyes.

IV

Doux reflet d'un globe de flamme,
Sweet reflection of a globe of flame,

Charmant rayon, que me veux-tu?
Charming ray, what of me want you?

Viens-tu dans mon sein abattu
Come you in my heart despondent

Porter la lumière à mon âme?
To carry the illumination of my soul?

V

Descends-tu pour me révéler
Descend you for me to reveal

Des mondes le divin mystère?
Of the worlds the divine mystery?

Ces secrets cachés dans la sphère
These secrets hidden in the sphere

Où le jour va te rappeler?
Where the day goes you to recall?

VI

Viens-tu dévoiler l'avenir
Come you to disclose the future

Au cœur fatigué qui t'implore?
To the heart tired that you implores?

Rayon divin, es tu l'aurore

Ray divine, are you the dawn

Du jour qui ne doit pas finir?

Of day not able to finish?

Poetic Equivalent

Evening brings silence. Seated on these deserted stones, I follow the chariot that delivers the night through the empty air. Venus lifts herself to the horizon: at my feet the star of love spreads its mysterious light across the carpet of grass. Suddenly, a beam from the evening star glides across my face, gently touching my eyes. The ball of fire has a sweet reflection. What is it wishing for? Have you come to life my sad heart and illuminate my soul? Have you come down to earth to share with me the hidden secrets of the sphere forgotten in the day? Are you come to predict the future to this tired heart who cries out to you? Divine glow, are you the dawning of an endless day?

Comparative Performances

Listen to the performances of the Australian soprano Yvonne Kenny with collaborative pianist Malcolm Martineau and British soprano Felicity Lott with collaborative pianist Graham Johnson. What are the similarities in these two interpretations? How are they different?

Comparative Listening

Perhaps one of the most popular of Gounod's songs is the "Sérénade." It is a strophic setting that invites pleasant hours of mindful waking and peaceful sleep.

"Sérénade" ("Serenade") set to music by Charles Gounod
(Text by Victor Hugo [1802–1885].)

Before you listen, implement your dictation strategies:

1. Spellings: Look for IPA spellings you already know such as the articles *le, les,* and *un*; the conjunction *et*; prepositions *quand, sans,* and *dans*; and pronouns *tu, te,* and *me.*

2. Familiar Words: Look for words you may recognize such as *soir, chantez, toujours, amour, coeur, ma belle, calme, ombre, mes yeux, murmure, beau,* and *dormez.*

3. Rhyming Words: Follow down the right side of the text to identify rhymes such as *bercée/pensée, bras/bas, rappelle/belle, jours/toujours, bouche/farouche, s'épanouit/s'évanouit, fidèle/belle, detours/toujours, pure/murmure, yeux/harmonieux, révèle/belle,* and *atours/toujours.* Use the same IPA spellings for the rhyming pairs.

4. Expressive Possibilities: Circle expressive words such as *chantez, riez,* and *dormez.*

5. Manner of Performance: A serenade is performed outside, under the window of someone whose attention is desired. Imagine how the verses would be

sung to entice the listener. Notice the dynamic changes suggested with each successive verse.

I

Quand tu chantes, bercée
When you sing, cradled

Le soir entre mes bras,
In the evening in my arms,

Entends-tu ma pensée
Hear you my thoughts

Qui te répond tout bas?
Who to responds softly?

Ton doux chant me rappelle
Your sweet song me recalls

Les plus beaux de mes jours . . .
The most beautiful of my days . . .

Chantez, ma belle,
Sing, my beauty,

Chantez toujours!
Sing always!

II

Quand tu ris, sur ta bouche
When you smile, on your lips

L'amour s'épanouit,
The love expands

Et soudain le farouche
And suddenly the wild

Soupçon s'évanouit.
Suspicion evaporates.

Ah! le rire fidèle
Ah! The smile faithful

Prouve un cœur sans détours . . .
Proves my heart without doubt . . .

Riez, ma belle,
Smile, my beauty,

Riez toujours!

Smile always!

III

Quand tu dors, calme et pure,

When you sleep, calmly and purely,

Dans l'ombre, sous mes yeux,

In the shadows, under my eyes,

Ton haleine murmure

Your breath murmurs

Des mots harmonieux.

Some words harmonious.

Ton beau corps se révèle

Your beautiful body itself reveals

Sans voile et sans atours . . .

Without veils and without adornments . . .

Dormez, ma belle,

Sleep, my beauty,

Dormez toujours!

Sleep always!

Poetic Equivalent

When you sing, cradled in my arms in the evening, can you discern my thoughts of you? Your sweet singing reminds me of the best days of my life. Sing on, my beloved! Sing always. When you smile, your lips spread the love from within you and any suspicions disappear. Ah! The smile of a trusted love reveals a sincere heart. Smile, my beloved, smile always! When you sleep, calmly and sweetly, in the shadows of my glance, your breath mutters melodious words. Your beautiful body is revealed in its innocence. Ah, sleep, my beloved! Sleep gently always!

Comparative Performances

Listen to performances by soprano Arleen Auger and baritone Gérard Souzay. Dalton Baldwin is the collaborative pianist for both performers. Do you notice any differences in the interpretation? In the diction? How does the collaborative pianist adapt himself to serve the music and the tastes of each performer?

Composers of the French Mélodie

Unlike the composers of the German Lied, the creators of French mélodie knew one another well. Paris was the center of all artistic endeavor. Musicians, artists, and literary figures met not only at school or in a concert hall; they also dined together and discussed the artistic trends of their time.

Camille Saint-Saëns (1835–1921)

Camille Saint-Saëns was considered a pioneer in setting the words of Victor Hugo (1802–1885) to music. An influential teacher, Saint-Saëns instructed the young Gabriel Fauré at the École Niedermeyer. It is thought that Fauré became acquainted with German lieder through this association. Below is a poem by Victor Hugo that was set to music by both Saint-Saëns and his pupil, Gabriel Fauré. Read the text and create a phonetic transcription.

Comparative Listening

"Puisqu'ici-bas Toute Âme" ("Since Down Here All Souls . . . ")

Before you listen, implement your dictation strategies:

1. Spellings: Look for IPA spellings you already know such as articles *la, un, une,* and *les*; conjunctions *ou, sans,* and *et*; prepositions *puisque, à, aux, sur,* and *comme*; and pronouns *je, te, toi,* and *tu*.

2. Familiar Words: Look for words you may recognize such as *âme, musique, flame, parfum, chose, rose, toujours, amours, branche, oiseau, rive, baiser, pleurs, jours, étoile, muse,* and *coeur*.

3. Rhyming Words: Follow down the right side of the text to identify rhymes such as *âme/flame, quelqu'un/parfum, chose/rose, toujours/amours, chênes/peines, charmant/dormant, heure/meilleure, toi/moi, pensée/rosée, d'ailleurs/pleurs, nombre/l'ombre, amours/jours, d'ivresses/caresses, soupçon/chansons, voile/étoile, hasard/regard, heures/pleures, rêvant/souvent, celeste/reste,* and *beauté/ôté*. Be sure to use identical IPA spellings for each rhyming pair.

4. Repeating Words: Study the text for common words that repeat such as *puisqu'ici-bas, toujours, amours, donne,* and *reçois*. Use the same IPA spelling for each repetition.

I

Puisqu'ici-bas toute âme
Since down here every soul

Donne à quelqu'un
Gives to someone

Sa musique, sa flamme,
His music, his flame,

Ou son parfum;
Or his perfume;

Puisqu'ici toute chose
Since down here every thing

Donne toujours
Gives always

Son épine ou sa rose
Its thorn or its rose

À ses amours;
To its loves;

Puisqu'avril donne aux chênes
Since April gives to the oak trees

Un bruit charmant;
A sound charming;

Que la nuit donne aux peines
That the night gives to the pains

L'oubli dormant;
The forgetfulness sleeping;

Puisque l'air à la branche
Since the air to the branch

Donne l'oiseau;
Gives the bird;

Que l'aube à la pervenche
Which the dawn to the periwinkle

Donne un peu d'eau;
Gives a little water;

Puisque, lorsqu'elle arrive
Since, when it arrives

S'y reposer,
Itself there to rest,

L'onde amère à la rive
The wave bitter to the shoreline

Donne un baiser;
Gives a kiss;

Je te donne à cette heure,
I you give at this hour,

Penché sur toi,
Bent over you

La chose la meilleure
The thing the best

Que j'ai en moi!
That I have in me!

II

Reçois donc ma pensée,
Receive then my thought

Triste d'ailleurs,
Sad besides,

Qui, comme une rosée,
Which, like a dew droplet,

T'arrive en pleurs!
You reaches in tears!

Reçois mes voeux sans nombre,
Receive my vows without number,

O mes amours!
O my love!

Reçois la flamme ou l'ombre
Receive the flame or the shadow

De tout mes jours!
Of all my days!

Mes transports pleins d'ivresses,
My rapture filled with exhilaration,

Pur de soupçons,
Pure of suspicions,

Et toutes les caresses
And all the caresses

De mes chansons!
Of my songs!

Mon esprit qui sans voile
My spirit which without sail

Vogue au hasard,
Wanders at random,

Et qui n'a pour étoile
And which not has for (its) star

Que ton regard!
But your glance!

Ma muse, que les heures
My muse, that the hours

Bercent rêvant,
Cradling dreamily,

Qui, pleurant quand tu pleures,
Who, weeping when you weep,

Pleure souvent!
Weeps often!

Reçois, mon bien céleste,
Receive, my dear celestial one,

O ma beauté,
O my beauty,

Mon coeur, dont rien ne reste,
My heart, in which nothing else rests,

L'amour ôté!
The love having taken away!

Poetic Equivalent

Since down here every soul gives another its music, its passion, or its scent; since down here all things are either thorns or roses to those who love; since April offers the oak trees the charming sounds of spring, let a night's rest allow some forgetting. Since the air gives birds to the branches, the dawn waters the thirsty periwinkles, since the wave kisses the shore and I give you at this hour the best I have to offer, receive my thoughts, even though they be sad and full of tears. Receive my numerous vows, o my love! Receive the flame or the shadow from all my days! My rapture is full of exhilaration, devoid of any suspicions. Accept all the caresses that my songs afford you. My spirit wanders aimlessly having neither sail nor star. My muse, that the hours pass dreamily. That we weep when the other weeps. Receive, my dear heavenly creature, oh my beauty, receive my heart in which nothing remains if love is taken from it.

Comparative Settings

The mélodie "Revêrie" by Saint-Saëns and a duet by Fauré entitled "Puisqu'ici-bas Toute Âme" were composed on the same text. Various stanzas of the poem have been set by Reynaldo Hahn, Edouard Lalo, and Louis Niedermeyer. Investigate these settings to develop new insights into possible interpretations.

Gabriel Fauré (1845–1924)

Gabriel Fauré began his training at the École Niedermeyer, a school founded for the training of church musicians. The curriculum emphasized the sacred traditions of plainchant and counterpoint. Fauré spoke of his musical training as one in which the masterpieces of J. S. Bach constituted "our daily bread" (Nectoux, 1991). During his professional career as an organist and teacher, Fauré had little time for composing except during summer vacations. His compositional output included piano, chamber, orchestral, and choral works along with more than 100 songs. His most famous student, Nadia Boulanger, described her teacher's inventive compositional style in the following way: "You never know to what key he is leading you, but when you reach your tonal destination, there is never any doubt as to its location. Indeed, you feel almost as though it would have been impossible to have gone elsewhere and you wonder only at the beauty of the voyage and the skill of your guide who, in coming has led you so quickly and surely through so many lands" (Campbell, 1984).

Comparative Listening

Note the use of "lydian" mode in the creation of this tribute to "Lydia." Read the text and create a phonetic transcription.

"Lydia"
(Text by Leconte de Lisle [1818–1894].)

<u>Before you listen, implement your dictation strategies:</u>

1. Spellings: Look for IPA spellings you already know such as articles *le*, *un*, and *une*; conjunctions *et* and *sans*; prepositions *sur* and *comme*; possessive adjectives *tes*, *ton*, *mes*, and *mon*; and pronouns *tu*, *toi*, and *je*.

2. Familiar Words: Look for words you may recognize such as *roses*, *blanc*, *jour*, *tombe*, *chanter*, *fleur*, *lys*, *odeur*, *sein*, *jeune*, *amours*, *âme*, *baisers*, and *toujours*.

3. Rhyming Words: Follow down the right side of the text to identify rhymes such as *joues/dénoues*, *blanc/étincelant*, *meilleur/fleur*, *tombe/colombe*, *cesse/déesse*,

sein/essaim, amours/toujours, and *ravie/vie.* Mark each pair with the same IPA spellings.

4. Expressive Possibilities: Circle the words that invite expression such as *je t'aime et meurs, rends-moi la vie,* and *mourir toujours.*

Lydia sur tes roses joues
Lydia, on your rosy cheeks

Et sur ton col frais et si blanc,
And on your neck fresh and so white,

Roule étincelant
Rolls glistening

L'or fluide que tu dénoues;
The gold fluid that you unfasten;

Le jour qui luit est le meilleur,
The day that lights up is the best,

Oublions l'éternelle tombe.
Let us forget the eternal tomb.

Laisse tes baisers de colombe
Allow your kisses of the dove

Chanter sur ta lèvre en fleur.
To sing on your lip in flower.

Un lys caché répand sans cesse
A lily hidden pours out without ceasing

Une odeur divine en ton sein;
An odor divine in your heart/breast;

Les délices comme un essaim
The delicacies like a swarm

Sortent de toi, jeune déesse.
Emerge from you, young goddess.

Je t'aime et meurs, ô mes amours.
I love you and I die, o my love.

Mon âme en baisers m'est ravie!
My soul on your kisses me have ravished!

O Lydia, rends-moi la vie,
O Lydia, return to me the (my) life,

Que je puisse mourir, mourir toujours!
That I am able to die, die forever!

Poetic Equivalent

Lydia, on your rosy cheeks and neck, so fresh and white, the liquid gold of your tresses you unwind in cascades of glittering down. This day as it dawns is the very best; let's forget our fate. Let your dovelike kisses sing forth on your flowery lips. I sense a divine scent of lilies hidden in your heart. There are countless delights that emanate from you, my young goddess! I love you and I die, o my love! My soul is in rapture from your kisses. O Lydia, give me back my life that I may forever die!

Comparative Performances

Compare performances of Frederica von Stade, Véronique Gens, and Souzay with their respective collaborative pianists, Jean Philippe Collard, Roger Vignoles, and Dalton Baldwin. Consider the similarities and differences. For this mélodie, do you prefer the voice of a male singer? A female singer? Why?

Who Wrote the Poems that Inspired French Mélodie?

In the excellent resource, *A French Song Companion* (Johnson & Stokes, 2000), we discover that the poets most preferred by French song composers are Paul Verlaine, Victor Hugo, Charles Baudelaire, and Théophile Gautier. More than 75 poems by Paul Verlaine have been set to music. Victor Hugo, well known in English-speaking countries for his novels, wrote 51 poems that attracted the attention of composers. Both Baudelaire and Gautier wrote more than 30 poems that have been set to music.

Paul Verlaine (1844–916)

Paul Verlaine (1844–1916) was already writing poetry by age 14. His first published work, *Poèmes Saturiens*, was published in 1866. The works of greatest interest to singers are found in Verlaine's subsequent collections entitled *Fêtes Galantes* (1869) and *La Bonne Chanson* (1872). Verlaine's life was complicated by addiction and emotional upheaval. His distress is perhaps best documented in a poem from *Romances sans Paroles* (1874). Fauré gave his musical setting of the poem the title "Prison," while Hahn called his "D'une Prison." Both titles acknowledge the poet's circumstances.

Why was Verlaine's poetry pivotal in the creative process of composers like Fauré, Debussy, and Hahn? Was it because, as William Rees suggests, Verlaine's poetry is " . . . a brilliant, original art of extreme musicality *'sur le mode mineur'* (in a minor key) a subtle transmission of intimate nuances of mood and feeling through sound patterns rhythms and images arranged in an incantatory tone poem. It has no finality but lingers as a dream-like a *paysage intérieur* (journey inward), the objective yet deliberately blurred expression of an inner state" (Rees, 1992).

Comparative Listening

Debussy and Fauré entitled their settings of the following poem "Green." Hahn chose to call his "Offrande" ("Offering"). It is from Verlaine's collection known as *Romances sans Paroles*. Read the text and create a phonetic transcription.

"Green" or "Offrande" ("Green"/"Offering")

Before you listen, implement your dictation strategies:

1. Spellings: Look for IPA spellings you already know such as the articles *le*, *la*, and *un*; the conjunctions *et* and *avec*; possessive adjectives *mon*, *vos*, *ma*, and *votre*; prepositions *de*, *du*, and *à*; and the pronouns *je* and *vous*. If you may recognize nasal vowels by their spellings, mark them.

2. Familiar Words: Look for words you may recognize such as *fruits*, *fleurs*, *feuilles*, *branches*, *coeur*, *rêve*, *tête*, and *yeux*.

3. Rhyming Words: Follow down the right side of the text to identify rhymes such as *branches/blanches*, *vous/doux*, *front/delasseront*, *rosée/reposée*, *tête/tempête*, and *baisers/reposez*. Use the same IPA spellings for each rhyming pair.

4. Repeating Words: Study the text for common words that repeat such as *des*, *et*, *de*, *le*, and *que*. Mark each repetition with the same IPA symbols.

5. Liaison Possibilities: Circle the words that might contain a liaison or elision.

Voici des fruits, des fleurs, des feuilles et des branches
Here are some fruits, some flowers, some leaves, and some branches

Et puis voici mon coeur qui ne bat que pour vous.
And then here my heart that beats only for you.

Ne le déchirez pas avec vos deux mains blanches
Do it not break with your two hands white

Et qu'à vos yeux si beaux l'humble present soit doux.
And that to your eyes so beautiful the humble present be sweet.

J'arrive tout couvert encore de rosée
I arrive all covered again with dew

Que le vent du matin vient glacer à mon front.
That the wind of the morning comes to freeze on my face/brow.

Souffrez que ma fatigue à vos pieds reposée
Suffer that my weariness at your feet reposes

Rêve des chers instants qui la délasseront.
Dream of dear instances that it refreshes.

Sur votre jeune sein laissez rouler ma tête

On your young heart allow to roll my head

Toute sonore encore de vos derniers baisers;

Totally resounding again from you last kisses;

Laissez-la s'apaiser de la bonne tempête,

Allow it to calm from the good tempest,

Et que je dorme un peu puisque vous reposez.

And that I sleep a little since you are resting.

Poetic Equivalent

Here are fruits, flowers, leaves, and branches, and with them, a heart that beats only for you. Do not crush my heart with your beautiful white hands. May this humble gift be seen as something sweet in your beautiful eyes. I arrive here, all covered with dew from the frozen morning wind. Let me rest at your feet and dream of our shared, dear moments. Let me roll my head upon your breast that still resonates from our kisses. Let me calm down from the lovely storm of our affection and sleep a little, while you also repose.

Comparative Settings

Compare first settings of "Green" composed by Fauré and Debussy. Multiple performances sung by baritone Souzay, soprano Ameling, and mezzo soprano von Stade are available. Compare the same text set by Hahn entitled "Offrande" in representative performances sung by mezzo soprano Susan Graham and by tenor Martyn Hill. What are the similarities and differences?

Comparative Listening

The term "spleen" is used in French poetry to describe a lethargic state of being, one that is not completely understood by the poet. The following poem from Verlaine's *Romances sans Paroles*, "Il Pleure dans mon Coeur" ("It Weeps in My Heart") was set to music by Debussy for his cycle, *Ariettes Oublièe* (*Forgotten Airs*). When Fauré chose to set the same poem, he gave it the title "Spleen." The term "spleen" was introduced to French society by the poet Baudelaire. Spleen is a nondescript state of despair and lethargy. Be aware that Verlaine also wrote a poem entitled "Spleen." That Verlaine poem is set to music by Debussy using the poet's title "Spleen." This can be very confusing. Read the text and create a phonetic transcription.

"Il Pleure dans Mon Coeur" ("It Weeps in My Heart"), also called "Spleen"

Before you listen, implement your dictation strategies:

1. Spellings: Look for IPA spellings you already know such as *il, dans, de le,* and *sur,* as well as nasal vowels *mon, langueur, un, sans/dans, raison/trahison, bien,* and *tant.* Also look for auxiliary verbs *est* and *a.*

2. Familiar Words: Look for words you may recognize such as *coeur, amour, ville,* and *peine.*

3. Rhyming Words: Identify rhymes such as *coeur/languer, s'ennuie/pluie, raison/trahison,* and *peine/haine.* Use the same IPA symbols for each rhyming vowel pair.

4. Repeating Words: Study the text for common words that repeat such as *pleure/pleut, coeur,* and *sans.* Mark each repetition with the same IPA symbols.

5. Liaison Possibilities: Circle the words that might contain a liaison or elision.

Il pleure dans mon coeur comme il pleut sur la ville.

Tears fall in my heart like rain upon the town.

Quelle est cette langueur qui pénétre mon coeur?

what is this languor that pervades my heart?

O bruit doux de la pluie par terre et sur les toits!

O sound gentle of the rain on the earth and on the roofs!

Pour un coeur qui s'ennuie O le bruit de la pluie!

For a heart that is bored O the sound and the rain!

Il pleure sans raison dans ce coeur qui s'écoeure.

Tears fall without reason in this heart that is ill.

Quoi! nulle trahison?

What! No treason?

Ce deuil est sans raison. C'est bien la pire peine

This sorrow has no reason. It is the worst kind of pain

De ne savoir pourquoi, sans amour et sans haine,

not to know why, without love and without hate,

Mon coeur a tant de peine.

My heart feels so much pain.

Poetic Equivalent

My heart weeps as the rain weeps upon the city. What is this languishing that penetrates my heart? Oh, the soft sounds of the rain as it falls on the earth and roofs! For this weary heart, Oh what a sound! The tears are falling without reason from this disheartened spirit. What! Was there no treason? This grief comes without reason. This is the worst pain of all: to feel this way without cause, without love or hate. Yet, my heart feels such pain.

Comparative Settings

The mélodie created from this text by Debussy constrasts sharply with the one composed by Fauré. There are many listening possibilities. Try comparing Debussy's "Il Pleure dans

Mon Coeur" sung by soprano Dawn Upshaw with the 1904 performanceby Mary Garden with the composer at the piano. Listen to countertenor Philippe Jaroussky sing Fauré's "Spleen" and compare the performance to that of mezzo soprano Nathalie Stutzmann. Notice the differences in the musical settings and the performances.

Comparative Listening

A memorable poetic description of moonlight and its impact on human emotions is found in Verlaine's "La Lune Blanche," a poem from the collection *La Bonne Chanson* (*The Good Song*).

Read the text and create a phonetic transcription.

"La Lune Blanche" ("The White Moon")

Before you listen, implement your dictation strategies:

1. Spellings: Look for IPA spellings you already know such as the articles *la*, *les*, *une*, and *un*; the preposition *sous*; the nasal vowels *blanche*, *dans*, *branche*, *bien*, *étang*, *profond*, *vent*, *rêvons*, *un*, *apaisement*, *semble*, *descendre*, and *firmament*; and the auxiliary verb *c'est*.
2. Familiar Words: Look for words you may recognize such as *lune*, *blanche/branche*, *voix*, and *bien-aimée*.
3. Rhyming Words: Follow down the right side of the text to identify rhymes such as *bois/voix*, *miroir/noir*, *pleure/l'heure*, *apaisement/firmament*, and *irise/exquise*. Be sure to use the same IPA spellings to insure rhyming pairs.
4. Repeating Words: Study the text for common words that repeat such as *la*, *de*, *le*, and *du*.
5. Liaison Possibilities: Circle the words that might contain a liaison or elision.

La lune blanche luit dans les bois;
The moon white shines on the woods;

De chaque branche part une voix
From every branch comes a voice

Sous la ramée . . . o bien-aimée.
Under the bough . . . o my beloved.

L'étang reflète, profond miroir,
The pool reflects, profound mirror,

La silhouette du saule noir
The silhouette of the willow black

Où le vent pleure . . . rêvons, c'est l'heure.
Where the wind weeps . . . we dream, this is the hour.

Un vaste et tendre apaisement

A vast and tender appeasement

Semble descendre du firmament

Seems to descend from the firmament

Que l'astre irise.

That the stars illuminate.

C'est l'heure exquise!

This is the exquisite hour!

Poetic Equivalent

The white moon shines through the trees and every branch seems to have a voice under the bough . . . o my beloved! The pool, a profound mirror, reflects the silhouette of a black willow, where the wind cries . . . let us dream, for this is the hour. A vast and tender calmness has fallen from heaven, illumined by the stars . . . this is the exquisite hour!

Comparative Setting

Compare the musical settings of this text by Hahn entitled "L'heure Exquise" and that of Fauré entitled "La Lune Blanche." The Fauré setting is a part of his song cycle *La Bonne Chanson*. There is also a version of the Fauré setting arranged for voice with string quartet sung by tenor Ian Bostridge that might interest you.

Discussion Questions

1. Why do you think Paul Verlaine's poems evoked such contrasting musical treatments?

2. Why do you think Verlaine's poetry Verlaine was so inspiring to French composers of the 19th and 20th centuries?

3. How do Verlaine's writings compare with other French poets whose works you have sung?

4. Is there a phrase from a Verlaine poem you consider characteristic of his writing?

5. Verlaine's poetry evokes a profound sadness that contains tender images. How will you use your musical skills and your diction strategies to interpret these poems?

Victor Hugo (1802–1885)

Though best known among English-speaking readers as a novelist, Victor Hugo referred to himself primarily as a poet. It is said that Hugo wrote verse daily from a young age. Over the span of his lifetime, Hugo wrote more than 158,000 lines of poetry (Blackmore, 2001). He was one of France's most prolific poets, choosing for his topics matters of politics as well as those of the heart. His fervor as political activist is not noticeable in the verse selected for musical elevation. Typical of Hugo's poetry, the following poem describes outward and inward beauty. Read the text and create a phonetic transcription.

Comparative Listening

XXXI. "Puisque Mai Tout en Fleurs . . . " ("Since May All in Flower . . . ")
(From *Les Chants du crepuscule* or *Songs from the Half-Light* [1835]; Music by Gabriel Fauré and entitled "Mai" ["May"].)

<u>Before you listen, implement your dictation strategies:</u>

1. Spellings: Look for IPA spellings you already know such as the articles *les, la, le, ce,* and *une*; the conjunction *et*; prepositions *dans, au, de, des, sur,* and *à*; the possessive adjective *ton*; and the pronoun *te*. Note also the words with nasal vowel spellings you may recognize such as <u>en</u>, d<u>ans</u>, vi<u>ens</u>, c<u>am</u>pagne, <u>om</u>brages charm<u>ants</u>, dorm<u>ants</u>, s<u>en</u>tier, comm<u>en</u>ce, print<u>em</u>ps, horiz<u>on</u> imm<u>en</u>se, m<u>on</u>de h<u>um</u>ble t<u>om</u>be, t<u>ant</u>, ch<u>ant</u>, ch<u>amps</u>, <u>em</u>brasé, l'<u>om</u>bre, rayonnem<u>ent</u>, t<u>on</u>, and fr<u>ont</u>.

2. Familiar Words: Look for words you may recognize such as *âme, bois, claire de lune, l'air, printemps, l'horizon, immense, humble, robe, cieux, étoiles, tombe, terre, l'arbre, parfums, chants, l'ombre, soleil, l'onde, verdure, nature, double, fleur, amour, coeur.*

3. Rhyming Words: Follow down the right side of the text to identify rhymes such as *réclame/âme, charmants/dormants, commence/immense, joyeux/cieux, étoiles/voiles, chants/champs, verdure/nature,* and *fleur/coeur*. Mark each pair with the same IPA spellings.

4. Liaison Possibilities: Circle the words that might contain a liaison or elision.

Puisque Mai tout en fleurs dans les prés nous réclame,
Since Mai all in flower in the meadows us reclaims,

Viens! ne te lasse pas de mêler à ton âme
Come! not you grow tired ever of mingling with your soul

La campagne, les bois, les ombrages charmants,
The countryside, the woods, the shadows charming,

Les larges clairs de lune au bord des flots dormants,
The large moonlight on the banks of the waters sleeping

Le sentier qui finit où le chemin commence,
The path that finishes where the road commences,

Et l'air et le printemps et l'horizon immense,
And the air and the spring and the horizon immense,

L'horizon que ce monde attache humble et joyeux
The horizon that this world is attached humbly and joyously

Comme une lèvre au bas de la robe des cieux!
Like a lip at the base of the robe of the skies!

Viens! et que le regard des pudiques étoiles
Come! and that the gaze of the modest stars

Qui tombe sur la terre à travers tant de voiles,
Which buries (itself) into the earth across so many veils,

Que l'arbre pénétré de parfums et de chants,
That the tree penetrated by perfumes and by songs,

Que le souffle embrasé de midi dans les champs,
That the breeze embraced by the midday in the fields,

Et l'ombre et le soleil et l'onde et la verdure,
And the shade and the sun and the wave and the green-ness,

Et le rayonnement de toute la nature
And the radiance of all the Nature

Fassent épanouir, comme une double fleur,
Causes to blossom, like a double flower,

La beauté sur ton front et l'amour dans ton coeur!
The beauty on your face and the love in your heart!

Poetic Equivalent

Since May, all in flower, calls us outside—come! Mingle your soul with the meadow, the woods, and the charming shadows, the spreading moonlight on the waters flowing banks, the paths that end where the roads begin, the air and the springtime, the immense horizon that attaches itself to the world humbly and joyfully like a lip that nudges the edge of the sky's robe. Come! Allow yourself to see the modest stars that bury themselves in the earth full of veils, the trees penetrated by perfume and songs, the soft embrace of midday in the valleys and the shadows and the sun and the waves and the greenery, and the radiance of all Nature revealed, like a double flower, in the beauty of your countenance and the love in your heart.

Comparative Performances

Compare the recordings of performances by Irish soprano Allish Tynan, French mezzo soprano Stutzmann, and British mezzo soprano Sarah Walker performing with their respective collaborative pianists, Iain Burnside, Catherine Collard, and Malcolm Martineau. Note the range of differences in tempo, interpretation, and diction.

Charles Baudelaire (1811–1867)

"Les Fleurs du Mal" ("The Flowers of Evil") is often considered to be the pivotal book in the history of modern, if not of all, French poetry (Appelbaum, 1969). Baudelaire was fascinated by the powers of his intellect, while discouraged by the fragility of the human body. His writings probe the psychological aspects of his dilemma. His contemplations range from childhood memories and dream reflections to sensual and sexual experiences. Baudelaire suffered from a kind of melancholy known as "spleen," a weariness mingled with irritation or even anger. It is often referred to as "peevish boredom." In his poems, "Spleen I, II, III, and IV," Baudelaire introduced the state of being to his reader. Baudelaire's writing contributed his own unique sense of melody and imagery to French poetry. Baudelaire's first published works (1845) chronicled his views on art and aesthetics. In 1853, he began translating the poetry of Edgar Allan Poe. *Petits Poèmes en Prose* (*Short Poems and Prose*), commonly called *Le Spleen de Paris*, appeared in 1869. *Les Fleurs du Mal*, published in 1857 with a dedication to Théophile Gautier, was deemed a work of decadence. Parts of it were censored and Baudelaire was fined. The following poem will acquaint you with Baudelaire's poetic style. Read the text and create a phonetic transcription.

Comparative Listening

"La Vie Antérieure" ("The Former Life")
(Music by Henri Duparc.)

<u>Before you listen, implement your dictation strategies:</u>

1. Spellings: Look for IPA spellings you already know such as the articles *les, le,* and *une*; the conjunctions *et* and *avec*; the prepositions *sous, aux, de, du,* and *dans*; the pronoun *m;,* and the auxiliary verb expressions *j'ai* and *c'est*. Note the nasal vowel spellings you already know such as <u>longtemps</u>, <u>marins</u>, <u>grands</u>, <u>rendaient</u>, <u>roulant</u>, <u>façon</u>, <u>puissants</u>, <u>couchant</u>, <u>dans</u>, <u>splendeurs</u>, <u>imprégnés</u>, <u>front</u>, <u>dont</u>, and *d'approfondir*.

2. Familiar Words: Look for words you may recognize such as *soleils, soir, images, cieux, mystique, musique, couchant, front, palmes, unique,* and *secret*.

3. Rhyming Words: Follow down the right side of the text to identify rhymes such as *portiques/basaltiques/feux/majestueux/cieux/yeux, mystique/musique, calmes/palmes, splendeurs/d'odeurs,* and *d'approfondir/languir*. Give rhyming pairs the same IPA spellings.

4. Liaison Possibilities: Circle the words that might contain a liaison or elision.

J'ai longtemps habité sous de vastes portiques
I have for a long time dwelt under the vast porticos

Que les soleils marins teignaient de mille feux,
That the sun maritime tinges in thousands of fires,

Et que leurs grand piliers, droits et majestueux,
And that their grand pillars, straight and majestic,

Rendaient pareils, le soir, aux grottes basaltiques.
Rendered parallel, (in) the evening, to the grottos basaltic.

Les houles, en roulant les images des cieux,
The tides, in rolling, the images of the skies,

Mêlaient d'une façon solennelle et mystique
Meld in a fashion, solemn and mystical

Les tout-puissants accords de leur riche musique
The all-powerful chords of their rich music

Aux couleurs du couchant reflété par mes yeux.
With colors of sunset reflected in my eyes.

C'est là que j'ai vécu dans les voluptés calmes,
It is there that I have lived in the voluptuous calm,

Au milieu de l'azur, des vagues, des splendeurs
Amid the azure, the waves, the splendors

Et des esclaves nus, tout imprégnés d'odeurs,
And the slaves naked, all permeated with scents,

Qui me rafraîchissaient le front avec des palmes,
Who me refreshed the brow with palm fronds,

Et dont l'unique soin était d'approfondir
And whose only care was to deepen

Le secret douloureux qui me faisait languir.
The secret sadness that me makes languourous.

Poetic Equivalent

For a long time, I lived beneath vast porticos that the ocean suns tinted with a thousand fires.

Their great pillars, straight and majestic, made them similar, by evening, to basaltic grottos.

The surf, rolling the images of the skies, in solemn and mystic fashion melded the all-powerful chords of its rich music with the colors of the setting sun that reflected in my eyes. It is there that I lived in calm delights. I lived by the azure waves and its splendors, amid the naked slaves, thoroughly steeped in perfumes, who cooled my brow with palm leaves. Their sole concern was to penetrate the painful secret which made me languish.

Comparative Performances

It would be informative for you to compare performances of this mélodie sung by American soprano Barbara Hendricks, German tenor Jonas Kaufmann, French soprano Regine

Crespin, and French baritone Souzay. Some of the available recordings present orchestrated versions of the accompaniment. Compare the settings with piano to the colors made available through the orchestration. Note the differences in the liaison choices of each singer. Which interpretation is most pleasing to you? Why?

Theophile Gautier (1811–1872)

Theophile Gautier, a contemporary of Hugo and Baudelaire, distinguished himself as a believer in "art for the sake of art." Had he not suffered from poor eyesight, his energies might have been devoted totally to the visual arts. His depiction of scenes and circumstances are vivid and sometimes even macabre. Gautier's poetry attracted many composers. Not only did Berlioz appreciate Gautier's words, but Gautier's poems inspired song settings by Georges Bizet, Ernest Chausson, Debussy, Duparc, Fauré, Gounod, Hahn, Jules Massenet, Jacques Offenbach, and Émile Paladilhe, to name only a few.

Claude Debussy (1862–1918)

For many singers, Claude Debussy's mélodies define the perfect union of French music and poetry. Considered by peers to be a revolutionary, Debussy invented his own compositional "voice" by incorporating myriad elements to formulate a new musical language. Debussy was capable of composing "singable" melodic lines, woven among rhythmic and harmonic threads that elevate the text through music. A recent biography of the composer is entitled *Debussy: A Painter in Sound*. Its author, Stephen Walsh, embraces the belief that Debussy's gift as a composer was enhanced significantly by his musical interpretation of visual stimulus (Walsh, 2018). As you study Debussy's mélodies, study how changes of vocal and harmonic colors relate to the description of tangible elements. Read this text and create a phonetic transcription.

Comparative Listening

Little is known about the poet André Girod, who wrote the words Debussy used to compose this early mélodie titled "Fleur des Blés" ("Flower of Wheat") (1881). The words and music paint a vivid scene. Read the text and create a phonetic transcription.

"Fleur des Blés" ("Flower of Wheat")
(Text by André Girod?)

Before you listen, implement your dictation strategies:

1. Spellings: Look for IPA spellings you already know such as the articles *le*, *la*, and *un*; the conjunction *et*; the possessives *ton*, *ta*, and *tes*; prepositions *en*, *à*, *pour*, *de*, *au*, *sur*, and *des*;, the pronoun *toi*; and the auxiliary verbs *j'ai*, *t'a*, *c'est*, and *est*. Look for the nasal vowel spellings such as *long*, *onduler*, *temps*, *l'onde*, *blonde*, *fronde*, *sang*, *point*, *rien*, *sont*, *qu'on*, and *tombés*.

2. Familiar Words: Look for words you may recognize such as *brise, bonne, bouquet, corsage, image, temps, blonde, bouche, beau, yeux, terre, deux,* and *cieux.*

3. Rhyming Words: Follow down the right side of the text to identify rhymes such as *brise/prise/défrise, coquet/bouquet, corsage/image/gage, toi/pourquoi, l'onde/ blonde/fronde, soleil/vermeil, mystère/n'altère/terre,* and *yeux/cieux.* Mark each rhyming pair with the same IPA spellings.

4. Liaison Possibilities: Circle the words that might contain a liaison or elision.

Le long des blés que la brise
Along the wheat that the breeze

Fait onduler puis défrise
Makes to undulate then straightens

En un désordre coquet,
In a disorder coquettish,

J'ai trouvé de bonne prise
I have found a good catch

De t'y cueillir un bouquet.
Of (something) for you from which to gather a bouquet.

Mets le vite à ton corsage,
Fasten it quickly to your bodice,

Il est fait à ton image
It is made in your image/likeness

En même temps que pour toi . . .
At the same time (made) for you . . .

Ton petit doigt, je le gage,
Your little finger, I it wager,

T'a déjà soufflé pourquoi:
You have already whispered why:

Ces épis dorés, c'est l'onde
This grain golden, it is the wave

De ta chevelure blonde
Of your hair blond

Toute d'or et de soleil;
All golden and of the sun;

Ce coquelicot qui fronde,
The poppy which bobs,

C'est ta bouche au sang vermeil.
It is your mouth of blood red.

Et ces bluets, beau mystère!
And these cornflowers, beautiful mystery!

Point d'azur que rien n'altère,
Points of azure (blue) that nothing can alter,

Ces bluets ce sont tes yeux,
These cornflowers these are your eyes,

Si bleus qu'on dirait, sur terre,
So blue that one says to the earth

Deux éclats tombés des cieux.
Two slivers fallen from the skies.

Poetic Equivalent

Among the wheat that the breeze ripples and straightens in a coquettish disorder, I was able to gather a bouquet for you. Attach it quickly to your bodice, because it looks just like you. While I was making it for you, I bet you have already figured why: The golden grain is like your beautiful blond hair glowing golden in the sunlight. The poppy of brilliant red is like your mouth. And those cornflowers—such a gorgeous mystery—those specks of azure blue that never fail. Those cornflowers are your eyes, so blue, that some would say they are bits of heaven that have fallen from the sky.

Comparative Performances

Compare the performances of Ameling and Gens, accompanied by collaborative pianists Baldwin and Vignoles, respectively. Contrast these performances with that from a live concert with Diana Damrau accompanied by harpist Xavier de Maistre. What differences do you notice? Is the French language easier to comprehend with the harp than with the piano accompaniment? Discuss the atmosphere created by the harp.

Ernest Chausson (1855–1899)

A student of Massenet and Franck, Ernest Chausson began a serious study of music in his mid-twenties. He was a gentleman of means, a collector of great artworks, and a well-traveled man of the world. Because of these factors, Chausson was able to regularly attend Wagner's opera performances in Bayreuth, Germany. You will recognize the influence of his mentors in the setting below. It is a tribute to Shakespeare's Ophelia from *Hamlet*. Study the text and create a phonetic transcription.

Comparative Listening

"Chanson d'Ophélie" ("Ophelia's Song")
(Text by Maurice Bouchor [1855–1929];
Based upon words from *Hamlet* by William Shakespeare [1564–1616].)

<u>Before you listen, implement your dictation strategies:</u>

1. Spellings: Look for IPA spellings you already know such as the articles *une, un, le,* and *les;* the conjunctions *et, avec,* and *sans;* the prepositions *pour, à, dans, comme,* and *du;* the possessive adjectives *ses, sa,* and *leur;* the auxiliary verbs *est, c'est,* and *ont;* and the pronouns *il* and *lui.* Look for the nasal vowel spellings such as *ay<u>an</u>t, l<u>in</u>ceul, m<u>ain</u>s, s<u>an</u>s, d<u>an</u>s,* and *s<u>in</u>cère.*

2. Familiar Words: Look for words you may recognize such as *mort, Madame, chose, pieds, tête, neige, fleurs, terre, larmes, sincere,* and *amour.*

3. Rhyming Words: Follow down the right side of the text to identify rhymes such as *faite/tête, semées/parfumées, retour/amour,* and *épanouie/pluie.* Use the same IPA spellings for each pair.

4. Liaison Possibilities: Circle the words that might contain a liaison or elision.

Il est mort ayant bien souffert, Madame;
He is dead, having well suffered, Milady;

Il es parti; c'est une chose faite.
He is departed; that is a thing certain.

Une pierre à ses pieds et pour poser sa tête,
A stone at his feet and for to rest his head,

Un tertre vert.
A turf green.

Sur le linceul de neige à pleines mains semées
On the blanket of snow with bare hands sewn

Mille fleurs parfumées,
Thousands of flowers perfumed,

Avant d'aller sous terre avec lui sans retour
Before going under the earth with him without return

Dans leur jeunesse épanouie
In their youth in blossom

Ont bu, comme une fraiche pluie,
Have drunk, as a fresh rain,

Les larmes du sincere amour.

The tears of sincere love.

Poetic Equivalent

He is dead, having suffered much, Milady; He is gone, that is a fact. At his feet a stone and at his head a grass-green turf. On the snow blanket are plentifully sewn a thousand scented flowers, Which, before going with him into the earth without return, in their bright youth drank, as if fresh raindrops, the tears of true love. (From *Hamlet*, Act IV, Scene 5.)

Comparative Performances

Compare the interpretations of British soprano Lynne Dawson with those of collaborative pianist Julius Drake, and the interpretations of Swiss mezzo soprano Brigitte Balleys versus those of collaborative pianist Bili Eidl. How does each singer use the French language to evoke the Shakespearean image of the dying Ophelia?

Henri Duparc (1848–1933)

Henri Duparc's legacy as a composer of mélodie consists of slightly more than a dozen works. It is thought that he destroyed some of his compositions, hoping to achieve perfection. For this reason, there are no recognizable "style periods" in his music. Each selection is its own work of art, as you will see in the following example. Read the text and create a phonetic transcription.

Comparative Listening

"Le Manoir de Rosamonde" ("Rosamonde's Manor")
(Text by Robert de Bonnières [1850–1905].)

Before you listen, implement your dictation strategies:

1. Spellings: Look for IPA spellings you already know such as the articles *un, la,* and *le*; the conjunctions *et, ou,* and *sans*; the possessive adjectives *mon* and *ma*; the prepositions *comme, en, de,* and *où*; the pronouns *tu, te,* and *je*; and the auxiliary verb *j'ai*. Note the nasal vowel spellings such as *dent, un, chien, suivant, mon, sang, répandu, prends, chemin, fondrière, sentier, passant, monde, qu'ainsi, m'en, bien, loin, sans,* and *Rosamonde*.

2. Familiar Words: Look for words you may recognize such as *amour, trace, race, course, passé, monde, mourir,* and *bleu*.

3. Rhyming Words: Follow down the right side of the text to identify rhymes such as *vorace/trace/race, mordu/répandu/ardu/perdu, passé/blessé, monde/Rosamonde,* and *mourir/découvrir*. Mark each rhyming pair with the same IPA spellings.

4. Liaison Possibilities: Circle the words that might contain a liaison or elision.

De sa dent soudaine et vorace,
With his tooth sudden and voracious,

Comme un chien l'amour m'a mordu . . .
Like a dog, love me has bitten . . .

En suivant mon sang répandu,
And following my blood spilling (out),

Va, tu pourras suivre ma trace . . .
Come, you can follow my traces/tracks . . .

Prends un cheval de bonne race,
Take a horse of good breeding,

Pars, et suis mon chemin ardu,
Set off, and follow my way arduous,

Fondrière ou sentier perdu,
Foundry or paths hidden,

Si la course ne te harasse!
If the course (does not) you exhaust!

En passant par où j'ai passé,
In passing by where I have passed,

Tu verras que seul et blessé
You will see that alone and pierced

J'ai parcouru ce triste monde.
I have traveled this sad world.

Et qu'ainsi je m'en fus mourir
And that thus I myself it went off to die.

Bien loin, bien loin, sans découvrir
A far distance, a far distance, without discovering

Le bleu manoir de Rosamonde.
The blue manor of Rosamonde.

Poetic Equivalent

With his vicious tooth, love has suddenly bitten me, like a dog. If you follow the trail of my blood, you will see the path I have followed. If you take a well-bred horse, you could traverse the arduous route. The obstacles are many and the journey could exhaust you! As you pass where I have been, you will see how, alone and wounded, I traveled this sad world. You will recognize why I risked death far away, without ever reaching the blue manor of Rosamonde.

Comparative Performances

There are many opportunities for you to compare interpretations of this text. Here are a few from which you should choose. You may wish to compare performances by French soprano Crespin, Belgian bass-baritone José Van Dam, German tenor Kaufmann, and Australian soprano Kiri te Kanawa with that of French baritone Souzay. Notice the use of the French language in each performance in developing the climatic moments of this mélodie. What are the challenges of singing the work in its orchestrated version? Which interpretation do you prefer? Why?

Emmanuel Chabrier (1841–1894)

Emmanuel Chabrier is best known for his sense of humor. It was apparently his intention to write a kind of French song that would not compete with his contemporaries. His works are strophic in form and unusual in harmonic language. As you read, see if you can recognize human behavior in the description of a typical day in the life of a turkey. Create a phonetic transcription.

Comparative Listening

"Ballade de Gros Dindons" ("Ballad of the Fat Turkeys")
(Text by Edmond Rostand [1868–1918].)

Before you listen, implement your dictation strategies:

1. Spellings: Look for IPA spellings you already know such as the articles *les*, *la*, *une*, *un*, and *le*; the conjunction *et*; the possessive adjectives *leur*, *leurs*, and *ses*; the prepositions *à*, *par*, *en de*, *parmi*, *comme*, *lorsqu'au*, *vers*, and *pour*; the pronouns *ils* and *vous*; and the auxiliary verbs *ont* and *sont*. Mark the nasal vowel spellings such as *dindons*, *champs*, *tranquille*, *matins*, *couchants*, *bêtement*, *devant*, *fredonnant*, *fredons*, *vont*, *procession*, *ont*, *marchands*, *remplis*, *imbécile*, *méchants*, *regardant*, *d'un*, *pendeloque*, *semblent*, *chardons*, *gravement*, *concile*, *touchants*, *sons*, *trébuchants*, *lointain*, *campanile*, *l'angélus*, *lents*, *penchants*, *sont*, *chants*, *passetemps*, *gent*, *arrondissant*, and *bedons*.

2. Familiar Words: Look for words you may recognize such as *tranquille*, *matins*, *procession*, *docile*, *hostile*, *rossignol*, *domicile*, *amour*, *chants*, *bourgeois*, and *dindons*.

3. Rhyming Words: Follow down the right side of the text to identify rhymes such as *champs/couchant/marchands/méchants/touchants/trébuchants/penchants/chants*, *tranquille/file/docile/imbécile/hostile/oscille/concile/file/édile/campanile/domicile/l'utile/futile/volatile/idylle*, and *fredons/dindons/chardons/dons/bedons/dindons*. Mark each rhyming unit with the same IPA spellings. Notice the humor in the continuous rhymes presented in this text.

4. Liaison Possibilities: Circle the words that might contain a liaison or elision.

Les gros dindons, à travers champs,
The fat turkeys, traversing (the) fields,

D'un pas solennel et tranquille,
With a step solemn and tranquille,

Par les matins, par les couchants,
During the mornings, during the evenings,

Bêtement marchent à la file,
Stupidly march (they) in a row (single file)

Devant la pastoure qui file,
In front of the shepherdess who turns around/spins,

En fredonnant de vieux fredons,
While humming some old tunes

Vont en procession docile
Go (they) in a procession docile

Les gros dindons!
The fat turkeys!

Ils vous ont l'air de gros marchands
They to you have the air of fat merchants

Remplis d'une morgue imbécile,
Filled of a pride absurd,

De baillis rogues et méchants
Of bailiffs rogue and spiteful

Vous regardant d'un oeil hostile;
You looking with an eye hostile;

Leur rouge pendeloque oscille;
Their red pendants oscillate;

Ils semblent, parmi les chardons,
They seem, among the thistles,

Gravement tenir un concile,
Gravely to be holding a council (meeting),

Les gros dindons!
The fat turkeys!

N'ayant jamais trouvé touchants
Not having ever been found to be moved

Les sons que le rossignol file,

The sounds that the nightingale spins out,

Ils suivent, lourds et trébuchants,

They follow, lumbering and stumbling,

L'un d'eux digne comme un édile;

One of them dignified as an elder (of the town council);

Et, lorsqu'au lointain campanile

And, when from a distant bell tower

L'angélus fait ses lents din! dons!

The angelus (bell) rings its slow Ding! Dong!

Ils regagnent leur domicile,

They return to their domicile,

Les gros dindons!

The fat turkeys!

Prud' hommes gras, leurs seuls penchants

Like pompous men fat, whose sole tendencies (penchants)

Sont vers le pratique et l'utile,

Are toward the practical and the useful,

Pour eux l'amour et les doux chants

For them, (the) love and the sweet songs

Sont un passetemps trop futile;

Are a pastime too futile;

Bourgeois de la gent volatile,

Bourgeois of the people flying,

Arrondissant de noirs bedons,

Rotund of black bellies,

Ils se fichent de toute idylle,

They themselves do not care for any romance,

Les gros dindons!

The fat turkeys!

Poetic Equivalent

The fat turkeys waddle clumsily across the fields. With solemn, tranquil steps, they march in single file behind a shepherdess who dances and sings old, familiar tunes. They follow her in a docile procession—those fat turkeys! They look like proud, absurd merchants or haughty magistrates who regard you with a hostile glance. Their red wattles shake, making them look as if they are holding a council meeting in the thistles—those fat turkeys! Never having been deeply moved by the song of the nightingale, they follow, lumbering and stumbling, behind their leader who looks like a dignified town councilor; and when the distant bell peals its "Ding! Dong!" from the tower they return to their homes—those fat turkeys! Pompous, fat fellows, they are more partial to the practical than to the trivial singing of sweet songs. They belong to the feathered bourgeois with their fat black bellies, caring nothing for romance—those fat turkeys!

Comparative Performances

Listen to baritone Kurt Ollman with collaborative pianist Mary Dibbern, and tenor Paul Sperry with collaborative pianist Ian Hobson, perform this song. Does the vocal timbre enhance the level of humor in the interpretation of this colorful text? Have you a preference? If so, why?

Reynaldo Hahn (1875–1947)

Reynaldo Hahn, a Venezuelan-born Parisian, was a singer, an opera conductor, a music critic, and a great friend to performing artists of his time. Because of his association with the literary giant Marcel Proust, Hahn was depicted as the musician in two of Proust's novels, *Jean Sauteuil* and *La Recherche du Temps Perdu*, known in English by the title *In Search of Lost Time*. Hahn's melodies are characterized by an uncommon tenderness, as you will see in the following mélodie. Read the following poem and create a phonetic transcription.

Comparative Listening

"L'énamourée" (The Beloved)
(Text by Théodore de Banville [1823-1891].)

Before you listen, implement your dictation strategies:

1. Spellings: Look for IPA spellings you already know such as the articles *la, une, les,* and *un;* the conjunction *et;* the demonstrative adjective *cette;* the possessive adjectives *ma, tes,* and *ta;* the prepositions *sous, par, dans, sur,* and *comme;* and the pronouns *ils, tu,* and *je.* Also mark the nasal vowel spellings such as *colombe, encore, tombe, pensive, bien-aimée, blanches, longs, mouvante, blondes,* and *ondes.*

2. Familiar Words: Look for words you may recognize such as *colombe, morte, encore, tombe, adore, blanches, nuits, d'étoiles, caresses, roses, blondes, voix, lyre,* and *pleure.*

3. Rhyming Words: Follow down the right side of the text to identify rhymes such as *colombe/tombe, encore/adore, ranimée/bien-aimée, d'étoiles/voiles, murmure/chevelure, demi-closes/roses, respire/lyre, blondes/ondes,* and *effleure/pleure.*

4. Liaison Possibilities: Circle the words that might contain a liaison or elision.

I

Ils se disent, ma colombe,
They themselves say, my dove,

Que tu rêves, morte encore,
That you dream, you are dead already,

Sous la pierre d'une tombe
Under the rock of a tomb

Mais pour l'âme qui t'adore!
But for the soul that adores you!

Tu t'éveilles ranimée
You awaken animated

O pensive bien-aimée!
O, pensive beloved!

II

Par les blanches nuits d'étoiles,
Through the sleepless star-filled night,

Dans la brise qui murmure,
In the breeze which murmurs,

Je caresse tes longs voiles,
I caress your long veils,

Ta mouvante chevelure
Your flowing hair

Et tes ailes demi-closes
And your wings half-closed

Qui voltigent sur les roses.
Which flutter among the roses.

III

O délices! Je respire
Oh delights! I breathe in

Tes divines tresses blondes;
Your divine tresses blond;

Ta voix pure, cette lyre,
Your voice pure, this lyre,

Suit la vague sur les ondes,

Follows the swell across the waters,

Et, suave, les effleure

And, softly, them touches

Comme un cygne qui se pleure!

Like a swan which is weeping!

Poetic Equivalent

There are those who tell me, my dove, that you dream as if you were dead under a gravestone: But for the soul who adores you awaken and return to life, o pensive beloved! During sleepless nights without stars, amid murmuring breezes, I caress your long veils, your streaming hair, and your half-folded wings that flutter over the roses! Oh, my delight! I inhale your divine blond curls! Your voice so pure, like a lyre that follows the waves across the sea and ripples them softly like a sorrowing swan!

Comparative Performances

Compare performances by soprano Anna Netrebko and mezzo soprano Susan Graham. How are their interpretations the same? Do they make similar diction choices?

Discussion Questions

1. The work of Camille Saint-Saëns is said to have had a significant influence on his student, Gabriel Fauré. What do you hear in the comparative settings by Fauré that is reminiscent of settings by Saint-Saëns? What is different?

2. How do the mélodies of Fauré compare with those of Debussy?

3. Ernest Chausson was a student of Henri Duparc. What characteristics do you notice in the Chausson example that might show the influence of his teacher?

4. The texts for mélodies of Emmanuel Chabrier are based on country life. What musical gestures make the texts most vivid?

5. How does the musical language of Claude Debussy contrast with that of his contemporaries, Chabrier, Fauré, Duparc, and Chausson?

The French Mélodies of Maurice Ravel, Francis Poulenc, and Erik Satie

Maurice Ravel (1875–1937)

Maurice Ravel was born in a small Basque fishing village. His father was Swiss, an inventor and amateur musician. Ravel's mother, a woman of the Basque region, is known to have been an independent spirit with a strong affinity for dance. Ravel entered the Paris Conservatoire for the first time in 1889, the year of the world exhibition that featured world music such as a gamelean orchestra. After an interruption in his studies, Ravel returned to Paris in 1896 and was accepted as a composition student of Fauré. Ravel wrote more than 40 songs, some of which are orchestrated and some are harmonizations of folksongs. Influenced by Chabrier and Satie, Ravel's writings are a rare melding of harmonies and rhythms. Below is the first song Ravel wrote after his return to the Conservatoire. The poet Stéphane Mallarmé was a member of the symbolist movement, a group that sought to open poetic language through visual and visceral images. The text is a hymn to St. Cecilia, the patron saint of music. Read the text and create a phonetic transcription.

Comparative Listening

"Sainte" ("Saint")
(Text by Stéphane Mallarmé [1842–1898].)

Before you listen, implement your dictation strategies:

1. Spellings: Look for IPA spellings you already know such as the articles *le*, *la*, and *une*; the auxiliary verb *est*; the conjunctions *ou* and *avec*; the prepositions *à*, *par*, and *sur*; and the pronoun *elle*. Identify the nasal vowel spellings such as *recélant*, *santal*, *étincelant*, *selon*, *sainte*, *étalant*, *ruisselant*, *complie*, *d'ostensoir*, *l'Ange*, *son*, *phalange*, *sans*, *balance*, *instrumental*, and *silence*.

2. Familiar Words: Look for words you may recognize such as *flûte*, *harpe*, *soir*, and *silence*.

3. Rhyming Words: Follow down the right side of the text to identify rhymes such as *recélant/étincelant/étalant/ruisselant/santal/instrumental*, *déplie/complie*, *d'ostensoir/soir*, and *balance/silence*. Use the same IPA spellings for each rhyming pair.

4. Repeating Words: Study the text for common words that repeat such as *vieux* and *livre*. Use the same IPA symbols for each repetition.

5. Liaison Possibilities: Circle the words that might contain a liaison or elision.

À la fenêtre recélant

At the window receiving/harboring

Le santal vieux qui se dédore

The sandalwood old that itself is-losing-its-gilded gold

De la viole étincelant

Of the viol sparkling

Jadis selon flûte ou mandora,

Once to flute or mandolin,

Est la sainte pale, étalant

Is the saint pale,

Le livre vieux qui se déplie
The book old that itself displays

Du Magnificat ruisselant
Of the Magnificat running down

Jadis selon vêpre ou complie:
Once to vesper or compline:

A ce vitrage d'ostensoir
At this glass ostensory

Que frôle une harpe par l'Ange
That touches a harp of the angel

Formée avec son vol du soir
Set upon his flight in the night

Pour la delicate phalange
For the delicate tip

Du doigt que, sans le vieux santal
Of (his) finger that, without the old sandalwood

Ni le vieux livre, elle balance
Neither the old book, she balances

Sur le plumage instrumental,
On the plumage instrumental,

Musicienne du silence.
Musician of silence.

Poetic Equivalent

At the window that holds the old sandalwood of flaking gold of the viol that once sparkled to flute or mandolin, stands the pale saint, showing the ancient open book of the Magnificat that once sparkled during vespers and compline: This ostensory was once brushed by a harp the angel forms during his evening flight for the delicate fingertip that, without the old sandalwood and the aged book, she poses on the instrument's plumage—a musician of silence.

Comparative Performances

Compare the performance of French baritone Souzay with that of Canadian baritone LaPlante. Notice the similarities and the differences. How does each singer achieve the atmosphere necessary to depict the "musician of silence"? What diction tools does each use?

Francis Poulenc (1899–1963)

Francis Poulenc is known as a member of *Les Six*, a group of young French intellectuals who sought to create a new approach to music and aesthetics. Poulenc found the sentiment of the following poem by Charles, Duc d'Orléans appropriate to a time of political strain preceding WW II. The baritone Pierre Bernac (1899–1979) premiered many of Poulenc's works with the composer at the piano. Be sure to avail yourself of opportunities to hear the collaborations of these artists. Read the text and create a phonetic transcription.

Comparative Listening

"Priez pour Paix" ("Pray for Peace")
(Text by Charles, Duc d'Orléans [1394–1465].)

Before you listen, implement your dictation strategies:

1. Spellings: Look for IPA spellings you already know such as the articles *de* and *le*; the conjunction *et*; the possessive adjectives *vostre* and *son*; the prepositions *pour*, *par*, and *vers*; and the pronoun *vous*. Identify the nasal spellings such as *monde*, *saints*, *saintes*, *requérant*, *son*, *sang*, *en*, and *deboutant*.

2. Familiar Words: Look for words you may recognize such as *paix*, *douce Vierge Marie*, *Saint*, *Saintes*, *fils*, and *prières*.

3. Rhyming Words: Follow down the right side of the text to identify rhymes such as *Marie/courtoisie*, *maîtresse/adresse/haultesse/lasser*, *regarder/racheter*, and *desvoye/joye*. Mark each pair with the same IPA spellings.

4. Repeating Words: Study the text for common words that repeat such as *priez*, *prier*, *prières*, and *priez pour paix*.

5. Liaison Possibilities: Circle the words that might contain a liaison or elision.

Priez pour paix, douce Vierge Marie,

Pray for peace, sweet Virgin Mary,

Reine des cieux et du monde maîtresse,

Queen of Heaven and of the world mistress,

Faites prier, par votre courtoisie,

Make/ask for prayers of your courtesy,

Saints et saintes, et prenez votre adresse

Saints (male) and saints (female) and make your address

Vers votre *Fils*, requérant sa Hautesse

To your son, requesting his Highness

Qu'il lui plaise son peuple regarder,
That he may be pleased his people to regard,

Que de son sang a voulu racheter
Whom with his blood he wished to redeem

En déboutant guerre qui tout dévoie.
In banishing war which everything disrupts.

De prières ne vous veuillez lasser.
Of the prayers not you want to become weary.

Priez pour paix, priez pour paix,
Pray for peace, pray for peace,

Le vrai trésor de joie.
The true treasure of joy.

Poetic Equivalent

Pray for peace, sweet Virgin Mary, Heaven's Queen and mistress of the world. In your goodness, ask all the saints to pray, and speak to your song, pleading that the Highest One will look down upon his people, those He chose to redeem through his blood, to banish the wars that destroy all. Pray without ceasing. Pray for peace, pray for peace, joy's true treasure.

Comparative Performances

Compare performances of mezzo soprano Stutzmann and baritone Bernac. What differences do you notice in the approaches of these two singers to this sensitive text?

Which performance do you prefer? Why?

Erik Satie (1866–1925)

The composer of ballets, piano pieces, and a drama entitled *Socrate*, Erik Satie is unusual among composers of song because of his eclectic output. Below you will find a short song in which the playful world of a precocious child is depicted. Read the text and create a phonetic transcription.

Comparative Listening

"Daphénéo" from *Trois Mélodies de 1916*
(Text by Mimi Godebska.)

Before you listen, implement your dictation strategies:

1. Spellings: Look for IPA spellings you already know such as the articles *un* and *les*; auxiliary verbs *est* and *sont*; and pronouns *moi* and *je*. Identify the nasal spellings such as d<u>on</u>c, d<u>on</u>t, s<u>on</u>t, pleur<u>an</u>t, and <u>un</u>.

2. Familiar Words: Look for words you may recognize such as *Oui! Daphénéo, Chrysaline, pleurant,* and *Ah!*

3. Rhyming Words: Follow down the right side of the text to identify rhymes such as *oisetier/noisetiers*. Use the same IPA symbols for each repetition.

4. Repeating Words: Study the text for words that repeat such as *Daphénéo, Chrysaline,* and derivatives of *donner, dont, donnaient,* and *donnent*.

5. Liaison Possibilities: Circle the words that might contain a liaison or elision.

Dis-moi, Daphénéo, quell est donc cet arbre
Tell me, Dapheneo, what is then that tree

Dont les fruits sont des oiseaux qui pleurant?
Whose (the) fruits are (of the) birds who weep?

Cet arbre, Chrysaline, est un oisetier.
This tree, Chrysaline, is a bird tree.

Ah! Je croyais que les noisetiers
Ah! I thought that the hazelnut trees

Donnaient des noisettes, Daphénéo,
Produce (give) hazelnuts, Dapheneo,

Oui, Chrysaline, les noisetiers donnent des noisettes,
Yes, Chrysaline, the hazelnut trees produce (give) hazelnuts,

Mais les oisetiers donnent des oiseaux qui pleurent.
But the bird trees produce (give) birds who weep.

Ah!
Ah!

Poetic Equivalent

Chrysaline: Tell me, Dapheneo, what you call a tree that produces weeping birds?

Dapheneo: That tree, Chrysaline, is called a bird tree.

Chrysaline: Ah! I thought that hazelnut trees produced hazelnuts.

Dapheneo: Yes, Chrysaline, a hazelnut tree does produce hazelnuts, but a bird tree produces birds who weep.

Chrysaline: Ah!

Comparative Performances

Compare the performances of mezzo soprano von Stade and soprano Upshaw. What does each singer do to create the dialogue between Daphénéo and Chrysaline? How does each singer deal with the diction challenges of this song?

French Diction Final Presentation Repertoire List

Each student will prepare the text with its word-by-word translation, poetic equivalent, and a thorough program note. The program note should place the work in time and give its historical and musical context. Important biographical information regarding the poet and composer are to be included. These materials will be submitted to the instructor for correction and grading. The materials will be duplicated for class use during the presentations. *Note.* Repertoire assignments should be approved by the studio teacher, who may suggest other selections for this project.

Villanelle des Petits Canards	Emmanuel Chabrier
Le Charme	Ernest Chausson
Le Colibri	Ernest Chausson
Les Papillons	Ernest Chausson
Beau Soir	Claude Debussy
Romance	Claude Debussy
Extase	Henri Duparc
Adieu	Gabriel Fauré
Après un Rêve	Gabriel Fauré
Chanson D'amour	Gabriel Fauré
Prison	Gabriel Fauré
Reve D'amour	Gabriel Fauré
Au Rossignol	Charles Gounod
Sérènade	Charles Gounod
D'une Prison	Reynaldo Hahn
L'heure Exquise	Reynaldo Hahn
Offrande	Reynaldo Hahn
Si Mes Vers	Reynaldo Hahn
O Quand Je Dors	Franz Liszt
Psyché	Emil Paladilhe

| Le Réveil de la Mariée | Maurice Ravel |
| Quel Galant | Maurice Ravel |

Conclusion

Bernac stated, "A French *mélodie* is a musico-literary work in which the heart plays its part, but which, in its poem and music, is an art infinitely more concerned with sensitive perceptions and impressions, more intellectual and more objective, than a German Lied, which is always subjective, both musically and poetically" (Bernac, 1970). The study of French art song involves a deep understanding of the visual and literary elements that interested the composers. Paris, where all the composers studied and worked, was the center of aesthetic, artistic, philosophical, and political activity. The younger composers enjoyed the mentorship of France's intellectual and musical giants such as Franck, Gounod, and Fauré. The art form known as the mélodie grew progressively, while maintaining a perceptive, sensitive objectivity.

References

Appelbaum, S. (Ed.). (1969). *Introduction to French poetry: A dual-language book* (p. 111). New York, NY: Dover Publications.

Bernac, P. (1970). *The interpretation of the French song* (p. 34). New York, NY: W. W. Norton.

Blackmore, E. H., & Blackmore, A. M. (Trans.). (2001). Introduction: Hugo V. In *Selected poems of Victor Hugo: A bilingual edition* (p. xv). Chicago, IL: University of Chicago Press.

Campbell, D. (1984). *Master teacher—Nadia Boulanger* (p. 107). Portland, OR: Pastoral Press.

Grubb, T. (1979). *Singing in French: A manual of French diction and French vocal repertoire* (p. 3). Belmont, CA: Schirmer Books.

Johnson, G., & Stokes, R. (2000). *A French song companion.* New York, NY: Oxford University Press.

Nectoux, J. M. (1991). *Gabriel Fauré: A musical life* (R. Nichols, Trans., p. 228). Cambridge, UK: Cambridge University Press.

Rees, W. (1992). *The Penguin book of French poetry 1820–1950* (p. 225). London, UK: Penguin Books.

Walsh, S. (2018). *Debussy: A painter in sound* (p. 3). New York, NY: Knopf.

Concluding Thoughts

The phrase "to breathe is to sing" is attributed to the early *bel canto* masters. The words have significance for every singer, singing teacher, and listener. The late Dr. Joseph R. Flummerfelt, to whom this book is dedicated, often said that breathing is the "galvanizing force" that brings us together. Dr. R. Allen Shoaf, whose poem opens this textbook, tells us that "we evolved with melodies, they with us." I too believe that the experience of singing melodies coupled with language has life-giving power. Using the tools gleaned from this book, I hope you will delve deeply into the texts you sing and allow "music's mirror to call you." Let the mysteries of poetry and music intrigue you. Follow every shred of evidence and respond to every clue. Discover what the poem may have meant to the composer and, ultimately, what it means to you. Be diligent in your work. As singers, we are the vessels that deliver the innermost thoughts of poets and composers to a world in need of beauty and comfort. In the act of singing, we confirm two truths: "to breathe is to sing" and "to sing is to be."

Glossary

This glossary was adapted from a glossary developed from the experience of authors Brenda Smith and Robert T. Sataloff and also from a review of glossaries developed by Johan Sundberg (personal communication, June 1995), Ingo Titze (*Principles of Voice Production*, 1994, Englewood Cliffs, NJ: Prentice Hall Inc; 330–338), and other sources. It is used with permission of Plural Publishing. It is difficult to appropriately credit contributions to glossaries or dictionaries of general terms, as each new glossary builds on prior works. The authors are indebted to colleagues whose previous efforts have contributed to the compilation of this glossary.

This glossary contains definitions not only of terms in this text, but also of terminology encountered commonly in related literature. Readers are encouraged to consult other sources, and these additional definitions are included for the convenience of those who do so.

abduct: To move apart; separate.

abduction quotient: The ratio of the glottal half-width at the vocal processes to the amplitude of vibration of the vocal fold.

absolute voice rest: Total silence of the phonatory system.

Adam's apple: Prominence of the thyroid cartilage in males.

adduct: To bring together; approximate.

affricate: Combination of plosive and fricative.

alto: (See contralto)

antagonist (muscle): An opposing muscle.

anterior: Toward the front.

appoggio: translated as "support;" in the terminology of vocal technique, refers to the point of appoggio, whether it be of the abdominal or the thoracic region, where the maximum muscular tension is experienced in singing (appoggio at the diaphragm; appoggio at the chest).

articulation: Shaping of vocal tract by positioning of its mobile walls such as the lips, the lower jaw, the tongue body and tip, the velum, the epiglottis, the pharyngeal sidewalls, and the larynx.

arytenoid cartilages: Paired, ladle-shaped cartilages to which the vocal folds are attached.

aspiration: (1) In speech, the sound made by turbulent airflow preceding or following vocal fold vibration, as in [ha]. (2) In medicine, refers to breathing into the lungs substances that do not belong there such as food, water, or stomach contents following reflux. Aspiration may lead to infections such as pneumonia, commonly referred to as *aspiration pneumonia*.

baritone: The most common male vocal range; higher than bass and lower than tenor. Singer 's formant around 2600 Hz.

bass: (See basso)

bass baritone: In between a bass and a baritone. Not as heavy as basso profundo, but typically with greater flexibility. Must be able to sing at least as high as F4.

basso: The lowest male voice; singer 's formant around 2300 to 2400 Hz.

basso profundo: Deep bass; the lowest and heaviest of the bass voices. Can sing at least as low as D2 with full voice. Singer 's formant around 2200 to 2300 Hz.

bel canto: Literally means "beautiful singing;" refers to a method and philosophical approach to singing voice production.

Bernoulli's principle: If the energy in a confined fluid stream is constant, an increase in particle velocity must be accompanied by a decrease in pressure against the wall.

bleating: Fast vibrato, like the bleating of a sheep.

body: With regard to the vocal fold, the vocalis muscle.

bravura: Brilliant, elaborate, showy execution of musical or dramatic material.

breathy phonation: Phonation characterized by a lack of vocal fold closure, which causes air leakage (excessive airflow) during the quasiclosed phase, producing turbulence that is heard as noise mixed in the voice.

cartilage of Wrisberg: Cartilage attached in the mobile portion of each aryepiglottic fold.

castrato: A male singer castrated at around age 7 or 8, so as to retain alto or soprano vocal range.

chest voice: Heavy registration with excessive resonance in the lower formants.

coloratura: In common usage, refers to the highest of the female voices, with range well above C6; may use more whistle tone than other female voices. In fact, coloratura actually refers to a style of florid, agile, complex singing that may apply to any voice classification. For example, the bass runs in Handel's *Messiah* require coloratura technique

complex sound: A combination of sinusoidal waveforms superimposed on each other. May be complex periodic sound (such as musical instruments) or complex aperiodic sound (such as random street noise).

complex tone: Tone composed of a series of simultaneously sounding partials.

component frequency: Mathematically, a sinusoid; perceptually, a pure tone. Also called a partial.

concert pitch: Also known as international concert pitch.

contraction: A decrease in length.

contralto: The lowest of the female voices; able to sing F3 below middle C, as well as the entire treble staff. The singer 's formant is at around 2800 to 2900 Hz.

corner vowels: [ɑ], [i], and [u]; vowels at the corners of a vowel triangle; they necessitate extreme placements of the tongue.

countertenor: A male voice that is primarily falsetto, singing in the contralto range.

cover: (1) In medicine, with regard to the vocal fold, the epithelium, and superficial layer of lamina propria. (2) In music, an alteration in technique that changes the resonance characteristics of a sung sound, generally darkening the sound.

creaky voice: The perceptual result of subharmonic or chaotic patterns in the glottal waveform. According to IR Titze, if a subharmonic is below about 70 Hz, creaky voice may be perceived as pulse register (vocal fry).

crescendo: To gradually get louder.

cricoid cartilage: A solid ring of cartilage located below and behind the thyroid cartilage.

cricothyroid muscle: An intrinsic laryngeal muscle that is used primarily to control pitch (paired).

crossover frequency: The fundamental frequency for which there is an equal probability for perception of two adjacent registers.

damp: To diminish or attenuate an oscillation.

dB: (See decibel)

decibel: One-tenth of a bel. The decibel is a unit of comparison between a reference and another point. It has no absolute value. Although decibels are used to measure sound, they are also used (with different references) to measure heat, light, and other physical phenomena. For sound pressure, the reference is 0.0002 microbar (millionths of one barometric pressure). In the past, this has also been referred to as 0.0002 dyne/cm^2 and by other terms.

decrescendo: (See diminuendo)

diaphragm: A large, dome-shaped muscle at the bottom of the rib cage that separates the lungs from the viscera. It is the primary muscle of inspiration and may be coactivated during singing.

diminuendo: Gradually reducing in loudness or force.

divisi: Literally "divided;" used in choral scores to indicate that a section is to be divided into two or more parts; generally intended for the rendering of fuller harmony.

dramatic soprano: A soprano with powerful, rich voice suitable for dramatic, heavily orchestrated operatic roles; sings at least to C$_6$.

dramatic tenor: A tenor with heavy voice, often with a suggestion of baritone quality; suitable for dramatic roles that are heavily orchestrated. Also referred to as *Heldentenor*, a term used typically for tenors who sing Wagnerian operatic roles.

dynamics: (1) In physics, a branch of mechanics that deals with the study of forces that accelerate object(s). (2) In music, it refers to changes in the loudness of musical performance.

edema: Excessive accumulation of fluid in tissues, or "swelling."

electroglottography (EGG): Recording of electrical conductance of vocal fold contact area versus time; EGG waveforms frequently have been used for the purpose of plotting voice source analysis.

electromyography (EMG): Recording of the electric potentials in a muscle, which are generated by the neural system and which control its degree of contraction; if rectified and smoothed, the EMG is closely related to the muscular force exerted by the muscle.

elongation: An increase in length.

embouchure: The shape of the lips, tongue, and related structures adopted while producing a musical tone, particularly while playing a wind instrument.

epiglottis: Cartilage that covers the larynx during the act of swallowing.

epithelium: The covering, or most superficial layer, of body surfaces.

extrinsic muscles of the larynx: The strap muscles in the neck, responsible for adjusting laryngeal height and for stabilizing the larynx.

Fach (German): Literally, subject or box. It is used to indicate voice classification. For example, lyric soprano and dramatic soprano are each a different Fach.

false vocal folds: Folds of tissue located slightly higher than and parallel to the vocal folds in the larynx.

falsetto: High, light register, applied primarily to men's voices singing in the soprano or alto range. Can also be applied to women's voices.

flow: The volume of fluid passing through a given cross-section of a tube or duct per second; also called volume velocity (measured in liters per second).

flow glottography (FLOGG): Recording of the transglottal airflow versus time; i.e., of the sound of the voice source. Generally obtained from inverse filtering, FLOGG is the acoustical representation of the voice source.

flow phonation: The optimal balance between vocal fold adductory forces and subglottic pressure, producing efficient sound production at the level of the vocal folds.

F_0: Fundamental frequency.

force: A push or pull; the physical quantity imparted to an object to change its momentum.

formant: Vocal tract resonance; the formant frequencies are tuned by the vocal tract shape and determine much of the vocal quality.

formant tuning: A boosting of vocal intensity when F0 or one of its harmonics coincides exactly with a formant frequency.

functional residual capacity (FRC): Lung volume at which the elastic inspiratory forces equal the elastic expiratory forces; in spontaneous quiet breathing, exhalation stops at FRC.

frequency tremor: A periodic (regular) pitch modulation of the voice (an element of vibrato).

fricative: A speech sound, generally a consonant, produced by a constriction of the vocal tract, particularly by directing the airstream against a hard surface, producing noisy air turbulence. Examples include "s" [z] produced with the teeth, "s" [s] produced with the lower lip and upper incisors, and "th" [θ] produced with the tongue tip and upper incisors.

functional voice disorder: An abnormality in voice sound and function in the absence of an anatomic or physiologic organic abnormality.

fundamental: Lowest partial of a spectrum; the frequency of which normally corresponds to the pitch perceived.

fundamental frequency (F_0): The lowest frequency in a periodic waveform; also called the first harmonic frequency.

glissando: A "slide" including all possible pitches between the initial and final pitch sounded. Similar to portamento and slur.

globus: Sensation of a lump in the throat.

glottal chink: Opening in the glottis during vocal fold adduction, most commonly posteriorly. It may be a normal variant in some cases.

glottal resistance: Ratio between transglottal airflow and subglottal pressure; mainly reflects the degree of glottal adduction.

glottal stop (or click): A transient sound caused by the sudden onset or offset of phonation.

glottis: The space between the vocal folds.

glottis vocalis: The portion of the glottis in the region of the membranous portions of the vocal folds.

harmonic: A frequency that is an integer multiple of a given fundamental. Harmonics of a fundamental are equally spaced in frequency; partial in a spectrum in which the frequency of each partial equals n times the fundamental frequency, n being the number of the harmonic.

harsh glottal attack: Initiating phonation of a word or sound with a glottal plosive.

Heldentenor: (See dramatic tenor)

hyoid bone: A horseshoe-shaped bone known as the "tongue bone." It is attached to the muscles of the tongue and related structures, and to the larynx and related structures.

hyperfunction: Excessive muscular effort; for example, pressed voice or muscular tension dysphonia.

hypernasal: Excessive nasal resonance.

hypofunction: Low muscular effort; for example, soft breathy voice.

hyponasal: Deficient nasal resonance.

infraglottic: Below the level of the glottis. This region includes the trachea, thorax, and related structures.

infraglottic vocal tract: Below the level of the vocal folds. This region includes the airways and muscles of support. (Infraglottic is synonymous with subglottic.)

infrahyoid muscle group: A collection of extrinsic muscles including the sternohyoid, sternothyroid, omohyoid, and thyroid muscles.

intensity: A measure of power per unit area. With respect to sound, it generally correlates with perceived loudness.

interarytenoid muscle: An intrinsic laryngeal muscle that connects the two arytenoid cartilages.

intercostal muscles: Muscles between the ribs.

interval: The difference between two pitches, expressed in terms of musical scale.

intrinsic laryngeal muscles: Muscles in the larynx responsible for abduction, adduction, and longitudinal tension of the vocal folds.

intrinsic pitch of vowels: Refers to the fact that in normal speech, certain vowels tend to be produced with a significantly higher or lower pitch than other vowels.

jitter: Irregularity in the period of time of vocal fold vibrations; cycle-to-cycle variation in fundamental frequency; jitter is often perceived as hoarseness.

lamina propria: With reference to the larynx, the tissue layers below the epithelium. In adult humans, the lamina propria consists of superficial, intermediate, and deep layers.

laryngeal ventricle: Cavity formed by the gap between the true and false vocal folds.

laryngitis: Inflammation of laryngeal tissues.

laryngologist: A physician specializing in disorders of the larynx and voice. In some areas of Europe, the laryngologist is primarily responsible for surgery, while diagnosis is performed by phoniatricians.

laryngopharyngeal reflux (LPR): A form of gastroesophageal relux disease in which gastric juice affects the larynx and adjacent structures. Commonly associated with hoarseness, frequent throat clearing, granulomas, and other laryngeal problems, even in the absence of heartburn.

larynx: The body organ in the neck that includes the vocal folds; also called the "voice box."

laser: An acronym for "light amplification by stimulated emission of radiation." A surgical tool using light energy to vaporize or cauterize tissue.

lateral cricoarytenoid muscle: Intrinsic laryngeal muscle that adducts the vocal folds through forward rocking and rotation of the arytenoids (paired).

lift: A transition point along a pitch scale where vocal production becomes easier.

loft: A suggested term for the highest (loftiest) register; usually referred to as falsetto voice.

Lombard effect: Modification of vocal loudness in response to auditory input; for example, the tendency to speak louder in the presence of background noise.

longitudinal: Along the length of a structure.

longitudinal tension: With reference to the larynx, stretching the vocal folds.

loudness: The amount of sound perceived by a listener; a perceptual quantity that can only be assessed with an auditory system. Loudness corresponds to intensity and to the amplitude of a sound wave.

lung volume: Volume contained in the subglottic air system; after a maximum inhalation following a maximum exhalation, the lung volume equals the vital capacity.

lyric soprano: A soprano with flexible, light vocal quality, but one who does not sing as high as a coloratura soprano.

lyric tenor: A tenor with a light, high, flexible voice.

marcato: Each note accented; a manner of performance frequently associated with music of the Baroque period.

marking: Using the voice gently (typically during rehearsals) to avoid injury or fatigue.

martellato: A technique for singing melismatic passages in music in which certain notes are accentuated within the context of legato singing, generally found in works of the Baroque period.

messa di voce: A traditional exercise in Italian singing tradition consisting of a prolonged crescendo and diminuendo on a sustained tone.

mezza voce: Literally means "half voice." In practice, means singing softly, but with proper support.

mezzo-soprano: A range of the female voice, higher than contralto but lower than soprano.

middle (or mixed): A mixture of qualities from various voice registers, cultivated to allow consistent quality throughout the frequency range.

middle C: C4 on the piano keyboard, with an international concert pitch frequency of 261.6 Hz.

modal: Used frequently in speech, refers to the voice quality used generally by healthy speakers, as opposed to a low, gravelly vocal fry or high falsetto. Modal register describes the laryngeal function in the range of fundamental frequencies most commonly used by untrained speakers (from about 75 to about 450 Hz in men; 130 to 520 Hz in women).

modulation: Periodic variation of a signal property; for example, as vibrato corresponds to a regular variation of fundamental frequency, it can be regarded as a modulation of that signal property.

mucosa: The covering of the surfaces of the respiratory tract, including the oral cavity and nasal cavities, as well as the pharynx, larynx, and lower airways. Mucosa also exists elsewhere, such as on the lining of the vagina.

muscle tension dysphonia: Also called muscular tension dysphonia. A form of voice abuse characterized by excessive muscular effort, and usually by pressed phonation. A form of voice misuse.

mutational dysphonia: A voice disorder. Most typically, it is characterized by persistent falsetto voice after puberty in a male. More generally, it is used to refer to voice with characteristics of the opposite gender.

myoelastic-aerodynamic theory of phonation: The currently accepted mechanism of vocal fold physiology. Compressed air exerts pressure on the undersurface of the closed vocal folds. The pressure overcomes adductory forces, causing the vocal folds to open.

The elasticity of the displaced tissues (along with the Bernoulli effect) causes the vocal folds to snap shut, resulting in sound. "Myoelastic" refers to the muscle (myo) and its properties. "Aerodynamic" refers to activities related to airflow.

nasal tract: Air cavity system of the nose.

nervous system: Organs of the body including the brain, spinal cord, and nerves. Responsible for motion, sensation, thought, and control of various other bodily functions.

neurotologist: Otolaryngologist specializing in disorders of the ear and ear-brain interface (including the skull base), particularly hearing loss, dizziness, tinnitus, and facial nerve dysfunction.

nodules: Benign growths on the surface of the vocal folds. Usually paired and fairly symmetric. They are generally caused by chronic, forceful vocal fold contact (voice abuse).

objective assessment: Demonstrable, reproducible, usually quantifiable evaluation, generally relying on instrumentation or other assessment techniques that do not involve primarily opinion, as opposed to subjective assessment.

open quotient: The ratio of the time the glottis is open to the length of the entire vibratory cycle.

organic voice disorder: Disorder for which a specific anatomic or physiologic cause can be identified, as opposed to psychogenic or functional voice disorders.

oscillation: Back-and-forth repeated movement.

oscillator: With regard to the larynx, the vibrator that is responsible for the sound source, specifically the vocal folds.

otolaryngologist: Ear, nose, and throat physician.

overtones: Partials above the fundamental in a spectrum.

partial: Sinusoid that is part of a complex tone; in voiced sounds, the partials are harmonic, implying that the frequency of the nth partial equals n times the fundamental frequency.

passaggio (Italian): The shift or break between vocal registers.

period: In physics, the time interval between repeating events; shortest pattern repeated in a regular undulation. A graph showing the period is called a waveform.

pharynx: The region above the larynx, below the velum, and posterior to the oral cavity.

phonation: Sound generation by means of vocal fold vibrations.

phonetics: The study of speech sounds.

phonosurgery: Originally, surgery designed to alter vocal quality or pitch. Now commonly used to also refer to all delicate microsurgical procedures of the vocal folds.

pitch: Perceived tone quality corresponding to its fundamental frequency.

plosive: A consonant produced by creating complete blockage of airflow, followed by the buildup of air pressure, which is then suddenly released, producing a consonant sound.

posterior: Toward the back.

posterior cricoarytenoid muscle: An intrinsic laryngeal muscle that is the primary abductor of the vocal folds (paired).

power source: The expiratory system including the muscles of the abdomen, back, thorax, and the lungs. The power source is responsible for producing a vector of force that results in efficient creation and control of subglottal pressure.

pressed phonation: A type of phonation characterized by low airflow, high adductory force, and high subglottal pressure; not an efficient form of voice production. Pressed voice is often associated with voice abuse and is common in patients with lesions such as nodules.

pulmonary system: The breathing apparatus including the lungs and related airways.

pulse register: The extreme low end of the phonatory range. Also known as vocal fry or Strohbass, characterized by a pattern of short glottal waves alternating with larger and longer ones, and with a long closed phase.

recurrent laryngeal nerves: The paired branches of the vagus nerve that supply all the intrinsic muscles of the larynx except for the cricothyroid muscles. The recurrent laryngeal nerves also carry sensory fibers (feeling) to the mucosa below the level of the vocal folds.

reflux laryngitis: Inflammation of the larynx due to irritation from gastric juice.

registers: A weakly defined term for vocal qualities; often, register refers to a series of adjacent tones on the scale that sound similar and seem to be generated by the same type of vocal fold vibrations and vocal tract adjustments. Examples of register are vocal fry, modal, and falsetto, but numerous other terms are also used.

relative voice rest: Restricted, cautious voice use.

resonance: Peak occurring at certain frequencies (resonance frequencies) in the vibration amplitude in a system that possesses compliance, inertia, and reflection; resonance occurs when the input and the reflected energy vibrate in phase. The resonances in the vocal tract are called formants.

resonator: With regard to the voice, refers primarily to the supraglottic vocal tract, which is responsible for timbre and projection.

sensory: Having to do with the feeling or detection of other nonmotor input. For example, nerves responsible for touch, proprioception (position in space), hearing, and so on.

singer's formant: A high-spectrum peak occurring between about 2.3 and 3.5 kHz in voiced sounds in Western operatic and concert singing. This acoustic phenomenon is associated with "ring" in a voice and with the voice's ability to project over background noise, such as a choir or an orchestra. A similar phenomenon may be seen in speaking voices, especially in actors. It is known as the speaker's formant.

singing teacher: Professional who teaches singing technique (as opposed to *voice coach*).

singing voice specialist: A singing teacher with additional training and specialization in working with injured voices, in conjunction with a medical voice team.

skeleton: The bony or cartilaginous framework to which muscle and other soft tissues are connected.

soft glottal attack: Gentle glottal approximation often obtained using an imaginary [h].

spectrum: Ensemble of simultaneously sounding sinusoidal partials constituting a complex tone, a display of relative magnitudes or phases of the component frequencies of a waveform.

spectrum analysis: Analysis of a signal showing its partials.

speech-language pathologist: A trained, medically affiliated professional who may be skilled in remediation of problems of the speaking voice, swallowing, articulation, language development, and other conditions.

spinto: Literally means "pushed." Usually applied to tenors or sopranos with a lighter voice than dramatic singers, but with aspects of particular dramatic excitement in their vocal quality, Enrico Caruso being a notable example.

staccato: Each note accented and separated.

stroboscopy: A technique that uses interrupted light to simulate slow motion. (See also strobovideolaryngoscopy)

strobovideolaryngoscopy: Evaluation of vocal folds utilizing simulated slow motion for detailed evaluation of vocal fold motion.

Strohbass (German): Literally "straw bass;" another term for *pulse register* or *vocal fry*.

subglottal pressure: Air pressure in the airway immediately below the level of the vocal folds. The unit most commonly used is centimeters of water: the distance in centimeters that a given pressure would raise a column of water in a tube.

subglottic: The region immediately below the level of the vocal folds.

subjective assessment: Evaluation that depends on perception and opinion, rather than independently reproducible quantifiable measures, as opposed to objective assessment.

support: Commonly used to refer to the power source of the voice; includes the mechanism responsible for creating a vector force that results in efficient subglottic pressure; includes the muscles of the abdomen and back, as well as the thorax and lungs; primarily the expiratory system.

superior laryngeal nerves: Paired branches of the vagus nerve that supply the cricothyroid muscle, and supply sensation from the level of the vocal folds superiorly.

supraglottic: Vocal tract above the level of the vocal folds. This region includes the resonance system of the vocal tract, including the pharynx, oral cavity, nose, and related structures.

suprahyoid muscle group: One of the two extrinsic muscle groups. Includes the stylohyoid muscle, the anterior and posterior bellies of the digastric muscle, the geniohyoid, the hyoglossus, and the mylohyoid muscles.

temporomandibular joint: The jaw joint; a synovial joint between the mandibular condyle and skull anterior to the ear canal.

tenor: The highest of the male voices, except countertenors; must be able to sing to C5. Singer's formant is around 2800 Hz.

thoracic: Pertaining to the chest.

thorax: The part of the body between the neck and abdomen.

thyroarytenoid muscle: An intrinsic laryngeal muscle that comprises the bulk of the vocal fold (paired). The medial belly constitutes the body of the vocal fold.

thyroid cartilage: The largest laryngeal cartilage. It is open posteriorly and made up of two plates (thyroid laminae) joined anteriorly at the midline. In males, there is an anterior, superior prominence known as the "Adam's apple."

tidal volume: The amount of air breathed in and out during respiration (measured in liters).

timbre: The quality of a sound. Associated with complexity or the number, nature, and interaction of overtones.

tracheobronchial tree: The air passages of the lungs and trachea (commonly referred to as the windpipe).

tremolo: An aesthetically displeasing, excessively wide vibrato.

trill: A vocal or instrumental ornament involving an oscillation of pitch within a discrete range.

trillo: The repetition of a given pitch with frequent interruptions; a vocal ornament of the late Medieval and early Renaissance periods.

tympanic membrane: The eardrum.

velar: Relating to the velum or palate.

velum: A general term that means "veil" or "covering." With regard to the vocal tract, it refers to the region of the soft palate and adjacent nasopharynx that closes together under normal circumstances during swallowing and phonation of certain sounds.

ventricular folds: The "false vocal folds," situated above the true vocal folds.

vibrato: In classical singing, vibrato is a periodic modulation of the frequency of phonation. Its regularity increases with training. The rate of vibrato (number of modulations per second) is usually in the range of 5 to 6 per second. Vibrato rates over 7 to 8 seconds are aesthetically displeasing to most people and sound "nervous." The extent of vibrato (amount of variation above and below the center frequency) is usually 1 or 2 semitones. Vibrato extending less than ±50.5 semitone is rarely noted in singers, although it is encountered in wind-instrument playing. Vibrato rates greater than 2 semitones are usually aesthetically unacceptable and are typical of elderly singers in poor artistic vocal condition, in whom the excessively wide vibrato extent is often combined with excessively slow rate.

viscera: The internal organs of the body, particularly the contents of the abdomen.

visceral pleura: The innermost of two membranes surrounding the lungs.

vital capacity: The maximum volume of air that can be exchanged by the lungs with the outside; it includes the expiratory reserve volume, tidal volume, and inspiratory reserve volume (measured in liters).

vocal cord: An old term for vocal fold.

vocal folds: A paired system of tissue layers in the larynx that can oscillate to produce sound.

vocal fry: A register with perceived temporal gaps; also known as *pulse register* and *Strohbass.*

vocal ligament: Intermediate and deep layers of the lamina propria. Also forms the superior end of the conus elasticus.

vocal tract: Resonator system constituted by the larynx, the pharynx, and the mouth cavity.

vocalis muscle: The medial belly of the thyroarytenoid muscle.

voce coperta: Covered registration.

voce di petto: Chest voice.

voce di testa: Head voice.

voce mista: Mixed voice.

voice abuse: Use of the voice in specific activities that are deleterious to vocal health, such as screaming.

voice coach: (1) In singing, a professional who works with singers, teaching repertoire, language pronunciation, and other artistic components of performance (as opposed to a singing teacher, who teaches singing technique). (2) The term *voice coach* is also used by acting and voice teachers who specialize in vocal, bodily, and interpretive techniques to enhance dramatic performance.

voice misuse: Habitual phonation using phonatory techniques that are not optimal and result in vocal strain. For example, speaking with inadequate support, excessive neck muscle tension, and suboptimal resonance. Muscular tension dysphonia is a form of voice misuse.

voice source: Sound generated by the pulsating transglottal airflow; the sound is generated when the vocal fold vibrations chop the airstream into a pulsating airflow.

volume: Amount of sound, best measured in terms of acoustic power or intensity.

wavelength: The initial distance between any point on one vibratory cycle and a corresponding point of the next vibratory cycle.

whisper: Sound created by turbulent glottal airflow in the absence of vocal fold vibration.

whistle voice: The highest of all registers (in pitch); it is observed only in females, extending the pitch range beyond F6.

wobble: A slow, irregular vibrato; aesthetically unsatisfactory. Sometimes referred to as a *tremolo*, having a rate of less than 4 oscillations per second and an extent of greater than ±2 semitones.

Appendix A

PRACTICE DRILLS, ASSESSMENT FORMS, AND QUIZZES

English Diction

English Diction Practicing Vowel Spellings Answer Sheet

Here are the answers to the English Diction Vowel Spellings Practice Drill found on page 51 in Chapter 2.

B<u>a</u>nk	[æ]		H<u>ee</u>d	[i]
Bl<u>ue</u>	[u]		L<u>a</u>st	[æ]
B<u>u</u>d	[ʌ]		L<u>oo</u>k	[ʊ]
Ch<u>ee</u>k	[i]		L<u>u</u>te	[ju]
D<u>a</u>m<u>a</u>sk	[æ] [æ]		M<u>a</u>d	[æ]
D<u>i</u>m	[ɪ]		M<u>ee</u>t	[i]
D<u>o</u>	[u]		M<u>i</u>d	[ɪ]
Dr<u>e</u>ss	[ɛ]		R<u>oo</u>t	[u:]
D<u>ue</u>	[ju]		S<u>i</u>t	[ɪ]
<u>Ea</u>t	[i]		S<u>o</u>ng	[ɑ]
F<u>a</u>lse	[ɑ]		Tr<u>ee</u>	[i]
F<u>ie</u>ld	[i]		W<u>ee</u>p	[i]
F<u>o</u>rsw<u>o</u>rn	[ɔ] [ɔ:]		Wh<u>a</u>t<u>e</u>v<u>er</u>	[ɑ] [ɛ] [ɚ]
F<u>u</u>ll	[ʊ]		W<u>i</u>nd	[ɪ]
G<u>o</u>ne	[ɔ]		<u>You</u>	[ju]

English Diction Practice Drills

Practicing Stressed and Unstressed Syllables in English

In English, the vowels [ɪ], [ə] and [o] appear in unstressed syllables. In the words given below, the unstressed syllable is underlined. Identify the appropriate vowel symbol for the unstressed syllable. Note its context in the phrase example provided.

1. Above

2. Again

3. Asleep

4. Before

5. Belief

6. Beloved

7. Beside

8. Delight

9. Desire

10. Enough

11. Enrich

12. Eternal

13. Obey

14. Omit

15. Pretend

16. Remember

17. Return

18. Secure

English Diction Practice Drills

Vowels in Poetic and Musical Context

Determine the International Phonetic Alphabet symbols for the vowels found in the following words as you would sing them:

1. animal   [   ] [   ] [   ]—"half-man, half-animal . . . "
   ("Memory," Theodore Roethke/Ned Rorem)

2. beloved   [   ] [   ] [   ]—"are heaped for the beloved's bed, and so thy thoughts . . . "
   ("Music, When Soft Voice Die," Shelley/Ernest Gold, Roger Quilter, et al.)

3. cathedral   [   ] [   ] [   ]—" . . . in a cathedral aisle . . . "
   ("I heard an Organ Talk Sometime" in *Twelve Poems of Emily Dickinson,* Emily Dickinson/Aaron Copland)

4. deadly   [   ] [   ]—" . . . in deadly pain and endless misery"
   ("Come Again, Sweet Love," John Dowland)

5. eternal   [   ] [   ] [   ]—"from their eternal bands . . . ."
   ("If Music Be the Food of Love," versions I and III, William Shakespeare/Henry Purcell)

6. grief   [   ]—"killing care and grief of heart"
   ("Orpheus With His Lute," William Shakespeare/ William Schuman, Arthur Sullivan, Richard Hundley)

7. heart   [   ]—"Heart, we will forget him . . . "
   ("Heart, We Will Forget Him" in *Twelve Poems of Emily Dickinson,* Emily Dickinson/Aaron Copland)

8. kissing   [   ] [   ]—"they fell a kissing..."
   ("Fair Phyllis," a madrigal/John Farmer)

9. merry   [   ] [   ]—"and tune his merry note, unto the sweet bird's throat"
   ("Under the Greenwood Tree," William Shakespeare/Roger Quilter, Douglas Moore)

10. pretty   [   ] [   ]—" . . . these pretty countryfolk did lie in Springtime"
    ("It Was a Lover and His Lass," William Shakespeare/ Thomas Morley, Roger Quilter, Gerald Finzi, et al.)

11. queer   [   ] [   ] —" . . . the little horse must think it queer . . . "
                 ("Stopping by Woods," Robert Frost/Ned Rorem)

12. scented   [   ] [   ] —" . . . in the scented bud of the morning, O!"
                 ("The Daisies," James Stephen/Samuel Barber)

13. triumph   [   ] [   ] —" . . . while she for triumphs laughs"
                 ("Come Again, Sweet Love Does Now Invite," John Dowland)

14. village   [   ] [   ] —" . . . the village seems asleep or dead . . . "
                 {"My Mother Bids Me Bind My Hair," Franz Josef Haydn)

15. wondrous   [   ] [   ] —"What wondrous love is this?"
                 (American Folk Hymn)

English Diction Practice Drills

Practicing the Letter "R"

In the following passage, <u>circle</u> the "r" letters that are *pronounced* and <u>underline</u> the ones that are *silent*. Note in the margin the reasons for your answers.

Ring out, wild bells, to the wild sky,

The flying cloud, the frosty light:

The year is dying in the night;

Ring out, wild bells, and let him die.

Ring out the old, ring in the new,

Ring, happy bells, across the snow:

The year is going, let him go;

Ring out the false, ring in the true.

Ring out the grief that saps the mind,

For those that here we see no more;

Ring out the feud of rich and poor,

Ring in redress to all mankind.

Ring out a slowly dying cause,

And ancient forms of party strife;

Ring in the nobler modes of life,

With sweeter manners, purer laws.

(From *In Memoriam* by
Alfred, Lord Tennyson [1809–1892].)

English Diction Practice Drills

Consonants

Stop Plosives and Fricatives

I. Stop Plosives:

Read each tongue twister silently. Notice the underlined consonants as you read.

Read aloud each tongue twister, noticing the use of the tip of your tongue for the letter "d" and the letter "t" and the inner surface of your lips for the letters "b" and "p."

Repeat the practice patterns to memorize the sensations.

Chant each tongue twister on one pitch. Strive for an efficient use of your articulators.

1. Does it matter that she gets madder ever moment we delay? (Practice "matter/madder.")

2. I bet it is time for bed. (Practice "bet/bed.")

3. The latter held the ladder, while the former scrambled up the tree. (Practice "latter/ladder.")

4. Rhoda wrote regularly about her reactions to events along the road. (Practice "wrote/road.")

5. Tightly seal the top and keep it tidy. (Practice "tightly/tidy.")

6. Happy the abbots who lived peacefully in the abbey. (Practice "happy/abbey.")

7. Let the red cap hail our cab. (Practice "cap/cab.")

8. No pest is best. Even the best pest is not a good guest. (Practice "pest/best.")

9. Peg did beg us to bring the buggy to the park. (Practice "beg/buggy.")

10. Put the bell, the book and the candle next to the bed and barely puff up the pillow. (Practice "put/bed.")

II. Fricatives:

Read each tongue twister silently. Notice the underlined consonants as you read.

Read aloud each tongue twister, noticing how your lips and tongue shape themselves to form the consonant clusters [ʒ], [ʃ], and [θ], [ð], and the letters "f" and "v."

Repeat the practice patterns to memorize the sensations.

Chant each tongue twister on one pitch. Strive for an efficient use of your articulators.

1. After the test, everyone breathes a sigh of relief. (Practice "after/every/relief" and "breathes/sigh.")

2. Do not fail to lift the veil. (Practice "fail/lift/veil.")

3. Only proof can prove your case. (Practice "proof/prove.")

4. Refer him to me and I will reveal the answer. (Practice "refer/reveal.")

5. With half a cake, you have more joy than with no cake at all. (Practice "half/have.")

6. Should you have earthly treasures, show them forth. (Practice "should/show" and "earthly/forth.")

7. Measure your vision by the leisure it affords. (Practice "measure/vision" and "measure/leisure.")

8. Have you thousands of thoughts of thin things? (Practice "thousands/thoughts" and "thin/things.")

9. Very few shun fortune or value shadows. (Practice "very/value," "few/fortune," and "shun/shadows.")

10. Breath thrives on a vital flow of heartfelt rhythm. (Practice "breath/thrives/rhythm" and "flow/felt.")

English Diction Presentation Assessments

Here is a list of comparative possibilities for first presentations to second presentations:

"Drink to Me Only With Thine Eyes," Ben Jonson and Roger Quilter

"Fain Would I Change That Note," Tobias Hume and Fair House of Joy/Quilter

"It Was a Lover and His Lass," Thomas Morley and Roger Quilter

"Sally in Our Alley," Anonymous, attr. Henry Carey and Benjamin Britten

"Weep You No More, Sad Fountains," John Dowland and Roger Quilter

Here is list of comparative possibilities for works assigned for the second presentations:

"Down by the Salley Gardens," Benjamin Britten/Ivor Gurney/Rebecca Clarke/John Ireland

"O Mistress Mine," Gerald Finzi and Roger Quilter

"Orpheus With His Lute," William Schuman/Arthur Sullivan and the setting by Richard Hundley entitled "When Orpheus Played"

"Sure on This Shining Night.," Samuel Barber (solo and choral versions)

"Under the Greenwood Tree," Roger Quilter/Douglas Moore

"Who Is Sylvia?" Gerald Finzi and "Was Ist Sylvia?" Franz Schubert. (Note that the Schubert version can be sung in English or German.)

Quiz on English Vowel Sounds: The Cornerstone of Singer's Diction

From the options given in the study guides, select for yourself one word per symbol that you associate directly with the sound the symbol represents. Make your choice a word you will recall gladly. The associative word you memorize will be the one you will use as a point of departure for remembering comparable sounds in foreign languages. Diphthongs and triphthongs are combinations of some of these basic vowel sounds. Check your choices with the study guide list to be sure you have chosen rightly. It might help you to make flash cards to reinforce your memory. Your thorough mastery of the initial vowel symbols forms the cornerstone for your study of singer's diction.

[æ] _____

[ɪ] _____

[ɛ] _____

[ɑ] _____

[o] _____

[e] _____

[u] _____

[ɝ] _____

[ə] _____

[ʌ] _____

[ɔ] _____

[ʊ] _____

[e] _____

English Diction Quiz on Classification of Consonants

Name _____

Match the definitions with the appropriate terms:

◆ Points of Articulation

Bilabial	Point of orientation; opening of vocal folds
Labiodental	Blade of tongue and hard palate
Dental	Lips
Alveolar	Back of tongue and soft palate
Prepalatal	Ridge behind front, upper teeth
Palatal	Low lip and upper row of teeth
Velar	Tip/blade of tongue between ridge and hard palate
Glottal	Tip of tongue and back of upper teeth

◆ Manner of Articulation

Stop	Tip of tongue curls up
Fricative	Momentary closure of air flow
Affricative	Tongue taps against upper teeth
Nasal	Airflow creates friction through articulators
Lateral	Airflow without friction through articulators
Glide	Stop followed by a fricative
Trill	Vocalized airflow through nasal passages
Retroflex	Vocalized airflow over sides of tongue

English Diction Quiz on English Consonant Sounds

From the options given in the study guide, select for yourself one word per symbol that you associate directly with the consonant sounds the symbol represents. Make your choice a word you will recall gladly. The associative word you memorize will be the one you will use as a point of departure for remembering comparable sounds in foreign languages. Check your choices with the study guide list to be sure you have chosen rightly. It might help you to make flash cards to reinforce your memory.

[ʒ]   —————————

[ʧ]   —————————

[ŋg]   —————————

[ʤ]   —————————

[θ]   —————————

[ŋk]   —————————

[ʃ]   —————————

[ɲ]   —————————

[ð]   —————————

[j]   —————————

◆ Voiced and Voiceless Consonants
Circle the consonants that are voiced and underline the ones that are voiceless:

[p]   [t]   [z]   [b]   [d]   [g]   [k]   [m]   [ʍ]   [v]   [θ]

[s]   [l]   [j]   [ɲ]   [ʒ]   [ʃ]   [ʧ]   [ʤ]   [w]   [n]   [f]

◆ Diacritical Marks
Define each of the following symbols:

[ʔ]

[ˈ]

[ˌ]

◆ Symbols for the letter "r"
Explain the use of each of the following symbols:

[ɹ]

[ɾ]

[r]

Italian Diction Quiz

Auxiliary Verb and Musical Terms

Give the present tense in Italian or English for the following verbs:

1. hanno _____   7. abbiamo _____

2. siete _____   8. è _____

3. avere _____   9. I am/they are _____

4. sei _____   10. essere _____

5. avete _____   11. I have _____

6. hai _____   12. siamo _____

In the space below, give the English equivalent for the following terms:

1. allargando   _____

2. meno mosso   _____

3. scherzando   _____

4. poco a poco   _____

5. accelerando   _____

6. cantabile   _____

7. rallentando   _____

8. prestissimo   _____

9. andante   _____

10. adagio   _____

German Diction Quiz on Auxiliary Verbs, Pronunciation Rules, and Question Words

Name _____

Auxiliary Verbs

In the space provided, translate each of the verb forms:

1. ich bin   _____

2. wir sind   _____

3. es ist   _____

4. du hast   _____

5. wir haben   _____

6. sein   _____

In the space provided, give the German equivalent of each English verb:

7. they are   _____

8. they have   _____

9. he has   _____

10. she is   _____

11. to have   _____

12. we are   _____

Pronunciation of Consonants

In German, the written letter "b" at the end of a word is pronounced [ ].

In German, the written letter "d" at the end of a word is pronounced [ ].

In German, the letters "f" and "v" are generally pronounced [ ].

In German, the letter "w" is pronounced [ ].

In German, the written cluster "ch" in the word *ich* is pronounced [ ].

In German, the written letters "ie" in the word *Lied* are pronounced [ ].

Extra Credit

When the consonant cluster "st" appears at the beginning of a word, it is pronounced [ ].

Question Words

In the spaces below, give the German words for the following question words:

Wann?   _____   What?   _____

Why?   _____   Where?   _____

In the spaces below, give the English equivalent for the German question words:

Wozu?   _____   Wer?   _____

Was für?   _____   Wie?   _____

Dictation

In the spaces below, please write the IPA symbols for each word of the dictation. Please be certain your symbols are legible.

1. [   ]

2. [   ]

3. [   ]

4. [   ]

5. [   ]

6. [   ]

7. [   ]

8. [   ]

9. [   ]

10. [   ]

Singer's Diction: Class Presentation Assessment Form

English

MUSICAL PREPARATION   1   2   3   4   5

(Please note: To receive full credit, you must have presented a clean copy of your selection to the accompanist at the coaching session.)

PHONETIC READING   6   7   8   9   10

(Please note: The grade for reading includes your spoken text, the punctuality of your written assignment, and the citing of sources where appropriate.)

POETIC INTERPRETATION   1   2   3   4   5

PROGRAM NOTES: POET/COMPOSER   1   2   3   4   5

(REMINDER: For all work, written and oral, you must cite your sources to receive full credit for the work done.)

OVERALL PRESENTATION SCORE   TOTAL =

    A = 25–24

    A– = 23–22

    B+ = 21

    B = 20–19

    B– = 18

    C+ = 17

    C = 16–15

    C– = 14

COMMENTS:

Singer's Diction: Class Presentation Assessment Form

Foreign Languages

MUSICAL PREPARATION   1   2   3   4   5

(Please note: To receive full credit, you must have presented a clean copy of your selection to the accompanist at the coaching session.)

PHONETIC READING/IPA   1   2   3   4   5

(Please note: The grade for reading includes your spoken text, the punctuality of your written assignment and the citing of sources, where appropriate.)

TRANSLATIONS: WORD-BY-WORD   1   2   3   4   5

               POETIC   1   2   3   4   5

PROGRAM NOTES: POET/COMPOSER/WORK   1   2   3   4   5

(REMINDER: For all work, written and oral, you must cite your sources to receive full credit for the work done.)

OVERALL PRESENTATION SCORE   TOTAL =

     A = 25–24

     A– = 23–22

     B+ = 21

     B = 20–19

     B– = 18

     C+ = 17

     C = 16–15

     C– = 14

COMMENTS:

Comparative Musical Terms

Italian, German, and English

Most musical scores use the Italian terms that describe the tempo and character of the music. Scores published in Germany present often the German equivalent of the Italian term. Here is a list of the Italian terms with the German and English definitions.

Italian	German	English
adagio	langsam	slow
ad libitum	nach Belieben	as you like
accelerando	schneller, rascher	getting faster
allegretto	beweglich, munter	agile, spirited
allegro	lebhaft, sehr lebhaft, heiter	lively, happy
assai	sehr	very
con brio	feurig, mit Schwung	fiery, spirited
espressione	Ausdruck	expression
espressivo	ausdrucksvoll	expressive
forte	stark	strong
giusto	angemessen	appropriate
instante	drängend	urgently, pressing
l'istesso tempo	in selben Zeitmass	in the same tempo
mensura	in Mass	measured; a tempo
meno/calando	nachlässig, weniger bewegt	relax the tempo
moderato	beweglich, mässig	moving, moderate
moderato	mässig bewegt	moderate movement
molto	viel, sehr	very
passione, passionato	Leidenschaft, leidenschaftlich	passionately
piacere	nach Belieben	as you like
placidamente	ruhig	restfully
presto	schnell	fast
religioso	andächtig	meditatively
replica	Wiederholung	repeat

Italian	German	English
rigore	unerbittlich	relentless
serioso	ernsthaft	serious, heavy
spirituoso	geistvoll; witzig	spirited, jokingly
tenerezza, dolce	zart, sanft	tender, delicate
innig	(German only)intimate	

French Diction Quiz

Auxiliary Verbs

French to English

In the space below, please write the English equivalent of each of the following French verb forms:

1. je suis _____
2. nous sommes _____
3. tu es _____
4. j'ai _____
5. elle a _____
6. tu as _____

7. vous avez _____
8. ils sont _____
9. il a _____
10. ils ont _____
11. nous avons _____
12. vous êtes _____

English to French

In the space below, give the French equivalent of the following English verb forms: (Be careful to spell the French equivalents with care.)

1. you are (sing.) _____
2. he has _____
3. they have (fem.) _____

4. to be _____
5. I am _____
6. he/it is _____

French Diction Quiz on Nasal Vowel Spellings

Can you identify the nasal vowel spellings? Give the IPA symbols for the nasal vowels in the following words:

1. parfum   [ ]   7. symbole   [ ]

2. plaintif   [ ]   8. balance   [ ]

3. monde   [ ]   9. bamboo   [ ]

4. plein   [ ]   10. timbre   [ ]

5. silence   [ ]   11. un   [ ]

6. somber   [ ]   12. syncope   [ ]

Nasal Vowel Spellings:

In the space below, give the possible spellings for the nasal vowels indicated:

13. [ɑ̃]   _____, _____, _____, _____.

14. [ɛ̃]   _____, _____, _____, _____, _____, _____, _____.

15. [õ]   _____, _____.

16. [œ̃]   _____, _____.

17. [wɛ̃]   _____, _____.

18. [jɛ̃]   _____.

19. A tool for the sound of the nasal vowel [œ̃] is the word _____.

20. A tool for the sound of the nasal vowel [ɛ̃] is the word _____.

INDEX OF WORKS CITED

MATERIALS FOR FURTHER LEARNING

International Phonetic Alphabet

https://www.internationalphoneticassociation.org

http://www.dictiondomain.com/

Cartier, F., & Todaro, M. (1971). *The phonetic alphabet* (2nd ed.). Dubuque, IA: Wm. C. Brown Publishers.

International Phonetic Association. (2003). *Handbook of the International Phonetic Association: A guide to the use of the International Phonetic Alphabet.* Cambridge, UK: Cambridge University Press.

Websites for International Phonetic Alphabet Transcriptions of Songs and Arias

http://www.artsongcentral.com

http://www.dictiondomain.com

http://www.leyerlepublications.com/?v=song_texts

http://www.halleonard.com

http://www.ipasource.com

http://www.stmpublishers.com

http://www.blugs.com/IPAPalette/

Books Containing Texts and Translations

Coffin, B. (1982). *Phonetic readings of songs and arias* (2nd ed.). Lanham, MD: Scarecrow Press.

Miller, P. (1973). *The ring of words: An anthology of song texts.* New York, NY: W. W. Norton.

Retzlaff, J., & Montgomery, C. (2015). *Exploring art song's lyrics.* New York, NY: Oxford University Press.

Opera Libretti

Castel, N. (1999). *French opera libretti* (3 vols.).
Castel, N. (2000). *Italian bel canto opera libretti* (3 vols.).
Castel, N. (2000). *Italian verismo opera libretti* (2 vols.).

English Diction Textbooks

Cox, R. (1990). *Singing in English: A manual of English diction for singers and choral directors.* New York, NY: Schirmer Books.
LaBouff, K. (2008). *Singing and communicating in English: A singer's guide to English diction.* New York, NY: Oxford University Press.
Marshall, M. (1943). *The singer's manual of English diction.* New York, NY: Schirmer Books.
Uris, D. (1971). *To sing in English.* New York, NY: Boosey & Hawkes.

French Diction Textbooks

Davis, E. (2004). *Sing French: Diction for singers.* Ashland, OR: Eclairé Press.
Grubb, T. (1990). *Singing in French: A manual of French diction and French vocal repertoire.* New York, NY: Schirmer Books.

German Diction Textbooks

Johnston, A. (2011). *English and German diction: A comparative approach.* Lanham, MD: Scarecrow Press.
Odom, W. (1997). *German for singers: A textbook of diction and phonetics* (2nd ed.). New York, NY: Schirmer Books.
Paton, J. G. (1999). *Gateway to German diction.* Alfred Publishing.

Italian Diction Textbooks

Colorni, E. (1995). *Singer's Italian.* New York, NY: Schirmer Books.
Paton, J. G. (2004). *Gateway to Italian diction.* Alfred Publishing.

Multiple Languages Diction Textbooks

Adams, D. (2008). *A handbook of diction for singers: Italian, German, French* (2nd ed.). New York, NY: Oxford University Press.
Moriarty, J. (1975). *Diction: Italian, Latin, French, German.* Boston, MA: E. C. Schirmer Books.

Sheil, R. (2004). *A singer's manual of foreign language dictions* (6th ed.). New York, NY: YBK Publishers.

Wall, J. (1990). *Diction for singers: A concise reference for English, Italian, Latin, German, French, and Spanish.* Dallas, TX: Pst. Inc.

Wall, J. (1989). *International phonetic alphabet for singers: A manual for English and foreign language diction.* Dallas, TX: Pst. Inc.

Books on Interpretation of Songs and Arias

English

Barzun, J. (1985). *Simple & direct: A rhetoric for writers* (Rev. ed.). Chicago, IL: University of Chicago Press.

Bryson, B. (1990). *The mother tongue: English and how it got that way.* New York, NY: Perennial.

Butterfield, J. (Ed.). (2015). *Modern English usage* (4th ed.). Oxford, U.K.: Oxford University Press.

Carmen, J., Gaeddert, W., Myers, G., & Resch, R. (2001). *Art song in the United States, 1759–1999* (3rd ed.). Lanham, MD: Scarecrow Press.

Clifton, K. (2008). *Recent American art song.* Lanham, MD: Scarecrow Press.

Fogiel, M. (1996). *REA's handbook of English grammar, style, and writing.* Piscataway, NJ: Research and Education Association.

Forward, G., & Howard, E. (2001). *American diction for singers: Standard American diction for singers and speakers.* Van Nuys, CA: Alfred Publishing.

Friedberg, R. (1981). *American art song and American poetry* (3 Vols.). Metuchen, NJ: Scarecrow Press.

Harrison, N. (2016). The songs of Roger Quilter. In *The wordsmith's guide to English song: Poetry, music, & imagination* (Vol. 1). Oxford, UK: Compton Publishing.

Heyman, B. (1992). *Samuel Barber: The composer and his music.* New York, NY: Oxford University Press.

Hold, T. (2002). *Parry to Finzi: Twenty English song-composers.* Suffolk, UK: The Boydell Press.

Jorgens, E. (1982). *The well-tun'd word: Musical interpretation of English poetry 1597–1651.* Minneapolis, MN: University of Minnesota Press.

McCrum, R., Cran, W., & MacNeil, R. (1986) *The story of English* (Rev. ed.). New York, NY: Viking.

Pilkington, M. (1989). *Gurney, Ireland, Quilter, and Warlock.* Bloomington, IN: Indiana University Press.

Pilkington, M. (1989). *Campion, Dowland, and the Lutenist songwriters.* Bloomington, IN: Indiana University Press.

Resick, G. (2018). *French vocal literature: Repertoire in context.* Lanham, MD: Rowman & Littlefield.

Villamil, V. (1993). *A singer's guide to the American art song: 1870–1980.* Lanham, MD: Scarecrow Press.

A website that offers in-depth information about the American Art Song is Song of America: http://www.songofamerica.net

Websites of Contemporary American Composers

Judith Cloud	http://www.judithcloud.com
Ricky Ian Gordon	http://www.rickyiangordon.com
Jake Heggie	http://www.jakeheggie.com
Lori Laitman	http://www.artsongs.com
Libby Larsen	http://www.libbylarsen.com
Ned Rorem	http://www.nedrorem.com

French

Bathori, J. (1998). *On the interpretation of the melodies of Claude Debussy.* New York, NY: Pendragon Press.

Bernac, P. (1977). *Francis Poulenc: The man and his songs.* New York, NY: Norton.

Bernac, P. (1978). *The interpretation of the French song.* New York, NY: Norton.

Cobb, M. (1982). *The poetic Debussy: A collection of his song texts and selected letters* (R. Miller, Trans.). Boston, MA: Northeastern University Press.

Davies, L. (1967). *The Gallic muse.* New York, NY: A. S. Barnes.

Gartside, R. (1992). *Interpreting the songs of Maurice Ravel.* Geneseo, NY: Leyerle Publications.

Gartside, R. (1996). *Interpreting the songs of Gabriel Fauré.* Geneseo, NY: Leyerle Publications.

Hahn, R. (1990). *On singers and singing* (L. Simoneau, Trans.). Portland, OR: Amadeus Press.

Johnson, G., & Stokes, R. (2000). *A French art song companion.* Oxford, UK: Oxford University Press.

Johnson, G., & Stokes R, (2009). *Gabriel Fauré: The songs and their poets.* Burlington, VT: Ashgate Publishing.

LeVan, T. (1991). *Masters of the French art song: Translations of the complete songs of Chausson, Debussy, Duparc, Fauré, and Ravel.* Metuchen, NJ: Scarecrow Press.

Leyerle, A., & Leyerle, W. (1983). *French diction songs: From the 17th to the 20th centuries.* Geneseo, NY: Leyerle Publications.

Meister, B. (1980). *Nineteenth-century French song: Fauré, Chausson, Duparc, and Debussy.* Bloomington, IN: Indiana University Press.

Nectoux, J. (1991). *Gabriel Fauré: A musical life.* (R. Nichols, Trans.) Cambridge, UK: Cambridge University Press.

Nichols, R. (1987). *Ravel remembered.* New York, NY: W. W. Norton.

Northcote, S. (1949). *The songs of Henri Duparc.* London, UK: Dennis Dobson.

Noske, F. (1970). *French song from Berlioz to Duparc.* New York, NY: Dover.

Orenstein, A. (1975). *Ravel: Man and musician.* New York, NY: Columbia University Press.

Panzéra, C. (1964). *Mélodies Françaises: Fifty lessons in style and interpretation.* Brussels, Belgium: Schott.

Poulenc, F. (1989). *Diary of my songs* (W. Radford, Trans.). London, UK: Victor Gollancz.

Rohinsky, M. (1987). *The singer's Debussy.* New York, NY: Pelion Press.

Vuillermoz, E. (1960). *Gabriel Fauré.* Philadelphia, PA: Chilton Book Company.

Walsh, S. (2018). *Debussy: A painter in sound.* New York, NY: Knopf.

Wenk, A. (1976). *Claude Debussy and the poets.* Berkeley, CA: University of California Press.

German

Bell, A. C. (1954). *The songs of Schubert*. London, UK: Alston Books.

Brody, E., & Fowkes, R. (1971). *The German lied and its poetry*. New York, NY: New York University Press.

Chernaik, J. (2018). *Schumann: The faces and the masks*. New York, NY: Knopf.

Cooper, J. M. (2007). *Mendelssohn, Goethe, and the Walpurgis Nacht: The heathen muse in European culture, 1700–1850*. Rochester, NY: University of Rochester Press.

Fischer-Dieskau, D. (1977). *Schubert: A biographical study of his songs*. New York, NY: Alfred A. Knopf.

Fischer-Dieskau, D. (1984). *The Fischer-Dieskau book of lieder*. New York, NY: Limelight Editions.

Fischer-Dieskau, D. (1988). *Robert Schumann: Words and music, the vocal compositions*. Portland, OR: Amadeus Press.

Glass, B. (1996). *Brahms' complete song texts*. Geneseo, NY: Leyerle Publications.

Glass, B. (2000). *Hugo Wolf's complete song texts*. Geneseo, NY: Leyerle Publications.

Glass, B. (2002). *Schumann's complete song texts*. Geneseo, NY: Leyerle Publications.

Glass, B. (2004). *Strauss's complete song texts*. Geneseo, NY: Leyerle Publications.

Gorrell, L. (1993). *The nineteenth-century German lied*. Portland, OR: Amadeus Press.

Harrison, M. (1972). *The lieder of Brahms*. New York, NY: Praeger.

Jefferson A, (1971). *The lieder of Richard Strauss*. New York, NY: Praeger.

Jensen, E. F. (2001). *Schumann*. New York, NY: Oxford University Press.

Loges, N. (2017). *Brahms and his poets: A handbook*. Suffolk, UK: The Boydell Press.

Loges, N., & Hamilton, K. (Eds.). (2014). *Brahms in the home and the concert hall: Between private and public performances*. Cambridge, UK: Cambridge University Press.

Miller, R. (2005). *Singing Schumann: An interpretive guide for performers*. New York, NY: Oxford University Press.

Moore, G. (1975). *The Schubert song cycles*. London, UK: Hamish Hamilton.

Moore, G. (1981). *Poet's love: The songs and cycles of Schumann*. New York, NY: Taplinger.

Parsons, J. (Ed.). (2004). *The Cambridge companion to the lied*. New York, NY: Cambridge University Press.

Reich, N. (2001). *Clara Schumann: The artist and the woman* (Rev. ed.). Ithaca, NY: Cornell University Press.

Reinhard, T. (1988). *The singer's Schumann*. New York, NY: Pelion Press.

Sams, E. (1973). *Brahms songs*. Seattle, WA: University of Washington Press.

Sams, E. (1992). *The songs of Hugo Wolf* (Rev. ed.). London, UK: Methuen.

Sams, E. (1993). *The songs of Robert Schumann* (3rd ed.). London, UK: Methuen.

Snyder, L. (1995). *German poetry in song*. Berkeley, CA: Fallen Leaf Press.

Stein, D., & Spillman, R. (1996). *Poetry into song: Performance and analysis of lieder*. New York, NY: Oxford University Press.

Swafford, J. (1998). *Johannes Brahms: A biography*. New York, NY: Knopf.

Youens, S. (1991). *Retracing a winter's journey: Schubert's Winterreise*. Ithaca, NY: Cornell University Press.

Youens, S. (1992). *Hugo Wolf: The vocal music*. Princeton, NJ: Princeton University Press.

Youens, S. (1992). *Schubert: Die Schöne Müllerin*. Cambridge, UK: Cambridge University Press.

Youens, S. (1996). *Schubert's poets and the making of lieder*. Cambridge, UK: Cambridge University Press.

Italian

Gerhart, M. (2003). *Italian song texts from the 17th through the 20th centuries* (2 Vols.). Geneseo, NY: Leyerle Publications.

Lakeway, R., & White, R. (1989). *Italian art song*. Bloomington, IN: Indiana University Press.

LeVan, T. (1991). *Masters of the Italian song*. Metuchen, NJ: Scarecrow Press.

Resources for Vocal Repertoire and Style

Coffin, B. (Ed.). (1962). *Singer's repertoire* (2nd ed.). New York, NY: Scarecrow Press.

Elliott, M. (2006). *Singing in style: A guide to vocal performance practices*. New Haven, CT: Yale University Press.

Emmons, S., & Sonntag, S. (2001). *The art of the song recital* (Rev. ed.). New York, NY: Schirmer Books.

Emmon, S., & Watkins, W. (2006). *Researching the song*. New York, NY: Oxford University Press.

Espina, N. (1977). *Repertoire for the solo voice*. Metuchen, NJ: Scarecrow Press.

Goleeke, T. (2002). *Literature for voice, Vols. I and II: An index to songs in collections and source book for teachers of singing*. Lanham, MD: Scarecrow Press.

Hall, J. (1953). *The art song*. Norman, OK: University of Oklahoma Press.

Holoman, D. K. (1988). *Writing about music*. Berkeley, CA: University of California Press.

Ivey, D. (1970). *Song: Anatomy, imagery, and styles*. New York, NY: Free Press.

Kagen, S. (1968). *Music for the voice* (Rev. ed.). Bloomington, IN: Indiana University Press.

Katz, M. (2009). *The complete collaborator: The pianist as partner*. New York, NY: Oxford University Press.

Kimball, C. (2013). *Art song: Linking poetry to song*. Milwaukee, WI: Hal Leonard Corp.

Kimball, C. (2015). *Song: A guide to art song style and literature* (2nd ed.). Milwaukee, WI: Hal Leonard Corp.

Kramer, L. (1984). *Music and poetry: The nineteenth century and after*. Berkeley, CA: University of California Press.

Lehmann, L. (1972). *More than singing: The interpretation of songs*. New York, NY: Praeger.

Lowenberg, C. (1991). *Musicians wrestle everywhere: Emily Dickinson and music*. Berkeley, CA: Fallen Leaf Press.

MacClintock, C. (1973). *The solo song, 1580–1730*. New York, NY: W. W. Norton & Co.

Mabry, S. (2002). *Exploring twentieth-century vocal music: A practical guide to innovations in performance and repertoire*. New York, NY: Oxford University Press.

Meister, B. (1980). *An introduction to the art song*. New York, NY: Taplinger Publishing.

Meister, B. (1992). *Art song: The marriage of music and poetry*. Wakefield, NH: Hollowbrook Publishing.

Miller, R. (1996). *On the art of singing*. New York, NY: Oxford University Press.

Moore, G. (1975). *Singer and accompanist: The performance of fifty songs*. Westport, CT: Greenwood Press.

Nix, J. (Ed.). (2002). *From studio to stage: Repertoire for the voice*. Lanham, MD: Scarecrow Press.

Rosen, C. (1995). *The romantic generation.* Cambridge, MA: Harvard University Press.

Schiøtz, A. (1970). *The singer and his art.* New York, NY: Harper & Row.

Seaton, D. (1987). *The art song: A research and information guide.* New York, NY: Garland Publishing.

Stein, D., & Spillman, R. (1996). *Poetry into song: Performance and analysis of lieder.* New York, NY: Oxford University Press.

Stein, J. (1971). *Poem and music in the German lied from Gluck to Hugo Wolf.* Cambridge, MA: Harvard University Press.

Stevens, D. (1970). *A history of song* (Rev. ed.). New York, NY: W. W. Norton & Co.

Resources for the Study of Poetry

Appelbaum, S. (1969). *Introduction to French poetry: A dual-language book.* New York, NY: Dover Publications.

Hirsch, E. (1999). *How to read a poem and fall in love with poetry.* New York, NY: Harvest Books.

Hollander, J. (1996). *Committed to memory: 100 best poems to memorize.* New York, NY: Riverhead Books.

Oliver, M. (1994). *A poetry handbook: A prose guide to understanding and writing poetry,* New York, NY: Houghton Mifflin.

Pinsky, R. (1998) *The handbook of heartbreak.* New York, NY: William Morrow.

Biographical and Historical Materials

Alighieri, D. (2011). *Vita nuova* (A. Mortimer, Trans.). Surrey, U.K.: Alma Classics.

Alighieri, D. (2003). *Divine comedy* (J. Ciardi, Trans.). New York, NY: New American Library.

Armstrong, J. (2006). *Love, life, Goethe: Lessons of the imagination from the great German Poet.* New York, NY: Farrar, Straus, & Giroux.

Baudelaire, C. (1982). *Les fleurs du mal* (R. Howard, Trans.). Boston, MA: David R. Godine.

Bell, M. (Ed.). (2016). *The essential Goethe.* Princeton, NJ: Princeton University Press.

Benjamin, W. (1973). *Charles Baudelaire.* London, UK: Verso Classics.

Bodley, L. B. (2009). *Goethe and Zelter: Musical dialogues.* Surrey, UK: Ashgate Publishing.

Boyle, N. (1992). *Goethe: The poet and the age: The poetry of desire, 1749–1790* (Vol. 1). New York, NY: Oxford University Press.

Boyle, N. (2000). *Goethe: The poet and the age: Revolution and renunciation, 1790–1803.* New York, NY: Oxford University Press.

Burckhardt, J. (1954). *The civilization of the Renaissance in Italy.* New York, NY: The Modern Library.

Celenza, C. (2017). *Petrarch: Everywhere a wanderer.* London, UK: Reaktion Books.

Gautier, T. (2011). *Selected lyrics* (N. R. Shapiro, Trans.). New Haven, CT: Yale University Press.

Heine, H. (n.d.). *Werke in drei Bänden, band I: Gedichte.* Munich, Germany: Winkler Verlag.

Housman, A. E. (2010). *A Shropshire lad and other poems.* London, UK: Penguin Books.

Hugo, V. (2001). *Selected poems of Victor Hugo: A bilingual edition* (E. H. Blackmore & A. M. Blackmore, Trans.). Chicago IL: University of Chicago Press.

Hunter, D. (2012). *Understanding French verse: A guide for singers*. London, UK: Oxford University Press.

Perraudin, M. (1989). *Heinrich Heine. Poetry in context: A study of the Buch der Lieder*. New York, NY: St. Martin's Press.

Petrarch. (1985). *Selections from Canzoniere and other work* (M. Musa, Trans.). New York, NY: Oxford University Press.

Rees, W. (1990). *The Penguin book of French poetry 1820–1950*. London, UK: Penguin Books.

Reeves, N. (1994). *Heinrich Heine:Poetry and politics*. London, UK: Libris.

Safranski, R. (2017). *Goethe: Life as a work of art* (D. Dollenmayer, Trans.). New York, NY: Liveright.

Sammons, J. (1979). *Heinrich Heine: A modern biography*. Princeton, NJ: Princeton University Press.

Shaw, P. (2015). *Reading Dante: From here to eternity*. New York, NY: Liveright.

Sternfeld, F. W. (1979). *Goethe and music: A list of parodies and Goethe's relationship to music*. New York, NY: DaCapo Press.

Tudor, J. M. (2011). *Sound and sense: Music and musical metaphor in the thought and writing of Goethe and his age*. Bern, Switzerland: Peter Lang International Academic Publishers.

Verlaine, P. (1999). *One hundred and one poems by Paul Verlaine: A bilingual edition* (N. R. Shapiro, Trans.). Chicago IL: University of Chicago Press.

Verlaine, P. (2003). *The cursed poets* (C. Madar, Trans.). Los Angeles, CA: Green Integer.

Williams, C. (1943). *The figure of Beatrice*. Berkeley, CA: Apocryphile Press.

Wilson, A. N. (2011). *Dante in love*. New York, NY: Farrar, Strauss, & Giroux.

Zweig, S. (2018). *Paul Verlaine*. CreateSpace Independent Publishing Platform.

Index